KB070127

세상이 변해도
배움의 즐거움은
변함없도록

시대는 빠르게 변해도
배움의 즐거움은
변함없어야 하기에

어제의 비상은
남다른 교재부터
결이 다른 콘텐츠
전에 없던 교육 플랫폼까지

변함없는 혁신으로
교육 문화 환경의 새로운 전형을
실현해왔습니다.

비상은 오늘, 다시 한번
새로운 교육 문화 환경을 실현하기 위한
또 하나의 혁신을 시작합니다.

오늘의 내가 어제의 나를 초월하고
오늘의 교육이 어제의 교육을 초월하여
배움의 즐거움을 지속하는 혁신,

바로, 메타인지 기반 완전 학습을.

상상을 실현하는 교육 문화 기업 비상

메타인지 기반 완전 학습

초월을 뜻하는 meta와 생각을 뜻하는 인지가 결합한 메타인지는
자신이 알고 모르는 것을 스스로 구분하고 학습계획을 세우도록 하는
궁극의 학습 능력입니다. 비상의 메타인지 기반 완전 학습 시스템은
잠들어 있는 메타인지를 깨워 공부를 100% 내 것으로 만들도록 합니다.

GRAMMAR TAPA

TAPA

LEVEL 3

How to Study

구성과 특장

STEP 1

Chapter의 전체적인 내용을 파악하세요.

챕터 미리 보기

공부할 내용을 미리 파악하면서 〈용어 사전〉으로
어려운 문법 용어의 의미를 익히세요.

STEP 2

핵심 문법 Focus를 공부하고
이해도를 점검하세요.

핵심 문법 Focus

문법 Focus를 다양한 유형의 문제로 반복 학습하고,
〈교과서 문장 응용하기〉로 Writing 실력을 높이세요.

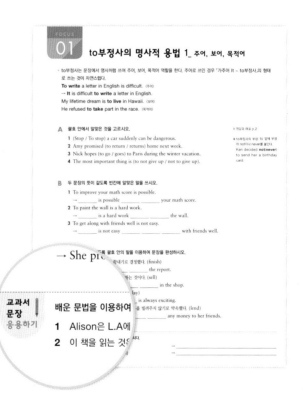

STEP 3

내신적중 실전문제로 문법을 학습하며 내신도 대비하세요.

〈내신적중 실전문제〉로 학교 시험 빈출 유형을 파악하고, 해당 Chapter의 문법을 이용한 〈서술형 평가〉의 Writing, Reading 문제를 통해 내신을 완벽하게 대비하세요.

STEP 4

Workbook으로 한 번 더 정리하세요.

공부한 내용은 〈요점정리 노트〉로 Chapter별 핵심 문법 사항을 다시 한 번 정리한 후, 문제를 통해 복습하여 완벽하게 이해하고 넘어가세요.

Contents
차례

CHAPTER 01

to부정사

FOCUS 01	to부정사의 명사적 용법 1_ 주어, 보어, 목적어	11
FOCUS 02	to부정사의 명사적 용법 2_ 의문사+to부정사	12
FOCUS 03	to부정사의 형용사적 용법	13
FOCUS 04	to부정사의 부사적 용법	14
FOCUS 05	too ~ to부정사 / enough +to부정사	15
FOCUS 06	to부정사의 의미상 주어	16
FOCUS 07	to부정사의 시제	17
FOCUS 08	원형부정사	18
FOCUS 09	대부정사	19
FOCUS 10	독립부정사	20

CHAPTER 02

동명사

FOCUS 11	동명사의 쓰임	27
FOCUS 12	동명사의 의미상 주어	28
FOCUS 13	동명사와 현재분사	29
FOCUS 14	동명사와 to부정사를 목적어로 쓰는 동사	30
FOCUS 15	동명사의 관용 표현	31

CHAPTER 03

분사

FOCUS 16	분사의 역할	39
FOCUS 17	분사구문	40
FOCUS 18	분사구문의 의미 1_ 시간, 이유	41
FOCUS 19	분사구문의 의미 2_ 조건, 양보	42
FOCUS 20	분사구문의 의미 3_ 동시동작, 연속상황	43
FOCUS 21	완료형 분사구문	44
FOCUS 22	being, having been의 생략	45
FOCUS 23	독립분사구문, 비인칭 독립분사구문	46
FOCUS 24	with +명사+분사	47

CHAPTER 04 시제

FOCUS 25	현재완료의 쓰임과 형태	57
FOCUS 26	현재완료의 의미 1_ 완료, 결과	58
FOCUS 27	현재완료의 의미 2_ 경험, 계속	59
FOCUS 28	현재완료진행형	60
FOCUS 29	과거완료의 쓰임과 형태	61
FOCUS 30	과거완료진행형	62

CHAPTER 05 조동사

FOCUS 31	can, could	69
FOCUS 32	may, might	70
FOCUS 33	must, have to	71
FOCUS 34	should, ought to	72
FOCUS 35	had better, would rather	73
FOCUS 36	used to, would	74
FOCUS 37	조동사+have+과거분사	75

CHAPTER 06 수동태

FOCUS 38	단순 수동태	83
FOCUS 39	조동사가 있는 수동태	84
FOCUS 40	진행·완료 시제 수동태	85
FOCUS 41	4형식 문장의 수동태	86
FOCUS 42	5형식 문장의 수동태	87
FOCUS 43	동사구의 수동태	88
FOCUS 44	목적어로 쓰인 that절의 수동태	89
FOCUS 45	by 이외의 전치사를 쓰는 수동태	90

CHAPTER 07	비교 구문		
	FOCUS 46	원급·비교급·최상급 비교	97
	FOCUS 47	as+원급+as+주어+can / 배수사를 이용한 비교	98
	FOCUS 48	less+원급+than	99
	FOCUS 49	비교급+and+비교급 / the+비교급, the+비교급	100
	FOCUS 50	one of the+최상급 / 원급과 비교급을 이용한 최상급	101

CHAPTER 08	관계사		
	FOCUS 51	주격 관계대명사_ who, which	109
	FOCUS 52	소유격 관계대명사_ whose	110
	FOCUS 53	목적격 관계대명사_ who(m), which	111
	FOCUS 54	관계대명사 that	112
	FOCUS 55	관계대명사 what	113
	FOCUS 56	관계대명사의 계속적 용법	114
	FOCUS 57	전치사+관계대명사	115
	FOCUS 58	관계대명사의 생략	116
	FOCUS 59	관계부사 1_ when, where	117
	FOCUS 60	관계부사 2_ why, how	118
	FOCUS 61	관계부사와 선행사의 생략	119
	FOCUS 62	복합관계대명사	120
	FOCUS 63	복합관계부사	121

CHAPTER 09	접속사		
	FOCUS 64	명사절을 이끄는 접속사	129
	FOCUS 65	시간의 접속사 1	130
	FOCUS 66	시간의 접속사 2	131
	FOCUS 67	조건·이유의 접속사	132
	FOCUS 68	양보의 접속사	133
	FOCUS 69	상관접속사 1	134
	FOCUS 70	상관접속사 2	135
	FOCUS 71	접속부사	136

CHAPTER 10

가정법

FOCUS 72	가정법 과거	143
FOCUS 73	가정법 과거완료	144
FOCUS 74	I wish 가정법	145
FOCUS 75	as if 가정법	146
FOCUS 76	Without(But for) 가정법	147
FOCUS 77	혼합가정법	148

CHAPTER 11

일치와 화법

FOCUS 78	수의 일치 1_ 단수	155
FOCUS 79	수의 일치 2_ 복수	156
FOCUS 80	시제 일치	157
FOCUS 81	시제 일치의 예외	158
FOCUS 82	평서문의 간접화법	159
FOCUS 83	의문문의 간접화법	160
FOCUS 84	명령문의 간접화법	161
FOCUS 85	간접화법과 간접의문문	162

CHAPTER 12

특수 구문

FOCUS 86	강조 1_ 동사 강조	169
FOCUS 87	강조 2_ 명사, 부정어 강조	170
FOCUS 88	강조 3_ It ~ that ... 강조	171
FOCUS 89	도치 1_ 부사(구)·부정어 도치	172
FOCUS 90	도치 2_ so / neither+동사+주어	173
FOCUS 91	부정_ 부분·전체부정	174
FOCUS 92	생략 1_ 공통 부분의 생략	175
FOCUS 93	생략 2_ 「주어+be동사」의 생략	176

When you have a dream,
you've got to grap it and
never let go.

by Carol Burnett

꿈이 있다면, 그 꿈을 잡고 절대 놓아주지 마라.

캐롤 버넷

CHAPTER

01

to부정사

FOCUS 01   to부정사의 명사적 용법 1_주어, 보어, 목적어

FOCUS 02   to부정사의 명사적 용법 2_의문사+to부정사

FOCUS 03   to부정사의 형용사적 용법

FOCUS 04   to부정사의 부사적 용법

FOCUS 05   too ~ to부정사 / enough +to부정사

FOCUS 06   to부정사의 의미상 주어

FOCUS 07   to부정사의 시제

FOCUS 08   원형부정사

FOCUS 09   대부정사

FOCUS 10   독립부정사

to부정사는 어떤 역할을 하는가?

to부정사는 「to+동사원형」의 형태로 문장에서 명사, 형용사, 부사의 역할을 한다.

명사 역할

주어 역할: ~하는 것은, ~하기는
> **To read** three books is my homework.
> 책 세 권을 읽는 것이 나의 숙제이다.

보어 역할: ~하는 것(이다), ~하기(이다)
> His wish is **to meet** her again.
> 그의 소원은 그녀를 다시 만나는 것이다.

목적어 역할: ~하는 것을, ~하기를
> She expects **to take** a trip abroad.
> 그녀는 해외로 여행가기를 기대한다.

의문사+to부정사: 주어, 목적어, 보어 역할
(주로 목적어로 쓰임)
> I don't know **where to put** the chair.
> 나는 의자를 어디에 두어야 할지 모르겠다.

형용사 역할

(대)명사+to부정사(+전치사): ~할, ~하는
> She has a proper skirt **to wear**.
> 그녀는 입을 적당한 치마가 있다.

부사 역할

목적의 의미: ~하기 위해
> I turned off the light **to save** energy.
> 나는 에너지를 절약하기 위해 전등을 껐다.

감정의 원인의 의미: ~해서, ~하게 되어
> My father was surprised **to see** our present.
> 나의 아버지는 우리의 선물을 보고 놀랐다.

결과의 의미: ~해서 (결국) …하다
> Thomas grew up **to be** a vet.
> Thomas는 자라서 수의사가 되었다.

형용사 수식
> French is not easy **to learn**.
> 프랑스어는 배우기가 쉽지 않다.

판단의 근거: ~하다니
> She must be smart **to solve** the puzzle.
> 그녀는 그 퍼즐을 푼 것을 보아 똑똑한 것이 틀림없다.

to부정사의 주어는 어떻게 나타내는가?

to부정사의 *의미상 주어가 문장의 주어 또는 목적어와 같거나 일반인일 경우에는 따로 쓰지 않는다. 그러나 문장의 주어와 다를 경우에는 일반적으로 「for+목적격」의 형태로, 사람의 성질·성격을 나타내는 형용사가 올 경우에는 「of+목적격」의 형태로 쓴다.

용어 사전

* **의미상 주어**: to부정사가 나타내는 동작이나 상태의 주체를 의미한다.

to부정사의 명사적 용법 1_ 주어, 보어, 목적어

■ to부정사는 문장에서 명사처럼 쓰여 주어, 보어, 목적어 역할을 한다. 주어로 쓰인 경우 「가주어 It ~ to부정사」의 형태로 쓰는 것이 자연스럽다.

To write a letter in English is difficult. 〈주어〉

→ **It** is difficult **to write** a letter in English.

My lifetime dream is **to live** in Hawaii. 〈보어〉

He refused **to take** part in the race. 〈목적어〉

A 괄호 안에서 알맞은 것을 고르시오.

1 (Stop / To stop) a car suddenly can be dangerous.

2 Amy promised (to return / returns) home next week.

3 Nick hopes (to go / goes) to Paris during the winter vacation.

4 The most important thing is (to not give up / not to give up).

》 정답과 해설 p.2

◆ **to**부정사의 부정: to 앞에 부정어 not이나 never를 붙인다.
Ken decided **not(never)** to send her a birthday card.

B 두 문장의 뜻이 같도록 빈칸에 알맞은 말을 쓰시오.

1 To improve your math score is possible.

→ _____ is possible _____ _____ your math score.

2 To paint the wall is a hard work.

→ _____ is a hard work _____ _____ the wall.

3 To get along with friends well is not easy.

→ _____ is not easy _____ _____ _____ with friends well.

C 우리말과 뜻이 같도록 괄호 안의 말을 이용하여 문장을 완성하시오.

1 James는 그 보고서를 끝내기로 결정했다. (finish)

→ James decided _____ _____ the report.

2 그의 직업은 가게에서 신발을 파는 것이다. (sell)

→ His job is _____ _____ _____ in the shop.

3 축구하는 것은 항상 신이 난다. (play)

→ _____ _____ _____ is always exciting.

4 그녀는 절대로 그녀의 친구들에게 돈을 빌려주지 않기로 약속했다. (lend)

→ She promised _____ _____ _____ any money to her friends.

교과서
문장
응용하기

배운 문법을 이용하여 영어 문장을 써 봅시다.

1 Alison은 L.A에 가기를 원한다. → _____

2 이 책을 읽는 것은 쉽지 않다. (it) → _____

to부정사의 명사적 용법 2_ 의문사+to부정사

- 「의문사+to부정사」는 명사처럼 쓰이며 의문사의 종류에 따라 그 뜻이 달라진다.

what+to부정사	how+to부정사	where+to부정사	when+to부정사	who(m)+to부정사
무엇을 ~할지	어떻게 ~할지	어디로 ~할지	언제 ~할지	누가(누구를) ~할지

You have to think about **what to wear**.　　He'll explain **where to go** tonight.

- 「의문사+to부정사」는 「의문사+주어+should+동사원형」으로 바꿔 쓸 수 있다.

I don't know **how to drive** a car.　→ I don't know **how I should drive** a car.

A 괄호 안의 말을 바르게 배열하여 문장을 완성하시오.

1 He's learning ＿＿＿＿＿＿＿＿＿＿ Spanish. (speak, how, to)

2 She didn't tell me ＿＿＿＿＿＿＿＿＿＿ to the party. (to, invite, who)

3 I asked the bus driver ＿＿＿＿＿＿＿＿＿＿. (where, get, should, I, off)

4 Let me know ＿＿＿＿＿＿＿＿＿＿ to bed. (when, go, should, I)

» 정답과 해설 p.2

◆ 의문사 why는 「why+to부정사」의 형태로 쓰지 않는다.
I don't know why to go there. (×)

B 다음 문장을 |보기|와 같이 바꿔 쓰시오.

> **보기**
> Please teach me how to play chess.
> → Please teach me how I should play chess.

1 Could you tell me what to bring to your house?

→ Could you tell me ＿＿＿＿＿＿＿＿＿＿＿?

2 Children usually ask when to finish their homework.

→ Children usually ask ＿＿＿＿＿＿＿＿＿＿＿.

C 우리말과 뜻이 같도록 빈칸에 알맞은 말을 쓰시오.

1 Chris는 나에게 무엇을 먼저 읽어야 할지 조언해 주었다.

→ Chris advised me ＿＿＿＿ ＿＿＿＿ ＿＿＿＿ first.

2 Sue는 그 상자를 어떻게 여는지 알지 못했다.

→ Sue didn't know ＿＿＿＿ ＿＿＿＿ ＿＿＿＿ the box.

3 나는 누구에게 그 책을 빌려주었는지 기억하지 못한다.

→ I don't remember ＿＿＿＿ ＿＿＿＿ ＿＿＿＿ the book to.

교과서 문장 응용하기 | 배운 문법을 이용하여 영어 문장을 써 봅시다.

1 그 꽃을 어디로 보내야 할지 나에게 말해 줘. (to send)　→ ＿＿＿＿＿＿＿＿＿＿

2 너는 그 문제를 푸는 방법을 아니? (should)　→ ＿＿＿＿＿＿＿＿＿＿

03 to부정사의 형용사적 용법

- **명사 수식**: to부정사는 형용사처럼 쓰여 (대)명사를 꾸며준다. 이때 수식하는 (대)명사가 전치사의 목적어인 경우에는 전치사를 반드시 써야 한다.

I have a lot of friends **to advise** me.　　　　　The old man doesn't have a house **to live in**.

- **be to 용법**: 「be동사+to부정사」의 형태로 다양한 의미를 나타낸다.

의미	예문	의미	예문
예정 (~할 예정이다)	She **is to come** at seven.	가능 (~할 수 있다)	Stars **are to be** seen at night.
의무 (~해야 한다)	You **are to study** English.	운명 (~할 운명이다)	He **was** not **to stay** with her.
의지 (~하려고 하다)	If you **are to succeed**, you must work hard.		

A 우리말과 뜻이 같도록 괄호 안의 말을 이용하여 문장을 완성하시오.　　　　　≫ 정답과 해설 p.2

1 나는 너에게 할 말이 있다. (something)

→ I have ＿＿＿＿＿ ＿＿＿＿＿ ＿＿＿＿＿ you.

2 나는 앉을 의자가 필요했다. (chair)

→ I needed a ＿＿＿＿＿ ＿＿＿＿＿ ＿＿＿＿＿ ＿＿＿＿＿.

3 그들은 돌봐야 할 아이들이 없다. (no children)

→ They have ＿＿＿＿＿ ＿＿＿＿＿ ＿＿＿＿＿ ＿＿＿＿＿ ＿＿＿＿＿.

B 두 문장의 뜻이 같도록 be to용법을 이용하여 문장을 완성하시오.

1 You must not smoke in the library.

→ You ＿＿＿＿＿＿＿＿＿＿＿＿ in the library.

2 The president is going to speak on TV tonight.

→ The president ＿＿＿＿＿＿＿＿＿＿＿＿ on TV tonight.

3 She thought that he was destined for her husband.

→ She thought that he ＿＿＿＿＿＿＿＿＿＿＿＿ her husband.

4 We can see a variety of paintings in the gallery.

→ We ＿＿＿＿＿＿＿＿＿＿＿＿ a variety of paintings in the gallery.

5 If you want to pass the test, you must study harder.

→ If you ＿＿＿＿＿＿＿＿＿＿＿＿, you must study harder.

교과서 문장 응용하기　배운 문법을 이용하여 영어 문장을 써 봅시다.

1 Amy는 가지고 먹을 스푼이 필요했다. (spoon)　　→ ＿＿＿＿＿＿＿＿＿＿＿＿＿＿

2 우리는 오후 3시에 그를 만날 예정이다. (meet)　　→ ＿＿＿＿＿＿＿＿＿＿＿＿＿＿

to부정사의 부사적 용법

의미	예문
목적 (~하기 위해)	She came home **to take** a rest.
감정의 원인 (~해서, ~하게 되어)	I was surprised **to hear** the news.
결과 (~해서 결국 …하다)	Grace grew up **to be** a movie director.
형용사 수식 (~하기에)	The explanation in this book is easy **to understand**.
판단의 근거 (~하다니, ~하는 것을 보니)	The man must be rich **to have** that car.
조건 (~한다면)	He would be delighted **to see** you.

A 빈칸에 알맞은 말을 |보기|에서 골라 알맞은 형태로 쓰시오.

» 정답과 해설 p.2

보기
send   see   help   have   fail

1 Ben was happy _____ people in need.
2 She is lucky _____ such good parents.
3 I stopped _____ a letter on my way home.
4 We will be very pleased _____ you tomorrow.
5 He studied very hard, only _____ the examination.

◆ 「~, only / never +to부정사」는
결과의 의미를 나타낸다.
I rushed to the bus stop,
only to miss the bus. (나
는 버스 정류장까지 뛰었으나 결
국 그 버스를 놓쳤다.)

B 우리말과 뜻이 같도록 괄호 안의 말을 이용하여 문장을 완성하시오.

1 그는 그런 일을 하는 것을 보아 바보임에 틀림없다. (do)
   → He must be a fool _____ _____ such a thing.
2 그녀는 자라서 훌륭한 건축가가 되었다. (grow up)
   → She _____ _____ _____ _____ a great architect.
3 독일어는 단 시간에 배우기 어렵다. (difficult)
   → German is _____ _____ _____ in a short time.
4 우리 아버지는 그 소식을 듣고 실망하셨다. (disappointed)
   → My father was _____ _____ _____ the news.
5 그 형사는 너에게 몇 가지 질문을 하기 위해 여기에 왔다.
   → The detective came here _____ _____ _____ some questions.
6 James가 그 좋은 기회를 놓치게 된다면 슬플 것이다. (miss)
   → James would be _____ _____ _____ the great opportunity.

교과서
문장
응용하기

배운 문법을 이용하여 영어 문장을 써 봅시다.

1 그녀는 책을 읽기 위해 앉았다. (sit down)   → _____
2 나는 너를 다시 만나게 되어 행복하다. (happy)   → _____

05 too ~ to부정사 / enough+to부정사

- 「too+형용사(부사)+to부정사」: '너무 ~해서 …할 수 없다'의 뜻으로 「so+형용사(부사)+that+주어+can't」로 바꿔 쓸 수 있다.

  Alex was **too** sick **to get** asleep.

  → Alex was **so** sick **that he couldn't** get asleep.

- 「형용사(부사)+enough+to부정사」: '~할 만큼 충분히 …하다'의 뜻으로 「so+형용사(부사)+that+주어+can」으로 바꿔 쓸 수 있다.

  Julie is tall **enough to reach** the top shelf.

  → Julie is **so** tall **that she can** reach the top shelf.

A 두 문장의 뜻이 같도록 too나 enough를 이용하여 빈칸에 알맞은 말을 쓰시오.   » 정답과 해설 p.2

1 My suitcase is so light that I can carry it by myself.

  → My suitcase is light _____ _____ _____ by myself.

2 Mike is so tired that he can't work anymore.

  → Mike is _____ _____ _____ _____ anymore.

3 The book was so big that I couldn't put it in my bag.

  → The book was _____ _____ _____ _____ in my bag.

4 The woman is so rich that she can travel around the world.

  → The woman is rich _____ _____ _____ around the world.

B 괄호 안에서 알맞은 것을 고르시오.

1 A Let's go to the cinema.

  B No, it's (too late / late enough) to go to the cinema.

2 A Did you swim in the river?

  B Yes, the water was (too warm / warm enough) to swim in.

C 우리말과 뜻이 같도록 괄호 안의 말을 이용하여 문장을 완성하시오.

1 그 자동차는 너무 비싸서 살 수 없다. (expensive, buy)

  → The car is _____ _____ _____ _____.

2 나는 그를 믿을 정도로 충분히 어리석었다. (foolish, trust)

  → I was _____ _____ _____ _____ him.

3 이 딸기는 먹을 수 있을 정도로 충분히 달다. (sweet, eat)

  → This strawberry is _____ _____ _____ _____.

교과서
문장
응용하기 | 배운 문법을 이용하여 영어 문장을 써 봅시다.

1 이 커피는 너무 뜨거워서 마실 수가 없다. → _____

2 내 여동생은 학교에 갈 만큼 충분히 나이가 들지 않았다. → _____

to부정사의 의미상 주어

- **to부정사의 의미상 주어를 쓰는 경우:** 일반적으로 「for+목적격」의 형태로 쓰지만, 사람의 성질·성격을 나타내는 형용사가 오면 「of+목적격」의 형태로 쓴다.

  The table is too heavy **for him** to move.　　　　It was very stupid **of you** to leave the change.

- **to부정사의 의미상 주어를 생략하는 경우:** 일반인이거나 문장 전체의 주어나 목적어와 같으면 생략한다.

  It is hard **to speak** foreign languages fast. 〈일반인인 경우〉

  I want **to answer** the question. 〈주어와 같은 경우〉

  We think **him to be** honest. 〈목적어(him)가 의미상 주어인 경우〉

A 괄호 안의 말을 이용하여 빈칸에 알맞은 말을 쓰시오.

    1 They allowed ＿＿＿＿ ＿＿＿＿ ＿＿＿＿ camping. (Brandon, go)

    2 It was wise ＿＿＿＿ ＿＿＿＿ ＿＿＿＿ ＿＿＿＿ the money. (she, spend)

    3 He ordered ＿＿＿＿ ＿＿＿＿ ＿＿＿＿ the soldiers with food. (we, provide)

    4 It's easy ＿＿＿＿ ＿＿＿＿ ＿＿＿＿ ＿＿＿＿ the way home. (he, find)

> » 정답과 해설 p.2
>
> ◆ 사람의 성질·성격을 나타내는 형용사: kind, bad, careless, wise, rude, silly, stupid, crazy, selfish, cruel, generous 등

B 두 문장의 뜻이 같도록 빈칸에 알맞은 말을 쓰시오.

    1 I wish that he would speak carefully.

    → I wish ＿＿＿＿ ＿＿＿＿ ＿＿＿＿ carefully.

    2 He believes that Grace is innocent.

    → He believes ＿＿＿＿ ＿＿＿＿ ＿＿＿＿ innocent.

    3 It is rude that you say so.

    → It is rude ＿＿＿＿ ＿＿＿＿ ＿＿＿＿ ＿＿＿＿ so.

C 우리말과 뜻이 같도록 괄호 안의 말을 이용하여 문장을 완성하시오.

    1 그들은 내게 물을 좀 가져오라고 요청했다. (bring)

    → They asked ＿＿＿＿ ＿＿＿＿ some water.

    2 네가 그녀의 실수를 비웃은 것은 잘못이었다. (laugh)

    → It was wrong ＿＿＿＿ ＿＿＿＿ ＿＿＿＿ ＿＿＿＿ at her mistake.

    3 우리들이 이 강에서 수영하는 것은 위험하다. (swim)

    → It is dangerous ＿＿＿＿ ＿＿＿＿ ＿＿＿＿ ＿＿＿＿ in this river.

교과서 문장 응용하기 | 배운 문법을 이용하여 영어 문장을 써 봅시다.

    1 그 책은 네가 역사를 이해하는 데 필요하다. (necessary)　→ ＿＿＿＿＿＿＿＿＿＿＿＿＿＿＿＿

    2 우리에게 진실을 이야기하다니 그녀는 정직하다. (it)　→ ＿＿＿＿＿＿＿＿＿＿＿＿＿＿＿＿

to부정사의 시제

to부정사의 시제	형태	예문
to부정사의 시제가 주절의 시제와 동일할 경우	to+동사원형 (단순부정사)	She seems **to be** a doctor. → It **seems** that she **is** a doctor. He seemed **to enjoy** writing his blog. → It **seemed** that he **enjoyed** writing his blog.
to부정사의 시제가 주절의 시제보다 앞설 경우	to have+과거분사 (완료부정사)	He appears **to have been** rich before. → It **appears** that he **was** rich before.

A 두 문장의 뜻이 같도록 빈칸에 알맞은 말을 쓰시오.

» 정답과 해설 p.2

1 It seems that Naomi was sick.

→ Naomi seems _____ _____ _____ sick.

2 It seemed that he was a fire fighter.

→ He seemed _____ _____ a fire fighter.

3 It appears that she was the leading role in the play.

→ She appears _____ _____ _____ the leading role in the play.

B 괄호 안의 말을 이용하여 빈칸에 알맞은 말을 쓰시오.

1 Ms. Smith seems _____ _____ _____ when she was young. (work)

2 He seems _____ _____ _____ to the music festival yesterday. (be)

3 Michael seems _____ _____ _____ the exam last month. (pass)

4 The accident seems _____ _____ _____ two weeks ago. (happen)

C 우리말과 뜻이 같도록 괄호 안의 말을 이용하여 문장을 완성하시오.

1 아이들은 잠든 것처럼 보인다. (be)

→ The children seem _____ _____ asleep.

2 그는 그 잡지를 읽는 것처럼 보였다. (read)

→ He seemed _____ _____ the magazine.

3 그녀는 그녀의 손목시계를 잃어버렸던 것처럼 보인다. (lose)

→ She seems _____ _____ _____ her wrist watch.

교과서
문장
응용하기 | 배운 문법을 이용하여 영어 문장을 써 봅시다.

1 그는 개를 좋아하는 것처럼 보인다. (seem to) → _____

2 그들은 전에 여기에 살았던 것처럼 보인다. (before) → _____

08 원형부정사

■ 원형부정사는 to 없이 동사원형만 쓰는 형태로, 사역동사와 지각동사의 목적격보어로 쓰인다.

동사의 종류	목적격보어	예문
사역동사 (make, have, let 등)	원형부정사	The police officer **made** Kelly **open** her bag.
지각동사 (see, watch, hear, smell, taste, feel 등)		I **heard** a dog **bark** at night.

cf. 동작의 진행 의미를 강조할 때는 지각동사의 목적격보어로 현재분사를 쓴다.
I **heard** a dog **barking** at night.

A 괄호 안에서 알맞은 것을 고르시오.

1 Jacob made her (to follow / follow) the rules.
2 I had my secretary (to call / call) the lawyer.
3 He felt someone (to touch / touch) his hair.
4 Amy watched the little girl (to cross / cross) the bridge.
5 We saw the cat (to steal / stealing) the fish.
6 They never let their children (to play / play) video games until late.

» 정답과 해설 p.2

◆ help는 목적격보어로 원형부정사와 to부정사 둘 다 쓸 수 있다. She **helped** her brother (**to**) **do** his homework.

B 괄호 안의 말을 바르게 배열하여 문장을 완성하시오.

1 They _____ to the grocery store. (go, made, him)
2 She _____ clothes. (wash, helped, her mother)
3 I _____. (knock, the window, on, him, heard)
4 We could _____ in the kitchen. (burning, the pie, smell)

C 우리말과 뜻이 같도록 괄호 안의 말을 이용하여 문장을 완성하시오.

1 Eric은 누군가가 그의 이름을 부르는 것을 들었다. (call)
   → Eric heard _____ _____ his name.
2 아무도 내 여동생이 나가는 것을 보지 못했다. (go out)
   → Nobody _____ _____ _____ _____ _____.
3 Molly는 어제 그녀의 남편에게 울타리를 수리하게 했다. (repair)
   → Molly had her husband _____ _____ _____ yesterday.

교과서 문장 응용하기

배운 문법을 이용하여 영어 문장을 써 봅시다.

1 나는 그가 드럼을 연주하는 것을 보았다. (watch) → _____
2 아빠는 내가 거실을 청소하게 했다. (make) → _____

09 대부정사

- **대부정사의 의미**: 앞에 나온 동사의 반복을 피하기 위해 to부정사에서 동사를 생략하고 to만 쓰는 것을 말한다. to만으로 to부정사를 대신한다는 의미이다.

  She wanted to *go to the concert*, but Peter told her not **to** (go to the concert).

- **대부정사의 쓰임**: 조동사처럼 쓰이는 have to, be going to, be able to 등의 부정사 구문에 자주 사용된다.

  I don't want to *go camping with him*, but I have **to** (go camping with him).

A 밑줄 친 to 뒤에 생략된 부분을 빈칸에 쓰시오.

» 정답과 해설 p.2

1 A Why didn't you have dinner?

   B Because I didn't want <u>to</u>.   to _____

2 A Do you want to go climbing?

   B Yes, I like <u>to</u>.   to _____

3 A Will they go abroad this summer?

   B No, they decided not <u>to</u>.   to _____

4 A Is she going to move into the new house?

   B No, she is not going <u>to</u>.   to _____

5 A Did he come home?

   B No, I asked him <u>to</u>, but he didn't want <u>to</u>.   to _____

B 우리말과 뜻이 같도록 괄호 안의 말과 대부정사를 이용하여 문장을 완성하시오.

1 네가 필요하다면 그 노트북 컴퓨터를 사용해도 된다. (need)

   → You may use the laptop if you _____ _____.

2 Noah는 가고 싶었지만 갈 수 없었다. (able)

   → Noah wanted to go, but he _____ _____ _____.

3 네가 원한다면 나의 제안을 거절해도 좋다. (would)

   → You may refuse my proposal if you _____ _____ _____.

4 나는 스마트폰을 끄고 싶지 않지만 꺼야만 한다. (have)

   → I don't want to turn off my smartphone, but I _____ _____.

5 그가 우리에게 가지 말라고 말했기 때문에 우리는 거기에 가지 않았다. (tell)

   → We didn't go there because he _____ _____ _____ _____.

**교과서
문장
응용하기** | 배운 문법을 이용하여 영어 문장을 써 봅시다.

1 네가 그것에 대해 말하고 싶지 않다면 말할 필요가 없다. (don't have to) → _____

2 나는 그곳에 가고 싶지만 갈 수 없을 것이다. (be able to) → _____

독립부정사

■ 독립부정사는 부사구처럼 독립된 의미를 가지며 문장 전체를 수식하는 to부정사이다.

to be frank(honest) with you	솔직히 말하면	to be sure	확실히
to make matters worse	설상가상으로	to begin with	우선, 먼저
to tell the truth	사실대로 말하면	so to speak	말하자면
that is to say	즉, 다시 말하면	strange to say	이상한 말이지만
not to mention	~은 말할 것도 없이	needless to say	말할 필요도 없이

Strange to say, I didn't sleep well.　　　　**To begin with**, I don't like his voice.

A 빈칸에 알맞은 말을 | 보기 |에서 골라 독립부정사 형태로 쓰시오.　　　》 정답과 해설 p.3

> | 보기 |
> say　　　tell　　　mention　　　make

1 _____ _____ the truth, I'm a little nervous.

2 _____ _____ matters worse, it began to snow.

3 He can speak French, not _____ _____ English.

4 Strange _____ _____, I'm not interested in movies.

B 괄호 안의 말과 독립부정사를 이용하여 문장을 완성하시오.

1 _____, the Earth is round. (needless)

2 Karen is, _____, a bookworm. (speak)

3 _____, I didn't do my homework. (honest)

4 _____, we do not have much money. (begin)

5 _____, she is the tallest girl in our school. (sure)

C 우리말과 뜻이 같도록 빈칸에 알맞은 말을 쓰시오.

1 다시 말하면, 우리는 기차를 놓쳤다.

　　→ _____ _____ _____ _____, we missed the train.

2 사실대로 말하면, 나는 오래된 책들을 버렸다.

　　→ _____ _____ _____ _____, I threw away the old books.

3 솔직히 말하면, 너는 잘생기지 않았다.

　　→ _____ _____ _____ _____ _____, you're not handsome.

교과서 문장 응용하기 배운 문법을 이용하여 영어 문장을 써 봅시다.

1 말할 필요도 없이, 그는 의사가 아니다. (needless)　　→ _____

2 확실히, 그 영화는 재미있다. (sure, interesting)　　→ _____

➡ 내신적중 실전문제를 풀기 전에 Workbook p.2에 있는 요점정리를 참고하세요.

내신적중 실전문제

» 정답과 해설 p.3

01 괄호 안에 주어진 말의 알맞은 형태가 바르게 짝지어진 것은?

> • (Help) the poor is important.
> • They have two old dogs (look after).

① Helping — look after
② To help — looking after
③ Help — to look after
④ To help — to look after
⑤ Helping — looking after

02 괄호 안의 말을 문맥에 맞게 빈칸에 알맞은 형태로 쓰시오. 주관식

> **A** Do you know how chopsticks are used in Korea?
> **B** Sure. Miso taught me _____ them. (use)

03 밑줄 친 부분의 쓰임이 | 보기 |와 같은 것은?

> ┌ 보기 ┐
> I was stupid to believe such a thing.

① She ordered a cup of coffee to take away.
② I want to have good friends at school.
③ It's dangerous to eat a lot of junk food.
④ He's very happy to meet a famous actor.
⑤ She has plans to take a trip during her vacation.

04 빈칸에 알맞지 <u>않은</u> 것은?

> He _____ us recycle cans and old clothes.

① made   ② told ③ let
④ watched   ⑤ helped

05 빈칸에 알맞은 말을 순서대로 쓰시오. 주관식

> • It is important _____ him to go to school every day.
> • It is smart _____ her to win a quiz game.

[06~07] 대화의 빈칸에 알맞은 것을 고르시오.

06
> **A** Do you want to improve your English?
> **B** Yes, I'd like _____.

① of   ② to   ③ in
④ that   ⑤ about

07
> **A** Can she speak foreign languages?
> **B** Sure, she can speak French and Spanish, _____ English.

① not to mention   ② so to speak
③ strange to say   ④ that is to say
⑤ to tell the truth

08 다음 문장과 의미가 같은 것은?

> All students are to take the final exam.

① All students may take the final exam.
② All students took the final exam.
③ All students were taking the final exam.
④ All students should take the final exam.
⑤ All students don't need to take the final exam.

09 빈칸에 알맞은 말이 나머지 넷과 다른 것은?

① This riddle is easy _____ you to solve.
② It is cruel _____ him to beat his dog.
③ It's necessary _____ Jenny to read this book.
④ This room is large enough _____ you to dance.
⑤ It's important _____ teenagers to get along with friends.

10 밑줄 친 부분의 우리말 뜻이 잘못된 것은?

① The plan is, <u>to be sure</u>, impossible. (확실히)
② <u>To begin with</u>, let's read the book aloud. (우선)
③ <u>Strange to say</u>, I'm not interested in clothes. (이상한 말이지만)
④ <u>To be frank with you</u>, Jack doesn't like you. (솔직히 말하자면)
⑤ <u>Needless to say</u>, I finished my homework without any help. (다시 말하면)

11 밑줄 친 부분의 쓰임이 나머지 넷과 다른 것은?

① I need friends <u>to play</u> with.
② Helen has some books <u>to read</u> tonight.
③ Mom didn't find a place <u>to park</u> the car.
④ There are a lot of places <u>to visit</u> in Rome.
⑤ She left for Japan, never <u>to come</u> back.

12 밑줄 친 부분 중 어법상 어색한 것은?

> When I was ① <u>walking</u> down the street, I ② <u>saw</u> Peter ③ <u>cross</u> the street and ④ <u>to enter</u> a bookstore ⑤ <u>with</u> his dog.

13 두 문장의 뜻이 같도록 할 때, 빈칸에 알맞은 것은?

> The sun was so bright that I couldn't open my eyes.
> → The sun was _____ my eyes.

① bright enough to open
② too bright to open
③ too bright me to open
④ too bright for me to open
⑤ bright enough for me to open

14 우리말과 뜻이 같도록 괄호 안의 말을 이용하여 문장을 완성하시오. (주관식)

> 내 방학은 지금부터 2주 후에 시작될 예정이다. (start)
> → My vacation _____ _____ _____ two weeks from now.

[15~16] 어법상 어색한 것을 고르시오.

15 ① People under 20 are not to smoke.

② He advised me to stop eating spicy food.

③ To play basketball is a lot of fun.

④ Mr. Jones seems to be a great player when he was young.

⑤ She didn't know where to stay for a week.

16 ① Mr. Brown heard the teenagers talking.

② Can you lend me a pen to write?

③ To make matters worse, it was getting dark.

④ The teacher was kind enough to give me advice.

⑤ You don't have to go to the party if you don't want to.

17 밑줄 친 부분의 쓰임이 같은 것끼리 짝지어진 것은?

ⓐ It is difficult to understand other people.

ⓑ My goal was to lose 10kg in three months.

ⓒ The girl cried hard only to make her mom angry.

ⓓ He must be kind to lend me some money.

ⓔ If you are to be a singer, you must practice a lot.

① ⓐ, ⓒ   ② ⓑ, ⓒ   ③ ⓑ, ⓒ, ⓓ

④ ⓒ, ⓓ   ⑤ ⓒ, ⓓ, ⓔ

18 괄호 안에서 알맞은 것을 골라 쓰시오. (주관식)

ⓐ The water is (too / to / so) cold for her to drink.

ⓑ Mr. Kim is skillful (too / so / enough) to manage the project by himself.

ⓐ _____ ⓑ _____

19 밑줄 친 부분을 잘못 고쳐 쓴 것은?

① They are being married in December.

    (→ are to be)

② It was generous for him to forgive the thief.   (→ of him)

③ Mom won't let me to watch TV for a long time.   (→ watch)

④ She walked carefully to fall not again.

    (→ to not fall)

⑤ The scientist appears to find the answer already.   (→ to have found)

20 짝지어진 두 문장의 의미가 같지 않은 것은?

① To travel to Paris takes all day.

    → It takes all day to travel to Paris.

② She was rude to behave like that.

    → It was rude of her to behave like that.

③ I expect to go to China someday.

    → I expect that I will go to China someday.

④ He doesn't know whom to believe.

    → He doesn't know whom he should believe.

⑤ The girl was so kind that she could show me the way.

    → The girl was too kind to show me the way.

서술형 평가

01 빈칸에 알맞은 말을 | 보기 |에서 골라 알맞은 형태로 쓰시오.

> 보기
> do   meet   arrive

(1) I'd like to invent a robot _____ my homework.

(2) Ann is _____ here the day after tomorrow.

(3) Sam went to Disneyland _____ Mickey Mouse.

02 두 문장의 뜻이 같도록 괄호 안의 말을 이용하여 문장을 완성하시오.

(1) Children eat well-balanced meals. (important)

   → It is _____ well-balanced meals.

(2) He wore blue jeans at the party. (careless)

   → It was _____ blue jeans at the party.

03 두 문장이 한 문장이 되도록 괄호 안의 지시대로 빈칸에 알맞은 말을 쓰시오.

> The world is a small place. We can travel anywhere in one day.

(1) The world is _____ anywhere in one day. (so ~ that 이용)

(2) The world is _____ anywhere in one day. (enough 이용)

04 우리말과 뜻이 같도록 문장을 완성하시오.

> 나의 삼촌은 내가 5살 때 수영하는 법을 가르쳐 주었다.

(1) My uncle taught me _____ when I was five years old. (3단어)

(2) My uncle taught me _____ when I was five years old. (4단어)

🔵 독해형 어법

[05~06] 다음 글을 읽고, 물음에 답하시오.

  Our lifestyles today are very busy. That is to saying, we have family, school, sports, leisure and social appointments ⓐ to fit into a limited time. We need to be healthy to cope with the demands of daily life. ⓑ To have a healthy lifestyle, we need to:
• eat a variety of healthy food most of the time
• get regular exercise
• go to bed early ⓒ to get enough sleep
  It is important ⓓ to balance these aspects of life, rather than put more emphasis on one aspect rather than another one.

05 밑줄 친 부분과 쓰임이 같은 것을 ⓐ~ⓓ 중에서 골라 쓰시오.

(1) They plan to reduce fats in the food.

_____

(2) Children were excited to see the show.

_____

(3) She knows many good ways to save things.

_____

06 어법상 어색한 부분을 찾아 바르게 고쳐 쓰시오.

_____ → _____

CHAPTER

02

동명사

FOCUS 11   동명사의 쓰임

FOCUS 12   동명사의 의미상 주어

FOCUS 13   동명사와 현재분사

FOCUS 14   동명사와 to부정사를 목적어로 쓰는 동사

FOCUS 15   동명사의 관용 표현

동명사는 어떤 역할을 하는가?

동명사는 「동사원형+-ing」의 형태로, 동사의 성격을 가지고 있으면서 문장에서 주어, 목적어, 보어와 같은 명사의 역할을 한다.

동명사의 역할

주어 역할: ~하는 것은, ~하기는

Playing in the street is dangerous.
거리에서 노는 것은 위험하다.

보어 역할: ~하는 것(이다)

My hobby is **collecting** stamps.
나의 취미는 우표를 수집하는 것이다.

목적어 역할: ~하는 것을

She finished **cleaning** her room.
그녀는 그녀의 방을 청소하는 것을 끝냈다.
I'm fond of **reading** novels.
나는 소설책을 읽는 것을 좋아한다.

동명사는 현재분사와 무엇이 다른가?

동명사와 *현재분사는 「동사원형+-ing」로 형태는 같지만 동명사는 명사 역할을, 현재분사는 형용사 역할을 한다. 또한 동명사와 현재분사가 명사 앞에 쓰일 때 동명사는 '~하기 위한'의 의미로 목적이나 용도를 나타내고, 현재분사는 '~하고 있는'의 의미로 동작이나 상태를 나타낸다.

a **singing** room 〈동명사〉
노래를 하기 위한 방

a **singing** girl 〈현재분사〉
노래하고 있는 소녀

동명사와 to부정사를 목적어로 취하는 동사에는 어떤 것들이 있는가?

동사는 동명사와 to부정사를 모두 목적어로 취할 수 있지만, 동명사만이나, to부정사만을 취하는 동사들이 있다. 또한 둘 다 목적어로 취하되, 목적어에 따라 그 의미가 달라지는 동사도 있다.

동명사만을 목적어로 취하는 동사	enjoy, finish, keep, mind, avoid, deny, stop ...
to부정사만을 목적어로 취하는 동사	want, wish, hope, expect, decide, plan, refuse ...
둘 다 목적어로 취하는 동사	begin, start, hate, love, like, continue ...
둘 다 목적어로 취하되 그 의미가 달라지는 동사	remember, forget, try ...

**용어
사전**

* **현재분사**: 「동사원형+-ing」의 형태로 동사의 성질을 가지고 있으면서 동시에 형용사의 역할도 하여, 명사를 수식하거나 보어 역할을 하는 동사의 변화형을 의미한다.

11 동명사의 쓰임

- 동명사는 명사처럼 쓰여 문장에서 주어, 보어, 목적어 역할을 한다. 주어와 보어로 쓰인 동명사는 단수 취급하며, to부정사로 바꿔 쓸 수 있다.

Walking late at night is dangerous. → **To walk** late at night is dangerous. 〈주어〉

My plan is **traveling** all around the world. → My plan is **to travel** all around the world. 〈보어〉

Most people *enjoy* **watching** TV. 〈동사의 목적어〉

She is afraid *of* **making** mistakes. 〈전치사의 목적어〉

A 괄호 안의 말을 바르게 배열하여 문장을 완성하시오.

》 정답과 해설 p.4

◆ 동명사의 부정은 동명사 앞에 부정어 not(never)을 쓴다.
Not overeating is one way to be healthy.

1 Her hobby _____.
(jazz, listening, is, to)

2 Julie _____ last year.
(junk food, eating, quit)

3 What are _____ in a big city?
(of, living, the, advantages)

4 _____ a popular activity today.
(mountains, is, cycling, on)

5 _____ your big mistake.
(his advice, not, was, following)

B 우리말과 뜻이 같도록 괄호 안의 말을 이용하여 문장을 완성하시오.

1 그녀는 뉴스기사 쓰는 것을 끝마쳤다. (write)
→ She _____ _____ news articles.

2 그의 직업은 새로운 소프트웨어 프로그램을 개발하는 것이다. (develop)
→ His job is _____ new software programs.

3 Mia는 옛날로 돌아가는 꿈을 꿨다. (go back)
→ Mia dreamed about _____ _____ to the old days.

4 미래의 계획을 세우는 것은 너의 삶을 더 낫게 만들 것이다. (make)
→ _____ _____ for the future will make your life better.

5 아침에 물 한 잔을 마시는 것은 너의 건강에 좋다. (drink)
→ _____ a cup of water in the morning is good for your health.

교과서
문장
응용하기 | 배운 문법을 이용하여 영어 문장을 써 봅시다.

1 노래하는 것은 그의 취미 중 하나이다. (sing) → _____

2 그녀는 농구를 잘한다. (good) → _____

12 동명사의 의미상 주어

- **의미상의 주어를 쓰는 경우:** 동명사의 주어가 문장의 주어와 일치하지 않을 때 동명사 앞에 소유격의 형태로 쓴다.

I am upset at **his breaking** the rule.

cf. 구어체에서는 의미상 주어로 목적격을 쓰기도 한다.

She was annoyed by **his(him) laughing** at her.

- **의미상 주어를 생략하는 경우:** 동명사의 주어가 문장 전체의 주어나 목적어와 같거나 일반인일 경우 생략한다.

Jacob doesn't mind **spending** money. 〈spending의 의미상 주어는 문장 전체의 주어인 Jacob〉

A | 보기 |와 같이 두 문장을 한 문장으로 쓸 때 빈칸에 알맞은 말을 쓰시오. » 정답과 해설 p.4

> 보기
> He goes there. + I like it. → I like his going there.

1 She talks loudly. + Thomas hates it.

　→ Thomas hates _____ _____ _____ .

2 He welcomed us. + We are thankful for it.

　→ We are thankful for _____ _____ _____ .

3 A dragonfly flew into the room. + Fiona stopped it.

　→ Fiona stopped _____ _____ _____ into the room.

4 The driver drove too fast. + I was afraid of it.

　→ I was afraid of _____ _____ _____ too fast.

B 우리말과 뜻이 같도록 괄호 안의 말을 이용하여 문장을 완성하시오.

1 우리는 네가 집에 돌아오는 것을 상상했다. (come)

　→ We imagined _____ _____ back home.

2 Alex는 그녀가 그에게 미소 지은 것을 기억한다. (smile)

　→ Alex remembers _____ _____ at him.

3 나는 내 남동생이 시험에 통과할 것을 확신한다. (pass)

　→ I am sure of _____ _____ _____ the test.

4 그녀가 그녀의 방 청소를 한 것이 온 가족을 놀라게 했다. (clean)

　→ _____ _____ her room surprised all her family.

5 Clara는 그가 그녀의 가방을 위층으로 운반해 준 것에 감동받았다. (carry)

　→ Clara was moved by _____ _____ her bag upstairs.

교과서 문장 응용하기 배운 문법을 이용하여 영어 문장을 써 봅시다.

1 그녀는 내가 금메달을 딴 것을 자랑스러워한다. (proud, win) → _____

2 Luke는 그 학생들이 규칙을 무시한 것을 인정했다. (admit, ignore) → _____

13 동명사와 현재분사

■ 동명사와 현재분사는 둘 다 「동사원형+-ing」의 형태이지만, 그 역할과 의미는 다르다.

동명사	용도·목적의 명사적 역할 (~하는 것)	a **sleeping** bag(= a bag for sleeping) Learning a foreign language is too difficult.
현재분사	동작, 상태의 형용사 역할 (~하고 있는)	a **sleeping** baby(= a baby who is sleeping) He is learning a foreign language.

A 밑줄 친 부분이 동명사인지 현재분사인지 쓰시오.

» 정답과 해설 p.4

1 (a) We bought a new <u>washing</u> machine. _____

   (b) We are <u>washing</u> our clothes. _____

2 (a) He is in the <u>dancing</u> room. _____

   (b) He knows the <u>dancing</u> girl. _____

B 다음 문장을 밑줄 친 부분에 유의하여 바르게 해석하시오.

1 <u>Exercising</u> regularly is a really good habit.

   → _____

2 <u>Cycling</u> in the morning makes you feel fresh.

   → _____

3 My grandmother went for a walk with a <u>walking</u> stick.

   → _____

C 우리말과 뜻이 같도록 괄호 안의 말을 이용하여 문장을 완성하시오.

1 그녀의 반짝이는 눈을 보아라. (twinkle)

   → Look at her _____ _____.

2 끓고 있는 물을 조심해라. (boil)

   → Be careful with the _____ _____.

3 역사책을 읽는 것은 시간여행을 하는 하나의 방법이다. (read)

   → _____ _____ _____ is a way to travel in time.

교과서
문장
응용하기 배운 문법을 이용하여 영어 문장을 써 봅시다.

1 그녀의 취미는 꽃 사진을 찍는 것이다. (take photos) → _____

2 Owen은 지금 에세이를 쓰고 있다. (write, essay) → _____

동명사와 to부정사를 목적어로 쓰는 동사

동명사만 목적어로 취하는 동사	enjoy, finish, keep, mind, avoid, deny, quit, stop, consider 등	I *enjoyed* **reading** the fashion magazine.
to부정사만 목적어로 취하는 동사	want, wish, hope, expect, promise, decide, plan, refuse, agree 등	Lily *wishes* **to be** the queen at the party.
동명사와 to부정사를 모두 목적어로 취하는 동사	begin, start, hate, love, like, continue 등	She *continued* **watching(to watch)** TV.

- 목적어의 형태에 따라 의미가 다른 동사

remember forget ＋동명사	(과거에) ~했던 것을 기억하다/잊다	remember forget ＋to부정사	(미래에) ~할 것을 기억하다/잊다
try＋동명사	시험 삼아 ~해 보다	try ＋to부정사	~하려고 노력하다

A 괄호 안에서 알맞은 것을 <u>모두</u> 고르시오.

    1 It began (to rain / raining) heavily.

    2 Leo quit (to drink / drinking) to stay fit.

    3 Luke loves (to work / working) at the marketing agency.

    4 Do you mind (to take / taking) care of my birds?

    5 Lucy expects (to pass / passing) her driving test tomorrow.

    6 Her father promised (to go / going) on a picnic this Sunday.

    7 Why did you decide (to become / becoming) a graphic designer?

》 정답과 해설 p.4

◆ 「stop＋동명사」는 '~하는 것을 멈추다'라는 의미를, 「stop＋to부정사」는 to부정사가 부사처럼 쓰여 '~하기 위해 멈추다'라는 의미를 나타낸다.
I stopped **going** to the gym. (나는 체육관에 가는 것을 멈추었다.)
I stopped **to buy** something to eat. (나는 먹을 것을 사기 위해 멈췄다.)

B 괄호 안의 말을 이용하여 빈칸에 알맞은 형태를 쓰시오.

    1 • He felt thirsty and stopped _____ water. (drink)

       • He stopped _____ and came down from the stage. (sing)

    2 • She often forgets _____ her hands before dinner. (wash)

       • She has forgotten _____ her friends to the party yesterday. (bring)

    3 • Hazel remembers _____ the report by Friday. (submit)

       • Hazel remembers _____ on a school trip in high school. (go)

교과서 문장 응용하기

배운 문법을 이용하여 영어 문장을 써 봅시다.

    1 Luna는 항상 그녀의 방을 청소하는 것을 피한다. (avoid) → _____

    2 나는 나의 할머니와 함께 살았던 것을 기억한다. → _____

동명사의 관용 표현

■ 동명사를 이용한 여러 가지 관용 표현들이 있다.

on(upon) -ing	~하자마자	be worth -ing	~할 가치가 있다
be busy -ing	~하느라 바쁘다	It's no use -ing	~해도 소용없다
look forward to -ing	~하기를 기대하다	be used to -ing	~하는 데 익숙하다
spend (on) -ing	(시간·돈을) ~하는 데 쓰다	have trouble -ing	~하는 데 어려움을 겪다
cannot help -ing	~하지 않을 수 없다	keep(prevent) ~ from -ing	~가 …하지 못하게 하다
feel like -ing	~하고 싶다	There is no -ing	~하는 것은 불가능하다

We **cannot help crying**.   This book **is worth reading**.

A 빈칸에 알맞은 말을 | 보기 |에서 골라 알맞은 형태로 쓰시오.

» 정답과 해설 p.5

| 보기 |
| prepare   watch   deny   draw |

1 It is no use _____ the fact.
2 The movie, *The Monster,* is worth _____ .
3 Alice spends most of her time on _____ cartoons.
4 My mother is used to _____ family dinner every night.

◆ 「used to+동사원형」: '~하곤 했다'의 의미로 과거의 규칙적인 습관을 나타낸다.
I **used to have** dinner with my pet. (나는 애완동물과 함께 저녁 식사를 하곤 했다.)

B 우리말과 뜻이 같도록 빈칸에 알맞은 말을 쓰시오.

1 Selena는 친구 집을 찾는 데 어려움을 겪고 있다.
→ Selena is _____ _____ _____ her friend's house.
2 Tom은 지금 전화하느라 바쁘다.
→ Tom is _____ _____ on the phone now.
3 나는 곧 당신과 같이 일하기를 기대한다.
→ I _____ _____ _____ _____ with you soon.

C 괄호 안의 말을 빈칸에 알맞은 형태로 쓰고 문장을 해석하시오.

1 We feel like _____ Mr. Brown next week. (visit)
→ _____
2 On _____ about the camping program, I wanted to join. (hear)
→ _____

교과서 문장 응용하기 | 배운 문법을 이용하여 영어 문장을 써 봅시다.

1 나는 지금 침대에서 자고 싶다. (on the bed)   → _____
2 그녀는 그 영화를 보는 동안 울지 않을 수 없다. (during the movie)   → _____

내신적중 실전문제

빈출유형 ★

[01~02] 괄호 안에 주어진 말의 알맞은 형태를 고르시오.

01

> (Open) your heart first is important to have many friends.

① Open   ② Opens
③ Opened   ④ Opening
⑤ To opening

02

> My dream once was (become) a fashion model.

① become   ② becoming
③ becomed   ④ became
⑤ to becoming

[03~04] 대화의 빈칸에 알맞은 것을 고르시오.

03

> **A** What do you like to do in your free time?
> **B** I enjoy _____ a walk with my dog.

① take   ② taking   ③ to take
④ took   ⑤ to taking

04

> **A** Why does he look sad?
> **B** He's worried about _____ healthy.

① not being   ② being not
③ not be   ④ to not be
⑤ not to be

05 빈칸에 공통으로 알맞지 <u>않은</u> 것은?

> •Harper _____ breathing the cool mountain air.
> •They _____ to look for some information about stars.

① liked   ② started   ③ began
④ loved   ⑤ finished

06 밑줄 친 부분의 알맞은 형태를 각각 쓰시오. 주관식

> ⓐ Remember <u>bring</u> a plastic bag for shopping.
> ⓑ I remember <u>bring</u> a plastic bag, but I can't find it.

ⓐ _____ ⓑ _____

07 밑줄 친 부분의 쓰임이 |보기|와 같은 것은?

> **보기**
> The first step is <u>understanding</u> different culture.

① I don't mind <u>making</u> dinner for you.
② I'm sick and tired of <u>arguing</u> with you.
③ <u>Wearing</u> a seat belt keeps drivers safe.
④ Grandmother enjoys <u>talking</u> to me about old times.
⑤ What he does first in the morning is <u>taking</u> a shower.

[08~09] 빈칸에 알맞은 말이 바르게 짝지어진 것을 고르시오.

08

> • I used to _____ a lot when I was young.
> • She is used to _____ speeches in public.

① travel — make
② travels — makes
③ travel — making
④ traveling — make
⑤ traveling — making

09

> • My mother feels like _____ a rest under the tree.
> • Ann looks forward _____ the badminton club.

① to take — to join
② to take — to joining
③ taking — to join
④ taking — joining
⑤ taking — to joining

[10~11] 밑줄 친 부분 중 어법상 어색한 것을 골라 바르게 고쳐 쓰시오. [주관식]

10

> Mary ①didn't ②go ③cycling yesterday. She ④wanted to avoid ⑤to meet Peter.

_____ → _____

11

> Jessy ① remembers ② inviting friends to her pajama party next week. ③ So, she ④ began ⑤ to make invitation cards.

_____ → _____

[12~13] 우리말을 바르게 영작한 것을 고르시오.

12

> Jack은 캠페인에 참여하지 않은 것에 대해 사과했다.

① Jack didn't apologize for take part in the campaign.
② Jack didn't apologize for taking part in the campaign.
③ Jack apologized for not take part in the campaign.
④ Jack apologized for not taking part in the campaign.
⑤ Jack apologized for taking not part in the campaign.

13

> 나는 그가 시험에 실패할 것이라고는 상상할 수 없다.

① I can't imagine failing the exam.
② I can't imagine to fail the exam.
③ I can't imagine his failing the exam.
④ I can't imagine him to fail the exam.
⑤ I can't imagine his fail the exam.

14 괄호 안의 동사를 동명사로 바꾸어야 하는 문장의 개수는?

> ⓐ I hope (take) pictures of beautiful flowers.
> ⓑ We arrived in the city after (drive) all night.
> ⓒ Mr. Miller decided not (stay) at a hotel on holidays.
> ⓓ The sun would not stop (produce) light and heat.
> ⓔ I spent my pocket money (buy) these shoes.

① 1개   ② 2개   ③ 3개
④ 4개   ⑤ 5개

15 빈칸에 알맞지 <u>않은</u> 것은?

> Jessica _____ reading science fiction books.

① wants   ② stops
③ finished   ④ gave up
⑤ minds

16 밑줄 친 부분을 바르게 고친 것은?

> Sophia likes I make dinner because she doesn't like cooking.

① I making   ② I to make
③ making my   ④ my making
⑤ me make

17 대화의 괄호 ⓐ, ⓑ안에 주어진 말의 알맞은 형태를 쓰시오.

> **A** Jessy, thank you for ⓐ (lend) me your digital camera. It was really useful.
> **B** Oh! I completely forgot ⓑ (lend) it to you.

ⓐ _____   ⓑ _____

18 밑줄 친 부분의 쓰임이 나머지 넷과 <u>다른</u> 것은?

① <u>Shopping</u> with friends makes me happy.
② The boys are <u>making</u> robots in the classroom.
③ What I like best is <u>listening</u> to popular music.
④ They enjoy <u>spending</u> their holiday in Spain.
⑤ Edward thinks of <u>climbing</u> trees this afternoon.

19 밑줄 친 부분을 동명사로 바꿔 쓸 수 <u>없는</u> 것은?

① It began <u>to snow</u> yesterday.
② They like <u>to travel</u> by bicycle.
③ She continued <u>to cook</u> the meal.
④ I hated <u>to walk</u> when I was a child.
⑤ Billy promised <u>to go</u> to the theater with me.

20 우리말을 영어로 <u>잘못</u> 옮긴 것은?

① 너는 스테이크를 먹고 싶니?
  → Do you feel like eating steak?
② 그는 공주와 사랑에 빠지지 않을 수 없다.
  → He can't help falling in love with the princess.
③ 나는 요즘 밤에 잠을 자는 데 어려움이 있다.
  → I have trouble to sleep at night these days.
④ 아빠는 부엌에서 저녁을 준비하느라 바쁘시다.
  → Dad is busy preparing dinner in the kitchen.
⑤ 그 아기는 나를 보자마자 울음을 터뜨렸다.
  → On seeing me, the baby bursted into tears.

21 어법상 옳은 것을 <u>모두</u> 고르면?

① Amy was happy with going not to school.
② I'm interested in helping the homeless.
③ She forgot reading the book in her childhood.
④ He tried explaining the situation, but his dad didn't listen to him.
⑤ I wouldn't mind he opening the window.

22 빈칸에 알맞은 것은?

Sophia denied _____ to the party yesterday.

① her going   ② her to go
③ her go   ④ she going
⑤ she to go

23 주어진 문장과 뜻이 같은 것은?

It's impossible to live on Mars.

① There is no living on Mars.
② There is not living on Mars.
③ There is no to live on Mars.
④ It is no good living on Mars.
⑤ It is no good to live on Mars.

24 밑줄 친 부분을 <u>잘못</u> 고쳐 쓴 것은?

① The rain kept me <u>to going</u> on a picnic.
                    (→ from going)
② Frank agreed <u>ride</u> our bicycles in the park.   (→ to ride)
③ It's no use <u>cry</u> over spilt milk.
                    (→ crying)
④ We felt sorry about <u>Anna</u> failing the exam.
                    (→ Anna's)
⑤ Mark stopped <u>take</u> a short break after a long walk.   (→ taking)

25 밑줄 친 부분의 쓰임이 같은 것끼리 짝지어 쓰시오.

ⓐ Sally is <u>working</u> on a computer in the library.
ⓑ I'm sure of his <u>passing</u> the exam.
ⓒ My mother enjoys <u>watching</u> comedy shows.
ⓓ Many people are <u>shopping</u> for new clothes.
ⓔ Will you try <u>eating</u> this soup?

_____ , _____

서술형 평가

01 괄호 안의 말을 이용하여 우리말을 영어로 쓰시오.

> 시각 장애인들은 보지 않고 물건을 다루는 데 익숙하다.
> (handle)

→ Blind people _____
 things without seeing them.

02 두 문장을 한 문장으로 쓸 때 빈칸에 알맞은 말을 쓰시오.

> • Sally takes care of her little sister.
> • I do not worry about it.

→ I do not worry about _____
 _____.

[03~04] 밑줄 친 부분을 우리말로 옮기시오.

03 (1) Jessica remembers bringing the coupons
 of the store.
 → _____

 (2) Jessica remembers to bring the coupons
 of the store.
 → _____

04 (1) Alan stopped talking to Jean about stars.
 → _____

 (2) Alan stopped to talk to Jean about stars.
 → _____

05 동사 **walk**를 이용하여 빈칸에 알맞은 형태로 쓰시오.

(1) _____ in the rain is interesting.
(2) Harry wants _____ in the rain.
(3) Harry enjoys _____ in the rain.
(4) Harry's hobby is _____ in the
 rain.
(5) Harry feels like _____ in the rain.

독해형 어법

[06~07] 다음 글을 읽고, 물음에 답하시오.

 아침에 일어나자마자, Miso went into the schoolroom. It was right next to her bedroom. The intelligent robot teacher was on and waiting for her. It is always on at the same time every day except for Saturday and Sunday. The screen was lit up, and it said; "Now, let's begin ⓐ (study) on the cloning. Don't forget ⓑ (insert) yesterday's homework in the proper slot." Miso inserted it. The intelligent robot teacher was flashing on the screen.

06 밑줄 친 우리말을 조건에 맞게 영어로 옮기시오.

> 조건
> get up과 전치사를 이용할 것

→ _____ in the morning

07 괄호 ⓐ, ⓑ 안의 말을 알맞은 형태로 쓰시오.

ⓐ _____   ⓑ _____

CHAPTER

03

분사

FOCUS 16   분사의 역할

FOCUS 17   분사구문

FOCUS 18   분사구문의 의미 1_ 시간, 이유

FOCUS 19   분사구문의 의미 2_ 조건, 양보

FOCUS 20   분사구문의 의미 3_ 동시동작, 연속상황

FOCUS 21   완료형 분사구문

FOCUS 22   being, having been의 생략

FOCUS 23   독립분사구문, 비인칭 독립분사구문

FOCUS 24   with+명사+분사

분사란 무엇인가?

분사는 동사를 동사의 성격을 유지하면서 형용사의 역할을 할 수 있게 변형한 것을 말한다. 분사에는 「동사원형+-ing」의 형태인 현재분사와 「동사원형+-ed」의 형태이거나 불규칙한 형태인 과거분사가 있다.

분사의 종류

현재분사: 동사원형+-ing 〈능동·진행의 의미〉

> Tom was **cleaning** the room then.
> Tom은 그때 방을 청소하고 있었다.

과거분사: 동사원형+-ed 〈수동·완료의 의미〉

> I have just **finished** doing the dishes.
> 나는 막 설거지를 끝냈다.

분사의 역할

명사의 앞, 뒤에서 명사를 수식함

> The **barking** dog is not mine.
> 그 짖고 있는 개는 나의 것이 아니다.

주어, 목적어를 설명하는 보어 역할

> She was **surprised** at the news.
> 그녀는 그 소식에 놀랐다.

분사구문이란 무엇인가?

분사구문이란 분사를 이용하여 *부사절을 부사구로 간단하게 나타낸 것을 말하며, 시간, 이유, 조건, 양보 등의 다양한 의미를 나타낸다.

〈부사절〉 **When I needed fresh air,** I went out for a walk. 나는 신선한 공기가 필요했을 때, 산책하러 나갔다.

① 접속사와 주어를 생략
② 동사를 「동사원형+-ing」 형태로 바꿈

〈분사구문〉 **Needing fresh air,** I went out for a walk.

용어 사전

* **부사절:** 문장에 꼭 필요한 성분인 주어, 동사, 목적어, 보어를 제외한 시간, 이유, 조건, 양보 등과 같은 부가적 정보를 제공하는 절을 말한다.

16 분사의 역할

- 현재분사는 「동사원형+-ing」 형태로 능동·진행의 의미를 갖고, 과거분사는 「동사원형+-ed」 형태로 수동·완료의 의미를 갖는다.

- **한정적 용법**: 명사를 꾸며주는 역할을 하며, 다른 수식어구와 함께 쓰이면 수식하는 명사의 뒤에 온다.

  He has a **hidden** card.   The girl **sitting on a bench** is my sister.

- **서술적 용법**: 문장에서 주격보어 또는 목적격보어 역할을 한다.

  You looked **excited** today. 〈주격보어〉   I saw the moon **rising** in the sky. 〈목적격보어〉

  cf. 감정을 나타내는 동사는 분사형으로 자주 쓰이며, '~한 감정을 느끼게 하는'의 뜻일 때는 현재분사를, '~한 감정을 느끼는'의 뜻일 때는 과거분사를 쓴다.

  The game was **exciting**.   I was **excited**.

A 괄호 안의 말을 빈칸에 알맞은 형태로 쓰시오.   » 정답과 해설 p.6

1 Mr. Johnson was _____. (delight)

2 The book was _____. (interest)

3 Her speech made us _____. (bore)

4 Who is that boy _____ a blue sweater? (wear)

5 _____ strawberries are her favorite dessert. (freeze)

6 I see her _____ out to dinner every Friday. (go)

7 The necklace _____ by a thief was found. (steal)

B 우리말과 뜻이 같도록 괄호 안의 말을 이용하여 문장을 완성하시오.

1 그는 그 방이 청소된 것을 발견했다. (clean)

  → He found _____ _____ _____.

2 겁에 질린 그 아이는 엄마 뒤에 숨었다. (frighten)

  → _____ _____ _____ _____ hid behind his mom.

3 Kate와 함께 달리고 있는 소녀는 누구니? (run)

  → Who is _____ _____ _____ with Kate?

4 Charlie는 그의 친구들이 거리에서 춤추고 있는 것을 보았다. (dance)

  → Charlie saw _____ _____ _____ in the street.

5 책상에서 책을 읽고 있는 그 소녀를 봐라. (read)

  → Look at _____ _____ _____ a book at the desk.

교과서 문장 응용하기

배운 문법을 이용하여 영어 문장을 써 봅시다.

1 그 영화는 실망스러웠다. (disappoint)   → _____

2 나는 고장 난 컴퓨터를 발견했다. (break)   → _____

17 분사구문

- 분사구문은 「접속사+주어+동사 ~」 형태의 부사절을 분사를 이용하여 부사구로 바꾼 구문이다.

- **분사구문 만드는 법**

1. 접속사를 생략한다.	<u>As</u> <u>he</u> works at the airport, he can get a free airline ticket.
2. 주절과 부사절의 주어가 같으면 주어를 생략한다.	(×) (×)
3. 동사를 「동사원형+-ing」 형태로 바꾼다.	⇩
	Working at the airport, he can get a free airline ticket.

cf. 분사구문의 부정은 분사 앞에 not(never)을 쓴다.
Not working at the airport, he can't get a free airline ticket.

A 두 문장의 뜻이 같도록 빈칸에 알맞은 말을 쓰시오.

» 정답과 해설 p.6

◆ being은 수동형의 분사구문에서는 생략할 수 있으며, 「be동사+-ing」의 진행형을 분사구문으로 만들 때도 생략한다.
(Being) Given a present from her, he felt so good.

1 After Olivia opened the fridge, she took out an orange.

→ _____ the fridge, Olivia took out an orange.

2 Since he was tired, he went to bed early.

→ _____ tired, he went to bed early.

3 When he entered the room, he saw his mom sleeping.

→ _____ the room, he saw his mom sleeping.

4 Because she wasn't busy, she could go to the movies.

→ _____ _____ busy, she could go to the movies.

B 괄호 안의 말을 빈칸에 알맞은 형태로 쓰시오.

1 _____ a bath, she fell asleep. (take)

2 _____ the house, he turned off the light. (leave)

3 _____ for the bus, I met my old friend. (wait)

C 우리말과 뜻이 같도록 빈칸에 알맞은 말을 쓰시오.

1 설거지를 하면서, Noah는 노래를 불렀다.

→ _____ the dishes, Noah sang songs.

2 왼쪽으로 돌면, 당신은 경찰서를 발견할 것입니다.

→ _____ left, you will find the police office.

3 초인종 소리를 듣지 못했기 때문에, 그녀는 문을 열지 않았다.

→ _____ _____ the doorbell, she didn't open the door.

교과서 문장 응용하기

배운 문법을 이용하여 영어 문장을 써 봅시다.

1 혼자 있을 때 그는 음악을 듣는다. (alone, listen) → _____

2 이 기차를 타면 너는 거기에 도착할 것이다. (take, get) → _____

18 분사구문의 의미 1_ 시간, 이유

- 시간의 분사구문: '~할 때(when)', '~하는 동안(while)', '~하기 전에(before)/후에(after)'로 해석한다.

  While I was walking down the street, I met my homeroom teacher.

  → **Walking** down the street, I met my homeroom teacher.

- 이유의 분사구문: '~때문에, ~이므로(because, since, as)' 등으로 해석한다.

  Since he didn't feel well, he stayed in bed.

  → **Not feeling** well, he stayed in bed.

A 괄호 안의 말을 빈칸에 알맞은 형태로 쓰시오.   » 정답과 해설 p.6

1 _____ baseball, Jude hurt his arm. (play)

2 _____ in Malaysia, I met many nice people. (travel)

3 _____ _____ a girlfriend, Tom felt lonely. (not, have)

4 _____ at me, my daughter opened her birthday present. (smile)

B 밑줄 친 부분을 분사구문으로 바꿔 쓰시오.

1 <u>When he opened the drawer,</u> he found it empty.

→ _____, he found it empty.

2 <u>After he took off his shirt,</u> he jumped into the sea.

→ _____, he jumped into the sea.

3 <u>As they had no time,</u> they couldn't prepare for the performance.

→ _____, they couldn't prepare for the performance.

4 <u>Since I was late for school,</u> I missed the English class.

→ _____, I missed the English class.

C 우리말과 뜻이 같도록 괄호 안의 말을 이용하여 문장을 완성하시오.

1 다리를 건널 때에, 너는 조심해야 한다. (cross)

→ _____ the bridge, you should be careful.

2 나는 지하철역으로 걸어가는 동안에, 파란색 차를 보았다. (walk)

→ _____ to the subway station, I saw a blue car.

3 Emma는 학교 근처에 살고 있으므로, 항상 가장 먼저 도착한다. (live)

→ _____ near the school, Emma always arrives first.

교과서 문장 응용하기

배운 문법을 이용하여 영어 문장을 써 봅시다.

1 우리는 우리의 숙제를 끝낸 후에 수영하러 갔다. (go swimming) → _____

2 그는 어린아이라서 운전할 수 없었다. (can't) → _____

분사구문의 의미 2_ 조건, 양보

- 조건의 분사구문: '~한다면, ~하면(if)'으로 해석한다.

  If I find Jenny's address, I'll send her an invitation card.

  → **Finding** Jenny's address, I'll send her an invitation card.

- 양보의 분사구문: '비록 ~일지라도, ~이지만(though, although)'으로 해석한다.

  Although I live next to his house, I don't know him well.

  → **Living** next to his house, I don't know him well.

A 밑줄 친 부분을 분사구문으로 바꿔 쓰시오.　　　　　　　　　　　　　　》정답과 해설 p.6

1 If you meet Brian, you will like him.

　→ _____, you will like him.

2 Though Mr. White worked hard, he didn't become rich.

　→ _____, Mr. White didn't become rich.

3 Although she is honest, she is not kind at all.

　→ _____, she is not kind at all.

4 If you don't study harder, you will fail the test.

　→ _____, you will fail the test.

5 If Sue is free in the afternoon, she will go shopping.

　→ _____, she will go shopping.

B 우리말과 뜻이 같도록 괄호 안의 말을 이용하여 문장을 완성하시오.

1 그 기차를 놓친다면, 그녀는 후회할 것이다. (miss)

　→ _____ the train, she will regret it.

2 비록 그녀는 나이가 많지만, 여전히 빨리 달릴 수 있다. (be)

　→ _____ old, she can still run fast.

3 비록 우리는 경기에 졌지만, 최선을 다했다. (lose)

　→ _____ the game, we did our best.

4 건강한 아침 식사를 한다면, 아침에 더 활력을 느낄 것이다. (eat)

　→ _____ healthy breakfast, you will feel more energized in the morning.

5 여름방학에 대한 어떤 계획도 없다면, 너는 지루할 것이다. (have)

　→ _____ _____ any plan for the summer vacation, you will be bored.

교과서 문장 응용하기 배운 문법을 이용하여 영어 문장을 써 봅시다.

1 이 길을 따라가면, 공원을 발견하게 될 것이다. (walk along)　→ _____

2 비록 그녀는 부자일지라도, 행복하지 않다. (be)　→ _____

20 분사구문의 의미 3_ 동시동작, 연속상황

- **동시동작의 분사구문**: 부사절의 동작이 주절의 동작과 동시에 일어나는 경우로, '~하면서(as, while)'로 해석한다.

  As(While) she was looking at me, she stood by the gate.

  → **Looking** at me, she stood by the gate.

- **연속상황의 분사구문**: 주절의 동작 다음에 부사절의 동작이 연속해서 일어나는 경우로, '~하고 나서', '그리고 ~하다 (and)'로 해석한다. 또한, 연속상황의 분사구문은 항상 주절 뒤에 온다.

  He studied very hard and passed the exam successfully.

  → He studied very hard, **passing** the exam successfully.

A 밑줄 친 부분을 동시동작이나 연속상황의 부사절로 바꿔 쓰시오.　　　　　　　　》 정답과 해설 p.6

1 <u>Walking slowly</u>, we started talking.

　→ _____ slowly, we started talking.

2 Noah turned off the TV, <u>going out for a walk</u>.

　→ Noah turned off the TV, _____ for a walk.

3 Emily arrived London in the morning, <u>leaving for Rome</u> at night.

　→ Emily arrived London in the morning, _____
　　at night.

4 <u>Saying good bye</u>, he bursted into tears.

　→ _____ good bye, he bursted into tears.

5 I dropped her off at the museum, <u>driving to the airport</u>.

　→ I dropped her off at the museum, _____.

B 우리말과 뜻이 같도록 빈칸에 알맞은 말을 쓰시오.

1 그 공연은 6시에 시작해서, 10시에 끝난다.

　→ The concert starts at 6, _____ at 10.

2 나는 일찍 일어나서, 학교에 갔다.

　→ I woke up early, _____ to school.

3 밝게 미소 지으면서, 그는 우리에게 도시 주변을 안내했다.

　→ _____ brightly, he guided us around the city.

4 영어 연설을 들으면서, Emma는 그것을 스페인어로 번역했다.

　→ _____ to the English speech, Emma translated it into Spanish.

교과서 문장 응용하기　배운 문법을 이용하여 영어 문장을 써 봅시다.

1 그 남자는 잡지를 읽으면서, 샌드위치를 먹었다. (magazine)　　→ _____

2 나는 기차역에 도착하고 나서, 택시를 탔다. (arrive)　　→ _____

완료형 분사구문

■ 완료형 분사구문은 부사절의 시제가 주절의 시제보다 앞 설 경우에 사용하며, 「having + 과거분사」의 형태로 쓴다. 수동태의 의미일 때는 「having been + 과거분사」의 형태로 쓴다.

Although he had heard the truth about the accident, he still didn't believe it.

→ **Having heard** the truth about the accident, he still didn't believe it.

As I had been invited to the party, I bought a new dress.

→ **Having been invited** to the party, I bought a new dress.

A 밑줄 친 부분을 분사구문으로 바꿔 쓰시오.

1 As he had watched the movie, he didn't want to watch it again.

→ _____, he didn't want to watch it again.

2 As she had been told the rumor, she was not interested.

→ _____, she was not interested.

3 Because Bella didn't read the book before, she doesn't know the story.

→ _____, she doesn't know the story.

» 정답과 해설 p.7

◆ 완료형 분사구문의 부정: not (never)을 having 앞에 쓴다.
Because I didn't eat anything all day, I am really hungry.
→ **Not having eaten** anything all day, I am really hungry.

B 빈칸에 알맞은 말을 | 보기 |에서 골라 완료형 분사구문을 완성하시오.

보기			
live	pass	teach	finish

1 _____ last year, Alan knew how to surf.

2 _____ his work, he went out to meet his friends.

3 _____ the job interview, I told my father the good news.

4 _____ in Spain in my youth, I can speak Spanish fluently.

C 우리말과 뜻이 같도록 괄호 안의 말을 이용하여 문장을 완성하시오.

1 그는 전에 정비소에서 일했기 때문에, 차에 대해 많이 안다. (work)

→ _____ _____ at a repair shop before, he knows a lot about cars.

2 Thomas에 의해 장식되고 나서, 그의 방은 멋져 보였다. (decorate)

→ _____ _____ _____ by Thomas, his room looked amazing.

3 Julia는 Jackson 씨를 전에 만나지 않았으므로, 그의 얼굴을 모른다.

→ _____ _____ _____ Mr. Jackson before, Julia doesn't know what he looks like.

교과서
문장
응용하기

배운 문법을 이용하여 영어 문장을 써 봅시다.

1 Tyler는 역에 도착한 후, 그 건물로 들어갔다. (arrive at) → _____

2 중국어로 쓰여졌기 때문에, 그 책은 어려워 보였다. (write) → _____

22 being, having been의 생략

■ 분사구문에 쓰인 being이나 having been은 생략 가능하다.

When she was left alone, she began to listen to music.
→ **(Being) Left** alone, she began to listen to music.
Since many houses were damaged lately, they need restoration.
→ **(Having been) Damaged** lately, many houses need restoration.

A 세 문장의 뜻이 같도록 빈칸에 알맞은 말을 쓰시오.

》 정답과 해설 p.7

1 When the Earth is seen from the moon, it looks like a ball.
→ _____ _____ from the moon, the Earth looks like a ball.
→ _____ from the moon, the Earth looks like a ball.

2 As the essay was written in haste, it has many mistakes.
→ _____ _____ _____ in haste, the essay has many mistakes.
→ _____ in haste, the essay has many mistakes.

B 괄호 안의 말을 빈칸에 알맞은 형태로 쓰시오.

1 _____ at the sight, she couldn't say a word. (shock)
2 _____ two days ago, the window needs repairing. (break)
3 _____ by the sea, Japan has a mild climate. (surround)
4 _____ in France, Violet speaks French very well. (bear)

C 우리말과 뜻이 같도록 괄호 안의 말을 이용하여 문장을 완성하시오.

1 새들은 총소리에 놀라서, 날아가 버렸다. (alarm)
→ _____ by the shot, the birds flew away.
2 그 소식에 기뻐서, 그녀는 방을 이리저리 뛰어다녔다. (delight)
→ _____ by the news, she jumped around the room.
3 그는 그 편지를 받았지만, 그것을 읽을 준비가 안 되어 있었다. (give)
→ _____ the letter, he was not ready to read it.
4 그 휴대전화는 수리점에 가져가자, 곧 수리가 되었다. (take)
→ _____ to the service center, the mobile phone was repaired soon.

교과서 문장 응용하기 배운 문법을 이용하여 영어 문장을 써 봅시다.

1 일 때문에 피곤했으므로, 나의 아버지는 휴식을 취했다. (from work) → _____
2 Luke에 의해 수리되었기 때문에, 그 기계는 잘 작동한다. (repair, work) → _____

독립분사구문, 비인칭 독립분사구문

■ **독립분사구문**: 분사구문의 주어가 주절의 주어와 일치하지 않을 때 분사구문의 주어를 생략하지 않고 쓴다.

As the day was fine, we decided to go swimming.

→ **The day being fine**, we decided to go swimming.

■ **비인칭 독립분사구문**: 분사구문의 주어가 일반인인 경우, 주절의 주어와 일치하지 않아도 주어를 생략하고 관용구처럼 쓴다.

strictly speaking	엄밀히 말해서	considering	~을 고려하면
generally speaking	일반적으로 말해서	judging from	~으로 판단하건대
frankly speaking	솔직히 말해서	speaking of	~에 대해 말하자면

A 밑줄 친 부분을 분사구문으로 바꿔 쓰시오.　　　　　　　　　　　　　　　　 » 정답과 해설 p.7

1 While my father was cooking, I did my homework.

→ _____, I did my homework.

2 As the sun had risen, she continued working.

→ _____, she continued working.

3 After their homework was done, the children rushed out.

→ _____, the children rushed out.

B 우리말과 뜻이 같도록 빈칸에 알맞은 말을 쓰시오.

1 날씨가 추웠기 때문에, 그는 더 따뜻한 코트를 입었다.

→ _____ _____ cold, he wore a warmer coat.

2 그녀의 억양으로 판단하건대, 그녀는 이탈리아인이 틀림없다.

→ _____ her accent, she must be an Italian.

3 그의 나이를 고려하면, 그는 어려 보인다.

→ _____ his age, he looks young.

4 엄밀히 말해서, 흡연은 허락되지 않는다.

→ _____ _____, smoking is not allowed.

5 일반적으로 말해서, 남자아이들이 여자아이들보다 더 빨리 달린다.

→ _____ _____, boys run faster than girls.

교과서
문장
응용하기

배운 문법을 이용하여 영어 문장을 써 봅시다.

1 그 그림이 완성되었을 때, 그녀는 만족감을 느꼈다. (complete, satisfied) → _____

2 스포츠에 대해 말하자면, 나는 야구를 가장 좋아한다. (best) → _____

24 with + 명사 + 분사

■ 「with+명사+분사」는 동시동작을 나타내며 '~인 채로', '~한 상태로' 등으로 해석한다. 이때 명사와 분사의 관계가 능동이면 현재분사를, 수동이면 과거분사를 쓴다.

Sally came into the room, and everyone stared at her.

→ Sally came into the room **with everyone staring** at her. 〈능동〉

He stood there, and his eyes were closed (by him).

→ He stood there **with his eyes closed**. 〈수동〉

A 두 문장의 뜻이 같도록 빈칸에 알맞은 말을 쓰시오.   » 정답과 해설 p.7

1 He listened to me, and his eyes were shining.

　→ He listened to me with his eyes _____.

2 She sat on the sofa, and her legs were crossed.

　→ She sat on the sofa with her legs _____.

3 I was reading the book, and tears were flowing.

　→ I was reading the book _____ _____ _____.

4 Luke studied all afternoon, and the door was locked.

　→ Luke studied all afternoon _____ _____ _____ _____.

5 It was a very busy day, and the phone was ringing all the time.

　→ It was a very busy day _____ _____ _____ _____ all the time.

B 우리말과 뜻이 같도록 괄호 안의 말을 이용하여 문장을 완성하시오.

1 그는 얼굴에 페인트가 묻은 상태로 일했다. (paint)

　→ He worked with his face _____.

2 그녀는 손가락으로 그를 가리킨 채로 서 있었다. (point)

　→ She was standing with her finger _____ at him.

3 아무도 눈을 감은 채로 자전거를 탈 수는 없다. (close)

　→ Nobody can ride a bicycle with his or her eyes _____.

4 Nick은 팔짱을 낀 채로 벤치에 앉아 있었다. (fold)

　→ Nick was sitting on the bench with his arms _____.

5 그 새는 다리가 부러진 채로 날아갔다. (break)

　→ The bird flew away with its leg _____.

- -

교과서
문장
응용하기

배운 문법을 이용하여 영어 문장을 써 봅시다.

1 Emma는 TV를 켜놓은 채로, 공부를 했다. (turn)　→ _____

2 그는 따라오는 그의 개와 함께 달리고 있었다. (follow)　→ _____

내신적중 실전문제 1회

[01~02] 괄호 안에 주어진 말의 알맞은 형태를 고르시오.

01

> Please turn off the (blink) light bulb.

① blink   ② blinking
③ blinked   ④ to blink
⑤ to blinking

02

> Brian likes to eat apple pies and (fry) potato chips.

① fry   ② frying
③ fried   ④ to fry
⑤ to frying

[03~04] 대화의 빈칸에 알맞은 것을 고르시오.

03

> **A** Did you go to the concert with Cathy?
> **B** Yes. _____ busy, we went there together.

① Being not   ② Not being
③ Not to be   ④ Be not
⑤ Not be

04

> **A** Why didn't you answer the phone 30 minutes ago?
> **B** Sorry. I didn't hear it. I was taking a bath, _____ songs.

① sing   ② to sing
③ singing   ④ sung
⑤ to singing

[05~06] 빈칸에 알맞은 말이 바르게 짝지어진 것을 고르시오.

05

> • _____ slowly, the girl started to talk about her dream.
> • _____ by the bad news, he couldn't sleep.

① To walk — To shock
② Walking — Shocked
③ Walking — To shock
④ Walked — Shocking
⑤ Walked — Shocked

06

> • Judy was standing at the gate with tears _____ down on her face.
> • _____ nothing to do, I went to bed.

① run — Being
② running — Being
③ running — There being
④ running — There been
⑤ run — There being

07 밑줄 친 부분이 의미하는 바로 알맞은 것은?

> <u>Being very hungry</u>, they started to eat the food.

① Since they were very hungry
② Though they were very hungry
③ If they were very hungry
④ After they were very hungry
⑤ While they were very hungry

08 대화의 빈칸에 동사 surprise의 알맞은 형태를 각각 쓰시오. 주관식

> **A** I was very _____ yesterday.
> **B** Why?
> **A** I watched a _____ program. A man rode a bike underwater for about five hours.

09 밑줄 친 부분을 바르게 고친 것은?

> Leaving alone, the dogs often get into a fight.

① Leave
② Left
③ Been leaving
④ Having been left
⑤ 고칠 필요 없음

[10~11] 밑줄 친 부분 중 어법상 어색한 것을 골라 바르게 고쳐 쓰시오. 주관식

10

> ① When I ② arrived, he was ③ dancing to music ④ with his radio ⑤ switching on.

_____ → _____

11

> The people ① made noise in the street ② were very ③ angry, and ④ they looked ⑤ shocked.

_____ → _____

[12~13] 밑줄 친 부분의 우리말 해석이 바르지 못한 것을 고르시오.

12 ① Using the fan, you'll be cool.
(선풍기를 사용한다면)
② Playing golf, Alex hurt his back.
(골프를 치는 도중에)
③ Standing up, the boy raised his hand.
(일어났기 때문에)
④ Being vegetarians, they don't eat meat.
(채식주의자라서)
⑤ Reading a paper, the man was sitting at the cafe. (신문을 읽으면서)

13 ① Speaking of Mike, he is so handsome.
(Mike에 대해 말하자면)
② Strictly speaking, this sentence is not grammatical. (엄밀히 말해서)
③ Considering it's 11 o'clock, Kate must go to bed. (~을 상상해 보면)
④ Generally speaking, women live longer than men. (일반적으로 말해서)
⑤ Judging from this plan, I have a busy week ahead. (~로 판단하건대)

14 밑줄 친 부분 중 어법상 옳은 것은?
① Painting by the famous artist, it is not good.
② Feeling not well, he didn't go out.
③ He was looking at her with his arms folding.
④ Seeing me, he waved his hands.
⑤ Living in Paris before, I have some friends there.

[15~16] 어법상 어색한 것을 고르시오.

15 ① He smelled the bread burning.

② I like to hear the noise of fallen rain.

③ They looked disappointed with his speech.

④ The goods made in Korea are nice.

⑤ The people dancing in the street are all very friendly.

16 ① Being Sunday, most shops were closed.

② Not having a car, she stayed at home.

③ Speaking of movies, I don't like action movies.

④ Having written down his address, I could contact him.

⑤ The festival will start at 10 o'clock, weather permitting.

17 우리말을 바르게 영작한 것은?

> 그녀가 돌아오지 않아서, Tom은 아직도 식사를 하지 않았다.

① Tom not coming back, she still didn't have meals.

② Tom coming back, she still didn't have meals.

③ She coming back, Tom still didn't have meals.

④ Not coming back, Tom still didn't have meals.

⑤ She not coming back, Tom still didn't have meals.

18 괄호 안에서 알맞은 말을 골라 쓰시오. 주관식

> ⓐ (Being / Dinner being) over, Sora and her sister left the table.
>
> ⓑ (Visiting / Having visited) his house before, I found it easily.

ⓐ _____　　　ⓑ _____

19 밑줄 친 부분이 의미하는 바가 같은 것끼리 짝지어진 것은?

> ⓐ <u>Living</u> next to his house, I've never met him.
>
> ⓑ <u>Cleaning</u> her room, she found some old photos.
>
> ⓒ <u>Being</u> short, Eric wants to be a professional basketball player.
>
> ⓓ <u>Not having</u> an umbrella, I got really wet.

① ⓐ, ⓑ　　　　② ⓐ, ⓓ　　　　③ ⓐ, ⓒ

④ ⓑ, ⓓ　　　　⑤ ⓒ, ⓓ

20 밑줄 친 부분을 잘못 바꾸어 쓴 것은?

① <u>Feeling</u> dizzy, I took a rest on the bed. (= Because I felt)

② <u>Being old</u>, he still works very hard. (= Though he is old)

③ <u>Taking</u> a bath in cold water, you'll catch a cold. (= If you take)

④ <u>Opening</u> the box, the boy found a pair of gloves. (= When he opened)

⑤ <u>Having finished</u> my homework, I played computer games. (= After I finished)

내신적중 실전문제 2회

[01~03] 빈칸에 알맞은 말을 고르시오.

01

> Be careful! You should not touch the
> _____.

① to boil kettle   ② boiling kettle
③ boiled kettle   ④ kettle boiling
⑤ kettle boiled

02

> I could see several _____ in
> the old building.

① break windows
② breaking windows
③ to break windows
④ broken windows
⑤ to breaking windows

03

> The TV program made me _____.

① bore   ② to bore   ③ boring
④ to boring   ⑤ bored

04 대화의 밑줄 친 부분을 바르게 고친 것은?

> **A** Have you ever talked to foreigners?
> **B** No. As live in the country, I rarely
> have a chance to meet them.

① Living   ② Lived
③ As I living   ④ As lived
⑤ 고칠 필요 없음

[05~06] 우리말을 영어로 옮길 때 빈칸에 알맞은 말을 고르시오.

05

> 이 책을 읽으면, UFO에 관한 많은 정보를 얻을 것
> 이다.
> → _____ this book, you'll get a lot of
> information about UFO.

① Read   ② Reading
③ To read   ④ If read
⑤ If you reading

06

> 새끼 고양이가 귀여워서 소라는 그것을 집으로 데려
> 가고 싶었다.
> → _____ cute, Sora wanted
>   to take it home.

① Being   ② Been
③ The kitten being   ④ The kitten been
⑤ As the kitten being

07 다음 문장의 밑줄 친 부분을 분사구문으로 바꿔 쓸 때
알맞은 것을 <u>모두</u> 고르면?

> <u>As we were frightened by the storm</u>, we
> couldn't sleep last night.

① Frightening by the storm
② Frightened by the storm
③ Being frightened by the storm
④ Been frightened by the storm
⑤ Having frightened by the storm

[08~09] 밑줄 친 부분 중 어법상 어색한 것을 고르시오.

08

① Looked down ② from the tower, we ③ saw ④ many people ⑤ walking in the streets.

09

With ① her eyes ② closing, the fortuneteller can ③ tell ④ who is who by ⑤ touching their faces.

10 밑줄 친 부분이 의미하는 바가 |보기|와 같은 것은?

|보기|
Being very rich, Mrs. Smith always feels sad.

① Having no time, I had to hurry up.
② Doing my best, I couldn't win the race.
③ Watching the comedy show, she laughed a lot.
④ Going ahead for a mile, you'll get to the park.
⑤ Holding the little girl's hand, Jenny crossed the road.

11 우리말과 뜻이 같도록 괄호 안의 말을 이용하여 문장을 완성하시오. 주관식

무엇을 해야 할지 몰라서 Sam은 나의 충고를 구하러 왔다. (know)

→ _____ _____ what to do, Sam came to ask for my advice.

12 우리말 뜻과 같도록 할 때 빈칸에 알맞은 것은?

솔직히 말하면, 그는 똑똑하지 않다.
→ _____, he is not smart.

① We speak frankly
② Frankly spoken
③ Speaking frankly
④ Spoken frankly
⑤ Frankly speaking

13 다음은 유리의 오답 노트이다. 잘못 고쳐진 부분을 찾아 바르게 고쳐 쓰시오. 주관식

ⓐ China and India are developed (→ developing) countries.
ⓑ Dave watched his sister to empty (→ emptying) the trash can.
ⓒ Been(→ Being) very hot, we went swimming.

_____ → _____

14 빈칸에 알맞은 말이 순서대로 짝지어진 것은?

ⓐ Did the boy find the _____ purse?
ⓑ Look at the kids _____ for a bigger piece of pizza.
ⓒ Peter saw the twins _____ in front of the theater.

① losing — fighting — stood
② lost — fighting — standing
③ lost — fighting — stood
④ losing — fought — stood
⑤ lost — fought — stood

15 밑줄 친 부분이 어법상 <u>어색한</u> 것은?

① My father was <u>pleased</u> with my gifts.

② This book was too <u>boring</u> to read.

③ Are you <u>satisfied</u> with your new bike?

④ Most boys are <u>interested</u> in soccer.

⑤ Have you ever heard about the <u>excited</u> new roller coaster?

16 어법상 옳은 것은?

① Hoped to meet the famous singer, they went to the concert.

② Wounding in the leg, she could not walk.

③ Spoken of Harry, he is always friendly to his friends.

④ He couldn't write well with his fingers bandaging.

⑤ Having done the homework for an hour, I am tired.

17 어법상 옳은 문장의 개수는?

ⓐ He rushed into the burning house.

ⓑ The police recovered the stealing paintings.

ⓒ Traveling around Ireland, I always stayed in small hotels.

ⓓ She watched TV, drinking coffee.

ⓔ Taking to the garage, the car was repaired within an hour.

① 1개　　　② 2개　　　③ 3개

④ 4개　　　⑤ 5개

[18~19] 괄호 안에 주어진 말의 알맞은 형태를 각각 쓰시오. **주관식**

18

> ⓐ The ship (sail) to India is leaving tomorrow.
> ⓑ People in Hong Kong have a special day in September (call) the Moon Festival.

ⓐ _____　ⓑ _____

19

> ⓐ (Clean) the old house, she found some gold coins.
> ⓑ (Locate) in a quiet part of the city, the hotel offers its guests a pleasant stay.

ⓐ _____　ⓑ _____

20 밑줄 친 부분을 <u>잘못</u> 바꾸어 쓴 것은?

① <u>Though she eats</u> lots of food, Sora doesn't gain weight. (= Eating)

② <u>As she was shocked</u> by the bad news, she bursted into tears. (= Shocking)

③ <u>When night came on</u>, Mom turned on the light. (= Night coming on)

④ <u>Because he didn't feel</u> well, he could not take a walk. (= Not feeling)

⑤ The teacher smiled at us, <u>as he said</u> that he agreed with Peter. (= saying)

서술형 평가

01 괄호 안의 말을 이용하여 빈칸에 알맞은 말을 쓰시오.

(1) The sitcom was so _____. Jack was _____ with it. (bore)

(2) The story was so _____. I was _____ by the main character. (move)

02 밑줄 친 부분을 우리말로 옮기시오.

(1) <u>Not having enough money</u>, they spent their holidays in Europe last year.

→ _____

(2) <u>Not having enough money</u>, they spent their holidays at home last year.

→ _____

03 밑줄 친 우리말을 조건에 맞게 영어로 옮기시오.

> <u>할리우드에서 태어나서</u>, 그녀는 모든 유명한 영화 배우들을 안다.

(1) _____ in Hollywood, she knows all the famous movie stars. (4단어)

(2) _____ in Hollywood, she knows all the famous movie stars. (3단어)

(3) _____ in Hollywood, she knows all the famous movie stars. (1단어)

04 내용에 맞게 A, B에서 한 개씩 골라 연결하여 한 문장으로 쓰시오. (단, 동사는 알맞은 형태로 쓸 것)

A	B
(1) Read the book. (2) Hear a big sound. (3) Wear his duck-down parka.	She went upstairs. I'll be very moved. He was very cold.

(1) _____

(2) _____

(3) _____

독해형 어법

[05~06] 다음 글을 읽고, 물음에 답하시오.

Verbal miscommunication can happen due to the differences in cultures and languages. Do you know that facial expressions can also be miscommunicated in different cultures? For example, a smile signals happiness or amusement in many cultures. However, ⓐ <u>when they are embarrassed</u>, people in some Asian countries smile or laugh. ⓑ <u>To see this, a Westerner might be confusing</u> and think the Asian person is laughing because he/she is amused.

05 밑줄 친 ⓐ를 분사구문으로 바꿔 쓰시오.

→ _____

06 밑줄 친 ⓑ에서 어법상 어색한 부분을 두 군데 찾아 바르게 고쳐 쓰시오.

(1) _____ → _____

(2) _____ → _____

CHAPTER

04

시제

FOCUS 25   현재완료의 쓰임과 형태

FOCUS 26   현재완료의 의미 1_ 완료, 결과

FOCUS 27   현재완료의 의미 2_ 경험, 계속

FOCUS 28   현재완료진행형

FOCUS 29   과거완료의 쓰임과 형태

FOCUS 30   과거완료진행형

시제란 무엇인가?

시제는 어떤 일에 대한 시간의 순서와 관계를 동사의 형태로 표현한 것이다. 시제에는 기본시제인 현재, 과거, 미래와 진행, 완료, 완료진행을 결합시켜 만든 12시제가 있다.

기본시제	기본+진행	기본+완료	기본+완료+진행
현재	현재진행	현재완료	현재완료진행
과거	과거진행	과거완료	과거완료진행
미래	미래진행	미래완료	미래완료진행

완료 시제란 무엇이고 어떤 것이 있는가?

완료 시제는 과거 또는*대과거에 발생한 일이 특정 시점까지 영향을 미치는 것을 의미한다. 완료 시제에는 과거의 일이 현재까지 영향을 미치는 것을 나타내는 현재완료와, 대과거의 일이 과거의 한 시점까지 영향을 미치는 것을 나타내는 과거완료가 있으며 '완료, 결과, 경험, 계속'의 의미로 쓰인다.

[현재완료] I **have studied** English for 6 years. 〈6년 전에 영어 공부를 시작해서 현재까지 해왔음〉
나는 6년 동안 영어를 공부해 왔다.
[과거완료] She **had** already **gone** when I returned home. 〈내가 돌아왔을 때 그녀는 이미 가고 없었음〉
내가 집으로 돌아왔을 때, 그녀는 이미 가버렸었다.

완료진행 시제란 무엇이고 어떤 것이 있는가?

완료진행 시제란 완료시제에 진행형을 더한 것으로, 현재완료진행형과 과거완료진행형이 있다.

[현재완료진행형] I **have been waiting** for him for an hour. 〈한 시간 전부터 지금까지 계속 그를 기다리고
나는 한 시간 동안 그를 기다리고 있다.   있는 중임〉
[과거완료진행형] I **had been doing** my homework when she arrived. 〈그녀가 도착했을 때까지 계속
나는 그녀가 도착했을 때 숙제를 하고 있는 중이었다.   숙제를 하고 있던 중이었음〉

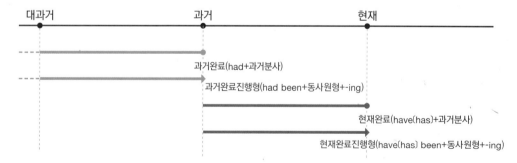

 * 대과거: 과거의 어떤 시점보다 더 이전의 과거를 말한다.

25 현재완료의 쓰임과 형태

- **현재완료의 쓰임**: 과거의 어느 시점에 일어난 동작이나 상태가 현재까지 영향을 미칠 때 「have(has)+과거분사」의 형태로 나타내며 '완료, 결과, 경험, 계속'의 의미가 있다.
  I have lost my purse. 〈현재완료 – 지금도 지갑을 찾지 못함〉

- **현재완료의 형태**: 부정문은 「have(has)+not(never)+과거분사」로, 의문문은 「Have(Has)+주어+과거분사 ~?」로 나타낸다.
  I have not lost my purse.   **Have** you **lost** your purse?

- 현재완료는 명백한 과거를 나타내는 ~ ago, just now, last ~ 등이나 의문사 when과는 같이 쓸 수 없다.
  When **have** you **arrived** at the hotel? (×)   When **did** you **arrive** at the hotel? (○)

A 빈칸에 알맞은 말을 | 보기 |에서 골라 현재완료 형태로 쓰시오. (한 번씩만 사용할 것)   » 정답과 해설 p.9

> | 보기 |
>
> know   go   write

1 She _____ _____ to Indonesia.

2 I _____ _____ a letter in Japanese.

3 Evan and Jude _____ _____ each other for 8 years.

◆ 과거시제는 과거에 시작되어 과거에 종료된 동작이나 상태를 나타낸다.
I lost my purse. 〈단순과거 – 지갑을 찾았는지 여부는 알 수 없음〉

B 두 문장의 뜻이 같도록 괄호 안의 말을 이용하여 문장을 완성하시오.

1 Isaac bought a watch, and he has the watch now.

→ Isaac _____ _____ the watch. (buy)

2 Natalie broke her leg yesterday, so she can't walk well now.

→ Natalie _____ _____ her leg. (break)

C 우리말과 뜻이 같도록 빈칸에 알맞은 말을 쓰시오.

1 나는 작년에 바르셀로나에 가지 않았다.

→ I _____ _____ to Barcelona last year.

2 그녀는 이틀 동안 아무것도 먹지 못했다.

→ She _____ _____ _____ anything for two days.

3 너는 그 예술 전시회에 대해 들어본 적 있니?

→ _____ you ever _____ of the art exhibition?

교과서
문장
응용하기

배운 문법을 이용하여 영어 문장을 써 봅시다.

1 나는 스마트폰을 하나 샀다. (지금도 가지고 있다.)   → _____

2 그녀는 부산에서 살아왔다. (지금도 살고 있다.)   → _____

현재완료의 의미 1_ 완료, 결과

■ **현재완료의 완료**: 과거에 시작된 동작이나 상태가 이제 막 완료되었을 때 쓴다. '막 ~했다'라는 의미로, just, already, yet 등과 함께 쓰인다.

She **has** *just* **finished** her work.   Kevin **has** *already* **finished** his homework.

■ **현재완료의 결과**: 과거에 했던 동작의 결과가 현재까지 남아있거나 영향을 미칠 때 쓰며, '~했다(그 결과 지금 …하다)'라는 의미를 나타낸다.

cf. have gone to는 결과의 의미로 '~에 가고 그 결과 지금 (여기에) 없다'는 뜻이며, have been to는 경험 또는 완료의 의미로 '~에 갔다 왔다, ~에 가본 적이 있다'는 뜻이다.

He **has gone** to New York. 〈결과〉   He **has been** to New York. 〈경험 또는 완료〉

A 괄호 안의 말을 이용하여 빈칸에 현재완료 형태를 쓰시오.   》 정답과 해설 p.9

1 My brother _____ _____ to Spain. (go)

2 I _____ already _____ the movie. (watch)

3 She _____ not _____ washing dishes yet. (finish)

4 Nicole _____ just _____ dinner at the restaurant. (have)

B 빈칸에 들어갈 말을 | 보기 |에서 골라 알맞은 형태로 쓰시오.

┌ 보기 ┐
| arrive   lose   send   leave |

1 He _____ _____ so much weight.

2 The plane _____ _____ for Tokyo.

3 Lily and I _____ just _____ at the train station.

4 She _____ already _____ the letter to her family.

C 우리말과 뜻이 같도록 빈칸에 알맞은 말을 쓰시오.

1 나는 어딘가에서 그 반지를 잃어버렸다. (그 결과 지금 갖고 있지 않다.)

→ I _____ _____ the ring somewhere.

2 그들은 아직 그 도시를 방문하지 않았다.

→ They _____ _____ _____ the city yet.

3 Oliver는 이미 샤워를 했니?

→ _____ Oliver already _____ a shower?

교과서
문장
응용하기 │ 배운 문법을 이용하여 영어 문장을 써 봅시다.

1 Gabriel은 런던에 갔다. (그래서 지금 여기에 없다.)   → _____

2 그녀는 지금 막 공항에 도착했다. (just)   → _____

현재완료의 의미 2_ 경험, 계속

- **현재완료의 경험**: 과거부터 현재까지의 경험을 나타낼 때 쓴다. '~한 적이 있다'라는 의미로, ever, never, before, ~ times 등과 함께 쓰인다.
  Have you *ever* **been** to Japan?

- **현재완료의 계속**: 과거에 시작된 동작이나 상태가 현재까지도 계속될 때 쓴다. '(계속) ~해왔다'의 의미로, for(~동안)이나 since(~이래로)처럼 기간을 나타내는 말과 함께 쓰인다.
  She **has lived** in the house *since* 2008.
  They **have learned** Chinese *for* 6 years.

A 괄호 안의 말을 이용하여 빈칸에 현재완료 형태를 쓰시오. 》 정답과 해설 p.9

1 She _____ _____ absent for a month. (be)
2 _____ you ever _____ Alex before? (meet)
3 He _____ never _____ the Indian food. (taste)
4 Mr. Porter _____ _____ science since last year. (teach)

B 빈칸에 들어갈 말을 | 보기 |에서 골라 알맞은 형태로 쓰시오.

보기				
swim	ride	see	wear	change

1 _____ you ever _____ a blue dress?
2 I _____ _____ a motorcycle before.
3 The woman _____ _____ in the lake since 3 o'clock.
4 Norah _____ not _____ the password for a year.
5 They _____ never _____ such a beautiful scenery.

C 우리말과 뜻이 같도록 빈칸에 알맞은 말을 쓰시오.

1 나는 며칠 동안 그녀를 보지 못하고 있다.
→ I _____ _____ _____ her for several days.
2 Lucy는 파리에 한 번 가본 적이 있다.
→ Lucy _____ _____ to Paris once.
3 어젯밤부터 계속 눈이 오고 있다.
→ It _____ _____ since last night.

교과서 문장 응용하기

배운 문법을 이용하여 영어 문장을 써 봅시다.

1 Daniel은 그 책을 세 번 읽은 적이 있다. → _____
2 그들은 7월 이래로 그 기숙사에서 살고 있다. (dormitory) → _____

현재완료진행형

- **현재완료진행형**: 과거의 어느 시점부터 현재까지 진행 중인 동작을 나타낼 때 쓴다. 「have(has) been＋동사원형＋ -ing」의 형태로 '(계속) ~하고 있다, ~하는 중이다'라는 의미를 나타낸다.
  It **has been snowing** for 2 weeks.

- 현재완료진행형의 부정문과 의문문

부정문	「have(has) not been＋동사원형＋-ing」	I **have not been using** his computer since 5 o'clock.
의문문	「Have(Has)＋주어＋been＋동사원형＋-ing ~?」	**Have** you **been using** his computer since 5 o'clock?

A 괄호 안의 말을 이용하여 빈칸에 현재완료 진행시제 형태를 쓰시오.　　　　　　　》 정답과 해설 p.10

1 It _____ _____ _____ for 6 hours. (rain)
2 I _____ _____ _____ French since childhood. (study)
3 How long _____ you _____ _____ here? (work)
4 They _____ not _____ _____ anything for 3 years. (learn)
5 _____ she _____ _____ outside until now? (play)

B 빈칸에 알맞은 말을 | 보기 |에서 골라 알맞은 형태로 쓰시오.

보기				
clean	exercise	talk	save	eat

1 Julie _____ _____ _____ lunch for 2 hours.
2 Bill _____ not _____ _____ outside since last week.
3 _____ Olivia _____ _____ the house all day?
4 Sam _____ _____ _____ about air pollution for an hour.
5 Peter _____ _____ _____ money for a week to buy a concert ticket.

C 우리말과 뜻이 같도록 빈칸에 알맞은 말을 쓰시오.

1 그녀는 오전 내내 자고 있는 중이니?
  → _____ _____ _____ _____ all morning?
2 우리는 네 달 동안 이 여행을 계속 계획하고 있는 중이다.
  → We _____ _____ _____ this trip for 4 months.
3 그들은 그를 5시간 동안 계속 찾고 있는 중이다.
  → They _____ _____ _____ for him for 5 hours.

교과서 문장 응용하기 | 배운 문법을 이용하여 영어 문장을 써 봅시다.

1 나는 한 시간 동안 계속해서 통화하고 있는 중이다.　→ _____
2 그들은 6월 이래로 그 도서관을 계속 짓지 않고 있다.　→ _____

29 과거완료의 쓰임과 형태

- **과거완료**: 과거의 어느 시점을 기준으로 그 이전에 일어난 동작이나 상태를 나타낼 때 쓴다. 「had + 과거분사」의 형태로, '완료, 결과, 경험, 계속'의 의미를 나타낸다.

  When I arrived at the airport, the plane **had** already **left**. 〈완료〉

  He **had** never **seen** a full moon until he was 10 years old. 〈경험〉

- **대과거**: 과거에 일어난 두 가지 일 중 먼저 일어난 일을 과거완료로 나타낸 것을 말한다.

  I *lost* the letter that he **had sent** me. 〈편지를 보낸 일이 잃어버린 일보다 먼저임〉

A 괄호 안의 말을 이용하여 빈칸에 과거완료 시제 형태를 쓰시오.   » 정답과 해설 p.10

1 David _____ _____ there for 4 years when he graduated. (live)

2 They knew that I _____ _____ the wrong bus. (take)

3 He _____ never _____ to Germany until he turned 20. (be)

4 She found a wallet that someone _____ _____. (leave)

B 괄호 안에서 알맞은 것을 고르시오.

1 Andrew lost the book that I (have lent / had lent) him.

2 Before she entered the room, her husband (has fallen / had fallen) asleep.

3 They (have gone / had gone) when she arrived at the party.

4 Gavin (has been / had been) sick before I gave him some medicine.

C 우리말과 뜻이 같도록 괄호 안의 말을 이용하여 문장을 완성하시오.

1 그는 그녀를 전에는 본 적이 없었다고 말했다. (see)

  → He said that he _____ _____ _____ her before.

2 Dylan은 내가 그에게 사 줬던 책을 팔았다. (buy)

  → Dylan sold the book that I _____ _____ for him.

3 그녀는 내가 그녀의 생일에 주었던 목걸이를 잃어버렸다. (give)

  → She lost the necklace I _____ _____ to her on her birthday.

4 경찰이 조사를 시작했을 때, 돈은 이미 사라진 뒤였다. (disappear)

  → When the police started an investigation, the money _____ already

    _____.

교과서 문장 응용하기 | 배운 문법을 이용하여 영어 문장을 써 봅시다.

1 나는 그녀가 쓴 보고서를 읽었다.   → _____

2 그가 돌아왔을 때, Carol은 그 차를 세차해 놓았었다. (wash, return)   → _____

과거완료진행형

■ 과거완료진행형은 과거의 어느 시점까지 동작이 계속될 때 쓰며, 「had been+동사원형+-ing」의 형태로 '(계속) ~하고 있었다, ~하는 중이었다'라는 의미를 나타낸다.

When she entered the room, I **had been playing** the piano for an hour.
I **hadn't been feeling** well for a few days, so I went to see a doctor.

| 대과거 | 〈과거완료 진행시제〉 | 과거 | 현재 |

A 괄호 안의 말을 이용하여 빈칸에 과거완료 진행시제 형태를 쓰시오.　　　　　》 정답과 해설 p.10

　1 Kate was tired because she _____ _____ _____. (surf)
　2 He gained weight because he _____ _____ _____. (overeat)
　3 I _____ _____ _____ alone until I got a new roommate. (live)

B 괄호 안의 말을 바르게 배열하여 문장을 완성하시오.

　1 The detective _____ for the clue. (looking, been, had)
　2 She _____ as a lawyer for 5 years. (working, had, been)
　3 I _____ TV for a long time. (been, had, not, watching)
　4 _____ when you arrived there? (praying, Jim, been, had)

C 우리말과 뜻이 같도록 빈칸에 알맞은 말을 쓰시오.

　1 그녀는 우리가 이곳에 도착하기 전까지 우리를 계속 기다리고 있었다.
　　→ She _____ _____ _____ for us until we arrived here.
　2 Henry는 하루 종일 서 있었기 때문에 앉고 싶었다.
　　→ Henry wanted to sit down because he _____ _____ _____ all day.
　3 그가 빗속에서 계속 노래를 부르고 있었기 때문에, 사람들은 그를 쳐다보았다.
　　→ Because he _____ _____ _____ in the rain, people stared at him.
　4 지원이는 LA에 가기 전에 얼마나 오랫동안 영어를 배우고 있었습니까?
　　→ How long _____ Jiwon _____ _____ English before she went to LA?

교과서
문장
응용하기 | 배운 문법을 이용하여 영어 문장을 써 봅시다.

　1 내가 오기 전에 누군가가 계속해서 담배를 피우고 있었다.　→ _____
　2 그들은 한 시간 동안 낚시를 하고 있었다고 말했다.　→ _____

➡ 내신적중 실전문제를 풀기 전에 Workbook p.16에 있는 요점정리를 참고하세요.

내신적중 실전문제

» 정답과 해설 p.10

[01~02] 빈칸에 알맞은 것을 고르시오.

01

> I'm not happy because I _____ Jim for two hours.

① waits　　　　② is waiting
③ will wait　　　④ will be waiting
⑤ have been waiting

02

> On the way to the school, Aron found that he _____ his English book at home.

① leaves　　　　② left
③ has left　　　④ will leave
⑤ had left

03 빈칸에 공통으로 알맞은 말을 쓰시오. 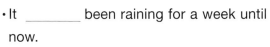 주관식

> • It _____ been raining for a week until now.
> • Tony _____ already bought the book on traditional costume.

04 밑줄 친 부분을 바르게 고친 것은?

> I couldn't wash my face because I break my arm.

① broke　　　　② will break
③ have broken　④ had broken
⑤ 고칠 필요 없음

05 우리말과 뜻이 같도록 할 때 빈칸에 알맞은 것은?

> 이것은 지금까지 내가 본 것 중 가장 재미있는 영화이다.
> → This is the most interesting movie that I _____.

① have ever see　　② have ever seen
③ am ever seeing　④ have never seen
⑤ never see

06 대화의 빈칸에 알맞은 것은?

> **A** Why didn't you come to the party yesterday?
> **B** My car broke down suddenly. It _____ well for a long time.

① runs　　　　　② is running
③ will have run　④ had been running
⑤ have been running

07 빈칸에 알맞은 말이 바르게 짝지어진 것은?

> • We _____ a plan for Lisa's birthday last night.
> • Tom and his brother _____ computer games since 10 o'clock.

① make — are playing
② made — are playing
③ have made — have played
④ make — have been playing
⑤ made — have been playing

08 밑줄 친 부분을 알맞은 형태로 고쳐 쓰시오. 주관식

> **A** How long has been Pam taking care of Jenny's dog?
> **B** She <u>takes care of</u> it for three days.

→ _____

09 밑줄 친 ①~⑤를 잘못 고쳐 쓴 것은?

> At that time, she ① <u>finds</u> him. She ② <u>has</u> been ③ <u>looks</u> for him ④ <u>during</u> 4 ⑤ <u>hour</u>.

① → found   ② → had
③ → look   ④ → for
⑤ → hours

10 우리말을 바르게 영작한 것은?

> 엄마가 전화하셨을 때 나는 이미 숙제를 다 했었다.

① I already finishes my homework when Mom calls me.
② I already finished my homework when Mom calls me.
③ I had already finished my homework when Mom called me.
④ I already finished my homework when Mom called me.
⑤ I have already finished my homework when Mom called me.

11 빈칸에 알맞은 말을 순서대로 쓰시오. 주관식

> • Jane and her sister have painted the wall _____ an hour.
> • People all around the world have loved his music _____ 2001.

12 다음 문장과 의미가 같은 것은?

> She went to France and she is not here.

① She is going to France.
② She has gone to France.
③ She has been to France.
④ She has not gone to France.
⑤ She had gone to France.

13 밑줄 친 부분의 쓰임이 |보기|와 같은 것은?

> 보기
> Eric <u>had been</u> to Italy once when he was young.

① He <u>had worked</u> with Ms. Smith until the new president came.
② Alex <u>had been</u> in hospital for a week when we visited him.
③ He <u>had injured</u> his leg and he couldn't play soccer.
④ When I arrived at the bus stop, the bus <u>had</u> already <u>left</u>.
⑤ Nick <u>had</u> never <u>drunk</u> beer before he went for a school trip.

14 두 문장을 한 문장으로 쓸 때 빈칸에 알맞은 말을 쓰시오. 주관식

> Ann and her sister began cleaning the street 2 hours ago. They are still cleaning it.
> → Ann and her sister _____ _____
> _____ the street for 2 hours.

15 어법상 어색한 것은?

① They have just had lunch.

② I have never touched a spider before.

③ She has gone to New York once.

④ He has heard of the famous comedian many times.

⑤ Has your grandfather arrived at the airport already?

16 빈칸에 들어갈 말이 나머지 넷과 다른 것은?

① I _____ not eaten anything since last night.

② They said that they _____ broken the chair.

③ I _____ just finished writing the post-card.

④ _____ you ever talked to the president in your life?

⑤ They _____ been watching the movie for 2 hours.

17 밑줄 친 부분을 어법에 맞게 고쳐 쓴 것이 아닌 것은?

① She has come here two days ago.
    (→ came)

② He has never seen a tiger until he visited the zoo. (→ had never seen)

③ Judy is running this website since 2010.
    (→ has been running)

④ It snowed in the morning, so the bus didn't arrive. (→ has snowed)

⑤ They were too tired because they have been jogging all day. (→ had been jogging)

18 밑줄 친 부분의 쓰임이 같은 것끼리 짝지어진 것은?

> ⓐ How long have you worked here?
> ⓑ Sam and Tony have already had dinner.
> ⓒ This air conditioner has not worked since last Monday.
> ⓓ Have you ever heard about the gray whale?

① ⓐ, ⓒ   ② ⓐ, ⓑ   ③ ⓐ, ⓓ
④ ⓑ, ⓒ   ⑤ ⓑ, ⓓ

19 괄호 안의 말을 빈칸에 알맞은 형태로 쓰시오. 주관식

> ⓐ We _____ _____ 5,000 words since last year. (learn)
> ⓑ Sue and Susie _____ _____ _____ in the sun for an hour. (lie)
> ⓒ She found a handbag that someone _____ _____. (leave)

20 어법상 옳은 문장을 모두 고르면?

① They have bought new shoes yesterday.

② Ann has stayed a night at a friend's house before.

③ Peter has been to Paris. He is on holiday.

④ The table that my father has repaired broke down again.

⑤ Mr. Benson has been working for the company since 2011.

서술형 평가

01 동사 act를 문맥에 맞게 이용하여 문장을 완성하시오.

(1) Eric _____ the play in his drama club since last year. (act)

(2) Eric _____ the play in his drama club until he was sixteen. (act)

02 두 문장의 뜻이 같도록 빈칸에 알맞은 말을 쓰시오.

(1) Sally went to Russia and she is not here
now.
→ Sally _____.

(2) Mr. Kim started teaching math 5 years
ago and he still teaches it now.
→ Mr. Kim _____.

03 두 문장을 한 문장으로 쓸 때 빈칸에 알맞은 말을 쓰시오.

(1)
> Pedro saw a hippo in the picture
> book. Then he went to the zoo.

→ _____
before he went to the zoo.

(2)
> My club members were discussing
> the project. Then I entered the room.

→ _____
when I entered the room.

04 괄호 안의 말을 이용하여 질문에 알맞은 답을 쓰시오.

> **Q** How long has Jessica been taking
> swimming lessons?

→ _____
(two years)

독해형 어법

[05~06] 다음 글을 읽고, 물음에 답하시오.

ⓐ Ms. Green was a science teacher in a
big city for twenty years. Last week, ⓑ she
has been appointed to a school in a remote
village. On her first day, she told about
modern science and how it helps human
progress. She told about space craft and
(인간이 어떻게 달 위를 걸었는지). When she finished
her lecture, she asked the students if there
were any questions. "Ma'am," one student
asked, "Could you please tell us when they
will start a bus service through our village?"

05 밑줄 친 ⓐ, ⓑ에서 어법상 어색한 부분을 찾아 바르게
고쳐 쓰시오.

ⓐ _____ → _____
ⓑ _____ → _____

06 주어진 말을 이용하여 괄호 안의 우리말을 영어로 옮기
시오. (단, 필요시 동사의 형태는 바꿔 쓸 것)

> walk　on　how　human　the moon

→ _____

CHAPTER

05

조동사

FOCUS 31   can, could

FOCUS 32   may, might

FOCUS 33   must, have to

FOCUS 34   should, ought to

FOCUS 35   had better, would rather

FOCUS 36   used to, would

FOCUS 37   조동사+have+과거분사

🍃 조동사란 무엇이고 어떤 특징을 가졌는가?

조동사는 동사만으로 표현하기 어려운 의미를 보충하여 말의 의도를 다양하게 해 주는 말이다. 의문문, 부정문을 만들기도 하고, 완료 등의 시제를 나타내기도 한다. 또한 '능력, 허가, 가능, 추측, 의무' 등의 의미를 보충해 주기도 한다.

Mina **did** not go to school. 〈부정문을 만드는 조동사〉 미나는 학교에 가지 않았다.
Have you seen the movie before? 〈완료시제를 나타내는 조동사〉 너는 전에 그 영화를 본 적이 있니?
Sally **couldn't** ride a horse last year. 〈의미를 보충해 주는 조동사〉 Sally는 작년에 말을 탈 수 없었다.

🍃 조동사에는 어떤 것들이 있는가?

조동사에는 크게 문법적인 역할을 주로 하는 have, do와 본동사에 다른 의미를 보충해 주는 can, may, must, should 등이 있다. have는 완료 시제를 나타낼 때 쓰며, do처럼 의문문과 부정문을 만들 수도 있다.
의미를 보충하는 조동사로는 다음과 같은 것들이 있다.

의미	종류	해석	예문
능력	can / could	~할 수 있다	We **can** see a lot of stars in the sky at night. 우리는 밤에 하늘에서 수많은 별들을 볼 수 있다.
추측, 가능성	may / might must can't / couldn't	~일지도 모른다 ~임에 틀림없다 ~일 리가 없다	He **might** be at the library. 그는 도서관에 있을지도 모른다. The movie **must** be boring. 그 영화는 지루한 것이 틀림없다. The rumor **can't** be true. 그 소문이 사실일 리가 없다.
허락, 허가	can / could may / might	~해도 된다	**Can** I have some cheesecake? 치즈 케이크를 먹어도 되나요? You **may** use my cellphone. 너는 내 휴대전화를 써도 된다.
요청	can / could	~해줄래?	**Can** you open this bottle for me? 날 위해 이 병을 따 줄래?
의무, 충고	must / have to should / ought to had better	~해야 한다 ~하는 게 낫다	I **must** finish the report by 3:00. 나는 3시까지 보고서를 끝내야 한다. You **have to** make money this year. 너는 올해 돈을 벌어야만 한다. He **should(ought to)** help the old. 그는 노인들을 도와야 한다. You **had better** meet your boyfriend now. 너는 네 남자친구를 지금 만나는 게 낫다.
과거의 습관	used to would	~하곤 했다	When I was in Korea, I **used to** visit my parents every weekend. 내가 한국에 있었을 때, 난 부모님을 주말마다 방문하곤 했다. She **would** ride her bike in the park when she was young. 그녀는 어렸을 때 공원에서 자전거를 타곤 했다.

can, could

- **can**: 능력, 허락, 요청, 가능성 등의 의미를 나타내며, 능력을 나타낼 때는 be able to로, 허락을 나타낼 때는 may 로 바꿔 쓸 수 있다. 부정형 can't(cannot)는 부정적인 추측의 의미를 나타낼 수 있다.

능력 (~할 수 있다)	I **can** swim in the sea.(= I **am able to** swim in the sea.)
허락 (~해도 된다)	**Can** I enter this room now?(= **May** I enter this room now?)
요청 (~해줄래?)	**Can** you carry the bag for me?
가능성 (~일(할) 수 있다)	Anyone **can** make such a mistake.
부정적인 추측 (~일 리가 없다)	He **can't(cannot)** be an elementary school student.

- **could**: can의 과거형으로 쓰이거나 can보다 공손한 요청을 나타낸다.

  A **Could** you tell me where the bank is? 〈공손한 요청〉　　B Sure.(Of course.) / Sorry, I can't.

A 괄호 안에서 알맞은 것을 고르시오.

》 정답과 해설 p.11

1 Can I (borrow / borrowed) your pen?
2 The rumor (can't / can) be true. I don't believe it.
3 (Will you be able to / Could you) tell me what time it is?
4 They played well, but they (can't / couldn't) beat their competitors.

◆ 조동사 뒤에는 항상 동사원형을 쓰며, 조동사는 두 개 이상을 나란히 쓸 수 없다.
She **will can** give me a ride to the hotel. (×)
She **will be able to** give me a ride to the hotel. (○)

B 괄호 안의 말을 바르게 배열하여 문장을 완성하시오.

1 Jackson _____ thirty miles a day. (walk, can)
2 _____ this box for me? (you, carry, can)
3 I _____ the violin someday. (play, able, to, will, be)
4 Sophia is very honest. She _____. (be, a, can't, liar)

C 우리말과 뜻이 같도록 빈칸에 알맞은 말을 쓰시오.

1 우리는 이 퍼즐을 풀 수 있다.
   → We _____ _____ this puzzle.
2 시청에 어떻게 가는지 말씀해 주시겠습니까?
   → _____ _____ _____ how to go to the city hall?
3 너는 완벽하게 중국어를 말할 수 있을 것이다.
   → You _____ _____ _____ _____ _____ Chinese perfectly.

교과서 문장 응용하기 배운 문법을 이용하여 영어 문장을 써 봅시다.

1 너는 그 질문에 대답할 수 있니?　　→ _____
2 너는 지루할 리가 없다.　　→ _____

32 may, might

* **may**: 허락, 불확실한 추측의 의미를 나타내며, 주어 앞에 써서 '바라건대 ~하소서'라는 의미의 기원문을 만들기도 한다. 허락을 나타내는 경우에는 can으로 바꿔 쓸 수 있다.

허락 (~해도 된다)	You **may** wear my new coat. (= You **can** wear my new coat.)
불확실한 추측 (~일지도 모른다)	The gentleman **may** be the mayor of New York.
기원문 (바라건대 ~하소서)	**May** the king live long!

* **might**: may의 과거형으로 쓰이거나 may보다 실현 가능성이 희박한 불확실한 추측을 나타낸다.

His excuse **might** be true, but I don't believe it. 〈실현 가능성이 희박한 추측〉

A 밑줄 친 부분을 may를 넣어 다시 쓰시오.   » 정답과 해설 p.12

1 Clara <u>goes</u> camping with her friends. _____

2 I think that he <u>has</u> no money. _____

3 <u>Do I have</u> some more dessert? _____

B 우리말과 뜻이 같도록 빈칸에 알맞은 말을 쓰시오.

1 너는 이 집 안에서 담배를 피우면 안 된다.

→ You _____ _____ _____ in this house.

2 내가 너의 사진첩을 봐도 되니?

→ _____ _____ _____ your photo album?

3 그들은 그가 친구 집에서 공부할지도 모른다고 생각했다.

→ They thought that he _____ _____ in his friend's house.

C 다음 문장을 바르게 해석하시오.

1 She may recognize the voice of her friend.

→ _____

2 May God help you!

→ _____

3 You may not speak loud in the library.

→ _____

교과서 문장 응용하기 | 배운 문법을 이용하여 영어 문장을 써 봅시다.

1 제가 여기 앉아도 되나요?   → _____

2 오늘 오후에는 비가 올지도 모른다.   → _____

33 must, have to

■ **must**: 강한 추측, 필요 · 의무의 의미를 나타내며, 필요 · 의무를 나타낼 때는 have to로 바꿔 쓸 수 있다.

강한 추측(~임에 틀림없다)	She has been crying for an hour. She **must** be very sad.
필요 · 의무(~해야 한다)	Students **must(have to)** follow the school rules.

cf. must는 과거형이나 미래형의 형태 변화가 없으므로, 과거의 필요·의무는 had to로, 미래의 필요·의무는 will have to로 쓴다.
   I **had to** take a bus this morning.   You **will have to** pay.

■ **must**와 **have to**의 부정형

부정형	의미	예문
must not	금지(~해서는 안 된다)	He **must not** cross the yellow line.
don't have to (= don't need to, need not)	불필요(~할 필요가 없다)	You **don't have to(don't need to / need not)** buy a backpack.

A 괄호 안에서 알맞은 것을 고르시오.   》 정답과 해설 p.12

1 Michael (must / had to) go home early last night.

2 They will (must / have to) wait in line like everyone else.

3 She hasn't eaten anything today. She (must / have to) be hungry.

4 The doctor says that I (must not / doesn't have to) eat high calorie foods.

B 우리말과 뜻이 같도록 빈칸에 알맞은 말을 쓰시오.

1 Daniel은 직장에서 넥타이를 매야 한다.
   → Daniel _____ _____ _____ a tie at work.

2 교실 안에서는 스마트폰을 사용해서는 안 된다.
   → You _____ _____ _____ your smartphone in the classroom.

3 그는 늦었기 때문에 택시를 타야만 했다.
   → He _____ _____ _____ a taxi because he was late.

4 그녀는 나를 기다릴 필요가 없다.
   → She _____ _____ _____ _____ for me.

5 Tompson 씨는 백발이다. 그는 나이가 아주 많은 것이 틀림없다.
   → Mr. Tompson's hair is white. He _____ _____ very old.

교과서
문장
응용하기
배운 문법을 이용하여 영어 문장을 써 봅시다.

1 너는 유령을 무서워하는 게 틀림없다. (be afraid of)   → _____

2 너는 밤에 나가서는 안 된다. (go out)   → _____

34 should, ought to

- should와 ought to는 '~해야 한다'는 의미로, 의무나 필요와 같은 당연한 행위를 나타낸다. 부정형은 「should not (ought not to)+동사원형」으로 쓰며 '~해서는 안 된다'라는 의미이다.

We **should(ought to)** keep our promises.

You **shouldn't(ought not to)** drink too many milkshakes.

cf. 제안·주장·요구·명령의 동사(suggest, insist, demand, order 등) 뒤의 that절에서는 대개 should를 생략하고 동사원형만 쓴다.

I *suggested* that she **(should) stay** here. 〈제안〉

A 괄호 안에서 알맞은 것을 고르시오.

» 정답과 해설 p.12

1 You (should / ought) be more careful when you jump into the water.

2 They (ought to not / ought not to) bring any animals into the building.

3 You (should not / don't have to) make so much noise in the hospital.

4 Olivia insists that he (attends / attend) the meeting today.

5 Charlie (should not / ought not) to spend too much time watching TV.

B 빈칸에 알맞은 말을 | 보기 |에서 골라 should나 ought to를 이용하여 쓰시오.

| 보기 |
| spend   follow   drink   call |

1 Drivers _____ the traffic laws.

2 Someone _____ an ambulance.

3 Mr. Brown _____ more time with his sons.

4 You _____ a lot of water in hot weather.

C 우리말과 뜻이 같도록 should나 ought to를 이용하여 문장을 완성하시오.

1 너는 점심값을 가져가야 한다.

→ You _____ _____ lunch money with you.

2 그녀는 거짓말을 해서는 안 된다.

→ She _____ _____ _____ _____ a lie.

3 나는 Dean에게 월요일에 사무실을 방문해야 한다고 제안했다.

→ I suggested that Dean _____ _____ the office on Monday.

교과서
문장
응용하기

배운 문법을 이용하여 영어 문장을 써 봅시다.

1 그는 담배를 끊어야 한다. (quit) → _____

2 너는 미술관에 있는 작품들을 만져서는 안 된다. (artwork, gallery) → _____

35 had better, would rather

- **had better**: '~하는 게 낫다, ~하는 게 좋다'라는 충고의 의미로 이때 쓰인 had는 have의 과거형이 아니다. 부정형은 「had better not+동사원형」으로 쓴다.
  You **had better not** be late.   You **had better** leave now.

- **would rather**: '~하는 게(차라리) 낫다, ~하고 싶다'라는 선택의 의미로, 부정형은 「would rather not+동사원형」으로 쓴다.
  I **would rather** tell him the truth.

A 괄호 안에서 알맞은 것을 고르시오.

1 I don't want to go for a walk. I (would / had) rather have a rest.
2 We (would rather / had better) eat here than take the food out.
3 I think you had (not better / better not) go skiing in this weather.
4 She would rather stay here than (goes / go) home.
5 You had (rather / better) leave now before it gets dark.

» 정답과 해설 p.12

◆ 「would rather A than B」는 'B 하느니 (차라리) A 하겠다'라는 의미이다.
I **would rather** watch TV **than** go to a movie.

B 빈칸에 알맞은 말을 | 보기 |에서 골라 괄호 안의 말을 이용하여 문장을 완성하시오.

┌ 보기 ┌
│   say   study   swim   wear   │

1 It's getting cold. You _____ _____ _____ your coat. (had better)
2 She _____ _____ _____ _____ in the river. (not, would rather)
3 You _____ _____ _____ _____ anything. (not, had better)
4 I _____ _____ _____ math than go on a picnic. (would rather)

C 우리말과 뜻이 같도록 빈칸에 알맞은 말을 쓰시오.

1 나는 그 영화를 보느니 차라리 그 책을 읽겠다.
  → I _____ _____ _____ the book than watch the movie.
2 너는 제시간에 기차를 타기 위해서 뛰는 게 낫겠다.
  → You _____ _____ _____ to take the train on time.
3 너는 네 가방을 거기에 놔두지 않는 게 좋겠다.
  → You _____ _____ _____ _____ your bag there.

교과서
문장
응용하기

배운 문법을 이용하여 영어 문장을 써 봅시다.

1 Mike는 잠깐 동안 조용히 하는 게 좋다. (for a while)   → _____
2 나는 차라리 붐비는 도시에서 살고 싶다. (a crowded city)   → _____

36 used to, would

- 「**used to**+동사원형」: 과거의 규칙적인 습관이나 상태를 나타낸다. 과거의 규칙적인 습관은 '~하곤 했다, 늘 ~했다'로, 과거의 상태는 '전에는 ~이었다'로 해석한다.

  He **used to** cook on Sundays. 〈과거의 규칙적인 습관 – 지금은 하지 않는다는 의미〉

  They **used to** live in that house. 〈과거의 상태 – 지금은 살지 않는다는 의미〉

- 「**would**+동사원형」: 과거의 불규칙적인 습관을 나타내며 '~하곤 했다'로 해석한다. 과거의 상태를 나타낼 때는 쓰지 않는다.

  In summer we **would** go to the seaside. 〈과거의 불규칙적인 습관 – 지금은 가지 않는다는 의미〉

A 괄호 안에서 알맞은 것을 고르시오.

1 Sometimes Susan would (visit / visited) her hometown.
2 When I was young, I (would / used) to have short hair.
3 There (would / used to) be a big bakery around the corner.
4 Ms. April (used to / is used to) work at the bank. Now she works at a flower shop.

» 정답과 해설 p.12

◆ used to의 쓰임
- 「used to+동사원형」: ~하곤 했다, 전에는 ~이었다
- 「be used to+동사원형+ -ing」: ~하는 데 익숙하다
  He **is used to getting** up early.
- 「be used to+동사원형」: ~하는 데 사용되다
  This song **is used to make** people happy.

B 빈칸에 알맞은 말을 |보기|에서 골라 used to를 넣어 쓰시오.

보기			
collect	go	have	watch

1 Bob _____ _____ _____ too much TV.
2 Emily _____ _____ _____ a fight with her brother.
3 I _____ _____ _____ to play badminton on weekends.
4 My sister _____ _____ _____ postcards when she was young.

C 우리말과 뜻이 같도록 빈칸에 알맞은 말을 쓰시오.

1 그는 전에는 여자친구가 있었다.
   → He _____ _____ _____ a girlfriend.
2 가끔씩 그녀는 이곳에서 그녀의 아들을 기다리곤 했다.
   → Sometimes she _____ _____ for her son here.
3 나는 과거에는 대학에서 물리학을 가르쳤었다.
   → I _____ _____ _____ physics at a university.

교과서
문장
응용하기

배운 문법을 이용하여 영어 문장을 써 봅시다.

1 저 방은 전에는 부엌이었다.   → _____
2 나는 주말마다 일하곤 했다.   → _____

조동사＋have＋과거분사

조동사+have+과거분사	의미	예문
must+have+과거분사	~이었음에 틀림없다 (과거에 대한 강한 추측)	It **must have been** impossible.
may(might)+have+과거분사	어쩌면 ~했을지도 모른다 (과거에 대한 약한 추측)	She **may(might) have been** right.
cannot+have+과거분사	~했을 리가 없다 (과거에 대한 강한 의심)	Jenny **cannot have eaten** my chocolate.
should+have+과거분사	~했어야 했는데 (못했다) (과거에 하지 못한 행동에 대한 후회, 안타까움)	The train **should have left** at 8 p.m.
should not+have+과거분사	~하지 말았어야 했는데 (했다)	You **should not have seen** the scene.

A 빈칸에 알맞은 말을 | 보기 |에서 골라 괄호 안의 말을 이용하여 문장을 완성하시오.　　》 정답과 해설 p.12

> 보기
> do　　arrive　　forget　　win　　decide

1 She _____ _____ the first prize. (may)
2 We _____ _____ _____ here early. (might)
3 They _____ _____ _____ their homework. (must)
4 You _____ _____ _____ to leave a message. (cannot)
5 He _____ _____ _____ to stay home last Sunday. (should)

B 우리말과 뜻이 같도록 빈칸에 알맞은 말을 쓰시오.

1 Evan은 경기에 졌음에 틀림없다.
　→ Evan _____ _____ _____ the game.
2 그 아이는 공원에서 그의 개를 잃어버렸을지도 모른다.
　→ The child _____ _____ _____ his dog in the park.
3 Emma는 그 차를 고쳤을 리가 없다.
　→ Emma _____ _____ _____ the car.
4 우리는 파티에 가지 말았어야 했는데.
　→ We _____ _____ _____ _____ to the party.
5 그는 지난 달에 그 차를 구입했음에 틀림없다.
　→ He _____ _____ _____ the car last month.

교과서
문장
응용하기

배운 문법을 이용하여 영어 문장을 써 봅시다.

1 내가 창문을 깼음에 틀림없다.　　　　　　　　→ _____
2 Joshua는 어젯밤에 자지 말았어야 했는데.　　→ _____

내신적중 실전문제

[01~02] 빈칸에 알맞은 것을 고르시오.

01

> Eric got the best prize. He _____ be proud of himself.

① could ② must
③ had better ④ used to
⑤ would rather

02

> She _____ bake cookies by herself than buy them at the store.

① should ② must
③ would ④ had better
⑤ would rather

[03~04] 빈칸에 공통으로 알맞은 것을 쓰시오. 주관식

03

> • You _____ use my dictionary.
> • The snail _____ be a slow animal, but it is an amazing creature.
> • _____ you always be happy!

04

> • She _____ listen to music while eating supper.
> • They _____ live in a small village, but now live in a big city.

[05~06] 우리말과 뜻이 같도록 빈칸에 알맞은 것을 고르시오.

05

> 대통령이 그들의 제안을 받아들일 리가 없다.
> → The president _____ accept their offer.

① must not ② cannot
③ should not ④ is not able to
⑤ doesn't have to

06

> 너는 똑같은 실수를 하지 않는 게 좋겠다.
> → You _____ the same mistakes.

① don't have better make
② don't had better make
③ had better not make
④ had better not making
⑤ had better not to make

07 다음 주어진 문장과 뜻이 같은 것은?

> It is possible that Seri dropped her earring somewhere.

① Seri may drop her earring somewhere.
② Seri must drop her earring somewhere.
③ Seri may have dropped her earring somewhere.
④ Seri must have dropped her earring somewhere.
⑤ Seri should have dropped her earring somewhere.

[08~09] 두 문장의 뜻이 같도록 빈칸에 알맞은 것을 고르시오.

08

James was a tour guide, but he isn't anymore.
→ James _____ a tour guide.

① might be
② could be
③ should be
④ used to be
⑤ had better be

09

I'm sorry we didn't keep calm in the emergency.
→ We _____ calm in the emergency.

① should keep
② should not keep
③ ought to keep
④ should have kept
⑤ should not have kept

10 밑줄 친 부분 중 어법상 어색한 것을 골라 바르게 고쳐 쓰시오. 주관식

I used to ① playing soccer ② when I ③ was young. I ④ am too old and fat ⑤ to play now.

_____ → _____

11 우리말을 영어로 옮길 때 다섯 번째 오는 말은?

나는 아침을 먹느니 차라리 잠을 자겠다.

① eat
② sleep
③ rather
④ than
⑤ would

[12~13] 빈칸에 알맞은 말이 바르게 짝지어진 것을 고르시오.

12

• You _____ take an umbrella with you.
• _____ you pick up a few oranges at the store?

① should — Might
② should — Could
③ might — Could
④ could — Might
⑤ should — Must

13

• He _____ have eaten the peanut pie. He is allergic to peanuts.
• She _____ have been tired because of the work. She looked sleepy.

① should — cannot
② cannot — must
③ could — cannot
④ should — must
⑤ cannot — should

14 밑줄 친 부분의 쓰임이 | 보기 |와 같은 것은?

| 보기 |
She would often go to the mountains when she was healthy.

① It would be nice to meet you again.
② Ms. Song told me that she would teach me.
③ He would be the last man to hear such news.
④ Would you mind my changing the channel?
⑤ When her parents were away, Sora would take care of her little brother.

[15~16] 빈칸에 알맞은 말이 바르게 짝지어진 것을 고르시오.

15

> Last week Jessy _____ go shopping, but this week she _____.

① can — can
② can — can't
③ could — can
④ could — can't
⑤ could — couldn't

16

> That dog _____ bite. You _____ touch it.

① may — don't have to
② must — don't have to
③ may — ought not to
④ should — ought not to
⑤ can't — had better not

17 어법상 어색한 것은?

① He will be able to come home tonight.
② They may have gone by airplane.
③ She doesn't have to buy expensive gifts.
④ You had not better read this book.
⑤ The baby is playing with a coin. She might swallow it.

18 우리말을 바르게 영작한 것은?

> 그들은 어제 줄을 서서 기다려야만 했다.

① They must wait in line yesterday.
② They might wait in line yesterday.
③ They had to wait in line yesterday.
④ They would wait in line yesterday.
⑤ They were able to wait in line yesterday.

19 밑줄 친 부분을 잘못 바꾸어 쓴 것은?

① This pine tree <u>must</u> be more than 100 years old.　(= has to)
② You <u>should</u> choose the best quality milk. (= ought to)
③ <u>Can</u> I open the window? (= May)
④ You <u>don't have to</u> get up early. (= need not)
⑤ He <u>can</u> swim faster than dolphins. (= is able to)

20 밑줄 친 부분의 쓰임이 나머지 넷과 다른 것은?

① He <u>must</u> show the salesclerk the receipt.
② I <u>must</u> take part in the marathon race.
③ We <u>must</u> give her our answer.
④ You <u>must</u> pay attention to the message.
⑤ Miso <u>must</u> be very tired because of the time difference.

21 밑줄 친 부분을 바르게 고친 것은?

> **A** Maria missed all the English classes last week.
> **B** I'm really surprised to hear that. She had never missed an English class before.
> **A** I know. She <u>must be</u> really sick last week.

① must have been
② should have been
③ could have been
④ ought not to have been
⑤ 고칠 필요 없음

22 밑줄 친 부분 중 어법상 어색한 것을 골라 바르게 고쳐 쓰시오. (주관식)

Steven ① lives in New York. But, he would rather live ② in the country than ③ lives in the city. He used to ④ live in the country ⑤ when he was young.

_____ → _____

23 밑줄 친 부분을 잘못 고쳐 쓴 것은?

① They have to take a school bus this morning. (→ had to)
② It's cloudy now. It should rain in the afternoon. (→ must)
③ You ought to not touch the paintings in the museum. (→ ought not to)
④ Simon is used to be very shy when he was young. (→ used to)
⑤ You don't have to drive so fast. The police will stop you. (→ must not)

24 괄호 안에서 알맞은 것끼리 짝지어진 것은?

ⓐ She should (see / seen / have seen) the fireworks. They were fantastic.
ⓑ Henry (would rather / had better) go to the beach than the mountain.

① see — would rather
② have seen — had better
③ seen — had better
④ seen — had better
⑤ have seen — would rather

25 어법상 옳은 것끼리 짝지어진 것은?

ⓐ I will able to use my time wisely.
ⓑ Last year, I had to babysit the twin boys twice a week.
ⓒ They had better take some cash with them when traveling.
ⓓ You ought to not swim straight after a meal.
ⓔ She used to be a reporter for her university newspaper.

① ⓐ, ⓑ, ⓓ
② ⓐ, ⓒ, ⓔ
③ ⓑ, ⓒ, ⓓ
④ ⓑ, ⓒ, ⓔ
⑤ ⓒ, ⓓ, ⓔ

26 두 문장의 뜻이 같지 않은 것은?

① It isn't necessary to cut the grass.
→ You don't have to cut the grass.
② Kate had long and brown hair, but she doesn't now.
→ Kate used to have long and brown hair.
③ Alex is sorry that he didn't leave 30 minutes earlier.
→ Alex shouldn't have left 30 minutes earlier.
④ I don't believe she paid so much for that shirt.
→ She cannot have paid so much for that shirt.
⑤ It's certain that Tony returned from a trip last Friday.
→ Tony must have returned from a trip last Friday.

서술형 평가

01 빈칸에 알맞은 말을 |보기|에서 골라 쓰시오.

> **보기**
> could   used to   had to   might   would

(1) The kids _____ be quiet in the restaurant yesterday.

(2) A long time ago, there _____ be many tigers in Korea.

(3) Jack _____ go out to see his friend if it doesn't rain.

02 밑줄 친 부분을 우리말로 옮긴 후 그 의미를 |보기|에서 골라 쓰시오.

> ⓐ You <u>may leave</u> the table when you finish your dinner.
> ⓑ He <u>may come</u> home earlier than usual.
> ⓒ <u>May I use</u> your cellphone?

> **보기**
> 요청   허락   추측

ⓐ _____ , _____

ⓑ _____ , _____

ⓒ _____ , _____

03 우리말과 뜻이 같도록 괄호 안에 주어진 말을 바르게 배열하고, 한 단어를 추가하여 문장을 쓰시오.

(1) Kate는 내일까지 쿠폰을 사용해야 한다.

(Kate, to, use, a coupon, by tomorrow).

→ _____

(2) 학생들은 자전거를 여기에 두면 안 된다.

(leave, students, here, not, bicycles).

→ _____

04 빈칸에 알맞은 말을 (A), (B)에서 골라 알맞은 형태로 쓰시오.

(A)	(B)
go call study	can should might

(1) Kate went to LA. She _____ by car.

(2) Harry looked sleepy. He _____ late.

(3) Sally didn't show up last night. She _____ us not to wait.

🗨️ 독해형 어법

[05~06] 다음 글을 읽고, 물음에 답하시오.

    Shopping on the Internet, or shopping on-line, is becoming more and more popular. More and more people are using the Internet to buy things. Why do people use the Internet to shop? Some people say it is more convenient. (A) <u>They must not leave their homes</u> to order something, and they _____ⓐ_____ shop for anything they want at any time, day or night. Other people say they _____ⓑ_____ find things for sale that they _____ⓒ_____ find in the stores near their homes. Still other people say they _____ⓓ_____ find better prices on the Internet.

05 밑줄 친 (A)에서 어법상 어색한 부분을 찾아 바르게 고쳐 문장을 다시 쓰시오.

→ _____

06 빈칸 ⓐ~ⓓ에 can의 알맞은 형태를 각각 쓰시오.

ⓐ _____   ⓒ _____

ⓑ _____   ⓓ _____

CHAPTER

06

수동태

FOCUS 38   단순 수동태

FOCUS 39   조동사가 있는 수동태

FOCUS 40   진행·완료 시제 수동태

FOCUS 41   4형식 문장의 수동태

FOCUS 42   5형식 문장의 수동태

FOCUS 43   동사구의 수동태

FOCUS 44   목적어로 쓰인 that절의 수동태

FOCUS 45   by 이외의 전치사를 쓰는 수동태

수동태란 무엇인가?

주어가 어떤 동작이나 상황을 '당하는' 문장을 수동태라고 한다. 수동태는 「주어+be동사+과거분사+by+목적격(행위자)」의 형태이며 '~가 …되어지다(당하다)'로 해석한다.

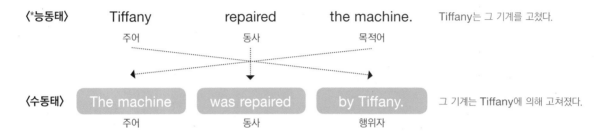

〈*능동태〉 Tiffany repaired the machine. Tiffany는 그 기계를 고쳤다.
          주어   동사   목적어

〈수동태〉 The machine was repaired by Tiffany. 그 기계는 Tiffany에 의해 고쳐졌다.
          주어   동사   행위자

수동태는 언제 어떻게 쓰이는가?

수동태는 행동을 당하는 대상에 초점을 맞추거나, 어떤 행위를 누가 했는지 모르거나 중요하지 않을 때 사용한다.

The *Mona Lisa* **was painted by** Leonardo da Vinci. 〈행동의 대상인 그림 Mona Lisa에 초점을 맞춤〉
'모나리자'는 레오나르도 다빈치에 의해 그려졌다.

수동태의 시제는 어떻게 나타내는가?

수동태의 시제		
	현재시제	The picture **is painted** by the boy. 그 그림은 그 소년에 의해 그려진다.
	과거시제	The picture **was painted** by the boy. 그 그림은 그 소년에 의해 그려졌다.
	미래시제	The picture **will be painted** by the boy. 그 그림은 그 소년에 의해 그려질 것이다.
	현재진행시제	The picture **is being painted** by the boy. 그 그림은 그 소년에 의해 그려지고 있다.
	과거진행시제	The picture **was being painted** by the boy. 그 그림은 그 소년에 의해 그려지고 있었다.
	현재완료시제	The picture **has been painted** by the boy. 그 그림은 그 소년에 의해 그려져 왔다.
	과거완료시제	The picture **had been painted** by the boy. 그 그림은 그 소년에 의해 그려져 왔었다.
	미래완료시제	The picture **will have been painted** by the boy. 그 그림은 그 소년에 의해 그려지게 될 것이다.

용어
사전

* **능동태**: 주어가 행동의 주체가 되는 문장으로 '~가 …하다'라고 해석한다.

38 단순 수동태

- 수동태는 「주어+be동사+과거분사+by+목적격(행위자)」의 형태이며, be동사를 통해 시제를 표현한다. 행위자가 일반인일 때, 혹은 중요하지 않거나 분명하지 않을 때 「by+목적격」은 생략할 수 있다.

The pitcher catches the ball.

The ball **is caught** by the pitcher.

Tower Bridge **was built** in 1894 (**by them**).

- 수동태의 부정문은 be동사 뒤에 not을 붙이고, 의문문은 be동사를 문장 맨 앞에 써서 만든다.

The car **was not moved** by him.

Was the chair **made** by her?

A 괄호 안에서 알맞은 것을 고르시오.
» 정답과 해설 p.14

1 My neighbor (bit / was bitten) by the dog.

2 She (is / was) invited to the party yesterday.

3 Was the window (opened / open) by him?

4 English (does not speak / is not spoken) in this country.

B 우리말과 뜻이 같도록 괄호 안의 말을 이용하여 문장을 완성하시오.

1 플루트는 그에 의해 연주된다. (play)

  → The flute _____ _____ by him.

2 그 건물은 허리케인에 의해 파괴되었다. (destroy)

  → The building _____ _____ by a hurricane.

3 그 기록은 누구에 의해서도 깨지지 않았다. (break)

  → The record _____ _____ _____ _____ anyone.

C 다음 능동태 문장을 수동태 문장으로 바꿔 쓰시오.

1 My sister found the key.

  → _____

2 The old man didn't catch the bug.

  → _____

3 Does she see the play?

  → _____

교과서 문장 응용하기

배운 문법을 이용하여 영어 문장을 써 봅시다.

1 그 탁자는 어제 그 여자에 의해 구입되었다.　　→ _____

2 그 컵들은 너에 의해 깨졌니?　　→ _____

조동사가 있는 수동태

■ 조동사가 있는 수동태는 조동사 뒤에 동사원형이 와야 하므로 「조동사+be+과거분사」의 형태로 나타내고, 부정문은 조동사 뒤에 not을 붙인다.

You must clean the room → The room **must be cleaned** by you.

He may not accept this lesson. → This lesson **may not be accepted** by him.

cf. 조동사가 있는 수동태의 의문문은 「조동사+주어+be+과거분사 ~?」의 형태이다.

Can the computer **be repaired**?

A 괄호 안의 말을 바르게 배열하여 문장을 완성하시오. 》 정답과 해설 p.14

1 The pants _____. (be, ought, washed, to)

2 Handball _____ the team. (played, be, by, might)

3 The situation_____ by her. (could, be, understood, not)

4 _____ to save our planet. (be, recycled, should, waste)

B 우리말과 뜻이 같도록 괄호 안의 말을 이용하여 문장을 완성하시오.

1 Jenny는 그 파티에 초대 받을지도 모른다. (invite)

→ Jenny _____ _____ _____ to the party.

2 너의 컴퓨터는 새로운 것으로 교체될 거니? (replace)

→ _____ your computer _____ _____ with a new one?

3 그 규칙들은 모든 사람들에 의해 준수되어야 한다. (obey)

→ The rules _____ _____ _____ _____ everybody.

C 다음 능동태 문장을 수동태 문장으로 바꿔 쓰시오.

1 We must protect our environment.

→ _____

2 Emily may not buy the blue ribbon.

→ _____

3 Everyone will love the new English teacher.

→ _____

4 Mr. Jones is going to open a new restaurant next week.

→ _____

교과서
문장
응용하기

배운 문법을 이용하여 영어 문장을 써 봅시다.

1 아이들은 그 선생님에 의해 가르침을 받을 수 있다. → _____

2 이 차는 도난 당하지 않을 것이다. → _____

40 진행·완료 시제 수동태

- **진행 시제 수동태:** 「be동사+being +과거분사」의 형태로 나타내며, 부정문은 be동사 뒤에 not을 붙인다.

  They are making the movie in Hollywood.

  → The movie **is being made** (by them) in Hollywood.

  Dinner **was not being prepared** by the chef.

- **완료 시제 수동태:** 「have(has/had) been +과거분사」의 형태로 나타내며, 부정문은 have(has/had) 뒤에 not을 붙인다.

  Steven has lost the umbrella.

  → The umbrella **has been lost** by Steven.

  The moon **has not been seen** in the backyard.

A 다음 능동태 문장을 수동태 문장으로 바꿔 쓰시오.
　　　　　　　　　　　　　　　　　　　　　　　　　　　　》 정답과 해설 p.14

1 Charlie is drinking a cup of water.

　→ _____

2 Were you painting the desk?

　→ _____

3 I have found my bike in the park.

　→ _____

4 He had worn blue shoes before he bought the new ones.

　→ _____

B 우리말과 뜻이 같도록 빈칸에 알맞은 말을 쓰시오.

1 그 탑은 Jane에 의해 건설되는 중이다.

　→ The tower _____ _____ _____ by Jane.

2 많은 개구리들이 연못에서 잡히고 있는 중이었다.

　→ A lot of frogs _____ _____ _____ in the pond.

3 그 접시들은 나의 여동생에 의해 설거지 되지 않은 상태이다.

　→ The dishes _____ _____ _____ _____ by my sister.

4 그녀가 도착했을 때, 그 탁자는 치워져 있었다.

　→ When she arrived, the table _____ _____ _____ .

교과서 문장 응용하기 배운 문법을 이용하여 영어 문장을 써 봅시다.

1 그 남자는 경찰에게 쫓기고 있는 중이었다. (chase)　　　→ _____

2 그녀의 노래들은 그에 의해 2달 동안 녹음되어 왔다. (record)　→ _____

4형식 문장의 수동태

- 4형식 문장은 간접목적어와 직접목적어를 각각 주어로 하는 두 개의 수동태 문장을 만들 수 있다. 직접목적어를 주어로 할 때에는 동사에 따라 간접목적어 앞에 전치사 to, for, of를 써야 한다.

  She gave Bill a present.
  → Bill **was given** a present by her. 〈간접목적어가 주어〉
  → A present **was given to** Bill by her. 〈직접목적어가 주어〉

- buy, make, write, read, sell, get 등의 동사는 간접목적어를 주어로 하는 수동태로는 쓸 수 없다.

  Sam makes me a chair. → A chair **is made for** me by Sam.

A 괄호 안에서 알맞은 것을 고르시오.

1 An invitation card (sent / was sent) to Helen by him.

2 A little cat (gives / is given) to her by James.

3 An apple pie will (make / be made) for you by her.

» 정답과 해설 p.14

◆ 간접목적어 앞에 쓰는 전치사
to: give, tell, send, teach, show 등
for: buy, get, make 등
of: ask, require 등

B 우리말과 뜻이 같도록 빈칸에 알맞은 말을 쓰시오.

1 그 목걸이는 누군가에 의해 나에게 보내졌다.
  → The necklace _____ _____ _____ me by someone.

2 그 새 신발은 나를 위해 나의 아버지에 의해 구입되었다.
  → The new shoes _____ _____ _____ me by my father.

3 너는 그녀에 의해 약간의 조언을 받게 될 것이다.
  → Some advice _____ _____ _____ _____ you by her.

C 다음 능동태 문장을 밑줄 친 부분을 주어로 하는 수동태 문장으로 바꿔 쓰시오.

1 Mrs. Brown teaches us science.
  → _____

2 He told me surprising news.
  → _____

3 Michael asked the students some questions.
  → _____

4 Victoria will make you a cup of coffee.
  → _____

**교과서
문장
응용하기** 배운 문법을 이용하여 영어 문장을 써 봅시다.

1 그는 한 손님에게서 질문 하나를 받았다. (ask) → _____

2 그 엽서는 Leo에 의해 내게 쓰여진 것이었다. (to) → _____

42 5형식 문장의 수동태

- 5형식 문장의 수동태는 목적어를 수동태의 주어로 하고, 목적격보어는 「be동사+과거분사」 뒤에 그대로 쓴다.
  The boys painted the room blue. → The room **was painted** blue by the boys.
  Andrew asked her *to leave*. → She **was asked** to leave by Andrew.

- 지각동사와 사역동사의 수동태는 목적격보어인 원형부정사를 to부정사로 바꿔 쓴다.
  They made him *go* there. → He **was made** *to go* there by them.

A 괄호 안에서 알맞은 것을 고르시오.
》 정답과 해설 p.14

1 He was never seen (walk / to walk) slowly.

2 I was told (to turn on / turned on) the radio by my grandfather.

3 Emma was (making to sign / made to sign) her name on the contract.

B 다음 능동태 문장을 수동태 문장으로 바꿔 쓰시오.

1 The members elected Lucy the vice president.

→ _____

2 We heard Kate shout at a man.

→ _____

3 He made her run faster for a good time.

→ _____

4 They advised him to exercise regularly.

→ _____

C 우리말과 뜻이 같도록 괄호 안의 말을 이용하여 문장을 완성하시오.

1 Tina는 Jack에게서 영화 보러 가자는 요청을 받았다. (ask)

→ Tina _____ _____ _____ _____ see a movie by Jack.

2 그녀의 인생은 그에 의해 행복하게 되었다. (make)

→ Her life _____ _____ _____ by him.

3 나는 어머니에 의해 꽃에 물을 주게 되었다. (make, water)

→ I _____ _____ _____ _____ the flowers by my mother.

교과서
문장
응용하기

배운 문법을 이용하여 영어 문장을 써 봅시다.

1 그 문은 열린 채로 내버려진 상태였다. (leave) → _____

2 Violet이 그 방에 들어가는 것이 목격되었다. (enter) → _____

동사구의 수동태

▪「동사+전치사」 또는 「동사+부사」의 동사구가 있는 문장을 수동태로 바꿀 때 동사구는 한 단어로 취급하여 쓴다.

The boys *laughed at* her.

→ She **was laughed at** by the boys.

He *turned off* the TV a few minutes ago.

→ The TV **was turned off** by him a few minutes ago.

A 다음 문장에서 동사구에 밑줄을 긋고, 수동태 문장으로 바꿔 쓰시오.

1 All parents take care of their children.

→ The children _____.

2 The company will set up a new branch.

→ A new branch _____.

3 She picked up Noah on her way to the office.

→ Noah _____.

》 정답과 해설 p.14

◆ 주요 동사구
• laugh at: 비웃다
• speak to: 말을 걸다
• take care of: 돌보다
• look down on: 무시[경멸]하다
• pick up: (도중에) 태워주다
• look up to: 존경하다
• set up: (계획 등을) 세우다
• hand in: 제출하다
• look after: 보살피다

B 우리말과 뜻이 같도록 괄호 안의 말을 이용하여 문장을 완성하시오.

1 Chloe는 그녀의 친구들로부터 존경을 받는다. (look up to)

→ Chloe _____ _____ _____ _____ by her friends.

2 그 보고서는 그 학생에 의해 제출되었다. (hand in)

→ The report _____ _____ _____ by the student.

3 새로운 마케팅 계획은 Johnson 씨에 의해 수행될 것이다. (carry out)

→ The new marketing plan _____ _____ _____ _____ by Ms. Johnson.

C 다음 능동태 문장을 수동태 문장으로 바꿔 쓰시오.

1 My brother looked after the birds.

→ _____

2 A stranger spoke to me on the street.

→ _____

3 Someone took away the broken chairs last night.

→ _____

교과서
문장
응용하기

배운 문법을 이용하여 영어 문장을 써 봅시다.

1 그 회의는 그녀에 의해 연기되었다. (put off)   → _____

2 그 남자는 모든 사람에게 무시를 당한다. (look down on)   → _____

목적어로 쓰인 that절의 수동태

- 목적어가 that절인 문장을 수동태로 바꿀 때는 가주어 it을 주어로 한 「It+be동사+과거분사+that ~」의 형태나 that 절을 주어로 한 「that절 주어+be동사+과거분사+to부정사 ~」의 형태로 쓸 수 있다.

Everyone says that *he* is a liar.
- → **It is said that** he is a liar. 〈가주어 it을 주어로 한 경우〉
- → He **is said to be** a liar. 〈that절을 주어로 한 경우〉

A 다음 능동태 문장을 밑줄 친 부분을 주어로 하는 수동태 문장으로 바꿔 쓰시오.　　　　》 정답과 해설 p.15

1 They say that <u>their marriage</u> is in trouble.
→ _____

2 Everyone hopes that <u>he</u> wins the gold medal.
→ _____

3 They think that <u>she</u> is the right person for the job.
→ _____

B 괄호 안의 말을 바르게 배열하여 문장을 완성하시오.

1 _____ he was the best actor in Korea. (that, is, said, it)
2 The plan _____ difficult. (be, found, to, was)
3 _____ the suspect ran away. (that, was, it, thought)

C 다음 문장을 |보기|와 같이 두 가지 형태의 수동태 문장으로 바꿔 쓰시오.

┌ 보기 ┐
Everyone says that honesty is the best policy.
→ It is said that honesty is the best policy.
→ Honesty is said to be the best policy.
└

1 We believed that he would come back soon.
→ _____
→ _____

2 Everyone thinks that turtles live longer than monkeys.
→ _____
→ _____

교과서 문장 응용하기 │ 배운 문법을 이용하여 영어 문장을 써 봅시다.

1 그들은 매우 친절하다고 믿어진다. (it, kind)　　　　→ _____
2 그 아이들은 시험에 합격할 것으로 기대되고 있다. (expect, to)　　→ _____

by 이외의 전치사를 쓰는 수동태

■ 수동태에서 행위자 앞에 쓰는 전치사는 주로 by이지만, 다른 전치사를 포함하여 관용구처럼 사용되는 수동태 표현들이 있다.

be interested in	~에 관심이 있다	be caught in	(눈, 비 등을) 만나다
be covered with	~로 덮여 있다	be worried about	~에 대해 걱정하다
be made of	~로 만들어지다 (모양만 바뀜)	be satisfied with	~에 만족하다
be made from	~로 만들어지다 (성질이 바뀜)	be disappointed at	~에 실망하다
be surprised at	~에 놀라다	be known for	~로 유명하다
be filled with	~로 가득 차 있다	be (well) known to	~에게 (잘) 알려져 있다
be crowded with	~로 붐비다	be known by	~에 의해 알려지다

She **is interested in** painting.　　　　His eyes **are filled with** tears.

A 빈칸에 알맞은 말을 |보기|에서 골라 쓰시오.

> 정답과 해설 p.15

보기
from　to
at　with

1 Their house was filled _____ happy memories.

2 We were surprised _____ the ending of the movie.

3 This wine was made _____ the best quality grapes.

4 She is known _____ everybody as a talented actor.

B 괄호 안의 말을 이용하여 현재시제 수동태 문장을 완성하시오.

1 Sora _____ _____ _____ drawing cartoon characters. (interest)

2 The main gate of this house _____ _____ _____ brass. (make)

3 Tim and Jenny _____ _____ _____ their jobs. (satisfy)

4 The hotel _____ _____ _____ its excellent cuisine. (know)

C 우리말과 뜻이 같도록 빈칸에 알맞은 말을 쓰시오.

1 그 음악 축제는 옷을 잘 입은 사람들로 붐볐다.

→ The music festival _____ _____ _____ well-dressed people.

2 그 산은 눈으로 덮여 있다.

→ The mountain _____ _____ _____ snow.

3 Cathy는 그녀의 가족에 대해 걱정을 한다.

→ Cathy _____ _____ _____ her family.

교과서
문장
응용하기 | 배운 문법을 이용하여 영어 문장을 써 봅시다.

1 그 배는 폭풍우를 만났다. (storm)　　→ _____

2 종이는 나무로 만들어진다. (wood)　　→ _____

　➜ 내신적중 실전문제를 풀기 전에 Workbook p.24에 있는 요점정리를 참고하세요.

내신적중 실전문제

» 정답과 해설 p.15

[01~02] 빈칸에 알맞은 말을 고르시오.

01
> Spanish _____ in most Latin American countries.

① speaks
② spoke
③ is speaking
④ will be spoke
⑤ is spoken

02
> Some experiments in space _____ by the astronauts.

① must do
② must done
③ must be do
④ must be done
⑤ must been done

03 빈칸에 공통으로 알맞은 말을 쓰시오. (주관식)
> • What kind of hobby are you interested _____?
> • Jessy was unfortunately caught _____ a shower.

04 우리말을 바르게 영작한 것은?
> Kevin은 모든 사람들로부터 비웃음을 당했다.

① Everyone laughed Kevin.
② Kevin was laughed at by everyone.
③ Kevin was laughed by everyone.
④ Kevin laughed at everyone.
⑤ Kevin has been laughed by everyone.

05 우리말과 뜻이 같도록 할 때 빈칸에 알맞은 것은?
> Bill은 내게 생일선물로 두 권의 만화책을 사 주었다.
> → Two comic books _____ me as my birthday present by Bill.

① were bought
② were bought for
③ was bought
④ have bought
⑤ bought for

06 빈칸에 알맞은 말이 바르게 짝지어진 것은?
> • An old lady _____ play golf.
> • I _____ take the exam by him.

① saw — made
② was seen — was made
③ was seen — was make
④ was seen to — was made
⑤ was seen to — was made to

07 주어진 문장을 수동태로 잘못 바꿔 쓴 것은?

① They call Vienna the 'City of Music.'
  → Vienna is called the 'City of Music.'
② Do students borrow many books from the library?
  → Are many books borrowed from the library by students?
③ Someone is following us.
  → We are being followed by someone.
④ My family had used the sports car.
  → The sports car had been used by my family.
⑤ Tim and I asked him to make the food.
  → He was asked make the food by Tim and me.

[08~09] 밑줄 친 부분 중 어법상 어색한 것을 골라 바르게 고쳐 쓰시오. 주관식

08

> The tree was ① been decorated when I ② arrived. Its color ③ was being ④ changed ⑤ beautifully!

_____ → _____

09

> The clock ① was broken by Jim. It couldn't ② be repaired by anybody. So a new clock needs ③ to buy and we ④ will go downtown ⑤ to get one.

_____ → _____

10 밑줄 친 부분을 바르게 고친 것은?

> **A** Harry was chosen "the leader of the month."
> **B** That's great! That's the second time he choose this year!

① was choosing   ② has chosen
③ have chosen   ④ has been chosen
⑤ 고칠 필요 없음

11 빈칸에 알맞은 말을 순서대로 쓰시오. 주관식

> ·A million dollars was given _____ Bill.
> ·A question was asked _____ my mother.

12 다음 문장을 수동태로 바르게 바꿔 쓴 것을 두 개 고르면?

> They thought that tomatoes were delicious.

① It thought that tomatoes were delicious.
② It was thought that tomatoes were delicious.
③ Tomatoes thought to be delicious.
④ Tomatoes were thought to be delicious.
⑤ Tomatoes were thought to have been delicious.

13 다음 문장을 수동태로 바꿔 쓸 때 빈칸에 알맞은 말이 바르게 짝지어진 것은?

> Because you can make a mistake during the test, you must bring your eraser.
> → Because a mistake _____ during the test, your eraser _____.

① can make — must bring
② can made — must brought
③ can be made — must be brought
④ can be made — must be bringing
⑤ can have made — must have brought

14 우리말과 뜻이 같도록 괄호 안의 말을 이용하여 빈칸에 알맞은 말을 쓰시오. 주관식

> 희생자들이 병원으로 이송되고 있나요? (take)
> → Are the victims _____ to the hospital?

15 밑줄 친 부분을 잘못 고쳐 쓴 것은?

① Paris is crowded of tourists.
(→ with)
② Elizabeth is worried of her little sister.
(→ about)
③ Those wine glasses were made from crystal.
(→ of)
④ The song is known to the kids all around the world. (→ by)
⑤ James is interested with Korean culture.
(→ in)

16 우리말과 뜻이 같도록 괄호 안의 말을 바르게 배열하시오. 〔주관식〕

그 도둑은 아직 경찰에 잡히지 않고 있다.
→ The thief _____
the police yet. (not, caught, by, been, has)

17 능동태는 수동태로, 수동태는 능동태로 바르게 바꿔 쓴 것이 <u>아닌</u> 것은?

① He will finish the report tomorrow.
→ The report will be finished tomorrow.
② The puppy was looked after by my sister.
→ My sister looked after the puppy.
③ It is believed that nuclear power stations are dangerous. → People believed that nuclear power stations are dangerous.
④ The raindrops were heard to fall on the roof.
→ We heard the raindrops fall on the roof.
⑤ Mr. Green taught P.E. to the students.
→ The students were taught P.E. by Mr. Green.

18 어법상 <u>어색한</u> 것은?

① The number 4 is considered unlucky by many Koreans.
② Breakfast is being prepared by him.
③ Were you picked from the airport by your father?
④ People were made to feel comfortable by music.
⑤ A letter is sent to me by someone.

19 밑줄 친 부분을 생략할 수 <u>없는</u> 것은?

① Stars can be seen at night by us.
② My bike has been stolen by someone.
③ English is spoken in Canada by them.
④ In many European countries, Euro(€) is used by people.
⑤ My rotten tooth was pulled out by the dentist.

20 〔고난도〕 어법상 알맞은 것끼리 짝지어진 것은?

ⓐ Ann's temperature was not taken by the nurse.
ⓑ Did milk been delivered to us by the boy since last year?
ⓒ Seafood spaghetti was made for us by Mom.
ⓓ A kangaroo was run over by a car.
ⓔ Your wet shirt should be dry in the hot sun.

① ⓐ, ⓑ, ⓔ   ② ⓐ, ⓒ, ⓓ   ③ ⓑ, ⓒ, ⓓ
④ ⓑ, ⓓ, ⓔ   ⑤ ⓒ, ⓓ, ⓔ

서술형 평가

[01~02] 괄호 안의 말을 이용하여 빈칸에 알맞은 말을 쓰시오.

01

> **A** Did Andersen write *The Old Man and the Sea*?
> **B** No. It _____.
> (Hemingway)

02

> **A** Has Mr. Smith painted the outside walls?
> **B** No. They _____.
> (his wife)

03 다음 문장을 수동태로 바꿔 쓸 때 빈칸에 알맞은 말을 쓰시오.

> The counsellor gave Jessica a piece of advice.

(1) Jessica _____ by the counsellor.

(2) A piece of advice _____ by the counsellor.

04 주어진 단어를 바르게 배열하여 문장을 완성하시오. (동사는 알맞은 형태로 쓸 것)

(1)
> hear, was, come up, the stairs

→ He _____ by Anna.

(2)
> was, made, in English, keep a diary

→ I _____ by Dad.

05 우리말과 뜻이 같도록 빈칸에 알맞은 말을 쓰시오.

(1) 아름다운 꽃들이 시장에서 판매되는 중이다.
→ Beautiful flowers _____ _____ _____ in the market.

(2) 그 고장 난 자전거가 Charlie에 의해 고쳐지고 있는 중이었다.
→ The broken bicycle _____ _____ _____ by Charlie.

독해형 어법

[06~07] 다음 글을 읽고, 물음에 답하시오.

A barking dog belonging to a family in the 400 block of Pear Tree Street was the source of problems of many neighbors. One Sunday afternoon, a complaint was raised to police by a family living next-door. <u>It was said that the dog's constant barking was always disturbing their peace.</u> They stated that they could not endure the noise and they wanted to have the dog removed from the owner. As a result, the dog (is, of, being, care, taken) temporarily at the City Animal Shelter.

06 밑줄 친 부분을 다음 지시대로 바꿔 쓰시오.

(1) 능동태로 쓸 것
→ _____
_____

(2) the dog's constant barking을 주어로 쓸 것
→ _____
_____

07 괄호 안에 주어진 말을 바르게 배열하시오.
→ _____

CHAPTER

07

비교 구문

FOCUS 46   원급·비교급·최상급 비교

FOCUS 47   as+원급+as+주어+can / 배수사를 이용한 비교

FOCUS 48   less+원급+than

FOCUS 49   비교급+and+비교급 / the+비교급, the+비교급

FOCUS 50   one of the+최상급 / 원급과 비교급을 이용한 최상급

🍃 **비교 구문이란 무엇인가?**

비교 구문은 둘 이상의 사람이나 사물의 성질, 상태, 분량 등의 차이를 비교해서 나타내는 구문이다.

🍃 **비교의 유형에는 어떤 것들이 있는가?**

형용사나 부사의 형태를 그대로 사용해 표현하는 *원급 비교, 형용사나 부사의 형태를 변화시키거나 다른 말을 넣어 표현하는 *비교급 비교와 *최상급 비교가 있다.

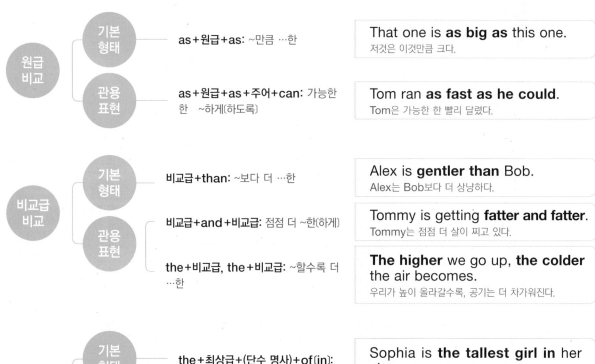

원급 비교	기본 형태	as+원급+as: ~만큼 …한	That one is **as big as** this one. 저것은 이것만큼 크다.
	관용 표현	as+원급+as+주어+can: 가능한 한 ~하게(하도록)	Tom ran **as fast as he could**. Tom은 가능한 한 빨리 달렸다.
비교급 비교	기본 형태	비교급+than: ~보다 더 …한	Alex is **gentler than** Bob. Alex는 Bob보다 더 상냥하다.
	관용 표현	비교급+and+비교급: 점점 더 ~한(하게)	Tommy is getting **fatter and fatter**. Tommy는 점점 더 살이 찌고 있다.
		the+비교급, the+비교급: ~할수록 더 …한	**The higher** we go up, **the colder** the air becomes. 우리가 높이 올라갈수록, 공기는 더 차가워진다.
최상급 비교	기본 형태	the+최상급+(단수 명사)+of(in): ~중에서 가장 …한(것)(셋 이상 비교시)	Sophia is **the tallest girl in** her class. Sophia는 그녀의 반에서 가장 키가 큰 소녀이다.
	관용 표현	one of the+최상급+복수 명사: 가장 ~한 (것)들 중 하나	A rose is **one of the prettiest flowers** in my garden. 장미는 나의 정원에서 가장 예쁜 꽃들 중의 하나이다.

* **원급**: 형용사나 부사의 정도를 나타내지 않는, 기준이 되는 급을 원급이라 한다.
* **비교급**: 원급보다는 더하고 최상급보다는 덜한 것을 표현하는 형용사나 부사의 형태 변화를 말한다.
* **최상급**: 비교 대상이 되는 것 가운데 성질이나 상태 따위의 정도가 가장 큰 것을 표시하는 형용사나 부사의 형태 변화를 말한다.

원급 · 비교급 · 최상급 비교

	형태	의미	예문
원급 비교	「as+형용사/부사의 원급+as」	~만큼 …한 (같은 성질의 것 비교)	Sam is 180cm tall. + Brian is 180cm tall. → Sam is **as tall as** Brian (is).
	「not as(so)+형용사/부사의 원급+as」	~만큼 …하지 않은	Sam is 170cm tall. + Brian is 180cm tall. → Sam is **not as(so) tall as** Brian (is).
비교급 비교	「비교급+than」	~보다 더 …한 (사물, 사람 등을 비교)	Light is **faster than** sound (is).
최상급 비교	「the+최상급+(단수 명사)+of(in) ~」	~중에서 가장 …한 (것)	Jennifer is **the prettiest girl in** my class.

cf. 비교급 강조: much, even, still, far, a lot 등은 비교급 앞에서 비교의 의미를 강조하며, '훨씬 더 ~한'이라는 뜻이다.
He looks **much younger** than his girlfriend.

A 괄호 안에서 알맞은 것을 고르시오. ≫ 정답과 해설 p.16

1 My kitten is as cute as (your / yours).

2 Julie goes shopping as often (as / than) Daniel.

3 The airplane is (faster / more faster) than the train.

4 George got the (higher / highest) score in the class.

5 This story had the(familiarest / most familiar) concept of all the stories.

6 The Sun is (a lot / more) bigger than the Earth.

B 우리말과 뜻이 같도록 괄호 안의 말을 이용하여 문장을 완성하시오.

1 Emily는 Peter만큼 예의가 바르지 않다. (polite)

→ Emily is not _____ _____ _____ Peter.

2 이 퍼즐은 저것보다 더 어렵다. (difficult)

→ This puzzle is _____ _____ _____ that one.

3 그 시험 결과는 내가 예상했던 것보다 훨씬 더 좋다. (much, good)

→ The result of the exam is _____ _____ _____ I expected.

4 철은 모든 금속 중에서 가장 유용하다. (useful)

→ Iron is _____ _____ _____ _____ all metals.

5 나는 내 남동생만큼 일찍 일어나지 않는다. (early)

→ I don't get up _____ _____ _____ my brother.

교과서 문장 응용하기

배운 문법을 이용하여 영어 문장을 써 봅시다.

1 그는 Susan만큼 건강하지 않다. (healthy) → _____

2 나는 내 친구들보다 훨씬 더 긍정적이다. (a lot, optimistic) → _____

FOCUS 47

as+원급+as+주어+can / 배수사를 이용한 비교

- 「as+원급+as+주어+can」: '가능한 한 ~하게[하도록]'라는 의미로 「as+원급+as possible」과 바꿔 쓸 수 있다.

  The man tries to explain it **as briefly as he can**.

  → The man tries to explain it **as briefly as possible**.

  The man *tried* to explain it **as briefly as he could**.

- 「배수사+as+원급+as」: '~보다 몇 배 더 …한'이라는 의미이다.

  His house is **twice as large as** mine.

A 두 문장의 뜻이 같도록 빈칸에 알맞은 말을 쓰시오.

1 Tony called me back as soon as he could.
   → Tony called me back as soon as _____.

2 They came home as quickly as possible.
   → They came home as quickly as _____ _____.

3 Lucy is 170cm tall. The baby is 85cm tall.
   → Lucy is _____ _____ _____ _____ the baby.

>> 정답과 해설 p.16

◆ 「배수사+as+원급+as」는 「배수사+비교급+than」으로 바꿔 쓸 수 있다.
   This bag is **three times as big as** your bag.
   → This bag is **three times bigger than** your bag.

B 괄호 안의 말을 이용하여 빈칸에 원급 비교의 형태를 쓰시오.

1 This box is _____ that box. (two, heavy)

2 My grandfather is _____ I am. (four, old)

3 Jane ran to the classroom _____. (fast, can)

4 Mr. Kim reads newspapers _____. (slowly, possible)

C 우리말과 뜻이 같도록 괄호 안의 말을 이용하여 문장을 완성하시오.

1 그는 다른 사람들보다 두 배 더 열심히 일한다. (hard)
   → He works _____ _____ _____ _____ others.

2 나는 가능한 한 자주 너를 보고 싶었다. (often)
   → I wanted to see you _____ _____ _____ _____.

3 이 건물은 저 건물보다 5배 더 크다. (tall)
   → This building is _____ _____ _____ _____ _____ that building.

◆ 비교급으로 '두 배 더 ~한[하게]'을 나타낼 때에는 「two+times+비교급+than」을 활용한다.

교과서 문장 응용하기

배운 문법을 이용하여 영어 문장을 써 봅시다.

1 그는 가능한 한 높이 점프했다. (high)   → _____

2 이 책상은 내 것보다 두 배 더 크다. (as, mine)   → _____

48 less+원급+than

- 「less+원급+than」은 '~보다 덜 …한'이라는 의미인 열등 비교의 표현으로 원급 앞에는 형용사의 음절 수에 상관없이 항상 less를 쓴다.

  Tom and Ann are **less old than** Becky.　　　　　His film is **less creative than** hers.

- '~만큼 …하지 않은'이라는 의미인 「not as(so)+원급+as」로 바꿔 쓸 수 있다.

  The actress is **less popular than** the actor.

  → The actress is **not as(so) popular as** the actor.

A 두 문장의 뜻이 같도록 less를 이용하여 빈칸에 알맞은 말을 쓰시오.　　　　》정답과 해설 p.16

1 Bella is not as brave as Lily.

→ Bella is _____ _____ _____ Lily.

2 He can't swim as fast as his sister.

→ He swims _____ _____ _____ his sister.

3 Brandon isn't as tired as his father.

→ Brandon is _____ _____ _____ his father.

4 Sarah is not as interested in the project as Luke is.

→ Sarah is _____ _____ in the project _____ Luke.

5 Owen is not so excited about the trip as Eva is.

→ Owen is _____ _____ about the trip _____ Eva.

B 우리말과 뜻이 같도록 빈칸에 들어갈 말을 |보기|에서 골라 알맞은 형태로 쓰시오.

보기
exciting　　comfortable　　clever　　adventurous

1 그녀의 차는 너의 것보다 덜 편안하다.

→ Her car is _____ _____ _____ yours.

2 그는 그의 형보다 덜 똑똑하다.

→ He is _____ _____ _____ his elder brother.

3 농구 경기는 축구 경기보다 덜 재미있다.

→ Basketball games are _____ _____ _____ soccer games.

4 Jackson은 Parker만큼 모험심이 강하지 않다.

→ Jackson is _____ _____ _____ _____ Parker.

교과서
문장
응용하기

배운 문법을 이용하여 영어 문장을 써 봅시다.

1 나의 고향은 런던보다 덜 유명하다. (than)　　　　→ _____

2 그는 그의 친구만큼 예의 바르지 않다. (as)　　　　→ _____

비교급+and+비교급 / the+비교급, the+비교급

- 「비교급+and+비교급」: '점점 더 ~한(하게)'이라는 의미로 비교급이 「more+원급」의 형태인 경우에는 「more and more+원급」으로 쓴다.

  The weather got **hotter and hotter** in the afternoon.

  Gas is becoming **more and more expensive**.

- 「the+비교급, the+비교급」: '~할수록 더 …한'이라는 의미이다.

  The older he grows, **the weaker** he becomes.

A 빈칸에 들어갈 말을 |보기|에서 골라 알맞은 형태로 쓰시오.　　　　　　　》 정답과 해설 p.16

> 보기
> smart　　　soon　　　little　　　high　　　busy

1 The faster we run, the _____ we'll get tired.

2 The new system is getting _____ and _____.

3 My father will get _____ and _____ this year.

4 The more electricity you use, the _____ your bill will be.

5 Violet started to eat _____ and _____ to lose weight.

B 밑줄 친 부분을 어법상 바르게 고쳐 쓰시오.

1 It's getting darker and <u>dark</u>.　　　　　　　　　　　　_____

2 The more you smile, <u>the more happy</u> you become.　　　_____

3 She is getting <u>more beautiful</u> and more beautiful.　　　_____

4 The harder you work, <u>much</u> opportunities you can get.　_____

5 If you study hard, your grade will get <u>good and good</u>.　_____

C 우리말과 뜻이 같도록 괄호 안의 말을 이용하여 문장을 완성하시오.

1 그는 오래 기다리면 기다릴수록, 더 화가 난다. (long, angry)

→ _____ _____ he waits, _____ _____ he gets.

2 그녀의 노래는 점점 더 인기 있어졌다. (popular)

→ Her song got _____ _____ _____ _____.

3 젊을수록 배우는 것이 더 쉽다. (young, easy)

→ The younger you are, _____ _____ it is to learn.

교과서
문장
응용하기

배운 문법을 이용하여 영어 문장을 써 봅시다.

1 세계는 점점 더 작아지고 있다. (get, small)　　→ _____

2 우리는 나이가 들수록 더 현명해진다. (wise)　　→ _____

one of the+최상급/원급과 비교급을 이용한 최상급

■ 「one of the+최상급+복수 명사」: '가장 ~한 것들 중 하나'라는 의미이다.
Betty is **one of the most successful people** that I know.

■ 원급과 비교급을 이용한 최상급 표현: 「비교급+than any other+단수 명사」와 「No (other) ~ 비교급+than」, 「No (other) ~ as+원급+as」로 최상급을 나타낼 수 있다.
Evan is **the strongest** boy in the class.
→ Evan is **stronger than any other boy** in the class.
→ **No** (**other**) boy in the class is **stronger than** Evan.
→ **No** (**other**) boy in the class is **as strong as** Evan.

A 우리말과 뜻이 같도록 괄호 안의 말을 이용하여 빈칸에 알맞은 말을 쓰시오. » 정답과 해설 p.17

1 '햄릿'은 가장 유명한 희곡들 중 하나이다. (famous)
→ *Hamlet* is _____ _____ _____ _____ _____ plays.

2 독도는 한국에서 가장 깨끗한 섬이다. (clean)
→ Dokdo is _____ _____ island in Korea.
→ Dokdo is _____ _____ _____ _____ island in Korea.
→ _____ other island in Korea is _____ _____ Dokdo.
→ _____ other island in Korea is _____ _____ _____ Dokdo.

B 다음 문장의 뜻이 같도록 빈칸에 알맞은 말을 쓰시오.

1 No other mountain in the world is as high as Mt. Everest.
→ No other mountain in the world is _____ _____ Mt. Everest.
→ Mt. Everest is _____ _____ _____ _____ mountain in the world.
→ Mt. Everest is _____ _____ _____ all the mountains in the world.

2 Madonna is the most famous singer in the United States.
→ No other singer in the United States is _____ _____ _____ Madonna.
→ Madonna is _____ _____ _____ _____ _____ singer in the United States.

교과서 문장 응용하기 배운 문법을 이용하여 영어 문장을 써 봅시다.

1 그 셔츠는 이 가게에서 가장 다채로운 색의 셔츠 중 하나이다. → _____
(colorful, shop)

2 Sam은 나의 반에서 다른 어떤 학생보다도 더 똑똑하다. (smart, any) → _____

내신적중 실전문제

[01~02] 빈칸에 알맞은 것을 고르시오.

01

> Female elephants aren't so _____ as male elephants.

① big
② bigger
③ biggest
④ the biggest
⑤ the most big

02

> It was _____ castle we've visited during our holidays.

① older
② the older
③ oldest
④ the oldest
⑤ the most old

[03~04] 두 문장의 뜻이 같도록 빈칸에 알맞은 말을 쓰시오. 주관식

03

> Kate visits her grandparents as often as possible.
> → Kate visits her grandparents as often as _____ _____.

04

> If you practice more, you can be on the stage sooner.
> → _____ _____ you practice, _____ _____ you can be on the stage.

[05~06] 괄호 안에 주어진 말의 알맞은 형태가 바르게 짝지어진 것을 고르시오.

05

> ⓐ What is (long) book in the world?
> ⓑ Actually, girls need (warm) clothes than boys.

① long — warm
② long — warmer
③ the longest — warm
④ the longest — warmer
⑤ the longest — the warmest

06

> ⓐ Today, it's less (hot) than yesterday.
> ⓑ Is the full moon twice as (bright) as the half moon?

① hot — bright
② hot — brighter
③ hotter — bright
④ hottest — brighter
⑤ hottest — brightest

07 의미하는 바가 나머지 넷과 다른 것은?

① Ethan is the luckiest person in the world.
② Ethan is luckier than any other person in the world.
③ Ethan is as lucky as other people in the world.
④ No other person in the world is as lucky as Ethan.
⑤ No other person in the world is luckier than Ethan.

08 밑줄 친 부분과 바꿔 쓸 수 <u>없는</u> 것은?

> Fruit and vegetables are <u>a lot</u> cheaper in the street market than in the supermarket.

① very   ② far   ③ still
④ much   ⑤ even

09 밑줄 친 부분 중 어법상 <u>어색한</u> 것은?

> Cars ① <u>are</u> more ② <u>expensive</u> than bikes, but ③ <u>they</u> are ④ <u>much</u> ⑤ <u>safe</u> than bikes.

10 |보기| 중 주어진 문장의 빈칸에 알맞지 <u>않은</u> 것의 개수는?

> |보기|
> hard   worse   merrily   fast   better

> Tina plays the flute as _____ as Ruby.

① 1개   ② 2개   ③ 3개
④ 4개   ⑤ 5개

11 다음 문장과 뜻이 같은 것을 <u>두 개</u> 고르면?

> Sofas are more comfortable than chairs.

① Sofas are as comfortable as chairs.
② Chairs are more comfortable than sofas.
③ Sofas are not as comfortable as chairs.
④ Chairs are less comfortable than sofas.
⑤ Chairs are not as comfortable as sofas.

12 우리말을 바르게 영작한 것은?

> 피자를 많이 주문할수록, 더 많은 쿠폰을 얻을 것이다.

① More pizza you order, more coupons you'll get.
② Most pizza you order, most coupons you'll get.
③ The more pizza you order, more coupons you'll get.
④ The more pizza you order, the more coupons you'll get.
⑤ The most pizza you order, the most coupons you'll get.

13 의미가 같은 문장을 골라 기호로 쓰시오. **주관식**

> ⓐ *Titanic* is the best of all movies.
> ⓑ *Titanic* is not as good as all the other movies.
> ⓒ No other movie is better than *Titanic*.
> ⓓ No other movie is as good as *Titanic*.
> ⓔ *Titanic* is less good than all the other movies.

_____

14 빈칸에 괄호 안의 말을 바르게 배열할 때 세 번째 오는 말은?

> New Guinea is _____ in the world. (one, islands, of, largest, the)

① of   ② the   ③ one
④ largest   ⑤ islands

[15~16] 두 문장을 비교하는 문장을 한 문장으로 쓸 때 빈칸에 알맞은 말을 쓰시오. 주관식

15

> This black umbrella is twenty dollars.
> That white umbrella is thirty dollars.

→ This black umbrella is _____ expensive _____ that white one.

16

> Aron has 30 comic books.
> Jack has 10 comic books.

→ Aron has _____ _____ _____ many books _____ Jack has.

17 밑줄 친 부분의 우리말 뜻이 잘못된 것은?

① The pollution problems are getting worse and worse. (가장 나쁘다)
② The colder the winter is, the warmer the spring gets. (추울수록 더 따뜻한)
③ He is one of the most popular musicians in the world. (가장 인기 있는 음악가들 중 하나)
④ They ran as fast as possible to catch up with her. (가능한 한 빨리)
⑤ More and more people in the world enjoy eating Korean food. (점점 더 많은)

18 우리말과 뜻이 같도록 할 때 빈칸에 알맞은 것은?

> Jessica는 그녀의 남동생보다 훨씬 덜 똑똑하다.
> → Jessica is _____ her brother.

① even less intelligent than
② not even less intelligent than
③ less even intelligent than
④ not less even intelligent than
⑤ less intelligent than even

19 밑줄 친 부분 중 어법상 어색한 것은?

① Greece is smaller than Turkey.
② Jessy speaks Korean better than Oliver.
③ No other state in the USA is larger than Alaska.
④ He became more generous and more generous to his students.
⑤ The film *Saw I* is more frightening than *Saw II*.

20 다음 표에 대한 설명으로 알맞지 않은 것은?

Package A	Package B	Package C	Package D
50 kg	55 kg	50 kg	60 kg

① Package A is as heavy as Package C.
② Package B is heavier than Package A and C.
③ Package D is the heaviest of all the packages.
④ Package D is not so heavy as the other packages.
⑤ Package B is less heavy than Package D.

21 우리말과 뜻이 같도록 할 때 빈칸에 알맞은 말을 모두 고르면?

> 우리는 깡통, 유리병 그리고 플라스틱을 가능한 한 많이 재활용해야 한다.
> → We should recycle cans, glass bottles, and plastics _____.

① much possible
② as much possible
③ as much as possible
④ as much as we can
⑤ as much as we could

22 어법상 어색한 것은?

① I watched the most recent movie yesterday.

② No car is faster than my car in the world.

③ Ken arrives at work the earliest of all.

④ Joy writes the most exciting books I've ever read.

⑤ The light bulb is one of the most useful invention that humans have invented.

23 밑줄 친 부분을 잘못 고쳐 쓴 것은?

① The richer he becomes, happier he is.
(→ the happier)

② It's best match they have ever played.
(→ the best)

③ His voice got loud and loud as he grew up. (→ louder and louder)

④ I wanted to improve my weak point as soon as I can. (→ as soon as I could)

⑤ This magazine is more interesting than any another magazines.
(→ any other magazines)

24 괄호 안에서 각각 알맞은 것을 골라 쓰시오. 주관식

ⓐ I wasn't so (tall as / taller than / the tallest) my mother last year.

ⓑ Did you know that penguins can walk (as fasts / faster than / the fastest) humans?

ⓒ The Pacific Ocean is (larger / largest / the largest) of the 5 oceans.

ⓐ _____

ⓑ _____

ⓒ _____

25 어법상 올바른 것의 개수는?

ⓐ Sugar is less sweet than honey.

ⓑ We're training three time as hard as last year.

ⓒ Whales are much bigger than buses!

ⓓ The weather is getting warm and warm.

ⓔ The deeper we go down the see, the colder it becomes.

ⓕ The Atacama desert in Chile is one of driest places in the world.

① 2개   ② 3개   ③ 4개
④ 5개   ⑤ 6개

26 짝지어진 두 문장의 뜻이 같지 않은 것은?

① Skiing isn't as easy as riding a bike.
= Riding a bike is easier than skiing.

② A canary is more colorful than an eagle.
= An eagle isn't less colorful than a canary.

③ Learn by heart as many idioms as you can.
= Learn by heart as many idioms as possible.

④ This computer is three times as fast as mine.
= This computer is three times faster than mine.

⑤ The Amazon is the longest river in the world.
= No other river in the world is longer than the Amazon.

서술형 평가

[01~02] 우리말과 뜻이 같도록 조건에 맞게 빈칸에 알맞은 말을 쓰시오.

01

> 조건
> fast를 사용하여 (1) 4단어 (2) 5단어로 쓸 것

> 멈추지 말고 가능한 한 빠르게 읽도록 노력해라.

(1) Try to read ＿＿＿＿＿＿＿ without stopping.

(2) Try to read ＿＿＿＿＿＿＿ without stopping.

02

> 조건
> nutritious를 사용하여 (1) 비교급 비교 (2) 원급 비교로 쓸 것

> 흰 밀가루 빵은 통밀 빵보다 영양가가 높지 않다.

(1) White bread ＿＿＿＿＿＿＿ whole wheat bread.

(2) White bread ＿＿＿＿＿＿＿ whole wheat bread.

03 취미 활동에 대한 인기 조사를 보고, popular를 사용하여 문장을 완성하시오.

인터넷 서핑	독서	운동하기	영화 감상	음악 감상
12명	7명	10명	14명	7명

(1) Surfing the Internet is ＿＿＿＿＿＿＿ than playing sports.

(2) Watching movies is the ＿＿＿＿＿＿＿ among them.

(3) Reading books is ＿＿＿＿＿＿＿ as listening to music.

04 다음 문장과 뜻이 같도록 조건에 맞게 완전한 문장을 쓰시오.

> The Vatican City is the smallest country in the world.

(1) 원급 사용

→ ＿＿＿＿＿＿＿＿＿＿＿＿

(2) 비교급 사용 – 부정 주어

→ ＿＿＿＿＿＿＿＿＿＿＿＿

(3) 비교급 사용

→ ＿＿＿＿＿＿＿＿＿＿＿＿

[05~06] 다음 글을 읽고, 물음에 답하시오.

Emily Dickinson was (of, the, one, poet, most, famous, American). The older Dickinson got, ⓐ more often she wanted to be alone. When someone came to the house, ⓑ she ran upstairs to hide as fast as she can. For the last 16 years of her life, she never left her home. The curtains were always closed. She dressed only in white. One day, ⓒ Dickinson was becoming most and most ill, but she did not let the doctor in her room. He could only see her from the doorway.

05 괄호 안에 주어진 말을 바르게 배열하시오. (단, 단어 하나의 형태를 알맞게 바꿀 것)

→ ＿＿＿＿＿＿＿＿＿＿＿＿

06 밑줄 친 ⓐ~ⓒ에서 어법상 어색한 부분을 바르게 고쳐 문장을 다시 쓰시오.

ⓐ ＿＿＿＿＿＿＿＿＿＿＿＿

ⓑ ＿＿＿＿＿＿＿＿＿＿＿＿

ⓒ ＿＿＿＿＿＿＿＿＿＿＿＿

CHAPTER

08

관계사

FOCUS 51   주격 관계대명사_ who, which

FOCUS 52   소유격 관계대명사_ whose

FOCUS 53   목적격 관계대명사_ who(m), which

FOCUS 54   관계대명사 that

FOCUS 55   관계대명사 what

FOCUS 56   관계대명사의 계속적 용법

FOCUS 57   전치사+관계대명사

FOCUS 58   관계대명사의 생략

FOCUS 59   관계부사 1_ when, where

FOCUS 60   관계부사 2_ why, how

FOCUS 61   관계부사와 선행사의 생략

FOCUS 62   복합관계대명사

FOCUS 63   복합관계부사

관계사란 무엇인가?

접속사와 대명사의 역할을 동시에 하는 말을 관계대명사, 접속사와 부사의 역할을 동시에 하는 말을 관계부사라고 하며, 이 둘을 관계사라고 한다. 관계사가 이끄는 절은 보통 앞의 명사인 *선행사를 수식하는 형용사의 기능을 한다.

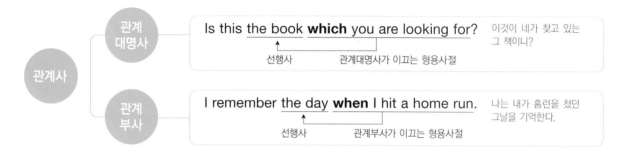

관계사 — 관계대명사

Is this the book **which** you are looking for?
선행사 / 관계대명사가 이끄는 형용사절
이것이 네가 찾고 있는 그 책이니?

관계사 — 관계부사

I remember the day **when** I hit a home run.
선행사 / 관계부사가 이끄는 형용사절
나는 내가 홈런을 쳤던 그날을 기억한다.

관계대명사와 관계부사는 어떻게 쓰이는가?

선행사가 사람, 사물, 동물 등일 때는 관계대명사를, 시간, 장소, 이유, 방법일 때는 관계부사를 쓴다.

	선행사	주격	소유격	목적격
관계대명사	사람	who	whose	who(m)
	사물, 동물	which	whose	which
	사람, 사물, 동물	that	–	that
	없음(선행사 포함)	what	–	what

	의미	선행사	종류
관계부사	시간	the time	when
	장소	the place	where
	이유	the reason	why
	방법	the way	how

복합관계사란 무엇인가?

관계사에 –ever를 붙인 것을 복합관계사라고 하며, 관계사와는 달리 명사절과 부사절을 이끈다.

You may invite **whomever** you like. 네가 좋아하는 사람은 누구든지 초대해도 된다.
동사의 목적어 역할을 하는 명사절

However hard you study, you can't pass the test. 네가 아무리 열심히 공부할지라도, 너는 그 시험을 통과할 수 없다.
양보의 의미를 나타내는 부사절

용어 사전

* **선행사:** 관계대명사 또는 관계부사가 이끄는 형용사절의 수식을 받는 형용사절 앞의 명사를 선행사라고 한다.

주격 관계대명사_ who, which

- 주격 관계대명사는 관계사절에서 주어 역할을 하며, 선행사가 사람일 때는 who, 사물이나 동물일 때는 which를 쓴다.

  I know the girl. + She speaks four languages.

  → I know *the girl* **who** speaks four languages.

- 주격 관계대명사 who와 which는 that으로 바꿔 쓸 수 있다.

  A lemon is a fruit. + The fruit is yellow and sour.

  → A lemon is *a fruit* **which(that)** is yellow and sour.

A 괄호 안에서 알맞은 것을 고르시오.   》 정답과 해설 p.18

1 I have two cats (which / who) have blue eyes.

2 The cellphone (who / which) was stolen was mine.

3 Judy gave me a doll (who / that) was made of plastic.

4 The woman (that / which) answered the door was very kind.

5 The tall man (who / whom) was leaning against the door is my uncle.

B 우리말과 뜻이 같도록 괄호 안의 말을 이용하여 빈칸에 알맞은 말을 쓰시오.

1 최 박사를 존경하는 그 소녀는 Emily이다. (admire)

 → The girl _____ _____ Dr. Choi is Emily.

2 나는 그가 집필했던 책을 읽고 있다. (write)

 → I'm reading a book _____ _____ _____ by him.

3 보라색 재킷을 입고 있는 그 남자는 박물관에서 일한다. (wear)

 → The man _____ _____ _____ a purple jacket works at a museum.

C 두 문장을 주격 관계대명사를 이용하여 한 문장으로 쓰시오.

1 I know Adam. + He lives in the Netherlands.

 → _____

2 Look at the house. + It has just one small window.

 → _____

3 The cafe is not open. + It sells the best milkshake in town.

 → _____

교과서 문장 응용하기 | 배운 문법을 이용하여 영어 문장을 써 봅시다.

1 Sally는 축구를 잘하는 소녀이다. (who)   → _____

2 원숭이는 나무에서 사는 동물이다. (that, in)   → _____

소유격 관계대명사_ whose

■ 소유격 관계대명사는 관계대명사 뒤의 명사와 소유의 관계를 나타내며, 선행사가 사람, 사물 또는 동물일 때 whose를 쓴다.

The woman is my teacher. + Her hair is brown.

→ *The woman* **whose** hair is brown is my teacher.

This is my bike. + Its wheels are red.

→ This is *my bike* **whose** wheels are red.

A 괄호 안에서 알맞은 것을 고르시오.

1 The man (who / whose) son was crying tried to calm him.

2 Look at the mountain (which / whose) top is covered with snow.

3 He is the man (which / whose) laptop was stolen last week.

4 The woman (who / whose) name was Scarlett died in 1603.

5 Evan met a friend (who / whose) job was to give advice to people.

» 정답과 해설 p.18

◆ 선행사가 사물 또는 동물일 때 소유격 관계대명사 whose를 of which로 바꿔 쓸 수 있으나 일상 회화에서는 거의 쓰이지 않는다.

B 우리말과 뜻이 같도록 괄호 안의 말을 이용하여 문장을 완성하시오.

1 나는 매우 어려운 수업을 하는 그 선생님을 안다. (course)

→ I know the teacher _____ _____ is very difficult.

2 내게 표지가 초록색인 책을 건네줘. (cover)

→ Pass me the book _____ _____ is green.

3 Ryan은 취미가 기타 연주인 그 소녀를 좋아한다. (hobby)

→ Ryan likes the girl _____ _____ is playing the guitar.

C 두 문장을 소유격 관계대명사를 이용하여 한 문장으로 쓰시오.

1 James knows a girl. + Her father is a TV producer.

→ _____

2 Look at the flower. + Its color is bright orange.

→ _____

3 The boy is over there. + His bike was broken yesterday.

→ _____

4 This is the picture. + Its price is really high.

→ _____

교과서
문장
응용하기

배운 문법을 이용하여 영어 문장을 써 봅시다.

1 이 사람은 어머니가 캐나다 출신인 소녀이다. (be from) → _____

2 그는 가격이 20달러인 가방을 가지고 있다. (price) → _____

53 목적격 관계대명사_ who(m), which

- 목적격 관계대명사는 관계사절에서 목적어 역할을 하며, 선행사가 사람일 때는 whom 또는 who를, 사물일 때는 which를 쓴다.

  I like the woman. + Cindy met her yesterday.

  → I like *the woman* **whom(who)** Cindy met yesterday.

- 목적격 관계대명사 whom(who)과 which는 that으로 바꿔 쓸 수 있다.

  This is the house. + Jack built it.

  → This is *the house* **which(that)** Jack built.

A 괄호 안에서 알맞은 것을 고르시오.

» 정답과 해설 p.18

◆ 주격 관계대명사 다음에는 동사가, 소유격 관계대명사 다음에는 명사가, 목적격 관계대명사 다음에는 「주어+동사」가 온다.

1 There is the street (that / whom) we have to cross.

2 Emma showed me the dress (whom / which) she had bought.

3 The man (whom / whose) you saw was not a famous actor.

4 Alex spoke in German (whom / which) we couldn't understand.

5 I received the letter (whom / which) he had sent last week.

B 우리말과 뜻이 같도록 괄호 안의 말을 이용하여 문장을 완성하시오.

1 그는 내가 어젯밤에 너에게 말했던 그 기자이다. (tell)

→ He is the reporter _____ _____ _____ you about last night.

2 나는 Olivia가 추천해 준 뮤지컬을 보러 갔다. (recommend)

→ I went to see the musical _____ _____ _____.

3 그녀가 나를 위해 작곡했던 그 노래들은 훌륭하다. (compose)

→ The songs _____ _____ _____ for me are wonderful.

C 두 문장을 목적격 관계대명사를 이용하여 한 문장으로 쓰시오.

1 The pizza was delicious. + Grace made it.

→ _____

2 The boy is very handsome. + My sister dated him.

→ _____

3 Is the movie scary? + You are watching it.

→ _____

교과서
문장
응용하기 | 배운 문법을 이용하여 영어 문장을 써 봅시다.

1 너는 네가 잃어버린 열쇠를 찾았니? (lose) → _____

2 내가 만난 그 여자는 유명한 가수였다. (meet) → _____

관계대명사 that

- 관계대명사 that은 주격 관계대명사 또는 목적격 관계대명사의 자리에 쓸 수 있다.
The waiter **who(that)** served us was very rude.

- 선행사가 다음과 같은 경우에는 주로 관계대명사 that을 쓴다.

「사람+동물」, 「사람+사물」인 경우	Look at *the boy and his* dog **that** are sitting on the bench.
형용사의 최상급이 수식하는 경우	This is *the fastest train* **that** I know.
all, no, any, -thing 등이 사용된 경우	We have *everything* **that** we need.
서수, the only, the same 등이 수식하는 경우	You are *the only man* **that** I want to marry.

A 괄호 안에서 알맞은 것을 <u>모두</u> 고르시오.   » 정답과 해설 p.19

1 The man (who / that / whose) is from Mexico works for the company.

2 Tylor is the only one (which / whose / that) I can trust.

3 The pigs ate all the apples (that / who / whom) were on the ground.

4 Mr. Brown is the wisest man (which / whose / that) lives in this town.

B 우리말과 뜻이 같도록 관계대명사 that과 괄호 안의 말을 이용하여 문장을 완성하시오.

1 나는 냉장고에 두었던 오렌지 주스를 찾을 수 없다. (put)

→ I can't find the orange juice _____ _____ _____ in the fridge.

2 Clara는 그 회의에 참석했던 유일한 학생이다. (attend)

→ Clara is the only student _____ _____ the conference.

3 그는 내가 아는 가장 귀여운 소년이다. (know)

→ He is the cutest _____ _____ _____ _____.

C 두 문장을 관계대명사 that을 이용하여 한 문장으로 쓰시오.

1 That's the same wallet. + I have lost the same wallet.

→ _____

2 Peter is the first boy. + Julie loved him in life.

→ _____

3 Did you see the man and his dog? + I am looking for them.

→ _____

교과서
문장
응용하기

배운 문법을 이용하여 영어 문장을 써 봅시다.

1 Daniel은 그녀가 좋아하는 유일한 사람이다. (person) → _____

2 너는 네가 원하는 어떤 책이든 가져가도 된다. (may, any) → _____

관계대명사 what

■ 관계대명사 what은 선행사를 포함하는 관계대명사로, 명사절을 이끌며 문장 내에서 주어, 목적어, 보어 역할을 한다.
What Anna needs might be attention. 〈주어〉
Do you remember **what** Tom likes best? 〈목적어〉
Going shopping is **what** she wants to do. 〈보어〉

■ 관계대명사 what은 the thing(s) which(that)의 의미를 나타내며 '~하는 것(들)'로 해석한다.
What he told me was not true at all.
→ **The thing which(that)** he told me was not true at all.

A 괄호 안에서 알맞은 것을 고르시오.   》 정답과 해설 p.19

1 Mike found (what / which) he had lost.
2 (That / What) I bought for you is good for your health.
3 I didn't know (that / what) she was going to do next.
4 The thing (which / what) you are seeing now is a painting by Van Gogh.

B 밑줄 친 부분을 어법상 바르게 고쳐 쓰시오.

1 <u>Which</u> you did yesterday was not right.   _____
2 Vegetable sandwich is <u>which</u> she ate for lunch.   _____
3 You may hear the thing <u>what</u> you want to hear.   _____

C 우리말과 뜻이 같도록 빈칸에 알맞은 말을 쓰시오.

1 우리에게 필요한 것은 커피 한 잔이다.
  → _____ we need is a cup of coffee.
  → _____ _____ _____ we need is a cup of coffee.
2 나는 그녀가 무엇에 대해 생각하는 중인지 이해할 수 없었다.
  → I couldn't understand _____ she was thinking about.
  → I couldn't understand _____ _____ _____ she was thinking about.
3 이것이 그가 너에게 말하려고 했던 것이다.
  → This is _____ he was going to tell you.
  → This is _____ _____ _____ he was going to tell you.

교과서 문장 응용하기 | 배운 문법을 이용하여 영어 문장을 써 봅시다.

1 그녀가 말한 것은 나를 행복하게 했다. (make)   → _____
2 나는 그가 내게 하라고 충고한 것을 듣지 않았다. (advise) → _____

관계대명사의 계속적 용법

■ 계속적 용법은 콤마(,)를 사용하여 관계대명사절이 선행사에 대해 부가적인 설명을 하거나 문장 전체를 수식하며, 관계
대명사를 「접속사+대명사」로 바꿀 수 있다. 단, 관계대명사 that과 what은 계속적 용법으로 쓸 수 없다.

Mr. Kim has *a sister*, **who**(= and she) is a soccer player.

I like *this show*, **which**(= for(as / because) it) is very exciting.

I wanted to buy *that car*, **which**(= but it) was too expensive.

cf. 제한적 용법: 관계대명사절이 선행사를 수식하거나 한정한다.

Mr. Kim has *a sister* **who** is a soccer player.

A 괄호 안에서 알맞은 것을 고르시오.   » 정답과 해설 p.19

1 Mr. Park likes this movie, (that / which) is very interesting.

2 I know Emily, (whose / whom) mother is a doctor in Japan.

3 Yesterday, she met Logan, (whom / that) she hadn't seen for a year.

4 Andrew, (who / that) was in a hurry, didn't finish his homework.

5 My house, (what / which) my grandfather built, needs repairing.

B 두 문장의 뜻이 같도록 밑줄 친 부분에 유의하여 빈칸에 알맞은 말을 쓰시오.

1 She likes him, who is very thoughtful.

→ She likes him, _____ _____ is very thoughtful.

2 I tried to change his mind, which I found impossible.

→ I tried to change his mind, _____ _____ found it impossible.

3 Evan passed the driving test, which surprised everyone.

→ Evan passed the driving test, _____ _____ surprised everyone.

C 우리말과 뜻이 같도록 빈칸에 알맞은 말을 쓰시오.

1 나는 그 사람에게 말했고, 그는 그 문제를 설명해 주었다.

→ I spoke to the man, _____ _____ the problem.

2 나는 비싼 호텔에서 머물렀지만, 그 호텔은 매우 더러웠다.

→ I stayed at an expensive hotel, _____ _____ very dirty.

3 그녀의 아버지는 그녀를 용서했는데, 그녀가 그에게 용서를 구했기 때문이다.

→ Her father forgave her, _____ _____ him forgiveness.

교과서
문장
응용하기

배운 문법을 이용하여 영어 문장을 써 봅시다.

1 Sarah는 나와 같은 반 친구지만, 나는 그녀를 좋아하지 않는다.   → _____

2 나는 친구가 한 명 있는데, 런던에 산다.   → _____

전치사+관계대명사

▪ 관계대명사가 전치사의 목적어일 때, 전치사는 관계대명사 앞이나 관계대명사절 끝에 온다. 단, 관계대명사 that은 전치사 뒤에 쓸 수 없다.

The boy is her brother. + I talked to him.

→ *The boy* **to whom** I talked is her brother. 〈to that은 불가〉

→ *The boy* (**whom**(**that**)) I talked **to** is her brother. 〈이때 목적격 관계대명사 whom(that)은 생략 가능〉

A 괄호 안에서 알맞은 것을 고르시오.   》정답과 해설 p.19

1 This is the school (to which / to that) Melody goes.

2 That's the girl (for that / for whom) I am waiting.

3 The music (which / to which) we listened was good.

4 I remember her (with whom / whom) I broke up with.

B 우리말과 뜻이 같도록 빈칸에 알맞은 말을 쓰시오.

1 내가 갔던 파티는 재미있었다.

   → The party _____ _____ I went was interesting.

2 David은 그가 태어난 프라하를 방문할 예정이다.

   → David is going to visit Prague _____ _____ he was born.

3 이 여자는 내가 함께 일했던 사람이다.

   → This is the woman _____ _____ I worked.

C 두 문장을 「전치사+관계대명사」 형태의 한 문장으로 쓰시오.

1 These are her cats. + She was looking for them.

   → _____

2 Do you know the man? + Spencer is speaking to him.

   → _____

3 The woman should follow the directions. + She asked for it.

   → _____

4 Victoria left him. + He fell in love with her.

   → _____

교과서
문장
응용하기

배운 문법을 이용하여 영어 문장을 써 봅시다. (「전치사+관계대명사」 형태를 활용하세요.)

1 네가 앉아있는 그 소파는 편안해 보인다. (comfortable)   → _____

2 나는 Jessica와 함께 놀았던 그 소녀를 안다. (play)   → _____

관계대명사의 생략

■ 제한적 용법의 목적격 관계대명사는 생략할 수 있지만, 앞에 전치사가 있거나 계속적 용법으로 쓰인 경우에는 생략할 수 없다.

The woman (**whom**(**that**)) you spoke to is my teacher.

The woman **to whom** you spoke is my teacher. 〈전치사 다음에는 생략 불가〉

■ 「주격 관계대명사+be동사」도 생략할 수 있다.

The woman (**who is**) speaking to you is my teacher.

A 밑줄 친 부분을 생략할 수 있으면 "○", 생략할 수 <u>없으면</u> "✕"를 쓰시오.　　　　》 정답과 해설 p.19

1 The wristwatch <u>which</u> she gave him is so cool.　　　　_____

2 I met the doctor <u>who</u> treats eye disease.　　　　_____

3 We know the girls <u>who are</u> dancing on the stage.　　　　_____

4 Where is the museum about <u>which</u> you told me?　　　　_____

B 우리말과 뜻이 같도록 빈칸에 알맞은 말을 쓰시오.

1 그는 믿을 수 있는 친구가 없다.

→ He has no friends _____ _____ trust.

2 그 점원은 내가 원하던 옷을 가져왔다.

→ The clerk brought the clothes _____ _____.

3 그가 묵었던 집은 Blake의 집이다.

→ The house _____ _____ at was Blake's.

C 두 문장을 관계대명사를 이용하여 한 문장으로 쓰고, 생략 가능한 부분에 괄호를 치시오.

1 The peaches are delicious. + I bought them yesterday.

→ _____

2 The lady is a science teacher. + Joe married her.

→ _____

3 The ice hockey match was exciting. + Sean played in it.

→ _____

4 It is a very old statue. + It was made of bronze.

→ _____

교과서 문장 응용하기

배운 문법을 이용하여 영어 문장을 써 봅시다.

1 그녀는 내가 작년에 만났던 여자이다.　　→ _____

2 내가 함께 살고 있는 나의 삼촌은 매우 친절하다.　　→ _____

59 관계부사 1_ when, where

관계부사는 선행사를 수식하는 절을 이끌며 접속사와 부사의 역할을 동시에 한다. 또한, 「전치사+관계대명사」로 바꿔 쓸 수 있다.

관계부사	선행사	예문
when	시간(the time, the day, the month, the year 등)	I can't forget the day. + We met on the day. → I can't forget *the day* **when** we met. → I can't forget *the day* **on which** we met.
where	장소(the place, the house, the city 등)	That's the house. + I grew up in the house. → That's *the house* **where** I grew up. → That's *the house* **in which** I grew up.

cf. 관계부사를 「전치사+관계대명사」로 바꿔 쓸 때 관계대명사 that은 쓸 수 없다.

A 괄호 안에서 알맞은 것을 고르시오. » 정답과 해설 p.19

1 I went to the park (where / that) I lost my backpack.

2 Amber called me at 11 o'clock (when / where) I was unable to answer.

3 The house (which / in which) Chopin was born is now a museum.

B 우리말과 뜻이 같도록 빈칸에 알맞은 말을 쓰시오.

1 나는 다리가 부러진 그 날을 기억하고 있다.

→ I remember the _____ _____ _____ I broke my leg.

2 너는 우리가 전에 갔었던 도서관을 기억하니?

→ Do you remember the _____ _____ we went before?

3 소포가 도착할 시간을 말해 주세요.

→ Please tell me the _____ _____ the package will arrive.

C 두 문장을 관계부사를 이용하여 한 문장으로 쓰시오.

1 She didn't forget the day. + Her son went to school on the day.

→ _____

2 This is the place. + The accident happened at the place.

→ _____

3 Do you know the time? + The soccer game will start at the time.

→ _____

교과서 문장 응용하기 배운 문법을 이용하여 영어 문장을 써 봅시다. (관계부사를 활용하세요.)

1 여기가 나의 어머니가 일하는 사무실이다. → _____

2 겨울은 산들이 눈으로 덮이는 계절이다. → _____

60 관계부사 2_ why, how

관계부사	선행사	예문
why	이유(the reason)	He didn't say the reason. + He was late for the reason. → He didn't say *the reason* **why** he was late. → He didn't say *the reason* **for which** he was late.
how	방법(the way) (단, the way와 how는 함께 쓸 수 없음)	Tell me the way. + She solved the problem in the way. → Tell me **how**(**the way**) she solved the problem. → Tell me *the way* **in which** she solved the problem.

A 괄호 안에서 알맞은 것을 고르시오.   » 정답과 해설 p.19

1 We discussed (the way how / how) we can improve the service.

2 What was the reason (why / when) you decided to travel all around the world?

3 That was the way (why / in which) Prince Leo got married.

4 He explained (the way / the way which) he persuaded his parents.

5 That's the reason (which / why) Grace was absent from school yesterday.

B 우리말과 뜻이 같도록 빈칸에 알맞은 말을 쓰시오.

1 우리는 그가 어떻게 이 모든 음식을 만들었는지 모른다.

   → We don't know _____ he made all this food.

2 네가 영어를 배운 방식을 나에게 말해 줄 수 있니?

   → Can you tell me _____ _____ you learned English?

3 나는 그녀가 파티에 오지 않았던 이유가 궁금하다.

   → I wonder _____ _____ _____ she didn't come to the party.

C 두 문장을 관계부사를 이용하여 한 문장으로 쓰시오.

1 There were some reasons. + I missed the train for some reasons.

   → _____

2 I know the way. + Emily operated the machine in the way.

   → _____

3 The horror movie was the reason. + Dylan couldn't sleep for the reason.

   → _____

교과서 문장 응용하기   배운 문법을 이용하여 영어 문장을 써 봅시다. (관계부사를 활용하세요.)

1 그것이 그가 그 길을 건넜던 이유이다. (road)   → _____

2 그는 그녀가 기타 연주를 배운 방법이 궁금했다. (wonder)   → _____

관계부사와 선행사의 생략

- 관계부사 앞에 일반적인 선행사가 오는 경우 관계부사 또는 선행사를 생략할 수 있다.

  Fall is *the time* **when** students come back to school.

  → Fall is *the time* students come back to school. 〈관계부사 생략〉

  → Fall is **when** students come back to school. 〈선행사 생략〉

- 관계부사가 계속적 용법으로 쓰인 경우에는 생략할 수 없다.

  I like *October*, **when** I was born. 〈관계부사 생략 불가〉

A 괄호 안에서 알맞은 것을 고르시오.

» 정답과 해설 p.20

1 (The day / The reason) I started to study for the exam was just yesterday.

2 Tell me (why / who) you didn't send my letter.

3 The drama club is (how / where) she met her boyfriend.

4 (How / The way how) he got the money is a secret.

5 July and August are (when / where) most people go on holiday.

◆ 구체적이면서 특정한 장소를 나타내는 관계부사 where는 가급적 생략하지 않는다.
I went back to the town **where** I grew up.

B 우리말과 뜻이 같도록 빈칸에 알맞은 말을 쓰시오.

1 나는 그가 프랑스에 간 이유를 모르겠다.

   → I don't know _____ _____ _____ to France.

2 Kate는 그 배우를 봤던 그 날을 잊을 수가 없다.

   → Kate can't forget _____ _____ _____ _____ the actor.

3 Tony는 어떻게 모형 배를 만드는지를 나에게 보여 주었다.

   → Tony showed me _____ _____ _____ a model ship.

C 다음 문장을 생략된 관계부사나 선행사를 넣어 다시 쓰시오.

1 Could you tell me when the train will leave?

   → _____

2 He wondered the reason she didn't invite him.

   → _____

3 I look forward to the day our school festival begins.

   → _____

교과서
문장
응용하기

배운 문법을 이용하여 영어 문장을 써 봅시다. (선행사를 생략하세요.)

1 그것이 그녀가 내게 화를 냈던 이유이다. (get angry)   → _____

2 이곳이 내가 나의 팔찌를 잃어버린 곳이다. (bracelet)   → _____

복합관계대명사

▪ 복합관계대명사는 「관계대명사+-ever」의 형태로 선행사를 포함하고 있으며, 명사절과 양보의 부사절을 이끈다.

복합관계대명사	명사절	양보의 부사절
whoever	anyone who (~하는 누구나)	no matter who (누가 ~할지라도)
whomever	anyone whom (~하는 누구나)	no matter whom (누구를 ~할지라도)
whichever	anything which (~하는 어느 것이나)	no matter which (어느 것을 ~할지라도)
whatever	anything that (~하는 무엇이나)	no matter what (무엇을 ~할지라도)

Whoever(= Anyone who) arrives first will be the winner. 〈명사절〉

Whoever(= No matter who) comes now, I won't open the door. 〈양보의 부사절〉

A 괄호 안에서 알맞은 것을 고르시오.   » 정답과 해설 p.20

1 (What / Whatever) happens, don't be surprised.

2 Give it to (whomever / whichever) you like.

3 Choose (which / whichever) you'd like to purchase.

4 (Whoever / Whomever) leaves last should turn off the computers.

B 우리말과 뜻이 같도록 빈칸에 알맞은 말을 쓰시오.

1 Luna가 무슨 말을 하더라도 나는 듣지 않을 것이다.

→ _____ Luna says, I will not listen.

2 누가 오더라도 나는 상관없다.

→ _____ _____ _____ comes, I don't care.

3 그는 그녀가 누구를 초대했더라도 꺼리지 않는다.

→ He doesn't mind _____ she invited.

C 두 문장의 뜻이 같도록 빈칸에 알맞은 말을 쓰시오.

1 Do anything that you want to do.

→ Do _____ you want to do.

2 I'll give the movie ticket to whoever loves movies.

→ I'll give the movie ticket to _____ _____ loves movies.

3 Whomever you ask, you'll not be able to get the answer.

→ _____ _____ _____ you ask, you'll not be able to get the answer.

교과서
문장
응용하기

배운 문법을 이용하여 영어 문장을 써 봅시다.

1 여기에 오는 사람은 누구든지 나의 친구가 될 것이다.   → _____

2 다른 사람들이 무슨 생각을 하더라도, 최선을 다해라.   → _____

복합관계부사

- 복합관계부사는 「관계부사+-ever」의 형태로 선행사를 포함하고 있으며, 부사절을 이끈다.

복합관계부사	시간·장소의 부사절	양보의 부사절
whenever	at any time when (~할 때마다)	no matter when (언제 ~해도)
wherever	at any place where (~하는 어디에나)	no matter where (어디에서 ~해도)
however	-	no matter how (아무리 ~해도)

Come and see me **whenever**(= at any time when) you like. 〈시간의 부사절〉
The baby follows his mom **wherever**(= at any place where) she goes. 〈장소의 부사절〉
However(= No matter how) hard he exercises, he never loses weight. 〈양보의 부사절〉

A 괄호 안에서 알맞은 것을 고르시오.   » 정답과 해설 p.20

1 (Wherever / However) brave he is, he can't do that.

2 (Wherever / Whenever) she is, she thinks of you.

3 Sally comes to me (whenever / however) she needs some advice.

4 I practice the guitar at any time (whenever / when) I can.

B 빈칸에 알맞은 복합관계부사를 쓰시오.

1 They always fight _____ they have a conversation.

2 _____ you come, I will wait for you.

3 _____ rich they are, they can't buy the whole country.

4 _____ he goes, he can meet many people.

C 우리말과 뜻이 같도록 빈칸에 알맞은 말을 쓰시오.

1 네가 그것을 아무리 완벽하게 해도, 나는 너를 믿지 않는다.
→ _____ perfectly you do it, I don't trust you.

2 내가 그 시를 읽을 때마다, 내 마음은 차분해진다.
→ _____ _____ _____ the poem, I feel relaxed.

3 Judy는 가는 곳 어디에서나 관심의 중심이 된다.
→ Judy is the center of interest _____ _____ _____.

4 그가 아무리 똑똑해도 그는 단지 어린 소년일 뿐이다.
→ _____ _____ _____ smart he is, he is just a little boy.

교과서 문장 응용하기 | 배운 문법을 이용하여 영어 문장을 써 봅시다.

1 네가 가는 어디에나 나는 너를 따라갈 것이다. (follow)   → _____

2 나는 아이스크림을 먹을 때마다 병이 난다. (get sick)   → _____

내신적중 실전문제

[01~02] 빈칸에 알맞은 것을 고르시오.

01

> I know many people _____ dream is
> to travel to outer space.

① who ② that ③ whom
④ when ⑤ whose

02

> Madrid, _____ is the capital of Spain,
> is one of the cities I want to visit.

① which ② that ③ where
④ what ⑤ who

[03~04] 우리말과 뜻이 같도록 빈칸에 알맞은 말을 쓰시오.

주관식

03

> Peter가 말한 것을 들은 후에, Anna는 모든 것을
> 이해했다.
> → After listening to _____ Peter said,
> Anna understood everything.

04

> 그 쇼에 참가하고 싶은 사람은 누구나 티켓을 신청할
> 수 있다.
> → _____ wants to join the show can
> apply for a ticket.

05 밑줄 친 부분 중 어법상 어색한 것은?

> My father, ① whom I helped ② install
> ③ his computer, always ④ forget his
> ⑤ password.

[06~07] 두 문장을 한 문장으로 쓸 때 빈칸에 알맞은 것을
고르시오.

06

> Jack told us the same joke again. + We
> had already heard it 100 times.
> → Jack told us the same joke _____
> we had already heard 100 times.

① who ② which ③ that
④ what ⑤ whose

07

> Do you know the year? + Korea got the
> first gold medal in the Olympics then.
> → Do you know the year _____
> Korea got the first gold medal in the
> Olympics?

① why ② when ③ how
④ where ⑤ what

빈출
유형
★

08 밑줄 친 부분과 괄호 안의 말의 의미가 다른 것은?

① Pat bought a book, which is popular for
its amazing characters. (= and it)
② You may do the things that you'd like to
do.   (= what)
③ I don't know the reason for which she
hates me.   (= why)
④ No matter who talks to him, he'll never
listen. (= Whoever)
⑤ You can take home anything that you like.
                (= which)

09 다음 문장에서 생략할 수 있는 말을 찾아 쓰시오. (주관식)

> Ms. May bought a cake which was decorated with fruit and peanuts.

_____

[10~11] 빈칸에 알맞은 말이 바르게 짝지어진 것을 고르시오.

10
> • I want to be a scientist _____ makes many surprising things.
> • Please tell me the shop _____ sells good fruit.

① whom — which
② which — that
③ that — who
④ which — who
⑤ who — that

11
> • Do you know the reason _____ so many people in the world learn English?
> • Please tell me _____ I can go to Insadong on this map.

① when — why
② why — when
③ why — how
④ where — how
⑤ how — why

12 주어진 말을 바르게 배열한 것은?

> this cake, made, whoever, a real artist, is

① A real artist is made whoever this cake.
② A real artist whoever is made this cake.
③ This cake is made a real artist whoever.
④ This cake is whoever a real artist made.
⑤ Whoever made this cake is a real artist.

13 우리말을 영어로 잘못 옮긴 것은?

> 나는 산타클로스에게 편지를 썼던 날을 기억하지 못한다.

① I do not remember the day when I wrote to Santa Claus.
② I do not remember the day on which I wrote to Santa Claus.
③ I do not remember the day which I wrote to Santa Claus on.
④ I do not remember the day on that I wrote to Santa Claus.
⑤ I do not remember the day that I wrote to Santa Claus on.

14 빈칸에 공통으로 알맞은 말을 쓰시오. (주관식)

> • _____ makes me angry is watching trash in the street.
> • These shoes are not _____ I'm looking for.
> • I'm sorry, but I can't understand _____ you're saying.

15 밑줄 친 부분을 다른 관계대명사로 바꿔 쓸 수 있는 것은?

① The Thames is a river <u>which</u> runs through London.
② You shouldn't believe everything <u>that</u> you read in the newspaper.
③ What's the name of the girl <u>whose</u> hair is very long?
④ The hotel at <u>which</u> we stayed was cheap and comfortable.
⑤ Harry bought a cellphone last month, <u>which</u> has recently broken down.

16 두 문장의 뜻이 같도록 빈칸에 알맞은 말을 쓰시오. (주관식)

Yuri came to meet her teacher, Mr. Kim, who was not at a teacher's room.
= Yuri came to meet her teacher, Mr. Kim, _____ _____ was not at a teacher's room.

17 밑줄 친 부분이 어법상 어색한 것은?

① Show me <u>how</u> this project got started.
② I know the place <u>where</u> she can make more friends.
③ Dr. Kim has studied <u>the way how</u> animals communicate.
④ I'm going to visit France in August <u>when</u> it is full of tourists.
⑤ He explained to me <u>the reason</u> he had made the system.

18 대화의 빈칸에 알맞은 것은?

A I'll follow _____ you go.
B Please, leave me alone.

① whomever
② whatever
③ wherever
④ whoever
⑤ whichever

19 우리말을 영어로 바르게 옮긴 것을 <u>두 개</u> 고르면?

무슨 일이 일어나든지 간에, 그녀의 얼굴에는 온화한 미소가 남아있었다.

① What happened, the gentle smile remained on her face.
② Whatever happened, the gentle smile remained on her face.
③ Whoever happened, the gentle smile remained on her face.
④ No matter what happened, the gentle smile remained on her face.
⑤ Anything what happened, the gentle smile remained on her face.

20 밑줄 친 부분의 쓰임이 나머지 넷과 <u>다른</u> 것은?

① These are all <u>that</u> I can do for you.
② The house <u>that</u> belongs to Julie is in New York.
③ They think <u>that</u> the exam will be difficult.
④ He is the man <u>that</u> lives next to my house.
⑤ Amy is the first woman <u>that</u> came to the party.

21 밑줄 친 부분 중 생략할 수 <u>없는</u> 것은?

① Who was the boy <u>who</u> you went to the movies with?

② An elephant is an animal <u>which</u> lives in hot countries.

③ The book <u>that</u> you recommended was good.

④ The black umbrella <u>which was</u> found at the bus stop belongs to Alan.

⑤ My mother asked me the reason <u>why</u> I got angry.

22 밑줄 친 부분을 <u>잘못</u> 고쳐 쓴 것은?

① The boy <u>who</u> bike was stolen was crying.
　　　　　　(→ whose)

② She knows the teacher, <u>which</u> can speak English very well. 　　(→ who)

③ Olympic Park is the place <u>which</u> we often take a walk after dinner. (→ where)

④ Look at the little boy <u>who playing</u> with a ball. 　　　　　　(→ playing)

⑤ <u>Whatever</u> old he is, Mr. Miller is still healthy and energetic. (→ whichever)

23 어법상 어색한 것끼리 짝지어진 것은?

ⓐ The girl is talking to him is my sister.

ⓑ Ben bought a book, that was very interesting.

ⓒ I visited the village where my parents lived.

ⓓ Eric told us the way how he helped the poor.

ⓔ What makes me happy is to go shopping with my mother.

① ⓐ, ⓓ　　　② ⓒ, ⓔ　　　③ ⓐ, ⓑ, ⓓ
④ ⓑ, ⓓ, ⓔ　　⑤ ⓑ, ⓒ, ⓓ, ⓔ

24 두 문장을 한 문장으로 바르게 연결한 것을 <u>두 개</u> 고르면?

Do you know the gallery? + We can see the traditional Korean paintings at the gallery.

① Do you know the gallery which we can see the traditional Korean paintings?

② Do you know the gallery where we can see the traditional Korean paintings?

③ Do you know the gallery where we can see the traditional Korean paintings at?

④ Do you know the gallery at that we can see the traditional Korean paintings?

⑤ Do you know the gallery which we can see the traditional Korean paintings at?

25 어법상 올바른 문장의 개수는?

ⓐ He has two brothers, whom are students.

ⓑ There is a house whose roof is high and looks bright.

ⓒ Look at the man and the cat who are running over there.

ⓓ This is the palace building in the early 1800s.

ⓔ Please tell me the reason why you didn't go to the camp.

ⓕ I don't have much money, so I'll take whichever is cheaper.

① 2개　　　　② 3개　　　　③ 4개
④ 5개　　　　⑤ 6개

서술형 평가

01 두 문장을 한 문장으로 쓸 때 빈칸에 알맞은 말을 쓰시오.

> The movie star received many gifts. +
> They were sent by his fans.

(1) The movie star received many gifts
_____ _____ _____ by his fans.

(2) The movie star received many gifts
_____ by his fans.

02 밑줄 친 부분을 우리말로 옮기고, 문장에서 어떤 역할을 하는지 쓰시오.

(1) What I want is to take a trip to Europe.
　→ _____, _____

(2) This book is what I wanted to read.
　→ _____, _____

03 다음 문장과 의미가 같도록 조건에 맞게 빈칸에 알맞은 말을 쓰시오.

> You grow plants in a greenhouse.

(1) A greenhouse is a glass building _____
_____. (전치사를 관계대명사 앞에 쓸 것)

(2) A greenhouse is a glass building _____
_____. (전치사를 뒤에 쓸 것)

(3) A greenhouse is a glass building _____
_____. (관계부사를 쓸 것)

04 A와 B에서 각각 알맞은 말을 골라 문장을 완성하시오.

A	the season, the reason, the shop
B	when, where, why

(1) I don't remember _____ I
bought the sandals.

(2) Spring is _____ many people
go on a picnic.

(3) Do you know _____ the South
Pole is colder than the North Pole?

🔵 독해형 어법

[05~06] 다음 글을 읽고, 물음에 답하시오.

　The human brain is divided into two sides,
ⓐ which are called the right brain and the
left brain. The left side of the brain ⓑ that
is more logical controls language. It names
things and puts them into groups. ⓒ Who
memorizes spelling and grammar rules
uses this side of the brain. The right side
of the brain is more creative. It receives the
information from the senses of sight, sound,
smell, touch, and taste. ⓓ No matter who
draw a picture or listen to music uses this
side of the brain.

05 밑줄 친 ⓐ, ⓑ를 다른 말로 바꿔 쓰시오.

ⓐ _____　　ⓑ _____

06 밑줄 친 ⓒ, ⓓ를 어법상 바르게 고쳐 쓰시오.

ⓒ _____　　ⓓ _____

CHAPTER

09

접속사

FOCUS 64   명사절을 이끄는 접속사

FOCUS 65   시간의 접속사 1

FOCUS 66   시간의 접속사 2

FOCUS 67   조건·이유의 접속사

FOCUS 68   양보의 접속사

FOCUS 69   상관접속사 1

FOCUS 70   상관접속사 2

FOCUS 71   접속부사

🍃 접속사란 무엇인가?

접속사는 단어, 구, 절을 서로 연결하는 말이다.

🍃 접속사에는 어떤 것이 있고 접속사는 어떻게 쓰이는가?

접속사에는 문법적 역할이 대등한 것을 연결하는 and, but, or, nor과 같은 등위접속사와 *주절에 *종속절을 연결하는 종속접속사, 그리고 두 요소가 짝이 되어 쓰이는 상관접속사가 있다.

종속 접속사	명사절을 이끄는 접속사: that, whether(if)	He wanted to know **whether** Betty passed the exam. 그는 Betty가 그 시험에 통과했는지 아닌지 알고 싶었다.
	조건의 부사절을 이끄는 접속사: if, unless	**Unless** you practice every day, you can't be the best player. 만약 네가 매일 연습하지 않는다면, 너는 최고의 선수가 될 수 없다.
	시간의 부사절을 이끄는 접속사: when, while, as, before, after, until, since	**While** she was having lunch, she read a newspaper. 그녀는 점심을 먹는 동안, 신문을 읽었다.
	이유의 부사절을 이끄는 접속사: because, as, since	I cancelled the appointment **as** I was very upset. 나는 매우 화가 나서 그 약속을 취소했다.
	양보의 부사절을 이끄는 접속사: though, although, even though, even if	He finished his homework **although** he had a bad cold. 그는 비록 독감에 걸렸지만 그의 숙제를 끝냈다.
상관 접속사	both A and B, not only A but (also) B	Harry **not only** cleaned the house, **but (also)** washed the clothes. Harry는 집을 청소했을 뿐 아니라 빨래도 했다.
	either A or B, neither A nor B	Her grade is **neither** the best, **nor** the worst. 그녀의 성적은 최상도 최하도 아니다.

* **주절**: 두 개의 문장이 종속접속사로 연결되었을 때 접속사가 붙어 있지 않고 「주어+동사」의 형식으로 문장에서 주가 되는 절을 말한다.
* **종속절**: 주절에 종속되어 의미를 전달하는 절로, 대체로 종속접속사 뒤에 쓰인다.

64 명사절을 이끄는 접속사_ that, whether(if)

- **that**: 문장에서 주어, 목적어, 보어 역할을 하는 명사절을 이끌며, 목적어절이나 보어절에서는 that을 생략할 수 있다.
  It is certain **that** he will come back. 〈가주어와 진주어〉
  We know **(that)** he left for America. 〈목적어 역할〉

- **whether(if)**: '~인지 아닌지'의 의미로 명사절을 이끌며, 뒤에 or not이 오기도 한다.
  I don't know **whether(if)** he will visit us (or not).

A 다음 문장에서 밑줄 친 부분이 주어, 목적어, 보어 중 어떤 역할을 하는지 쓰시오.

» 정답과 해설 p.21

1 It is his idea that I should get a haircut. ＿＿＿＿＿
2 Whether she will do it doesn't matter to me. ＿＿＿＿＿
3 Daniel didn't know that Jane didn't read the book. ＿＿＿＿＿
4 The problem is that the rumor turned out to be true. ＿＿＿＿＿

◆ whether *vs.* if

1. whether는 대부분 if로 바꿔 쓸 수 있지만, 명사절이 주어나 보어로 쓰인 경우에는 바꿔 쓸 수 없다. 즉 if는 목적절에서만 쓰인다.
   Ask them **if** they can swim.
2. whether or not ~처럼 or not이 바로 뒤에 올 때에는 if로 바꿔 쓸 수 없다.
   I don't know **whether or not** he will come.

B 괄호 안의 말을 바르게 배열하여 문장을 완성하시오.

1 ＿＿＿＿＿＿＿＿＿＿＿＿ is certain. (Mr. Johnson, not, will, return, that)
2 I heard ＿＿＿＿＿＿＿＿＿＿＿. (you, a traffic accident, that, had)
3 ＿＿＿＿＿＿＿＿＿＿＿ will require my advice. (wonder, Noah, if, I)
4 The question is ＿＿＿＿＿＿＿＿＿＿ or not.
  (the job, she, will quit, whether)
5 ＿＿＿＿＿＿＿＿＿＿＿ you should respect different cultures.
  (important, that, is, it)

C 우리말과 뜻이 같도록 괄호 안의 말을 이용하여 문장을 완성하시오.

1 사실은 우리가 충분한 시간을 갖고 있지 않다는 것이다. (enough)
  → The fact is ＿＿＿＿ we don't have ＿＿＿＿ ＿＿＿＿.
2 그녀는 시험이 어려울 것이라고 생각한다. (hard)
  → She thinks ＿＿＿＿ the exam ＿＿＿＿ ＿＿＿＿ ＿＿＿＿.
3 그가 동의할 것인지 아닌지는 중요하지 않다. (agree)
  → ＿＿＿＿ ＿＿＿＿ ＿＿＿＿ ＿＿＿＿ or not is not important.
4 우리는 그 회의에 참석할 것인지 아닌지 결정해야 한다. (attend, meeting)
  → We should decide ＿＿＿＿ we will ＿＿＿＿ ＿＿＿＿ ＿＿＿＿.

교과서
문장
응용하기

배운 문법을 이용하여 영어 문장을 써 봅시다.

1 Jeff는 그녀가 아프다는 것을 모른다. → ＿＿＿＿＿＿＿＿＿＿＿＿＿＿＿＿＿
2 Emily는 내가 선생님인지 아닌지 모른다. → ＿＿＿＿＿＿＿＿＿＿＿＿＿＿＿＿＿

시간의 접속사 1_ when, while, as

접속사	의미	특징	예문
when	~할 때	시간의 부사절에서는 현재시제로 미래를 표현함	He was talking on the phone **when** I arrived.
while	~하는 동안	별개의 사건이 동시에 일어남	**While** I was playing the piano, my brother was cooking dinner.
as	~할 때, ~하면서	관련이 있는 사건이 동시에 일어남	Ann ate an apple **as** she studied.

A 두 문장을 괄호 안의 접속사를 이용하여 한 문장으로 쓰시오. 》 정답과 해설 p.22

1 You seem very happy. + You help other people. (when)

→ You _____ .

2 Mom made some cookies. + I was taking care of my sister. (while)

→ Mom _____ .

3 Jack came up to me. + He was singing. (as)

→ Jack _____ .

4 I watched the movie. + Violet was taking a test. (while)

→ I _____ .

5 Mark got a lot of experience. + Time passed. (as)

→ Mark _____ .

6 I will tell her the truth. + She will come here tomorrow. (when)

→ I _____ .

B 우리말과 뜻이 같도록 괄호 안의 말을 이용하여 문장을 완성하시오.

1 너는 씹고 있을 때, 말을 해서는 안 된다. (as, chew)

→ _____ _____ _____ _____ , you shouldn't speak.

2 너는 여가 시간에 무엇을 하니? (when, free time)

→ What do you do _____ _____ _____ _____ _____ ?

3 그녀가 라디오를 듣는 동안, 그가 문을 두드렸다. (while, listen to)

→ _____ _____ _____ _____ _____ the radio, he knocked on the door.

교과서
문장
응용하기

배운 문법을 이용하여 영어 문장을 써 봅시다.

1 그녀는 더 젊었을 때, 서핑하는 것을 즐겼다. (enjoy) → _____

2 시간이 지나면서, 나는 너를 더욱 사랑한다. (go by) → _____

시간의 접속사 2_ before, after, until, since

접속사	의미	특징	예문
before / after	~하기 전에 / ~한 후에	뒤에 동명사나 명사구가 오는 전치사로 쓰이기도 함	I washed my hands **before** I had dinner. 〈접속사〉 I washed my hands **before** having dinner. 〈전치사〉
until(till)	~할 때까지	–	**Until(Till)** it stops raining, he won't leave.
since	~ 이후로 (줄곧)	주로 과거시제의 절을 이끌어 현재완료와 함께 쓰임	She has played tennis **since** she was young.

A 괄호 안의 말을 바르게 배열하여 문장을 완성하시오.　　　　　　　　　》 정답과 해설 p.22

1 I'll wait here _____. (opens, bakery, until, this)

2 We are going to go to Europe _____.
(we, after, graduate)

3 She has not seen Jake _____.
(he, his hometown, moved, since, to)

B 두 문장을 괄호 안의 접속사를 이용하여 한 문장으로 쓰시오.

1 Judy stayed outside. + The guests arrived. (until)
→ Judy _____.

2 I haven't seen him. + He went to the USA. (since)
→ I _____.

3 They packed their luggage. + They left for Thailand. (before)
→ They _____.

C 우리말과 뜻이 같도록 괄호 안의 말을 이용하여 문장을 완성하시오.

1 그가 말할 때까지, 나는 조용히 있었다. (speak)
→ _____ _____ _____, I kept silent.

2 그녀는 결혼한 이후로 줄곧 여기에 살고 있다. (get married)
→ She has lived here _____ _____ _____ _____.

3 그 경주가 끝난 후, 우리는 실망했다. (end)
→ _____ the race _____, we were disappointed.

교과서 문장 응용하기 | 배운 문법을 이용하여 영어 문장을 써 봅시다.

1 그가 오기 전에 돌아와라. (back)　　　　　　　→ _____

2 나는 Ben이 집에 도착할 때까지 그 책을 읽을 것이다. (arrive)　→ _____

조건·이유의 접속사_ if, unless / because, as, since

		의미	특징	예문
조건의 접속사	if	(만약) ~라면	조건의 부사절에서는 현재시제로 미래를 표현함	**If** he comes back, we will be happy.
	unless	(만약) ~하지 않는다면	if ~ not으로 바꿔 쓸 수 있음	**Unless** you work hard, you won't succeed. → If you don't work hard, you won't succeed.
이유의 접속사	because	~이기 때문에	because of일 때는 뒤에 동명사나 명사구가 옴	We couldn't go to the park **because** it was raining heavily.
	as, since	~이므로, ~해서	이유나 원인을 나타냄	**As** it was cold, I caught a cold. **Since** you helped me, I could finish the report.

A 괄호 안에서 알맞은 것을 고르시오.   》 정답과 해설 p.22

1 I ordered two pizzas (as / if) we were all hungry.

2 We can go to a movie (if / unless) you have other plans.

3 You should submit an application (if / unless) you want to get a job.

4 She wants to be a doctor (when / since) she likes to help the sick.

5 (Because / Because of) I didn't clean my room, my mother was angry.

B 우리말과 뜻이 같도록 괄호 안의 말을 이용하여 문장을 완성하시오.

1 날씨가 좋지 않으면, 나는 나가지 않겠다. (fine)

   → I will not go out _____ the weather _____ _____.

2 내가 네 스마트폰을 사용하면 나한테 화낼 거니? (use)

   → Are you going to be mad at me _____ I _____ your smartphone?

3 월요일은 공휴일이므로 나는 학교에 갈 필요가 없다. (since)

   → _____ _____ _____ a holiday, I don't have to go to school.

4 Alex는 오랫동안 밖에 서있었기 때문에 병이 났다. (because)

   → Alex got sick _____ _____ _____ _____ outside for a long time.

5 그들은 서로를 알았기 때문에, 자신들을 소개할 필요가 없었다. (as)

   → _____ _____ _____ each other, they didn't need to introduce themselves.

교과서 문장 응용하기

배운 문법을 이용하여 영어 문장을 써 봅시다.

1 네가 그 파티에 참석하지 않으면, 나는 가지 않겠다. (unless, attend)   → _____

2 그가 도착했으므로 그녀는 일찍 떠났다. (since)   → _____

68 양보의 접속사_ though, although, even though, even if

- **though(although)**: '비록 ~일지라도'라는 의미이며, even though는 더 강한 양보의 의미를 나타낸다.
  He went out **though(although)** it was raining.
  Even though I knew the truth, I didn't tell him.

- **even if**: '비록 ~일지라도', '(만약) ~할지라도', '~에도 불구하고' 등의 양보의 의미를 나타낸다.
  Even if I don't agree with him, I respect his opinion.

A 괄호 안에서 알맞은 것을 고르시오.

1 (If / Although) I got tired easily, I enjoyed hiking.
2 I won't mind (even if / but) Georgia doesn't come.
3 Chris went to school (as / though) he was sick.
4 (Even though / If) she is famous, she is still my friend.

» 정답과 해설 p.22

◆ 양보의 전치사 despite / in
spite of: '~에도 불구하고'의 뜻
으로 양보의 의미를 나타낸다.
· I love her **despite** her
faults.
· He went hiking **in spite
of** the heavy snowstorm.

B 두 문장을 괄호 안의 접속사를 이용하여 한 문장으로 쓰시오.

1 He went out without a coat. + It was very cold. (though)
  → He _____ .
2 The game will be played. + It rains. (even if)
  → The game _____ .
3 Martin won't give up. + He failed. (even though)
  → Martin _____ .
4 She has to do her homework. + She doesn't like doing it. (although)
  → She _____ .

C 우리말과 뜻이 같도록 괄호 안의 말을 이용하여 문장을 완성하시오.

1 비록 그녀는 겨우 네 살일지라도 바이올린을 켤 수 있다. (though, only)
  → She can play the violin _____ _____ _____ _____ .
2 네가 그를 좋아하지 않을지라도 너는 그와 친구가 되어야 한다. (if)
  → _____ _____ _____ _____ _____ him, you should be
  friends with him.
3 Jane은 비록 나보다 더 어릴지라도 그녀는 나보다 더 똑똑하다. (although)
  → _____ Jane _____ _____ _____ me, she is smarter than me.

교과서
문장
응용하기

배운 문법을 이용하여 영어 문장을 써 봅시다.

1 Tim은 비록 가난할지라도 정직하다. (although)   → _____
2 그녀는 배가 고플지라도 저녁을 먹지 않을 것이다. (even if)   → _____

상관접속사 1_ both *A* and *B*, not only *A* but (also) *B*

■ 「**both *A* and *B***」: 'A와 B 둘 다'라는 의미이며, 주어로 쓰인 경우 동사는 복수형으로 쓴다.
I can speak **both** Chinese **and** Japanese.
Both Jane **and** Mary *were* at the meeting.

■ 「**not only *A* but (also) *B***」: 'A뿐만 아니라 B도'라는 의미로 「*B* as well as *A*」와 바꿔 쓸 수 있다. 주어로 쓰인 경우 동사는 B의 수에 일치시킨다.
Not only you **but (also)** he likes soccer. → He **as well as** you likes soccer.

A 빈칸에 알맞은 상관접속사를 쓰시오.   》 정답과 해설 p.22

1 He can play _____ the piano _____ the flute.
2 It was _____ _____ hot _____ _____ cloudy yesterday.
3 Daniel _____ _____ _____ Eva learns Chinese at school.
4 Not only you _____ _____ Violet _____ going to join our club.

B 빈칸에 알맞은 말을 | 보기 |에서 골라 상관접속사를 이용하여 쓰시오.

┌─ 보기 ───┐
│   math   I   mine   attractive   │
└──┘

1 He is not only talented _____ _____ _____.
2 My daughter likes _____ history _____ _____.
3 _____ my brother and _____ are taking the class.
4 The boy ate not only his food _____ also _____.

C 우리말과 뜻이 같도록 빈칸에 알맞은 말을 쓰시오.

1 Jack과 Petra는 둘 다 회의에서 발표를 했다.
→ _____ _____ _____ _____ made a presentation at the
  meeting.
2 Karen은 파티장을 제공했을 뿐 아니라 그것을 장식도 했다.
→ Karen _____ _____ offered the party room _____ also decorated it.
3 선생님들뿐만 아니라 학생들도 공원에서 재미있는 시간을 보냈다.
→ Students _____ _____ _____ teachers had fun in the park.

┄┄

교과서 문장 응용하기 배운 문법을 이용하여 영어 문장을 써 봅시다.
  1 나는 Brian과 그의 아내 둘 다 만날 것이다.   → _____
  2 그녀는 영어뿐만 아니라 과학도 공부하고 있는 중이다. → _____

상관접속사 2_ either A or B, neither A nor B

- 「either A or B」는 'A 또는 B 둘 중 하나'라는 의미이며, 「neither A nor B」는 'A도 B도 둘 다 아닌'이라는 의미이다.
  He is **either** a doctor **or** a lawyer.
  I am **neither** angry **nor** excited.

- 「either A or B」와 「neither A nor B」가 주어로 쓰인 경우 동사는 B의 수에 일치시킨다.
  Either she **or** you *have* to call him.
  Neither he **nor** you *are* interested in the problem.

A 괄호 안에서 알맞은 것을 고르시오. » 정답과 해설 p.22

1 Either you (nor / or) she will be selected.

2 She speaks (neither / either) English nor Spanish.

3 I could find the book neither at the library (but / nor) the bookstore.

B 빈칸에 알맞은 말을 either ~ or, neither ~ nor를 이용하여 |보기|와 같이 바꿔 쓰시오.

> |보기|
> I will clean the toilet. + Or I will clean the living room.
> → I will clean either the toilet or the living room.

1 He doesn't read novels. + He doesn't read comic books, either.
  → He reads _____ novels _____ comic books.

2 Orange juice will be prepared. + Or apple juice will be prepared.
  → _____ orange juice _____ apple juice will be prepared.

3 She doesn't need to go. + You don't need to go, either.
  → _____ she _____ you need to go.

C 우리말과 뜻이 같도록 빈칸에 알맞은 말을 쓰시오.

1 실내는 덥지도 춥지도 않았다.
  → It was _____ _____ _____ cold inside.

2 너는 버스나 지하철 중 하나를 타면 된다.
  → You can take _____ _____ _____ _____ a subway.

3 Susan이나 Tom 중 한 사람이 그 보고서를 쓴다.
  → _____ Susan _____ _____ writes the report.

교과서
문장
응용하기

배운 문법을 이용하여 영어 문장을 써 봅시다.

1 그녀는 빵이나 샐러드 중 하나를 먹는다. (either) → _____

2 그들은 캠핑도 낚시도 가지 않았다. (neither) → _____

접속부사

■ 접속부사는 원래 부사(구)이면서 접속사처럼 문장과 문장을 연결하는 말이며, 연결부사라고도 한다.

대조	however (그러나), on the other hand (반면에)	첨가 (게다가)	in addition, besides, moreover
결과	therefore (그러므로), as a result (그 결과)	예시 (예를 들면)	for example, for instance

Karen is rich. **However**, her cousin, Kate, is poor.
Nick didn't study. **Therefore**, he failed the test.

A 괄호 안에서 알맞은 것을 고르시오. 》 정답과 해설 p.22

1 Lily did her best. (As a result / However), she lost the game.

2 I was nervous. (Therefore / Besides), I took a deep breath.

3 She is a beautiful woman. (In addition / Therefore), she is a brave person.

4 Justin practiced hard. (Moreover / As a result), he won the gold medal.

5 Mom can cook any dish. (For instance / However), she can even cook risotto.

B 빈칸에 알맞은 말을 | 보기 |에서 골라 쓰시오. (한 번씩만 사용할 것)

> 보기
> for example   however   moreover   therefore

1 Diana is smart. _____, she is ambitious.

2 We looked everywhere. _____, we could not find the money.

3 He has not paid the bill. _____, the electricity has been cut off.

4 I always help my mom. _____, I wash the dishes every night.

C 우리말과 뜻이 같도록 빈칸에 알맞은 말을 쓰시오.

1 Ian은 축구를 잘한다. 게다가 그는 스케이트도 잘 탄다.
→ Ian plays soccer well. _____, he skates well.

2 Kate는 숙제를 끝냈다. 그러므로 그녀는 놀러 나갈 수 있다.
→ Kate has finished her homework. _____, she can go out to play.

3 나는 과학을 잘한다. 반면에 나는 영어는 못한다.
→ I'm good at science. _____ _____ _____ _____, I'm not good at English.

교과서 문장 응용하기 | 배운 문법을 이용하여 영어 문장을 써 봅시다.

1 비가 억수로 내렸다. 그 결과 그 테니스 경기는 취소되었다. (heavily, cancel) → _____

2 그는 매우 인기 있다. 반면에 그는 친절하지 않다. (popular, other) → _____

➡ 내신적중 실전문제를 풀기 전에 Workbook p.39에 있는 요점정리를 참고하세요.

내신적중 실전문제

» 정답과 해설 p.23

[01~02] 빈칸에 알맞은 말이 바르게 짝지어진 것을 고르시오.

01

> • _____ the medicine is bitter, it is good for your health.
> • Edward's friends wonder _____ he can skate.

① Since — that
② Though — whether
③ Though — what
④ Before — whether
⑤ That — since

02

> • I couldn't go home _____ I finished cleaning my classroom.
> • I love May _____ it is such a wonderful month.

① while — since
② if — because
③ unless — since
④ although — when
⑤ until — because

[03~04] 빈칸에 공통으로 알맞은 말을 쓰시오. 주관식

03

> • We saw the boy singing _____ we were sitting on the bench.
> • She missed the meeting _____ her car broke down.

04

> • Keep yourself busy _____ you want to feel happy.
> • Do you know _____ birds can communicate with each other?

[05~06] 우리말과 뜻이 같도록 빈칸에 알맞은 것을 고르시오.

05

> 내가 버스 정류장에서 기다리는 동안에, 반대 방향에서는 세 대의 버스가 지나갔다.
> → _____ I was waiting at the bus stop, three buses went by in the opposite direction.

① Even if
② Until
③ Since
④ While
⑤ Because

06

> 만약 신발을 신지 않으면, 너는 발을 매우 쉽게 다칠 것이다.
> → _____ you wear shoes, you can hurt your feet very easily.

① As
② If
③ Whether
④ After
⑤ Unless

07 두 문장을 한 문장으로 바르게 연결한 것을 <u>두 개</u> 고르면?

> Peter is tired of action movies. + Kate is tired of action movies, too.

① Peter is tired of action movies, not Kate.
② Either Peter or Kate is tired of action movies.
③ Neither Peter nor Kate is tired of action movies.
④ Not only Peter, but also Kate is tired of action movies.
⑤ Kate as well as Peter is tired of action movies.

[08~09] 밑줄 친 부분 중 어법상 어색한 것을 고르시오.

08

> ① Before I came ② to Korea, I didn't ③ speak a word in Korean. ④ Therefore, now I ⑤ can speak Korean well.

09

> ① Since Justin loves Judy, he ② will only go ③ if she goes. He will ④ not go ⑤ while she goes.

[10~11] 두 문장의 뜻이 같도록 빈칸에 알맞은 말을 쓰시오. (주관식)

10

> Look both ways _____ you cross the street at a crosswalk.
> = Cross the street at a crosswalk _____ you look both ways.

11

> Dolphins can learn many cool tricks quickly _____ they are very smart.
> = Dolphins are very smart. _____, they can learn many cool tricks quickly.

12 밑줄 친 부분을 바르게 고친 것은?

> Harry will take this medicine until the doctor will tell him to stop.

① 고칠 필요 없음
② before the doctor tells
③ as the doctor will tell
④ until the doctor tells
⑤ after the doctor tells

13 밑줄 친 부분의 쓰임이 |보기|와 같은 것을 모두 고르면?

> |보기|
> I wonder if I turned off my reading lamp.

① I'd like to know if I could be a model.
② Eat these snacks if you feel hungry.
③ Miso will smile if she wins the contest.
④ Can you tell me if Mary is wearing her new jacket?
⑤ Even if he wants to give up, he will keep going.

14 다음 문장에 이어질 말로 알맞은 것은?

> His car doesn't start. _____

① Besides, he has another car.
② For example, the car is expensive.
③ As a result, he has to walk to work.
④ However, the car belongs to me.
⑤ Moreover, he doesn't need to repair the car.

15 두 문장을 한 문장으로 쓸 때 빈칸에 알맞은 것은?

> Harry doesn't like Italian food. + Jack doesn't like Italian food, either.
> → _____ likes Italian food.

① Both Harry and Jack
② Jack as well as Harry
③ Neither Harry nor Jack
④ Not Harry but Jack
⑤ Either Harry nor Jack

16 두 문장의 뜻이 같도록 빈칸에 알맞은 말을 쓰시오. 주관식

> If you don't want these clothes and hats, I'll throw them away.
> = _____ you want these clothes and hats, I'll throw them away.

17 다음 문장과 의미가 같은 것은?

> Although Mom was angry, she listened to me patiently.

① In spite of her anger, Mom listened to me patiently.
② Besides her anger, Mom listened to me patiently.
③ Mom was angry. As a result, she didn't listen to me patiently.
④ Mom was angry. However, she didn't listen to me patiently.
⑤ Mom was angry. Therefore, she didn't listen to me patiently.

18 어법상 어색한 것을 모두 고르면?

① Both Helen and Susan is scared.
② Parents as well as children need some protection.
③ Either you or he have to attend the meeting.
④ Neither he nor she is going to the library.
⑤ Not only Jane but also Mary was working on the project.

19 빈칸에 들어갈 접속사가 <u>아닌</u> 것은?

> • _____ it rained a lot, the trees grew well.
> • _____ the bell rang, we were ready to run to the cafeteria.
> • I'm sure _____ street lighting is bad for animals.
> • _____ she is very old, she always challenges new things.

① if   ② since   ③ that
④ when   ⑤ though

20 밑줄 친 부분의 의미가 같은 것끼리 짝지어진 것은?

> ⓐ <u>Since</u> there's no more snow here, the skiing season is over.
> ⓑ Sora has liked chocolate <u>since</u> she was a child.
> ⓒ We've been busy <u>since</u> the new semester started.
> ⓓ <u>Since</u> I couldn't find him, I left a message.
> ⓔ <u>Since</u> he won't help me, I have to do it myself.

① ⓐ, ⓑ — ⓒ, ⓓ, ⓔ   ② ⓐ, ⓑ, ⓔ — ⓒ, ⓓ
③ ⓐ, ⓒ, ⓔ — ⓑ, ⓓ   ④ ⓐ, ⓓ, ⓔ — ⓑ, ⓒ
⑤ ⓑ, ⓒ, ⓓ — ⓐ, ⓔ

서술형 평가

01 빈칸에 알맞은 말을 |보기|에서 골라 적절한 접속사를 이용하여 문장을 완성하시오.

> **보기**
> I got up   I didn't have breakfast
> I go to bed   I came to this city

(1) I write a diary _____.

(2) I haven't watched a movie _____
_____.

(3) I'm hungry _____.

(4) She kept crying _____.

02 괄호 안의 말을 이용하여 우리말을 영어로 쓰시오.

> 이 기사들을 읽지 않으면, 너는 아프리카에 대한 사실을 알지 못할 것이다. (article)

(1) _____, you will not know the facts about Africa. (5단어)

(2) _____, you will not know the facts about Africa. (6단어)

03 주어진 문장에 알맞은 접속사를 넣어 문장을 완성하시오.

(1)
> There are many bad people in the world.

→ It's true _____.

(2)
> They smell good.

→ When you buy fruits, check _____
_____.

04 두 문장을 조건에 맞게 한 문장으로 쓰시오.

> Jessy has tried scuba diving. + Her parents have tried scuba diving, too.

(1) _____ tried scuba diving. (both ~ and 사용)

(2) _____ tried scuba diving. (not only ~ but also 사용)

(3) _____ tried scuba diving. (as well as 사용)

[05~06] 다음 글을 읽고, 물음에 답하시오.

My name is Arpi. ____ⓐ____ I'm American, I grew up in Iran. Now I live in the United States. One day I met two sisters from Kuwait, but their family was American. I invited them to my home ____ⓑ____ I wanted to be their friend. ____ⓒ____ the girls arrived, we began to talk in a very friendly way. I immediately brought them cookies and fruit. Then I served them coffee. Suddenly, they looked confused. About twenty minutes ____ⓓ____ they arrived, they said goodbye and they left. <u>I didn't know it. + In Kuwait, people serve coffee at the end of a visit.</u>

05 빈칸 ⓐ~ⓓ에 알맞은 말을 쓰시오.

ⓐ _____ ⓒ _____
ⓑ _____ ⓓ _____

06 밑줄 친 두 문장을 한 문장으로 쓰시오.

→ _____

CHAPTER

10
가정법

FOCUS 72   가정법 과거

FOCUS 73   가정법 과거완료

FOCUS 74   I wish 가정법

FOCUS 75   as if 가정법

FOCUS 76   Without(But for) 가정법

FOCUS 77   혼합가정법

가정법이란 무엇인가?

가정법은 실제로 일어나지 않았거나 앞으로 일어나지 않을 것 같은 일에 대해 반대로 말하거나 상상하여 말할 때 사용하는 어법이다. 어느 시점의 사실이나 상황에 대해서 말하는지에 따라 동사의 시제를 바꿔서 표현하며, 주어의 수나 인칭에 관계없이 어느 정도 일정한 형태를 취한다.

가정법에는 어떤 것이 있으며 가정법은 어떻게 표현하는가?

가정법에는 동사의 시제로 표현하는 가정법 과거와 과거완료가 있으며, 대부분 if, I wish, as if 등과 함께 쓴다.

if 가정법 if절은 문장의 앞이나 뒤에 씀	과거	If+주어+동사의 과거형 ~, 주어+조동사의 과거형+동사원형 … (만약) ~라면, …일 텐데	**If I were** you, I **would obey** the company's regulations. 내가 너라면 회사의 규정을 준수할 텐데.
	과거완료	If+주어+had+과거분사 ~, 주어+조동사의 과거형+have+과거분사 … (만약) ~했다면, …했을 텐데	**If I had been** you, I **would have done** the homework. 내가 너였다면 숙제를 했을 텐데.
	*혼합가정	If+주어+had+과거분사 ~, 주어+조동사의 과거형+동사원형 … (만약) ~했다면, …일 텐데	**If I had gone** to bed early, I **would not be** late for school today. 만약 일찍 잤더라면, 오늘 학교에 지각하지 않을 텐데.
I wish 가정법 I wish 다음에 절이 옴	과거	I wish+주어+동사의 과거형 ~ ~라면 좋을 텐데	**I wish** I **could ride** a motorcycle. 내가 오토바이를 탈 수 있다면 좋을 텐데.
	과거완료	I wish+주어+had+과거분사 ~ ~였다면 좋았을 텐데	**I wish** my brother **had been** a teacher. 나의 오빠가 선생님이었다면 좋았을 텐데.
as if 가정법 as if(though)절은 주절 다음에 옴	과거	as if+주어+동사의 과거형 … 마치 …인 것처럼	Tina acts **as if** she **were** my sister. Tina는 마치 그녀가 내 여동생인 것처럼 행동한다.
	과거완료	as if+주어+had+과거분사 … 마치 …였던 것처럼	He talks **as if** he **had finished** the work by himself. 그는 마치 혼자 그 일을 마무리했던 것처럼 말한다.

용어
사전

* **혼합가정**: if절에는 주로 가정법 과거완료를, 주절에는 가정법 과거를 사용하여, 과거 사실이 현재까지 영향을 미치는 것을 나타내는 어법을 의미한다.

가정법 과거

■ 가정법 과거는 현재의 사실이나 상황에 반대되는 일을 가정하거나 상상할 때 쓰며, 「If+주어+동사의 과거형 ~, 주어+
조동사의 과거형+동사원형 …」의 형태로 '(만약) ~라면, …일 텐데'라는 의미이다. if절의 be동사가 과거형인 경우 주어
의 인칭이나 수에 상관없이 were를 사용한다.

If I **didn't know** his phone number, I **couldn't call** him.
→ As I know his phone number, I can call him. 〈직설법 전환〉
If she **were** rich, she **could buy** a boat.
→ As she is not rich, she can't buy a boat. 〈직설법 전환〉

A 괄호 안에서 알맞은 것을 고르시오. 》정답과 해설 p.24

1 If she (had / has) enough money, she could buy it.
2 If I were taller, I (could / can) join the basketball team.
3 If George (failed / were failed) again, he would never try again.
4 If it (were / is) not raining, I would go to see a movie.

B 두 문장의 뜻이 같도록 빈칸에 알맞은 말을 쓰시오.

1 As you don't try hard enough, you may not succeed.
 → If you _____ hard enough, you _____ _____.
2 As I am busy, I will not go to the concert.
 → If I _____ _____ busy, I _____ _____ to the concert.
3 If he had more time, he could learn judo.
 → As he _____ _____ more time, he _____ _____ judo.

C 우리말과 뜻이 같도록 빈칸에 알맞은 말을 쓰시오.

1 만약 내가 건축가라면, 멋진 집을 지을 텐데.
 → _____ I _____ an architect, I _____ _____ a great house.
2 만약 그가 교실에 있다면, 그를 만날 수 있을 텐데.
 → If he _____ in the classroom, I _____ _____ him.
3 만약 내가 카메라를 가지고 있다면, 이 아름다운 풍경을 찍을 수 있을 텐데.
 → _____ I _____ a camera with me, I _____ _____ a picture
 of this beautiful scenery.

교과서
문장
응용하기 | 배운 문법을 이용하여 영어 문장을 써 봅시다.

1 만약 그녀가 아프지 않으면, 내가 그녀를 파티에 초대할 텐데. → _____
2 만약 그가 그녀를 다시 만난다면, 더 행복할 텐데. → _____

가정법 과거완료

■ 가정법 과거완료는 과거의 사실이나 상황에 반대되는 일을 가정하거나 상상할 때 쓰며, 「If+주어+had+과거분사 ~, 주어+조동사의 과거형+have+과거분사 …」의 형태로 '만약 ~했다면, …했을 텐데'라는 의미이다.

If I **had left** the house on time, I **wouldn't have missed** the train.
→ As I didn't leave the house on time, I missed the train. 〈직설법 전환〉

A 두 문장의 뜻이 같도록 빈칸에 알맞은 말을 쓰시오.   》정답과 해설 p.24

1 If you had taken my advice, you would not have regretted.
→ As you _____ _____ my advice, you _____.

2 If he had not lost his money, Harry wouldn't have walked home.
→ As he _____ _____ _____, Harry _____ home.

3 As she was busy yesterday, I didn't invite her.
→ If she _____ _____ busy yesterday, I would _____ _____ her.

B 괄호 안의 말을 이용하여 가정법 과거완료 문장을 완성하시오.

1 If you had asked him, he _____ with you. (will, go)

2 If they _____ hard, they wouldn't have won. (not, train)

3 If I hadn't forgotten your address, I _____ you a gift. (can, send)

C 우리말과 뜻이 같도록 괄호 안의 말을 이용하여 문장을 완성하시오.

1 만약 네가 나를 격려해주지 않았다면, 나는 그 일을 끝낼 수 없었을 텐데.
(encourage, finish)
→ If you _____ _____ _____ me, I _____ _____ _____
_____ the work.

2 만약 내가 그 신발이 할인 중인 것을 몰랐다면, 그것을 사지 않았을 텐데. (know, buy)
→ If I _____ _____ the shoes were on sale, I _____ _____
_____ them.

3 만약 너무 춥지 않았다면, 나는 오늘 수영하러 갔을 텐데. (be, go)
→ If it _____ _____ _____ so cold, I _____ _____ _____
swimming today.

교과서
문장
응용하기

배운 문법을 이용하여 영어 문장을 써 봅시다.

1 만약 내가 Evan을 보았다면, 그의 스마트폰을 돌려주었을 텐데. (return)
→ _____

2 만약 그녀가 숙제를 했다면, 선생님이 그녀를 벌주지 않았을 텐데. (punish)
→ _____

I wish 가정법

- 「I wish+가정법 과거」: '~라면 좋을 텐데'라는 의미로 현재 사실과 반대되거나 실현 가능성이 희박한 것을 소망할 때 쓴다.

  I wish I **had** a big car.

  → I am sorry (that) I don't have a big car. 〈직설법 전환〉

- 「I wish+가정법 과거완료」: '~였다면 좋았을 텐데'라는 의미로 과거 사실과 반대되거나 실현 가능성이 희박한 것을 소망할 때 쓴다.

  I wish he **had seen** the TV program.

  → I am sorry (that) he didn't see the TV program. 〈직설법 전환〉

A 두 문장의 뜻이 같도록 빈칸에 알맞은 말을 쓰시오.   » 정답과 해설 p.24

1 I wish I owned a video recorder.

  → I am sorry I _____ _____ a video recorder.

2 I wish I had known the truth about Emma.

  → I am sorry I _____ _____ the truth about Emma.

3 I am sorry I didn't study hard in my school days.

  → I wish I _____ _____ hard in my school days.

4 I am sorry I don't have a lot of time to travel the world.

  → I wish I _____ a lot of time to travel the world.

B 괄호 안의 말을 이용하여 빈칸에 알맞은 형태를 쓰시오.

1 I wish I _____ good at drawing. (be)

2 I wish he _____ his laptop last night. (bring)

3 I wish I _____ my new roommates. (meet)

C 우리말과 뜻이 같도록 괄호 안의 말을 이용하여 문장을 완성하시오.

1 내가 그녀와 더 자주 말할 수 있으면 좋을 텐데. (talk)

  → I wish I _____ _____ with her more often.

2 우리가 그때 파리에서 더 많은 시간을 가졌으면 좋았을 텐데. (have)

  → I wish we _____ _____ more time in Paris then.

3 그가 어제 그렇게나 많은 돈을 쓰지 않았다면 좋았을 텐데. (spend)

  → I wish he _____ _____ so much money yesterday.

교과서
문장
응용하기

배운 문법을 이용하여 영어 문장을 써 봅시다.

1 내가 이탈리아어를 말할 수 있다면 좋을 텐데. (Italian)   → _____

2 그가 그 차를 사지 않았다면 좋았을 텐데. (buy)   → _____

as if 가정법

- 「**as if**+가정법 과거」: '마치 …인 것처럼'이라는 의미로 현재 사실과 반대되는 것을 가정하며, 가정법 과거는 주절의 동사와 같은 때를 나타낸다.

  She acts **as if** she **were** a queen.

  → In fact, she is not a queen. 〈직설법 전환〉

- 「**as if**+가정법 과거완료」: '마치 …였던 것처럼'이라는 의미로 과거 사실과 반대되는 것을 가정하며, 가정법 과거완료는 주절의 동사보다 앞선 때를 나타낸다.

  He talks **as if** he **had known** about the problem.

  → In fact, he didn't know about the problem. 〈직설법 전환〉

A |보기|를 참고하여 빈칸에 알맞은 말을 쓰시오.   » 정답과 해설 p.24

> 보기
>   She isn't my sister, but she speaks as if she were my sister.

1 Cathy isn't a singer, but she sings as if she _____ a singer.

2 Jude didn't visit London, but he talks as if he _____ _____ London.

3 He doesn't eat cucumbers, but he acts as if he _____ _____ .

B 다음 문장을 |보기|와 같이 가정법 문장으로 바꿀 때 빈칸에 알맞은 말을 쓰시오.

> 보기
>   In fact, he is smart.
>   → He talks as if he were not smart.

1 In fact, he didn't watch the movie.

  → He talks as if _____ .

2 In fact, she isn't a police officer.

  → She acts as if _____ .

C 우리말과 뜻이 같도록 빈칸에 알맞은 말을 쓰시오.

1 그는 마치 독일사람인 것처럼 말한다.

  → He talks as if he _____ _____ .

2 그녀는 마치 부자인 것처럼 행동한다.

  → She acts _____ _____ _____ _____ .

교과서
문장
응용하기

배운 문법을 이용하여 영어 문장을 써 봅시다.

1 Patrick은 마치 선생님인 것처럼 행동한다.   → _____

2 그녀는 마치 자신이 건축가였던 것처럼 행동한다. (architect)   → _____

Without(But for) 가정법

- 「**Without(But for)** ~, 가정법 과거」: '~가 없다면'이라는 의미로 If it were not for ~로 바꿔 쓸 수 있다.

  Without(But for) water, nothing **could survive**.

  → **If it were not for** water, nothing **could survive**.

- 「**Without(But for)** ~, 가정법 과거완료」: '~가 없었다면'이라는 의미로 If it had not been for ~로 바꿔 쓸 수 있다.

  Without(But for) your advice, I **would have failed**.

  → **If it had not been for** your advice, I **would have failed**.

A 두 문장의 뜻이 같도록 빈칸에 알맞은 말을 쓰시오.   » 정답과 해설 p.24

  1 If it had not been for the alarm, you might have been late for school.

  → _____ the alarm, you might have been late for school.

  2 If it were not for enough rain, all plants would die.

  → _____ _____ enough rain, all plants would die.

B 다음 문장을 if를 이용하여 바꿀 때 빈칸에 알맞은 말을 쓰시오.

  1 Without our hard work, we couldn't have succeeded.

  → _____ it _____ _____ _____ _____ our hard work, we couldn't have succeeded.

  2 But for her family, Emily might not overcome her fear.

  → _____ it _____ _____ _____ her family, Emily _____ _____ _____ her fear.

C 우리말과 뜻이 같도록 빈칸에 알맞은 말을 쓰시오.

  1 그가 없었다면, 우리는 그 시합에 졌을 것이다.

  → Without him, we _____ _____ _____ the game.

  2 그 돈이 없다면, 나는 엄마를 위한 선물을 살 수 없을 것이다.

  → Without the money, I _____ _____ the gift for my mom.

  3 그녀의 충고가 없었다면, 나는 담배를 끊지 못했을 것이다.

  → If it had not been for her advice, I _____ _____ _____ smoking.

교과서
문장
응용하기

배운 문법을 이용하여 영어 문장을 써 봅시다.

1 네 도움이 없다면, 나는 내 숙제를 할 수 없다. (without)   → _____

2 그 소방관이 없었다면, 그들은 죽었을 것이다. (but for)   → _____

혼합가정법

■ 혼합가정법은 주로 if절에 가정법 과거완료, 주절에 가정법 과거를 쓴 「If+주어+had+과거분사 ~, 주어+조동사의 과거형+동사원형 …」의 형태로 나타낸다. '만약 ~했다면, …일 텐데'라는 의미로, 과거에 실현되지 못한 일이 현재까지 영향을 미칠 때 쓴다. 보통 if절에는 과거, 주절에는 현재의 시간을 나타내는 부사(구)를 쓴다.

If she **had left** *yesterday*, she **wouldn't be** at home *today*.

→ As she didn't leave yesterday, she is at home today.

A 두 문장의 뜻이 같도록 빈칸에 알맞은 말을 쓰시오.　　　　　　　　　　　》 정답과 해설 p.24

1 As it didn't rain yesterday, I am watering the flowers now.

→ If it ＿＿＿＿＿＿ ＿＿＿＿＿＿ yesterday, I wouldn't be watering the flowers now.

2 As the driver wasn't careful last night, she is in hospital now.

→ If the driver had been careful last night, she ＿＿＿＿＿＿ ＿＿＿＿＿＿ ＿＿＿＿＿＿ in hospital now.

3 As I didn't take a Spanish in high school, I can't understand Spanish now.

→ If I ＿＿＿＿＿＿ ＿＿＿＿＿＿ a Spanish in high school, I ＿＿＿＿＿＿ ＿＿＿＿＿＿ Spanish now.

4 As I didn't take your advice then, I'm not satisfied now.

→ If I ＿＿＿＿＿＿ ＿＿＿＿＿＿ your advice then, I ＿＿＿＿＿＿ ＿＿＿＿＿＿ satisfied now.

B 우리말과 뜻이 같도록 빈칸에 알맞은 말을 쓰시오.

1 만약 그녀가 더 일찍 집을 떠났다면, 지금 비행기를 탈 수 있을 텐데.

→ If she ＿＿＿＿＿＿ ＿＿＿＿＿＿ home earlier, she could catch the plane now.

2 만약 내가 음악을 전공했다면, 나는 지금 작곡가일 텐데.

→ If I ＿＿＿＿＿＿ ＿＿＿＿＿＿ in music, I ＿＿＿＿＿＿ ＿＿＿＿＿＿ a composer now.

3 만약 내가 아침 식사를 했었다면, 지금 배가 고프지 않을 텐데.

→ If I ＿＿＿＿＿＿ ＿＿＿＿＿＿ breakfast, I would not be hungry now.

4 만약 내가 어제 더 일찍 잤다면, 지금 피곤하게 느끼지 않을 텐데.

→ If I had gone to bed earlier yesterday, I ＿＿＿＿＿＿ ＿＿＿＿＿＿ ＿＿＿＿＿＿ tired now.

교과서 문장 응용하기

배운 문법을 이용하여 영어 문장을 써 봅시다.

1 만약 내가 어젯밤에 공부를 열심히 했다면, 오늘 좋은 점수를 받을 텐데. (a good mark)

→ ＿＿＿＿＿＿＿＿＿＿＿＿＿＿＿＿＿＿＿＿＿＿＿＿＿＿＿＿＿＿＿＿＿＿＿

2 만약 그가 지난달에 팔이 부러지지 않았다면, 지금 농구를 할 수 있을 텐데. (break)

→ ＿＿＿＿＿＿＿＿＿＿＿＿＿＿＿＿＿＿＿＿＿＿＿＿＿＿＿＿＿＿＿＿＿＿＿

내신적중 실전문제

» 정답과 해설 p.25

[01~02] 괄호 안에 주어진 말의 알맞은 형태를 고르시오.

01

> If you (live) closer to the supermarket, you could walk there.

① live   ② lived
③ had lived   ④ would live
⑤ have lived

02

> Sora didn't take a trip to Rome. But she talks as if she (take) a trip there.

① take   ② takes
③ took   ④ have taken
⑤ had taken

03 대화의 빈칸에 알맞은 것은?

> **A** The washing machine is broken again.
> **B** I wish I _____ how to fix it.

① know   ② knew
③ will know   ④ have known
⑤ would known

04 빈칸에 공통으로 알맞은 말을 쓰시오. 주관식

> • _____ subway trains, life in Seoul would be very inconvenient.
> • _____ his help, Alice wouldn't have been a good student.

05 다음 문장과 의미가 같은 것은?

> I wish I had bought the wallet on sale.

① I'm sorry I buy the wallet on sale.
② I'm sorry I don't buy the wallet on sale.
③ I'm sorry I bought the wallet on sale.
④ I'm sorry I didn't buy the wallet on sale.
⑤ I'm sorry I haven't buy the wallet on sale.

06 밑줄 친 부분을 바르게 고친 것은?

> If I hadn't lost my cellphone yesterday, I <u>isn't buy</u> a new one now.

① didn't buy
② would not buy
③ would have bought
④ would not have bought
⑤ 고칠 필요 없음

07 우리말을 바르게 영작한 것은?

> 만약 네가 그 무서운 영화를 보았다면, 나쁜 꿈을 꾸었을 텐데.

① If you watch the scary movie, you would have had a bad dream.
② If you watched the scary movie, you would have had a bad dream.
③ If you watched the scary movie, you would had a bad dream.
④ If you had watched the scary movie, you would have had a bad dream.
⑤ If you had watched the scary movie, you would have a bad dream.

[08~09] 밑줄 친 부분 중 어법상 어색한 것을 골라 바르게 고쳐 쓰시오. 주관식

08

① When the young man ② begs for money, ③ he always ④ acts as if he ⑤ is an old man.

_____ → _____

09

If she ① learned English ② when she ③ was very young, ④ her pronunciation ⑤ would be perfect now.

_____ → _____

[10~11] 빈칸에 알맞은 것을 고르시오.

10

She speaks as if she were my mom. In fact, _____.

① I am not her mom
② I was her mom
③ she is my mom
④ she was my mom
⑤ she isn't my mom

11

I don't have any older sister. I wish _____.

① I have no older sister
② I have an older sister
③ I had an older sister
④ I have had an older sister
⑤ I didn't have any older sister

12 괄호 안에 알맞은 것끼리 짝지어진 것은?

• If I (be / were / had been) hungry, I would have eaten something.
• If I (do / did / had done) my homework, I wouldn't be worried now.

① be — do
② were — did
③ had been — did
④ had been — do
⑤ had been — had done

13 의미하는 바가 나머지 넷과 다른 것은?

① But for TV, we might read more books.
② Without TV, we might read more books.
③ If it were not for TV, we might read more books.
④ Were it not for TV, we might read more books.
⑤ Had it not been for TV, we might have read more books.

14 다음 직설법 문장을 가정법 문장으로 바르게 바꾼 것은?

As we didn't stay in Florida, we didn't go to the beach.

① If we stayed in Florida, we would go to the beach.
② If we had stayed in Florida, we would have gone to the beach.
③ If we didn't stay in Florida, we would go to the beach.
④ If we hadn't stayed in Florida, we would have gone to the beach.
⑤ If we hadn't stayed in Florida, we wouldn't have gone to the beach.

15 어법상 어색한 것은?

① But for sunlight, we could see nothing.

② I wish he had a lot of money now.

③ If I were taller, I could reach the shelf.

④ If she had tried again, she could have reached the top.

⑤ The salesclerk talks as if the diamond necklace is the original.

16 밑줄 친 부분을 잘못 고쳐 쓴 것은?

① If I speak Italian, I would live in Rome. (→ spoke)

② Nick feels as if he is flying in the air. (→ were flying)

③ I wish I don't eat a lot of candies last night. (→ didn't eat)

④ If you had gotten up early, you could see the beautiful sunrise. (→ could have seen)

⑤ Without her dog, Kate won't take a walk. (→ wouldn't take)

17 어법상 어색한 것의 개수는?

ⓐ If you asked me then, I would have helped you.

ⓑ I wish I won the first prize at the song festival.

ⓒ Mary talked as if she hadn't eaten lunch.

ⓓ If I had taken your advice last year, I would be successful now.

ⓔ If it is not for the sun, the Earth would be too cold.

① 1개 ② 2개 ③ 3개 ④ 4개 ⑤ 5개

18 괄호 안의 말을 빈칸에 알맞은 형태로 쓰시오. 주관식

A It's a very expensive ring.
B If I were you, I _____ it. (buy)

19 어법상 어색한 것끼리 짝지어진 것은?

ⓐ Paula would be disappointed if Kevin refused her proposal.

ⓑ I wish I had taken a hot bath last night.

ⓒ He looks as if he haven't slept for two days.

ⓓ If he had not broken his leg, he could have been running here now.

ⓔ But for the air, no one could breathe.

① ⓐ, ⓑ ② ⓐ, ⓒ ③ ⓑ, ⓒ
④ ⓒ, ⓓ ⑤ ⓓ, ⓔ

20 다음 가정법 문장을 잘못 바꿔 쓴 것은?

① I wish I knew how to jazz dance.
→ I'm sorry I don't know how to jazz dance.

② Ann acts as if she were a princess.
→ In fact, Ann is a princess.

③ If you clicked the red button, you'd cancel the download.
→ As you don't click the red button, you won't cancel the download.

④ If there had been enough snow, they could have made a snowman.
→ There wasn't enough snow, so they couldn't make a snowman.

⑤ But for the soft pillow, I couldn't have slept well.
→ If it had not been for the soft pillow, I couldn't have slept well.

서술형 평가

01 괄호 안의 말을 이용하여 조건에 맞게 우리말을 영어로 옮기시오.

> 타임머신이 있다면, 나는 과거로 돌아갈 수 있을 텐데. (time machine, go)

(1) _____ , I _____ back to the past. (if를 쓸 것)

(2) _____ , I _____ back to the past. (as를 쓸 것)

02 대화에서 어법상 어색한 부분을 두 군데 찾아 바르게 고쳐 쓰시오.

> **A** I wonder why Jimmy got sick last night.
>
> **B** He must have eaten too much. If he didn't eat too much, he wouldn't get sick.

(1) _____ → _____

(2) _____ → _____

03 밑줄 친 부분과 의미가 같도록 빈칸에 알맞은 말을 세 가지 쓰시오.

> But for your help, I would not finish the report.
>
> → _____ your help, I would not finish the report.

(1) _____

(2) _____

(3) _____

04 두 문장의 의미가 같도록 문장을 완성하시오.

(1) I can't eat peaches because I have an allergy to them.

　→ If I _____ to peaches, I _____ them.

(2) I forgot to buy eggs this morning because I didn't have my shopping list with me.

　→ If I _____ with me this morning, I _____ eggs.

 독해형 어법

[05~06] 다음 글을 읽고, 물음에 답하시오.

　Molly is worried. Her best friend, Sally, invited her to spend a week at Lake House, but it is the same week as Space Camp! Molly has always dreamed of becoming an astronaut someday. ⓐ If she goes to Lake House, Molly would swim and sleep outdoors. On the other hand, if she went to Space Camp, ⓑ she might have gotten to spend time in real space capsule. Both trips would be a lot of fun. ⓒ Molly wishes she could go to the both places. What should she do?

05 밑줄 친 ⓐ, ⓑ에서 어법상 어색한 부분을 찾아 바르게 고쳐 문장을 다시 쓰시오.

ⓐ _____

ⓑ _____

06 밑줄 친 ⓒ를 다음과 같이 바꿔 쓸 때 빈칸에 알맞은 말을 쓰시오.

→ Molly is sorry _____ .

CHAPTER

11

일치와 화법

FOCUS 78   수의 일치 1_ 단수

FOCUS 79   수의 일치 2_ 복수

FOCUS 80   시제 일치

FOCUS 81   시제 일치의 예외

FOCUS 82   평서문의 간접화법

FOCUS 83   의문문의 간접화법

FOCUS 84   명령문의 간접화법

FOCUS 85   간접화법과 간접의문문

일치란 무엇인가?

문장 내에서 서로 밀접한 관계가 있는 어구끼리는 수, 인칭, 시제 등을 일치시켜야 한다. 대표적으로 주어와 동사의 수의 일치, 시제의 일치가 있다.

일치

수의 일치
- **단수**: 주어가 단수이면 단수 동사
- **복수**: 주어가 복수이면 복수 동사

시제의 일치: 일반적으로 주절의 시제와 종속절의 시제를 일치시킨다.

> *The girl* **goes** to the concert.
> 그 소녀는 콘서트에 간다.

> *The girls* **go** to the concert.
> 그 소녀들은 콘서트에 간다.

> I *thought* that she **was** right.
> 나는 그녀가 옳다고 생각했다.

화법이란 무엇이며 화법에는 어떤 것이 있는가?

화법이란 어떤 사람이 말한 것을 다른 사람에게 전달하는 방법으로, 화법에는 직접화법과 간접화법이 있다.

화법

직접화법: *인용 부호(" ")를 사용하여 다른 사람이 말한 내용을 그대로 전달하는 방법

간접화법: 다른 사람이 말한 내용을, 전달하는 사람의 입장에서 적절히 바꿔서 전달하는 방법

> She **said**, "I like the shoes."
> 그녀는 "나는 그 신발이 마음에 들어."라고 말했다.

> She **said that she liked** the shoes.
> 그녀는 그 신발이 마음에 든다고 말했다.

화법은 어떻게 전환하는가?

직접화법을 간접화법으로, 간접화법을 직접화법으로 전환할 때는 종속절의 주어와 시제 등을 주절에 일치시킨다.

He said, "I want to play the guitar." 〈직접화법〉 그는 "나는 기타를 연주하고 싶어."라고 말했다.
　전달동사　　　　　피전달문

He said that he wanted to play the guitar. 〈간접화법 - 피전달문의 주어와 시제가 바뀜〉
　전달동사　　　　　피전달문　　　　　　　　　그는 기타를 연주하고 싶다고 말했다.

용어 사전

* **인용 부호**: 문장 부호의 하나로, 다른 사람의 말이나 글을 자신의 말이나 글에 가져다 쓸 때 사용하는 부호이다.

수의 일치 1_ 단수

■ 단수 취급하는 단어

every, each, -thing, -one, -body	Every room **is** clean. Each girl **has** her own dream.
시간·거리·금액·무게의 명사	Thirty dollars **is** expensive for a meal.
학문 이름	Mathematics **is** my favorite subject.

■ 단수 취급하는 구문

「분수, some(most / half / the rest) of the+단수 명사」	Some of the pie **is** missing.
「the number of+복수 명사」 (~의 수)	The number of patients **increases** day by day.

A 괄호 안에서 알맞은 것을 고르시오. » 정답과 해설 p.26

1 Economics (is / are) one of my favorite subjects.

2 Everybody (was / were) curious about the result.

3 Five miles (is / are) a long distance to walk.

4 Most of the building (has / have) been destroyed by a tornado.

B 괄호 안의 말을 이용하여 빈칸에 알맞은 형태로 쓰시오. (현재시제로 쓸 것)

1 Half of the bread _____ rotten. (be)

2 Each of my brothers _____ glasses. (wear)

3 One fourth of an iceberg _____ underwater. (be)

4 Three hours _____ enough time to watch a movie. (be)

5 Physics _____ a natural science based on experiments. (be)

6 The rest of the team _____ disappointed at the result. (feel)

C 우리말과 뜻이 같도록 괄호 안의 말을 이용하여 문장을 완성하시오.

1 모든 사람이 너만큼 신이 나있다. (be)
→ _____ _____ as excited as you.

2 그 노래의 일부분이 불법적으로 모방되었다. (be)
→ _____ _____ the song _____ copied illegally.

3 지원자의 수가 증가하고 있다. (increase)
→ _____ _____ of candidates _____ _____ .

교과서
문장
응용하기

배운 문법을 이용하여 영어 문장을 써 봅시다.

1 각 학생은 역사 보고서를 내야 한다. (have to, submit) → _____

2 그 강의의 대부분이 매우 어려웠다. (lecture) → _____

수의 일치 2_ 복수

▪ 복수 취급하는 경우

「분수, some(most / half / the rest) of the+복수 명사」	*Some of the animals* **are** still hungry.
「a number of+복수 명사」 (많은 ~)	*A number of cars* **are** on the road.
「(both) A and B」	*Both Tom and Jerry* **have** been to Europe.
항상 짝을 이루는 명사	**Are** there *any socks* in the drawer?

▪ 「There+be동사+주어」 형태의 수 일치는 주어가 복수이면 be동사는 복수형, 단수이면 단수형을 쓴다.

There **are** *three magazines* on the couch.
There **is** *a bus stop* over there.

A 빈칸에 현재시제 be동사를 알맞은 형태로 쓰시오.

» 정답과 해설 p.26

1 One third of the students _____ in the classroom.
2 Forty percent of the people in my school _____ boys.
3 Both men and women _____ allowed to join the club.
4 There _____ several reasons why I can't come.
5 A number of players _____ entering the stadium.
6 Your glasses _____ different from hers.

B 어법상 어색한 부분을 찾아 고쳐 쓰시오.

1 There was five women in the cafe. _____ → _____
2 Chopsticks is useful to pick up little things. _____ → _____
3 A number of tourists visits the palace every year. _____ → _____
4 Three fourths of the apples is his. _____ → _____
5 Some of the girls is playing in the playground. _____ → _____

C 우리말과 뜻이 같도록 괄호 안의 말을 이용하여 문장을 완성하시오.

1 Kate와 그녀의 여동생 둘 다 골프 치는 것을 좋아한다. (like)
  → _____ Kate _____ her sister _____ to play golf.
2 그 자동차들 중 일부는 한국의 광주에서 만들어졌다. (make)
  → _____ _____ the cars _____ _____ in Gwangju, Korea.

교과서
문장
응용하기

배운 문법을 이용하여 영어 문장을 써 봅시다.

1 많은 건물들이 붕괴되었다. (number, destroy)   → _____
2 그 박물관 안에는 많은 사람들이 있었다. (there, many)   → _____

80 시제 일치

■ 주절의 동사가 현재시제인 경우 종속절에는 모든 시제를 쓸 수 있다.

He *thinks* that he **is**(was / will be) happy.

■ 주절의 동사가 과거시제인 경우 종속절의 시제는 과거나 과거완료가 온다.

He *said* that he **supported** the soccer team.

He *said* that he **had supported** the soccer team before.

A 괄호 안에서 알맞은 것을 고르시오. 　》 정답과 해설 p.26

1 She never thought that she (will / would) meet him again.

2 Molly (says / said) that she had missed the last train.

3 Nobody knows what (can / could) happen in the future.

4 He said that the famous designer (makes / had made) the jacket.

5 They believed that she (is / had been) honest and brave.

6 James hopes that he (completed / will complete) the project by tomorrow.

B 밑줄 친 부분이 어법상 맞으면 ○표, 틀리면 ×표를 한 후 바르게 고쳐 쓰시오.

1 Hazel couldn't understand what <u>was</u> happening. ＿＿＿＿＿＿＿＿

2 She asks me whether I <u>like</u> Chinese food. ＿＿＿＿＿＿＿＿

3 When I <u>am</u> young, I joined the school band. ＿＿＿＿＿＿＿＿

4 I told them that I <u>have been</u> to Hong Kong. ＿＿＿＿＿＿＿＿

5 Owen said that he <u>had already written</u> a letter. ＿＿＿＿＿＿＿＿

C 다음 문장의 시제를 바꿀 때 빈칸에 알맞은 말을 쓰시오.

1 Henry argues that the price is not reasonable.

→ Henry argued that ＿＿＿＿ ＿＿＿＿ ＿＿＿＿ not reasonable.

2 Alice says that she will give a speech in front of people.

→ Alice said that she ＿＿＿＿ ＿＿＿＿ a speech in front of people.

3 I know that the twins visited Barcelona.

→ I knew that the twins ＿＿＿＿ ＿＿＿＿ Barcelona.

4 Stella believes that her little brother broke the window.

→ Stella believed that her little brother ＿＿＿＿ ＿＿＿＿ the window.

**교과서
문장
응용하기** | 배운 문법을 이용하여 영어 문장을 써 봅시다.

1 그는 그의 숙제를 끝마칠 수 있다고 말한다. (finish) → ＿＿＿＿＿＿＿＿＿＿＿＿＿

2 그는 그녀가 그를 존경했었다고 생각했다. (admire) → ＿＿＿＿＿＿＿＿＿＿＿＿＿

시제 일치의 예외

- 주절의 시제가 과거일지라도 종속절이 불변의 진리, 격언, 현재의 습관, 과학적 사실 등을 나타내면 현재시제를 쓴다.
I *learned* that light **travels** faster than sound. 〈불변의 진리〉
She *said* that he **takes** a walk every morning. 〈현재의 습관〉

- 역사적인 사실은 주절의 시제와 상관없이 과거시제를 쓴다.
He *says* that Apollo 11 **landed** on the Moon in 1969.

A 괄호 안에서 알맞은 것을 고르시오.

» 정답과 해설 p.26

1 The little boy answered that two and four (makes / made) six.
2 The student learned from a book that the moon (is / was) round.
3 We learned that the Korean War (was / had been) over in 1953.
4 She says that King Sejong (invents / invented) *Hangeul* in 1443.
5 Jessica told me that she always (gets / got) up at 7.

B 밑줄 친 부분을 과거시제로 바꿔 문장을 다시 쓰시오.

1 The teacher <u>says</u> that World War II ended in 1945.
   → _____

2 Lisa <u>tells</u> me that practice makes perfect.
   → _____

3 The scientists <u>say</u> that the Earth is getting warmer.
   → _____

4 My father <u>says</u> that Madrid is the capital of Spain.
   → _____

C 우리말과 뜻이 같도록 괄호 안의 말을 이용하여 문장을 완성하시오.

1 그는 지구가 태양 주위를 움직인다는 것을 증명했다. (move)
   → He proved that the Earth _____ around the sun.
2 그녀는 물이 100℃에서 끓는다는 것을 알고 있었다. (boil)
   → She knew that water _____ at 100℃.
3 Oliver는 정직이 최상의 방침이라고 말했다. (be)
   → Oliver said that honesty _____ the best policy.

교과서 문장 응용하기

배운 문법을 이용하여 영어 문장을 써 봅시다.

1 그녀는 지구가 둥글다고 내게 말했다.   → _____

2 나는 Edison이 전구를 발명했다는 것을 배웠다. (light bulb)   → _____

82 평서문의 간접화법

- **평서문의 화법 전환**

 1. 전달동사 say는 say (that)로, say to는 tell로 바꾼다.

 2. 쉼표(,)와 인용부호("")를 없앤 후, 접속사 that으로 연결한다.

 3. that절의 시제는 전달동사의 시제와 일치시키고, 인칭이나 지시대명사와 부사(구)도 알맞게 바꾼다.

 [직접화법] She **said**,　　　"**I** can repair the bike today."
　　　　　　　　↓　　　　　↓　　↓

 [간접화법] She **said** **(that)** **she could** repair the bike that day.

- **화법 전환 시 지시대명사와 부사(구)의 전환**

 this(these) → that(those), here → there, today → that day, tomorrow → the next day(the following day), ago → before, now → then, tonight → that night, yesterday → the day before(the previous day)

A 다음 문장을 간접화법으로 바꿀 때 빈칸에 알맞은 말을 쓰시오. 　　　　　　》 정답과 해설 p.26

 1 He said to me, "I am angry at Peter."

　→ He _____ me that _____ _____ angry at Peter.

 2 She said to me, "I have been inspired by his speech."

　→ She _____ me that she _____ _____ _____ by his speech.

 3 Clara said, "I don't do business this way."

　→ Clara _____ that she _____ do business _____ way.

 4 Luke said, "I will not go to work tomorrow."

　→ Luke _____ that he _____ _____ _____ to work _____ _____ _____.

B 다음 문장을 직접화법으로 바꿀 때 빈칸에 알맞은 말을 쓰시오.

 1 Jackson said that he wanted to visit his friends that weekend.

　→ Jackson said, "_____"

 2 They told me that they had lived there for a long time.

　→ They said to me, "_____"

 3 She told me that she would finish that report that night.

　→ She said to me, "_____"

교과서 문장 응용하기 | 배운 문법을 이용하여 영어 문장을 써 봅시다.

 1 Rose는 그에게 그녀가 그때 바빴다고 말했다.　　　　→ _____

 2 Noah는 그가 전날에 아팠다고 말했다.　　　　→ _____

의문문의 간접화법

■ 의문문의 간접화법 전환: say나 say to를 ask로 바꾸고 인용 부호를 없앤 후, 의문사의 유무에 따라 알맞은 형태로 바꾼다.

1. 의문사가 없는 의문문의 간접화법: 「ask(+목적어)+if(whether)+주어+동사」

He **said**, "Do you know Mr. Brown?" → He **asked if(whether) I knew** Mr. Brown.

2. 의문사가 있는 의문문의 간접화법: 「ask(+목적어)+의문사+주어+동사」

He **said to** her, "What are you reading?" → He **asked** her **what she was** reading.

cf. 의문사가 주어인 경우에는 「의문사+동사」의 어순을 그대로 유지한다.

She **said to** me, "Who has closed the door?" → She **asked** me **who had closed** the door.

A 다음 문장을 간접화법으로 바꿀 때 빈칸에 알맞은 말을 쓰시오.　　　　　　　　》 정답과 해설 p.27

1 Alex said to Eva, "Do you like chocolate?"

→ Alex asked Eva _____ _____ _____ chocolate.

2 He said to me, "Can you help me tomorrow?"

→ He asked me _____ _____ _____ help him _____ _____

_____.

3 Ivy said to him, "When did you move to California?"

→ Ivy asked him when he _____ _____ to California.

4 I said to him, "Who gave you this pen?"

→ I asked him _____ _____ _____ _____ _____ pen.

5 She said to me, "Are you free tonight?"

→ She asked me _____ _____ _____ _____ _____ _____.

B 우리말과 뜻이 같도록 괄호 안의 말을 이용하여 문장을 완성하시오.

1 그는 내게 누구를 기다리고 있는지 물었다. (be)

→ He _____ me _____ _____ _____ waiting for.

2 그녀는 내게 그날 무엇을 할건지 물었다. (do)

→ She _____ me what I _____ _____ _____ _____.

3 그는 Peter에게 이탈리아어를 잘할 수 있는지 물었다. (speak)

→ He asked Peter _____ _____ _____ _____ Italian well.

교과서 문장 응용하기 | 배운 문법을 이용하여 영어 문장을 써 봅시다.

1 그녀는 내게 나비를 좋아하는지 물었다. (butterflies)　　→ _____

2 나는 그녀에게 이틀 전에 무엇을 했는지 물었다.　　→ _____

명령문의 간접화법

■ 명령문의 간접화법 전환

1. 전달동사를 문맥에 맞게 tell, ask, order, advise 등으로 바꾼다.
2. 인용 부호를 없앤 후, 인용문의 동사를 to부정사로 바꾼다.
3. 「전달동사+목적어(+not)+to부정사」의 형태로 만든다.

He **said to** me, "**Do** your homework." → He **told(ordered)** me **to do** my homework.

Jenny **said to** them, "**Don't bother** me with questions."

→ Jenny **ordered** them **not to bother** her with questions.

A 다음 문장을 간접화법으로 바꿀 때 괄호 안의 말을 이용하여 빈칸에 알맞은 말을 쓰시오. » 정답과 해설 p.27

1 He said to me, "Try this again." (order)

→ He _____ me _____ _____ that again.

2 Mother said to me, "Help me in the kitchen." (tell)

→ Mother _____ me _____ _____ her in the kitchen.

3 She said to him, "Lend me some money." (ask)

→ She _____ him _____ _____ _____ some money.

4 The doctor said to me, "Don't skip breakfast." (advise)

→ The doctor _____ me _____ _____ _____ breakfast.

5 The teacher said to me, "Don't use smartphone in the class." (tell)

→ The teacher _____ me _____ _____ _____ smartphone in the class.

B 다음 문장을 직접화법으로 바꿀 때 빈칸에 알맞은 말을 쓰시오.

1 I ordered her to walk her dog.

→ I said to her, "_____"

2 The tour guide asked us not to be too noisy in the museum.

→ The tour guide said to us, "_____"

3 The doctor advised my mother to drink enough water.

→ The doctor said to my mother, "_____"

4 She told me to join the baseball team.

→ She said to me, "_____"

교과서
문장
응용하기

배운 문법을 이용하여 영어 문장을 써 봅시다.

1 그녀는 그에게 뛰지 말라고 명령했다. (order) → _____

2 나는 그녀에게 날 그 파티에 데려가 달라고 부탁했다. (ask) → _____

85 간접화법과 간접의문문

■ 간접화법은 다른 사람이 말한 내용을 전달하는 사람의 입장에서 적절히 바꿔서 전달하는 방법이고, 간접의문문은 직접적인 질문을 공손한 어조로 표현하는 방식이다.

■ 간접의문문의 어순

의문사가 없는 간접의문문	「if(whether)+주어+동사」	Can you tell me? + Is that girl your sister? → Can you tell me **if(whether) that girl is** your sister?
의문사가 있는 간접의문문	「의문사+주어+동사」	I wonder. + When will you come home? → I wonder **when you will come** home.

cf. 의문사가 있는 간접의문문에서 의문사가 주어로 쓰인 경우에는 직접의문문의 어순을 그대로 쓴다.

A 밑줄 친 부분을 어법상 바르게 고쳐 쓰시오.

1 I wonder how old <u>is the boy</u>. _____

2 Do you think <u>why</u> we support Emily? _____

3 Do you have any idea where <u>did he go</u>? _____

» 정답과 해설 p.27

◆ 간접의문문에서 주절의 동사가 think, believe, imagine, guess, suppose 등과 같이 생각이나 추측과 관련된 동사인 경우, 의문사를 맨 앞에 쓴다.
What do you **think** the book is about?

B 다음 문장을 간접의문문으로 바꿀 때 빈칸에 알맞은 말을 쓰시오.

1 Can he play the guitar?

→ I want to know _____ _____ _____ _____ the guitar.

2 Why were you late for the meeting?

→ Please tell me _____ _____ _____ late for the meeting.

3 Who will be here this afternoon?

→ _____ do you guess _____ _____ here this afternoon?

C 괄호 안의 말을 바르게 배열하여 문장을 완성하시오.

1 (who, know, this poem, you, wrote, do)?

→ _____

2 (happened, when, knows, the accident, nobody).

→ _____

3 (comes, she, do, where, suppose, you, from)?

→ _____

교과서 문장 응용하기 배운 문법을 이용하여 영어 문장을 써 봅시다.

1 너는 그녀가 무엇을 원했었는지 아니? → _____

2 너는 누가 그 경기를 이길 것이라고 생각하니? → _____

➜ 내신적중 실전문제를 풀기 전에 Workbook p.48에 있는 요점정리를 참고하세요.

내신적중 실전문제

» 정답과 해설 p.27

[01~02] 빈칸에 알맞은 것을 고르시오.

01

> Yesterday each of the students _____ interviewed before the test.

① is   ② are   ③ was
④ were   ⑤ am

02

> Two days _____ a short time for me to finish the work.

① are   ② is   ③ have
④ has   ⑤ had

03 빈칸에 공통으로 알맞은 말을 쓰시오. (주관식)

> • The doctor asked me _____ I had an allergy to nuts.
> • Can you tell me _____ Sally exercises to keep slim?

04 우리말과 뜻이 같도록 할 때 빈칸에 알맞은 것은?

> 민호는 Molly에게 부엌에서 무엇을 하고 있는지를 물었다.
> → Minho asked Molly _____ in the kitchen.

① what are you doing
② what you are doing
③ what she is doing
④ what she was doing
⑤ what was she doing

05 빈칸에 들어갈 말로 <u>어색한</u> 것은?

> Alan said that he _____.

① was baking cookies
② took part in the campaign
③ will read the cookbook
④ had visited his grandparents
⑤ makes it a rule to take a walk every day

06 다음 문장을 간접화법으로 바르게 바꾼 것은?

> Mom said to me, "Don't surf the Internet until late at night."

① Mom said that I didn't surf the Internet until late at night.
② Mom told me that she didn't surf the Internet until late at night.
③ Mom told me don't surf the Internet until late at night.
④ Mom told me not to surf the Internet until late at night.
⑤ Mom asked me if I didn't surf the Internet until late at night.

07 다음 문장을 직접화법으로 바르게 바꾼 것은?

> Sam asked me if I was reading it.

① Sam asked me, "Are you reading it?"
② Sam asked me, "Were you reading it?"
③ Sam said to me, "Was I reading it?"
④ Sam said to me, "Are you reading it?"
⑤ Sam said to me, "Were you reading it?""

08 밑줄 친 부분 중 어법상 어색한 것은?

> A ① number of ② student ③ are present at the meeting. Some of ④ them ⑤ are my friends.

[09~10] 다음 간접화법으로 바꿔 쓴 문장에서 밑줄 친 ①~⑤ 중 어법상 어색한 부분을 찾아 바르게 고쳐 쓰시오. 주관식

09

> Richard said, "I'm going to visit my uncle tomorrow."
> → Richard said that he was going to visit
>   ①   ②   ③
>   my uncle the next day.
>   ④   ⑤

_____ → _____

10

> Linda said to me, "Did Harry fly to Rome two weeks ago?"
> → Linda asked if Harry flew to Rome two
>   ① ② ③   ④
>   weeks before.
>   ⑤

_____ → _____

11 괄호 안에서 알맞은 말을 골라 쓰시오.

> ⓐ Three-fourths of our body (is / are) made up of water.
> ⓑ Most of my friends (keep / keeps) pets at home.
> ⓒ Some of her free time (was / were) spent on watching movies.

ⓐ _____ ⓑ _____ ⓒ _____

[12~13] 대화의 빈칸에 알맞은 것을 고르시오.

12

> A Who knows the secret?
> B Maybe both Julian and his brothers _____ it.

① done   ② does   ③ knowing
④ knows   ⑤ know

13

> A What did the doctor say to Peter?
> B He advised _____ regularly.

① to him to exercise   ② to him exercise
③ him exercises   ④ him exercising
⑤ him to exercise

14 두 문장을 간접의문문으로 쓸 때 어색한 것은?

① I don't remember. + Does he live in Seoul?
   → I don't remember if he lives in Seoul.
② I wonder. + Can Jack come to the farewell party?
   → I wonder whether Jack can come to the farewell party.
③ Can you tell me? + What time does the train leave?
   → Can you tell me what time the train leaves?
④ I want to know. + Who solved this quiz?
   → I want to know who solved this quiz.
⑤ Do you guess? + How can she get first prize?
   → How do you guess can she get first prize?

15 밑줄 친 부분이 어법상 어색한 것은?

① The watch and chain <u>are</u> too expensive.
② The number of bookstores <u>have</u> decreased rapidly.
③ There <u>are</u> some actors on the stage.
④ Every room in the hotel <u>has</u> a bathroom.
⑤ Your shoes <u>are</u> different from mine.

16 어법상 어색한 것은?

① Luke said he had bought the shirt on sale.
② Did you know the fact that Earth moves around the Sun?
③ Eva learned that knowledge is power.
④ Jessica said that she was cleaning her room then.
⑤ Yuri learned that Einstein had discovered the special theory of relativity.

17 다음 문장을 직접화법으로 바르게 바꾼 것은?

① Kate told me that she was watering the flowers. → Kate said to me, "She is watering the flowers."
② He told me that he would be back the next day. → He said to me, "I will be back the next day."
③ I asked the man not to park there. → I said to the man, "Park here."
④ Mr. Smith asked me if I knew the history of that tower.→ Mr. Smith said to me, "Did you know the history of this tower?"
⑤ My wife said that she had lost her wedding ring the day before. → My wife said, "I lost my wedding ring yesterday."

18 빈칸에 알맞지 <u>않은</u> 것은?

> What _____ the students did at the senior center?

① do you think
② do you know
③ do you imagine
④ do you guess
⑤ do you suppose

19 어법상 옳은 것끼리 짝지어진 것은?

> ⓐ 5,280 feet are a mile.
> ⓑ Economics is about more than just money.
> ⓒ Most of the dogs in town were barking.
> ⓓ She said that she had waited for the bus for ten minutes.
> ⓔ My grandfather told me that a good medicine tasted bitter.

① ⓐ, ⓑ, ⓒ
② ⓐ, ⓒ, ⓓ
③ ⓑ, ⓒ, ⓓ
④ ⓑ, ⓓ, ⓔ
⑤ ⓒ, ⓓ, ⓔ

20 화법 전환이 <u>잘못된</u> 것은?

① I said to my brother, "Turn off the TV." → I told my brother to turn off the TV.
② I said to him, "You have to drive a car." → I told him that he had to drive a car.
③ His mother said to him, "I'll tell you the truth." → His mother told him that she would tell him the truth.
④ Mark said to me, "Don't sing the song loud in the room!" → Mark told me sing the song loud in the room.
⑤ She said to me, "Where did you go yesterday?" → She asked me where I had gone the day before.

서술형 평가

01 밑줄 친 부분을 괄호 안의 말로 바꿔 문장을 다시 쓰시오.

(1) Some of the pumpkin pie is missing. (pies)

→ _____

(2) Sora as well as Bill wants to ride a camel around the desert. (Both Bill and Sora)

→ _____

02 주어진 문장을 바꿔 쓸 때 빈칸에 알맞은 말을 쓰시오.

(1) He discovers that the prisoners escaped through the window.

→ He discovered that the prisoners _____ _____ through the window.

(2) Jenny tells me that the telescope was invented by Galileo.

→ Jenny told me that the telescope _____ by Galileo.

03 문맥에 맞게 대화를 완성하시오.

(1) **A** I wonder _____ lunch outside.

B Well, he doesn't. Ted eats lunch at school cafeteria.

(2) **A** Do you know what Sally is doing in the kitchen?

B No, I don't know _____ in the kitchen.

04 우리말과 뜻이 같도록 괄호 안의 말을 이용하여 간접화법 문장으로 쓰시오.

Ann은 Peter에게 그 도서관 사서가 그에게 무슨 말을 했었는지 물었다. (librarian)

→ _____

05 대화의 내용과 일치하도록 문장을 완성하시오.

Eric Are you reading the detective novel now?

Jessy Yes. It is very exciting.

(1) Eric asked Jessy _____

_____.

(2) Jessy told Eric _____.

[06~07] 다음 글을 읽고, 물음에 답하시오.

Did you know the Moon ⓐ had one-sixth the gravity of the Earth? Everything ⓑ weigh six times less on the Moon. One woman weighs 120 pounds on Earth. ⓒ Do you think? How much does the same woman weigh on the Moon? Right. She would weigh only 20 pounds there. She could jump higher on the Moon than she could on Earth. A blue whale weighs 150 tons. If a blue whale could go to the moon, it would weigh just 25 tons.

06 밑줄 친 ⓐ, ⓑ의 알맞은 형태를 쓰시오.

ⓐ _____ ⓑ _____

07 밑줄 친 ⓒ를 연결하여 한 문장으로 쓰시오.

→ _____

CHAPTER

12
특수 구문

FOCUS 86   강조 1_ 동사 강조

FOCUS 87   강조 2_ 명사, 부정어 강조

FOCUS 88   강조 3_ It ~ that ... 강조

FOCUS 89   도치 1_ 부사(구)·부정어 도치

FOCUS 90   도치 2_ so / neither+동사+주어

FOCUS 91   부정_ 부분·전체부정

FOCUS 92   생략 1_ 공통 부분의 생략

FOCUS 93   생략 2_ 「주어+be동사」의 생략

특수 구문이란 무엇인가?

특별히 강조하고 싶은 말에 조동사를 추가하거나, 강조하고 싶은 말을 먼저 말하거나, 혹은 반복된 말을 생략하기 위해 문장의 *어순이나 형태가 달라지는 문장 형식을 특수 구문이라고 한다.

특수 구문에는 어떤 것이 있는가?

강조
어떤 사실이나 대상에 대한 관심을 유도하기 위해 새로운 말을 넣거나 형식을 변형하는 것

| 동사 강조 | do(does / did)+동사원형 | John **did** speak to Mary.
John은 Mary에게 정말로 말을 했다. |

| 명사, 부정어 강조 | the very+명사 / not ~ at all, in the least | This is **not** the book **at all** that I have read. 이것은 내가 읽었던 책이 전혀 아니다. |

| It ~ that ... 강조 | It+be동사+강조의 말+that | **It was** Judy **that** called you last night. 어젯밤 너에게 전화한 사람은 바로 Judy였다. |

도치
어떤 사실이나 생각 또는 관점을 강조하기 위해 어순을 바꾸거나 다른 문장 형태로 바꾸는 것

| 부사(구) 도치 | 부사(구)+동사+주어 | **Under the table** sings a boy.
탁자 밑에서 한 소년이 노래를 부른다. |

| 부정어 도치 | *부정어+조동사+주어+본동사 | **Never did I meet** him.
나는 결코 그를 만나지 않았다. |

| so/neither +동사+주어 | so / neither+동사+주어 | She didn't break the vase and **neither did I**. 그녀는 꽃병을 깨지 않았고 나도 깨지 않았다. |

생략
불필요한 말이나 반복을 피하기 위해 말을 생략하는 것

| 공통 부분 생략 | | We cannot live by (**ourselves**) and for ourselves.
우리는 혼자서도 혼자 힘으로도 살 수 없다. |

| 「주어+be동사」 생략 | | As (**she was**) a girl, she liked playing the piano.
그녀는 소녀였을 때, 피아노를 연주하는 것을 좋아했다. |

용어 사전
* **어순**: 문장 성분의 배열에 나타나는 일정한 순서를 뜻한다.
* **부정어**: '아니', '못', '아니다', '못하다'와 같이 부정하는 뜻을 가진 말을 의미한다.

강조 1_ 동사 강조

- **일반동사의 의미 강조**: 주어의 인칭과 수, 시제에 맞게 조동사 do를 이용하여 「do(does / did)+동사원형」의 형태로 쓰며, '정말로', '꼭' 등으로 해석한다.

I **do announce** the news every morning.

John **does set** the alarm clock before he goes to bed.

Ann **did eat** Mexican food when she visited Mexico.

A 밑줄 친 부분을 강조하는 표현이 되도록 빈칸에 알맞은 말을 쓰시오. 》 정답과 해설 p.28

1 My sister <u>likes</u> the jazz band.

   → My sister _____ _____ the jazz band.

2 I <u>believe</u> we have met somewhere before.

   → I _____ _____ we have met somewhere before.

3 Lily <u>waited</u> for three hours to see the president.

   → Lily _____ _____ for three hours to see the president.

4 All the athletes <u>trained</u> for the Olympics.

   → All the athletes _____ _____ for the Olympics.

5 He <u>became</u> the chef of the restaurant.

   → He _____ _____ the chef of the restaurant.

B 우리말과 뜻이 같도록 빈칸에 알맞은 말을 쓰시오.

1 그들은 그들의 가게를 정말로 팔았다.

   → They _____ _____ their store.

2 박물관에서 꼭 조용히 해라.

   → _____ _____ quiet in the museum.

3 Kate는 그에게 담배를 끊으라고 정말로 경고했다.

   → Kate _____ _____ him to quit smoking.

4 그 소년은 정말로 '햄릿'을 읽는다.

   → The boy _____ _____ *Hamlet*.

5 Evan은 일주일에 한 번 꼭 그 아이들을 돌본다.

   → Evan _____ _____ _____ _____ the children once a week.

6 나는 미국 문화와 관련된 모든 강의를 정말로 수강했다.

   → I _____ _____ all the courses related to American culture.

교과서
문장
응용하기

배운 문법을 이용하여 영어 문장을 써 봅시다.

1 그는 보스턴에서 음악을 정말로 공부한다.   → _____

2 나는 그녀에게 너의 편지와 선물을 정말로 주었다.   → _____

강조 2_ 명사, 부정어 강조

- **명사 강조**: 명사 뒤나 문장 끝에 재귀대명사를 쓰거나, 명사 앞에 the very를 쓴다. '직접', '바로' 등으로 해석한다.
  My sister made this table **herself**.
  This is **the very** *book* that I have lost.

- **부정어(not) 강조**: 문장에 at all, in the least 등을 쓰며, '전혀', '도무지' 등으로 해석한다.
  I was *not* surprised **at all**.
  My grandmother could *not* hear what others say **in the least**.

A 괄호 안에서 알맞은 것을 고르시오.

» 정답과 해설 p.28

1 I saw the thief (myself / herself).
2 I'm not happy (in the least / at the last).
3 They didn't see the accident (himself / at all).
4 He (himself / itself) went to the concert last night.
5 Molly is (a very / the very) woman that Ryan has been looking for.

B 빈칸에 알맞은 말을 | 보기 |에서 골라 쓰시오.

┌ 보기
│ the very   at all   themselves   in the least   herself
└

1 She _____ told me the news.
2 Emma can't eat anything _____ because of a stomachache.
3 I know _____ person that will be suitable for the job.
4 The boys _____ cut the grass once a week.
5 They are not satisfied _____ with the result.

C 우리말과 뜻이 같도록 빈칸에 알맞은 말을 쓰시오.

1 나는 그 이야기를 전혀 모른다.
  → I don't know the story _____ _____.
2 그는 집에 오는 길에 직접 그 목걸이를 샀다.
  → He _____ bought the necklace on his way home.
3 이곳이 우리가 30년 동안 살아온 바로 그 집이다.
  → This is _____ _____ _____ that we have lived in for 30 years.

───────────────────────────────────

교과서 문장 응용하기

배운 문법을 이용하여 영어 문장을 써 봅시다.

1 이것이 그녀가 찾고 있는 바로 그 책이다. (look for)   → _____
2 나는 영화에 전혀 관심이 없다. (be interested in, all)   → _____

강조 3_ It ~ that ... 강조

- 「It ~ that ...」 강조 구문: 주어, 목적어, 수식어구 등을 강조할 수 있으며, '…인 것은 바로 ~이다(였다)'로 해석한다.

  강조 대상에 따라 that 대신 who(m), which, where, when 등을 쓸 수 있다.

  Matt had coffee at the cafe yesterday.
  → **It was** *Matt* **that(who)** had coffee at the cafe yesterday. 〈주어 강조〉
  → **It was** *coffee* **that(which)** Matt had at the cafe yesterday. 〈목적어 강조〉
  → **It was** *at the cafe* **that(where)** Matt had coffee yesterday. 〈장소 강조〉
  → **It was** *yesterday* **that(when)** Matt had coffee at the cafe. 〈시간 강조〉

  cf. 동사는 「It ~ that ...」 강조 구문으로 강조할 수 없다.

A 밑줄 친 부분을 「It ~ that ...」 강조 구문을 이용하여 바꿔 쓰시오.　　　　　　　》 정답과 해설 p.29

1 She met the popular actor at the airport.

→ _____

2 Noah returned the money last night.

→ _____

3 They started a dancing class last week.

→ _____

4 This movie is based on a true story.

→ _____

B 우리말과 뜻이 같도록 빈칸에 알맞은 말을 쓰시오.

1 내가 사용한 것은 바로 그의 스마트폰이었다.

→ _____ was _____ _____ _____ I used.

2 그가 비웃었던 사람은 바로 Mike이었다.

→ _____ was _____ _____ he laughed at.

3 그녀가 그 상품을 광고한 것은 바로 어제였다.

→ _____ was _____ _____ she advertised the product.

4 내가 그를 처음 만난 곳은 바로 그 식당에서였다.

→ _____ was _____ _____ _____ _____ I met him first.

5 길에서 반지를 주운 사람은 바로 Helen이었다.

→ _____ was _____ _____ _____ _____ a ring on the road.

교과서 문장 응용하기 배운 문법을 이용하여 영어 문장을 써 봅시다.

1 그녀를 잘 아는 사람은 바로 Finn이다.　　　　　→ _____

2 그녀가 어제 산 것은 바로 이 자켓이었다.　　　　→ _____

도치 1_ 부사(구)·부정어 도치

* **도치 구문**: 평서문에서 동사가 주어 앞에 위치하는 구문을 말한다.

■ **부사(구) 도치**: 부사(구)를 문장 앞으로 도치시켜 강조할 경우 「부사(구)+동사+주어」의 어순이 된다. 「There / Here + 동사+주어」의 형태도 일종의 도치 구문이다.

Under the tree was sleeping an old man.　　　　**There** are two books on the table.
　　　　　　　　동사　　　　주어　　　　　　　　　　　　　　　　동사　　주어

　　cf. 주어가 대명사인 경우에는 「주어+동사」의 어순을 유지한다.
　　　　Here he comes.

■ **부정어 도치**: 부정어 never, little, hardly, seldom 등이 문장의 맨 앞으로 오면 「부정어+조동사+주어+본동사」의 형태가 된다.

　　I had never seen so many people in a room.
　　→ **Never had I seen** so many people in a room.

A　두 문장의 뜻이 같도록 빈칸에 알맞은 말을 쓰시오.　　　　　　　　》 정답과 해설 p.29

1 The meeting begins in the afternoon.
　　→ In the afternoon ＿＿＿＿ ＿＿＿＿ ＿＿＿＿.

2 Two bats are in the cave.
　　→ In the cave ＿＿＿＿ ＿＿＿＿ ＿＿＿＿.

3 She hardly makes a mistake.
　　→ Hardly ＿＿＿＿ ＿＿＿＿ ＿＿＿＿ a mistake.

4 I little dreamed that such a thing would happen.
　　→ Little ＿＿＿＿ ＿＿＿＿ ＿＿＿＿ that such a thing would happen.

B　우리말과 뜻이 같도록 괄호 안의 말을 이용하여 문장을 완성하시오.

1 탁자 위에 약간의 사과들이 있다. (some)
　　→ On the table ＿＿＿＿ ＿＿＿＿ ＿＿＿＿.

2 호텔 안으로 그 소녀가 뛰어 들어갔다. (rush)
　　→ Into the hotel ＿＿＿＿ ＿＿＿＿ ＿＿＿＿.

3 결코 나는 그렇게 큰 개를 본 적이 없다. (see)
　　→ Never ＿＿＿＿ ＿＿＿＿ ＿＿＿＿ such a big dog.

4 우리는 밤 9시 이후에는 거의 만나지 않았다. (meet)
　　→ Seldom ＿＿＿＿ ＿＿＿＿ ＿＿＿＿ after 9 p.m.

**교과서
문장
응용하기**

배운 문법을 이용하여 영어 문장을 써 봅시다.

1 접시 위에 그 치즈 케이크가 있다. (plate)　　→ ＿＿＿＿＿＿＿＿＿＿＿＿＿＿＿

2 그녀는 그를 거의 이해하지 못했다. (little)　　→ ＿＿＿＿＿＿＿＿＿＿＿＿＿＿＿

90

도치 2_ so / neither+동사+주어

도치 구문	의미	예문
「so+동사+주어」 (긍정문 다음에 씀)	~도 또한 그렇다	**A** He wants to take a rest. **B So does she.** (→ She wants to take a rest, too.)
「neither+동사+주어」 (부정문 다음에 씀)	~도 또한 아니다	I can't go to New York and **neither can she**. (→ I can't go to New York and she can't go to New York, either.)

cf. 「so / neither+동사+주어」의 동사는 앞의 말에 쓰인 동사의 종류, 시제와 일치시킨다.

A 대화의 빈칸에 알맞은 말을 so나 neither를 이용하여 쓰시오.　　　　　　　　　　» 정답과 해설 p.29

1 A He watched the movie.　**B** _____ _____ I.

2 A She won't be here.　**B** _____ _____ her brother.

3 A Tina has gone back to Japan.　**B** _____ _____ her husband.

4 A Evan doesn't want to go fishing.　**B** _____ _____ his sister.

B 두 문장의 뜻이 같도록 빈칸에 알맞은 말을 쓰시오.

1 She can't play the piano and her father can't, either.

　→ She can't play the piano and _____ _____ her father.

2 He is wearing a red jacket and I am, too.

　→ He is wearing a red jacket and _____ _____ I.

C 우리말과 뜻이 같도록 빈칸에 알맞은 말을 쓰시오.

1 A Peter는 프랑스어를 할 수 있어.　**B** Leo도 또한 그래.

　→ **A** Peter can speak French.　**B** _____ _____ _____.

2 A Grace는 공포영화를 좋아하지 않아.　**B** 나도 또한 그렇지 않아.

　→ **A** Grace doesn't like horror movies.　**B** _____ _____ _____.

3 A 그는 그런 것은 절대 말하지 않을 거야.　**B** 나도 또한 그러지 않을 거야.

　→ **A** He would never say such a thing.　**B** _____ _____ _____.

4 내 오렌지는 내가 생각했던 것만큼 맛있었고, 그의 것도 또한 그랬다.

　→ My orange tasted as good as I thought and _____ _____ _____.

5 Ben은 사용한 병을 재활용하지 않았고, Hannah 또한 그러지 않았다.

　→ Ben didn't recycle the used bottles and _____ _____ _____.

교과서 문장 응용하기 　배운 문법을 이용하여 영어 문장을 써 봅시다.

1 Fiona는 Brandon을 좋아하고, 우리도 또한 그렇다. (so)　　　→ _____

2 그는 그녀를 믿을 수가 없었으며, 나도 또한 그럴 수 없었다. (neither)　　→ _____

부정_ 부분·전체부정

- 부분부정: 「not+every / all / both / always」 등의 형태로 쓰여 '모두 / 둘 다 / 항상 ~인 것은 아니다'의 의미를 나타 낸다.

  Not all of them are high school students.

  Not both of them raised a dog.

  I do **not always** watch TV.

- 전체부정: none, never, neither 등의 부정어를 써서 '아무도 / 결코 / 둘 다 ~하지 않다'의 의미를 나타낸다.

  None of them are high school students.

  Neither of them raised a dog.

A 빈칸에 알맞은 말을 |보기|에서 골라 쓰시오. 》 정답과 해설 p.29

| 보기 |
| neither　　　　never　　　　all |

1 A Did you have a fight with your brother?

  B Yes. He _____ talks to me anymore.

2 A Did Aron and Cora pass the driving test?

  B Yes, they did. _____ of them failed the test.

3 A I think computer games are not good for you.

  B Not _____ of them are bad. Some of them are educational.

B 우리말과 뜻이 같도록 빈칸에 알맞은 말을 쓰시오.

1 우리 중 아무도 과학 선생님을 좋아하지 않는다.

  → _____ of us likes the science teacher.

2 그 아이들 둘 다 버섯을 먹는 것을 좋아하는 것은 아니다.

  → _____ of the children like eating mushrooms.

3 모든 사람이 유명한 영화 감독이 될 수 있는 것은 아니다.

  → _____ _____ can become a famous movie director.

4 돈이 우리에게 항상 행복을 주는 것은 아니다.

  → Money does _____ _____ give us happiness.

5 그 이야기들 둘 다 재미있지 않다.

  → _____ _____ _____ _____ is interesting.

교과서
문장
응용하기

배운 문법을 이용하여 영어 문장을 써 봅시다.

1 그녀가 항상 같은 시간에 저녁을 먹는 것은 아니다. (same time)　→ _____

2 그의 부모님 두 분 다 살아계시지 않다. (neither, alive)　→ _____

생략 1_ 공통 부분의 생략

- 반복되는 명사(구), 동사(구), 형용사(구)는 생략할 수 있다.
  The moon shines at night and the sun (**shines**) in the daytime.

- 질문에 대한 응답에서 동사가 반복될 때에는 조동사만 쓰고 나머지는 생략할 수 있다.
  A Did you meet John?   **B** Yes, I did (**meet John**).

- 비교 구문의 than이나 as 뒤의 말이 중복되면 생략할 수 있다.
  Jack walks faster than Sam (**does**).

- to부정사가 반복되면 to만 쓰고 동사원형 이하는 생략할 수 있다.
  You may come if you want to (**come**).

A 밑줄 친 부분을 생략된 어구를 넣어 다시 쓰시오.   》 정답과 해설 p.29

1 Rose can swim well, but I can't. _____
2 She can run faster than Gavin can. _____
3 Adam's is the longest hair in our class. _____
4 I'd like to go to concerts, but I don't have time to. _____

B 다음 문장에서 생략할 수 있는 부분을 생략하여 문장을 다시 쓰시오.

1 She met her friends and she ordered some food.

→ _____

2 Ivy does the dishes more often than Isaac does the dishes.

→ _____

3 This is the most beautiful hotel and the most expensive hotel in China.

→ _____

C 우리말과 뜻이 같도록 빈칸에 알맞은 말을 쓰시오.

1 이 집은 나의 집이 아니라 Susan의 집이야.
  → This is not my house but _____.
2 네가 이곳에 머무르고 싶으면 머물러도 된다.
  → You can stay here if you _____ _____.
3 나는 그의 사진을 찍고 싶었지만 찍을 수 없었다.
  → I wanted to take a picture of him, but _____ _____.

교과서
문장
응용하기 | 배운 문법을 이용하여 영어 문장을 써 봅시다.

1 그의 책과 Eva의 책이 책상 위에 있다. (on)   → _____
2 그녀의 드레스는 Sophia의 드레스보다 더 단순하다. (simple)   → _____

생략 2_ 「주어+be동사」의 생략

- 시간·조건·양보 부사절의 주어가 주절의 주어와 같을 때에는 종종 「주어+be동사」를 생략하기도 한다.
  Though (**she was**) poor, she was happy. 〈양보의 부사절〉
  As (**he was**) a boy, he liked playing tennis. 〈시간의 부사절〉

- if가 이끄는 「if+주어+be동사+necessary(possible / any 등)」 구문에서 부사절의 주어가 주절의 주어와 다르더라도 「주어+be동사」를 관용적으로 생략하기도 한다.
  Paint all the houses, if (**it is**) necessary.

A 다음 문장에서 생략할 수 있는 어구에 밑줄을 그으시오. 　　　　　　　　》 정답과 해설 p.29

1 When she was young, she used to ride a bicycle.
2 I fell asleep while I was reading a book.
3 Practice the flute every day before the performance, if it is necessary.
4 Though he was tired, he went out to meet his friends.
5 Meat will be good for a week, if it is put in the refrigerator.

B 다음 문장에서 생략된 어구를 넣어 문장을 다시 쓰시오.

1 As a young artist, she was not famous.
→ _____

2 When in danger, you should call me.
→ _____

3 If necessary, you can use a dictionary.
→ _____

4 Though in Paris, he has not visited the Louvre Museum.
→ _____

C 우리말과 뜻이 같도록 빈칸에 알맞은 말을 쓰시오.

1 가능하다면, 나와 함께 가자.
→ Come with me, _____ _____.

2 호수에서 수영할 때에는 조심해야 한다.
→ You should be careful _____ _____ in the lake.

3 그녀는 비록 게을렀지만, 점심 식사 후에 산책을 하곤 했다.
→ _____ _____, she used to take a walk after lunch.

교과서
문장
응용하기

배운 문법을 이용하여 영어 문장을 써 봅시다.

1 음악을 듣는 동안, 그녀는 그림을 그렸다. (draw) 　　→ _____
2 필요하다면, 오늘 밤에 내게 전화해라. (necessary) 　→ _____

내신적중 실전문제

[01~02] 대화의 빈칸에 알맞은 것을 고르시오.

01

> **A** Does Susie want to go to the dancing party?
> **B** Of course. She _____ to go there.

① want
② does want
③ do want
④ did want
⑤ wanted

02

> **A** Do you want to come with me?
> **B** Yes, if you allow me _____.

① for
② to
③ at
④ in
⑤ about

03 대화의 빈칸에 알맞은 말을 쓰시오.

> **A** I can't sleep well because of the noise from outside.
> **B** Neither _____ I.

04 밑줄 친 부분 중 생략할 수 있는 것은?

> ① Jimmy ② can ③ play basketball today but I ④ can't ⑤ play basketball today.

05 밑줄 친 부분을 바르게 고친 것은?

> Never Susan realized that she had lost her smartphone.

① realized Susan
② did Susan realized
③ did realize Susan
④ did Susan realize
⑤ 고칠 필요 없음

06 대화의 빈칸에 알맞은 말이 바르게 짝지어진 것은?

> **A** Mom, _____ is Amy who I want to invite to my birthday party.
> **B** Look outside. Here _____ comes!

① she — she
② it — Amy
③ she — Amy
④ it — it
⑤ it — she

07 밑줄 친 부분을 강조하는 문장으로 잘못 바꿔 쓴 것은?

> ① Tim ② bought ③ some apples ④ at the market ⑤ in the morning.

① It was Tim that bought some apples at the market in the morning.
② It was bought that Tim some apples at the market in the morning.
③ It was some apples that Tim bought at the market in the morning.
④ It was at the market that Tim bought some apples in the morning.
⑤ It was in the morning that Tim bought some apples at the market.

08 빈칸에 공통으로 알맞은 말을 쓰시오.

> • She went to Seattle and so _____ Jay.
> • They didn't have lunch but I _____.

09 밑줄 친 부분 중 어법상 어색한 것을 골라 바르게 고쳐 쓰시오. (주관식)

In the doorway ① stood Helen's father. ② He did ③ got angry at her ④ when he ⑤ saw her.

_____ → _____

[10~11] 우리말과 뜻이 같도록 빈칸에 알맞은 것을 고르시오.

10

우리 중 아무도 전에 대만에 가 본 적이 없다.
→ _____ has been to Taiwan before.

① Both of us   ② None of us
③ Neither of us   ④ All of us
⑤ Not all of us

11

그는 그런 노래는 결코 들어본 적이 없다.
→ _____ such a song.

① Never did he heard
② Never has he hear
③ Never he has heard
④ Never has he heard
⑤ Never have he heard

12 부분부정을 나타내는 문장이 아닌 것은?

① Not all of them are teachers.
② Not every man can be a hero.
③ None of the foreign guests are absent.
④ Bob doesn't go swimming every Sunday.
⑤ Computer games are not necessarily harmful.

13 밑줄 친 부분이 생략 가능한 문장의 개수는?

ⓐ He returns home earlier than David does.
ⓑ Give him some money, if it is possible.
ⓒ When I was in the room, the bell rang.
ⓓ **A** Would you like to have some tea?
   B Yes, I'd like to have some tea.
ⓔ I don't exercise much now, but I used to exercise a lot.

① 1개   ② 2개   ③ 3개   ④ 4개   ⑤ 5개

14 짝지어진 두 문장의 의미가 같지 않은 것은?

① I really hope you'll be happy.
   = I do hope you'll be happy.
② Not everybody knew that news.
   = Everybody didn't know that news.
③ Plastic bags are not always recyclable.
   = Sometimes plastic bags are recyclable.
④ Sam is the very person that I was looking for.
   = It is Sam that I was looking for.
⑤ Not all women are interested in fashion.
   = Some women are interested in fashion, but others aren't.

15 강조를 나타내는 문장이 아닌 것은?

① David didn't say a word at all.
② Jessica herself cleaned her room.
③ Yumi did her homework before supper.
④ It was last night that he wrote the letter.
⑤ He guided a stranger through the woods to the very house.

16 밑줄 친 It의 쓰임이 |보기|와 다른 하나는?

> It is music that she teaches at an art school.

① It was she that likes cookies more than cakes.
② It is her puppy that Pam wants to bring to the party.
③ It was in the street that a little girl was crying.
④ It was last Saturday that his family went to the amusement park.
⑤ It is surprising that she's going to marry a movie star.

17 두 문장의 뜻이 같도록 빈칸에 알맞은 말을 쓰시오. 주관식

> I'm good at math, and Jenny is, too.
> → I'm good at math and _____ _____ _____.

18 어법상 어색한 것은?

① Kate herself didn't live in Europe.
② It was the scientist who solved the mystery.
③ Here two apples and three oranges are.
④ He's not in the least worried about the result.
⑤ Seldom did I spend time with my family.

19 밑줄 친 부분을 생략할 수 있는 것을 골라 그 기호를 쓰시오. 주관식

> ⓐ When she was young, the building was not here.
> ⓑ Although he is old, he is still strong.
> ⓒ I wanted to eat Chinese food, but Carol wanted to eat Italian food.
> ⓓ She is much taller than her brother is.
> ⓔ Do your homework later if it is possible.

20 주어진 문장을 괄호 안의 지시대로 바꿔 쓸 때 잘못 쓴 것은?

① Walking in the morning is his rule. (밑줄 친 부분을 강조할 것)
→ It is walking in the morning that is his rule.
② While walking along the street, he met Ann. (생략된 말을 넣어 다시 쓸 것)
→ While he was walking along the street, he met Ann.
③ Some stories of this book are false. (부분부정으로 바꿀 것)
→ Not every story of this book is true.
④ You can play baseball only after lunch. (밑줄 친 부분을 문장 앞으로)
→ Only after lunch you can play baseball.
⑤ Nicole doesn't like action movies, and I don't like them, either. (밑줄 친 부분을 neither를 사용해 바꿀 것)
→ Nicole doesn't like action movies, and neither do I.

서술형 평가

01 밑줄 친 부분을 문장 맨 앞으로 보내 문장을 다시 쓰시오.

> A great castle stood <u>on a hill in front of the hotel.</u>

→ _____

02 다음 문장에서 생략된 부분을 넣어 다시 쓰시오.

(1) Some people went to the park on foot and others by bus.

→ _____

_____

(2) Always stay with your parents when camping in the woods.

→ _____

_____

03 표의 내용과 일치하도록 문장을 완성하시오.

(○: 찬성 ×: 반대)

Topic	A	B	C	D
using cellphones in school	○	○	×	○

(1) _____ students are for using cellphones in school.

(2) _____ student is for using cellphones in school.

04 대화의 밑줄 친 부분을 3단어로 바꿔 쓰시오.

> **A** I can't understand Ann's unusual expressions.
> **B** <u>I can't understand Ann's unusual expressions, either.</u>

→ _____

05 밑줄 친 부분을 강조하는 문장으로 다시 쓰시오.

> Sally met the prince at the party last night.
> (1) (2)   (3)   (4)   (5)

(1) _____

(2) _____

(3) _____

(4) _____

(5) _____

[06~07] 다음 글을 읽고, 물음에 답하시오.

Despite the bad weather, ⓐ (Jack) is determined to jog today, as he does every day. He began his exercise program two months ago, and never he wants it interrupted. Not only did Jack lose weight, but ⓑ he now (feels) better than he did in years. So, even though it might look foolish, ⓒ Jack begins jogging (in the rain).

06 밑줄 친 ⓐ~ⓒ를 괄호 안의 부분을 강조하는 문장으로 다시 쓰시오.

ⓐ _____

ⓑ _____

ⓒ _____

07 어법상 어색한 부분을 찾아 바르게 고쳐 쓰시오.

_____ → _____

Memo

TAPA

ABOVE IMAGINATION

우리는 남다른 상상과 혁신으로
교육 문화의 새로운 전형을 만들어
모든 이의 행복한 경험과 성장에 기여한다

GRAMMAR TAPA
WORKBOOK

LEVEL 3

CONTENTS

CHAPTER 01	2
CHAPTER 02	8
CHAPTER 03	11
CHAPTER 04	16
CHAPTER 05	20
CHAPTER 06	24
CHAPTER 07	29
CHAPTER 08	32
CHAPTER 09	39
CHAPTER 10	44
CHAPTER 11	48
CHAPTER 12	53
ANSWER	58

01	to부정사의 명사적 용법 1
02	to부정사의 명사적 용법 2_의문사+to부정사

- **to부정사의 명사적 용법**: 문장에서 주어, 보어, 목적어로 쓰이며, 주어일 경우 「가주어 ¹ _____ ~ to부정사」 형태로 나타낸다.

To write a letter in English is difficult.
→ It is difficult to write a letter in English.
영어로 편지를 쓰는 것은 어렵다.

- **「의문사+to부정사」**: 명사처럼 쓰여 의문사에 따라 다양하게 해석하며 「의문사+주어+should+동사원형」으로 바꿔 쓸 수 있다.

You have to think about ² _____ to wear.
너는 무엇을 입어야 할지에 대해 생각해야 한다.

I don't know how to drive a bus.
→ I don't know how ³ _____ _____ drive a bus. 나는 버스를 운전하는 방법을 모른다.

03	**to부정사의 형용사적 용법**

- **명사 수식**: '~할', '~하는'의 의미로 to부정사 앞에 오는 (대)명사를 수식한다. 또한 수식하는 (대)명사가 전치사의 목적어인 경우에는 전치사를 반드시 써야 한다.

I have a lot of friends to advise me.
나는 나에게 충고해 줄 친구들이 많다.

The old man doesn't have a house to live ⁴ _____.
그 노인은 살 집이 없다.

- **be to 용법**: 「be동사+to부정사」 형태이다.

예정 (~할 예정이다)	She is to come at seven. 그녀는 7시에 올 예정이다.
의무 (~해야 한다)	You are to study English. 너는 영어를 공부해야 한다.
가능 (~할 수 있다)	Stars are to be seen at night. 별은 밤에 목격될 수 있다.
운명 (~할 운명이다)	He was not to stay with her. 그는 그녀와 함께 머무를 운명이 아니었다.
의지 (~하려고 하다)	If you are to succeed, you must work hard. 네가 성공하려고 한다면, 열심히 일해야 한다.

04	**to부정사의 부사적 용법**

목적 (~하기 위해)	She came home to take a rest. 그녀는 휴식을 취하기 위해 집으로 왔다.
결과 (~해서 …하다)	Grace grew up to be a movie director. Grace는 자라서 영화감독이 되었다.
원인 (~해서, ~하게 되어)	I was surprised to hear the news. 나는 그 소식을 듣고 놀랐다.
형용사 수식 (~하기에)	The explanation in this book is easy to understand. 이 책의 설명은 이해하기 쉽다.
조건 (~한다면)	He would be delighted to see you. 그가 너를 본다면 기뻐할 것이다.
근거 (~하다니, ~하는 것을 보니)	The man must be rich to have that car. 그 남자는 저 차를 갖고 있는 것을 보니 부자임이 틀림없다.

cf. 「~, only/never+to부정사」는 ⁵ _____의 의미를 나타낸다.
I rushed to the bus stop, only to miss the bus.
나는 버스 정류장까지 뛰었으나 결국 그 버스를 놓쳤다.

05	**too ~ to부정사 / enough+to부정사**

- 「**too+형용사(부사)+to부정사**」: '너무 ~해서 ⁶ _____'
= 「so+형용사(부사)+that+주어+⁷ _____」

Alex was too sick to get asleep.
Alex는 너무 아파서 잠을 잘 수 없었다.
→ Alex was so sick that he couldn't get asleep.

- 「**형용사(부사)+enough+to부정사**」: '~할 만큼 ⁸ _____'
= 「so+형용사(부사)+that+주어+⁹ _____」

Julie is tall enough to reach the top shelf.
→ Julie is so tall that she can reach the top shelf.
Julie는 맨 위쪽 선반에 손이 닿을 만큼 충분히 키가 크다.

06	**to부정사의 의미상 주어**
07	**to부정사의 시제**

- **to부정사의 의미상 주어**: 일반적으로는 「¹⁰ _____+목적격」으로, 사람의 성질, 성격을 나타내는 형용사가 오면 「of+목적격」으로 쓴다.

The table is too heavy for him to move.
그 탁자는 그가 옮기기에는 너무 무겁다.

It was very stupid ¹¹ _____ you to leave the change. 잔돈을 두고 가다니 너는 매우 어리석었다.

» 정답 p.58

■ **to부정사의 시제**: 주절의 시제와 동일할 경우에는 「to+동사원형」으로, 주절의 시제보다 앞설 경우에는 「to have+과거분사」로 쓴다.
It seems that she is a doctor. 그녀는 의사인 것처럼 보인다.
→ She seems to ¹² _____ a doctor.
It appears that he was rich before.
→ He appears to ¹³ _____ _____ rich before.
그는 전에 부유했던 것 같다.

She wanted to go to the concert, but Peter told her not to (go to the concert).
그녀는 콘서트에 가고 싶었지만, Peter는 그녀에게 가지 말라고 했다.

08 원형부정사   09 대부정사

■ **원형부정사**: 사역동사(make, have, let)와 지각동사(see, watch, hear, smell, taste, feel)의 목적격보어로 쓰인다.
The police officer made Kelly ¹⁴ _____ her bag.
경찰관은 Kelly에게 그녀의 가방을 열게 했다.
I heard a dog ¹⁵ _____ at night.
나는 개가 밤에 짖는 것을 들었다.
cf. 동작이 진행 중임을 나타낼 때 지각동사의 목적격보어로 원형부정사 대신 현재분사를 쓴다.
I heard a dog barking at night.
나는 개가 밤에 짖고 있는 것을 들었다.
■ **대부정사**: 앞에 나온 동사의 반복을 피하기 위하여 반복되는 부분을 생략하고 to부정사의 ¹⁶ _____ 만 쓰는 형태이다.

10 독립부정사

■ 독립된 의미를 갖고 문장 전체를 수식하는 to부정사를 말한다.

to be frank(honest) with you	솔직히 말하면
to make matters worse	설상가상으로
to tell the truth	17 _____
that is to say	즉, 다시 말하면
not to mention	~은 말할 것도 없이
18 _____ _____ _____	확실히
to begin with	우선, 먼저
19 _____ _____ _____	말하자면
strange to say	이상한 말이지만
20 _____ _____ _____	말할 필요도 없이

FOCUS 01 to부정사의 명사적 용법 1

1 괄호 안에서 알맞은 것을 고르시오.
(1) (Study / To study) for the test was hard.
(2) (This / It) is not easy to be a famous actress.
(3) The important thing is (to solve / solved) the problem for yourself.

2 우리말과 뜻이 같도록 빈칸에 알맞은 말을 쓰시오.
(1) 그는 영어 이야기책을 읽기를 원한다.
→ He wants _____ _____ an English storybook.
(2) 나의 친구들과 여행하는 것은 매우 재미있다.
→ _____ is very interesting _____ _____ with my friends.
(3) 내 목표는 노래 대회에서 우승하는 것이다.
→ My goal is _____ _____ the singing contest.

3 괄호 안의 말을 바르게 배열하여 문장을 완성하시오.
(1) My dream _____.
(to, a, be, is, photographer)
(2) She decides _____.
(prepare, party, the, to, not)
(3) I hope _____.
(to, friends, with, be, you)

1 빈칸에 들어갈 말을 | 보기 |에서 골라 괄호 안의 말을 이용하여 알맞은 형태로 쓰시오.

| 보기 |
| what   how   when |

(1) Let's decide _____ _____ _____,
   today or tomorrow. (leave)
(2) She is not sure _____ _____ _____
   after graduation. (do)
(3) You should learn _____ _____ _____
   soccer. (play)

2 우리말과 뜻이 같도록 빈칸에 알맞은 말을 쓰시오.

(1) 그녀는 언제 자야 할지 몰랐다.
   → She didn't know _____.
(2) 그는 책을 어디에 두어야 할지 모른다.
   → He is not sure _____ _____ _____
   the book.
(3) 나는 무엇을 입어야 할지 결정을 할 수 없다.
   → I can't decide _____.

3 괄호 안의 말을 바르게 배열하여 문장을 완성하시오.

(1) I wonder _____.
   (to, dinner, to, invite, who)
(2) He didn't know _____.
   (to, get, where, off)

4 두 문장의 뜻이 같도록 빈칸에 알맞은 말을 쓰시오.

(1) She doesn't tell me what to study.
   → She doesn't tell me _____.
(2) I don't know how to apologize to you.
   → I don't know _____.

1 빈칸에 들어갈 말을 | 보기 |에서 골라 알맞은 형태로 쓰시오.

| 보기 |
| eat   visit   talk   do |

(1) He knows some places _____ in Seoul.
(2) She has a lot of homework _____ today.
(3) I need a fork _____ with.
(4) We have a big issue _____ about.

2 우리말과 뜻이 같도록 빈칸에 알맞은 말을 쓰시오.

(1) 그녀는 3년 후에 그녀의 나라로 돌아갈 것이다.
   → She _____ _____ _____ back to
   her country in 3 years.
(2) 그의 스마트폰은 찾을 수 없었다.
   → His smartphone _____ _____
   _____ _____ found.
(3) Tom은 왕이 될 운명이다.
   → Tom _____ _____ _____ a king.

3 괄호 안의 말을 바르게 배열하여 문장을 완성하시오.

(1) He has _____.
   (friends, to, no, to, talk)
(2) You don't have _____.
   (time, to, enough, do, it)
(3) _____ there on time,
   we had better hurry. (are, get, to, we, if)

4 어법상 어색한 부분을 찾아 고쳐 쓰시오.

(1) Brian wants something to drinking.
   _____ → _____
(2) She has a baby to take care.
   _____ → _____
(3) I don't have many books reading.
   _____ → _____

FOCUS 04 to부정사의 부사적 용법

1 빈칸에 들어갈 말을 |보기|에서 골라 알맞은 형태로 쓰시오.

| 보기 |
| ask   borrow   read |

(1) She cannot be rich _____ for some money.

(2) _____ his letter, you can understand him.

(3) She went to the library _____ some books.

2 다음 문장을 밑줄 친 부분에 유의하여 바르게 해석하시오.

(1) I'm glad to see you again.

→ _____

(2) He grew up to be an English teacher.

→ _____

(3) Mary went to Paris to study art.

→ _____

3 두 문장을 to부정사를 이용하여 한 문장으로 쓰시오.

(1) He is a thief. He stole a ring.

→ _____

(2) He was sad. He heard the bad news.

→ _____

4 우리말과 뜻이 같도록 빈칸에 알맞은 말을 쓰시오.

(1) 나는 일기를 쓰기 위해서 컴퓨터를 사용했다.

→ I used the computer _____.

(2) 그녀는 그 게임에 져서 실망했다.

→ She was disappointed _____.

FOCUS 05 too ~ to부정사 / enough +to부정사

1 괄호 안에서 알맞은 것을 고르시오.

(1) She was (so / too) hungry to run.

(2) He is (good enough / enough good) to be a leader.

(3) I am (so / too) strong that I can lift that heavy box.

2 괄호 안의 말을 바르게 배열하여 문장을 완성하시오.

(1) The book is _____.
(difficult, to, too, understand)

(2) She is _____.
(married, old, to, get, enough)

(3) The gloves were _____ them on. (small, that, couldn't, so, put, I)

3 우리말과 뜻이 같도록 빈칸에 알맞은 말을 쓰시오.

(1) 그는 너무 피곤해서 외출을 할 수 없었다.

→ He was _____ _____ to go out.

(2) Alice는 모델이 될 만큼 충분히 아름답다.

→ Alice is beautiful _____ _____ _____ a model.

(3) 너무 어두워서 나는 어떤 것도 볼 수 없었다.

→ It was _____ _____ that I _____ see anything.

4 두 문장의 뜻이 같도록 빈칸에 알맞은 말을 쓰시오.

(1) My sister is too young to ride a bike.

→ My sister is _____ _____ can't ride a bike.

(2) He was so rich that he could buy the car.

→ He was rich _____ the car.

1 괄호 안에서 알맞은 것을 고르시오.

(1) It is easy (of / for) him to learn English.

(2) It is kind (of / for) her to help the old man.

(3) It was foolish (of / for) you to waste time.

2 어법상 어색한 부분을 찾아 고쳐 쓰시오.

(1) It is difficult of me to lose weight.

_____ → _____

(2) It was cruel for him to beat the dog.

_____ → _____

(3) It was very nice for you to clean the blackboard.

_____ → _____

3 괄호 안의 말을 이용하여 빈칸에 알맞은 말을 쓰시오.

(1) It was foolish _____ _____ to give up the chance. (you)

(2) It is careless _____ _____ to lose his bag. (he)

(3) It is dangerous _____ _____ to play soccer on the street. (she)

4 우리말과 뜻이 같도록 빈칸에 알맞은 말을 쓰시오.

(1) 그가 밖에 나가는 것은 불가능하다.

→ It is impossible _____ _____ _____ outside.

(2) 내가 공부를 하는 것은 중요하다.

→ It is important _____ _____ _____ _____.

(3) 나의 집을 방문하다니 너는 정말 친절하다.

→ It is very nice _____ _____ _____ my house.

1 두 문장의 뜻이 같도록 빈칸에 알맞은 말을 쓰시오.

(1) It seemed that he was tall.

→ He seemed _____ _____ tall.

(2) You seem to be satisfied now.

→ It _____ that _____ _____ _____ satisfied now.

(3) He appears to have been happy.

→ It appears _____ _____ _____ happy.

2 빈칸에 괄호 안의 말을 알맞은 형태로 쓰시오.

(1) He seems _____ _____ sick now. (be)

(2) She seemed _____ _____ many friends to help her. (have)

(3) He seems _____ _____ _____ handsome when young. (be)

3 우리말과 뜻이 같도록 괄호 안의 말을 이용하여 문장을 완성하시오.

(1) 너는 이상한 꿈을 꿨던 것처럼 보인다. (have)

→ You seem _____ _____ a strange dream.

(2) 그는 그녀를 좋아하는 것처럼 보인다. (like)

→ He seems _____ _____ her.

1 괄호 안에서 알맞은 것을 고르시오.

(1) He saw her (play / to play) the piano.

(2) I helped my brother (cleaning / to clean) the room.

(3) He made me (pick / to pick) up the ball.

2 우리말과 뜻이 같도록 빈칸에 알맞은 말을 쓰시오.

(1) 네가 생각하고 있는 것을 알려줘.
   → Let me _____ what you are thinking.
(2) 아이들이 너무 많은 패스트푸드를 먹게 하지 마라.
   → Don't make the children _____ too much fast food.
(3) 나는 그들이 강에서 수영하는 것을 지켜보았다.
   → I watched them _____ in the river.

3 밑줄 친 부분을 어법상 바르게 고쳐 쓰시오.

(1) I had my son cleaning the bathroom.
   _____
(2) Funny stories make her to laugh.
   _____
(3) I felt something came to me. _____
(4) She heard him sang yesterday. _____

FOCUS 09 대부정사

1 생략할 수 있는 부분을 찾아 밑줄을 그으시오.

(1) You don't have to wear the cap if you don't want to wear the cap.
(2) She wanted to visit Rome, and she is going to visit Rome.
(3) You may read the book if you want to read the book.

2 밑줄 친 to 뒤에 생략된 말을 쓰시오.

(1) I didn't mean to, but I made her cry.
   → _____
(2) He can apply for the job if he wants to.
   → _____
(3) I will help her if she wants me to.
   → _____

3 다음 괄호 안의 말을 바르게 배열하여 문장을 완성하시오.

(1) Susan wanted to finish her report tonight, but _____.
   (to, wasn't, she, able)
(2) You can make your friend a dress _____
   _____. (you, to, want, if)

FOCUS 10 독립부정사

1 빈칸에 알맞은 말을 | 보기 |에서 골라 쓰시오.

보기
   to say   matters worse   begin with

(1) To _____, smoking is not good for your health.
(2) Strange _____, I have had the same dream for three nights.
(3) To make _____, the wind began to blow hard.

2 우리말과 뜻이 같도록 빈칸에 알맞은 말을 쓰시오.

(1) 솔직히 말하면, 그는 아주 잘생겼다.
   → To be _____ _____ _____, he is very handsome.
(2) 사실대로 말하면, 나는 아무것도 기억하지 못한다.
   → To _____ _____ _____, I can't remember anything.
(3) 다시 말해서, 그녀는 해고되었다.
   → _____ _____ _____ _____, she was fired.

3 다음 문장의 밑줄 친 부분을 바르게 해석하시오.

(1) To be sure, this story is interesting.
   _____
(2) To be honest with you, I've been here before. _____
(3) He's rich and not to mention, he's diligent, too. _____

4 괄호 안의 말을 이용하여 빈칸에 알맞은 말을 쓰시오. (독립부정사 형태로 쓸 것)

(1) She is, _____, a princess to me. (speak)
(2) _____, we are winning. (needless)

» 정답 pp.58~59

11 동명사의 쓰임

- 주어: 단수 취급하며 to부정사로 바꿔 쓸 수 있다.
  Going to parties is fun. 파티에 가는 것은 재미있다.
  → ¹_____ _____ to parties is fun.
- 보어: be동사 뒤에 오며 to부정사로 바꿔 쓸 수 있다.
  My job is teaching English.
  → My job is to teach English.
  나의 직업은 영어를 가르치는 것이다.
- 목적어: 동사나 전치사의 목적어로 쓰인다.
  I don't mind ²_____ up early.
  나는 일찍 일어나는 것을 개의치 않는다.
  She is afraid of making mistakes.
  그녀는 실수하는 것을 두려워한다.

12 동명사의 의미상 주어

- 문장의 주어와 일치하지 않을 때: 동명사 앞에 소유격 형태로 의미상의 주어를 쓴다.
  I am upset at ³_____ breaking the rule.
  나는 그가 규칙을 위반한 것에 대해 화가 난다.
  cf. 구어체에서는 목적격으로 쓰기도 한다.
- 문장의 주어나 목적어와 같거나 일반인일 때: 의미상의 주어는 생략한다.
  Jacob doesn't mind spending money.
  Jacob은 돈 쓰는 것을 꺼리지 않는다.

13 동명사와 현재분사

	기능	의미
동명사	용도, 목적(명사 역할)	~하는 것
현재분사	동작, 상태(형용사 역할)	~하고 있는

a sleeping bag 침낭 〈⁴_____〉
a sleeping baby 자고 있는 아기 〈⁵_____〉
Learning a foreign language is too difficult. 〈동명사〉
외국어를 배우는 것은 너무 어렵다.
He is learning a foreign language. 〈현재분사〉
그는 외국어를 배우고 있는 중이다.

14 동명사와 to부정사를 목적어로 쓰는 동사

동명사	enjoy, finish, keep, mind, avoid 등
to부정사	want, wish, hope, expect, promise 등
동명사 / to부정사	begin, start, hate, love, like, continue 등

I enjoyed ⁶_____ the fashion magazine.
나는 그 패션 잡지 읽는 것을 즐겼다.
Lily wishes ⁷_____ be(become) the queen at the party. Lily는 그 파티에서 여왕이 되기를 희망한다.
He continued ⁸_____ TV. 그는 TV 보기를 계속했다.

- 목적어의 형태에 따라 의미가 다른 동사

remember forget	+동명사	(과거에) ~했던 것을 기억하다/잊다
	+to부정사	(미래에) ~할 것을 기억하다/잊다
try	+동명사	⁹_____
	+to부정사	¹⁰_____
regret	+동명사	~했던 것을 후회하다
	+to부정사	¹¹_____

15 동명사의 관용 표현

on(upon) -ing	¹²_____
be busy -ing	~하느라 바쁘다
look forward to -ing	~하기를 기대하다
spend (on) -ing	(시간·돈을) ~하는 데 쓰다
cannot ¹³_____ -ing	~하지 않을 수 없다
feel like -ing	¹⁴_____
be ¹⁵_____ -ing	~할 가치가 있다
be used to -ing	¹⁶_____
have trouble -ing	~하는 데 어려움을 겪다
keep(prevent) ~ from -ing	~가 …하지 못하게 하다
¹⁷_____ is no -ing	~하는 것은 불가능하다
It's no use -ing	¹⁸_____

FOCUS 11 동명사의 쓰임

1 괄호 안에서 알맞은 것을 고르시오.

(1) (Become / Becoming) a lawyer is very hard.

(2) My problem is (eaten / eating) too much.

(3) Is your hobby (takes / taking) pictures of flowers?

(4) He is proud of (win / winning) the speech contest.

2 우리말과 뜻이 같도록 빈칸에 알맞은 말을 쓰시오.

(1) 나는 잡지를 읽는 것이 싫증난다.

→ I'm tired of _____ magazines.

(2) 걷는 것은 건강에 좋다.

→ _____ is good for health.

(3) Jenny가 가장 하기 좋아하는 것은 인터넷 검색이다.

→ Jenny's favorite thing to do is _____ the Internet.

3 어법상 어색한 부분을 찾아 고쳐 쓰시오.

(1) I don't mind to wear the old dress.

_____ → _____

(2) Go on holiday always makes me happy.

_____ → _____

(3) Having not my camera with me is my mistake.

_____ → _____

FOCUS 12 동명사의 의미상 주어

1 괄호 안에서 알맞은 것을 <u>모두</u> 고르시오.

(1) I'm sure of (he / his) failing in the exam.

(2) He doesn't like (I / my) singing songs at night.

(3) She minds (Tom / Tom's) leaving home.

2 괄호 안의 말을 바르게 배열하여 문장을 완성하시오.

(1) He is angry _____.

(him, her, about, ignoring)

(2) I'm afraid _____.

(of, late, being, her)

(3) She _____ her what to do. (like, doesn't, ordering, his)

3 다음 문장을 동명사를 이용한 문장으로 바꿀 때 빈칸에 알맞은 말을 쓰시오.

(1) I remembered that you waved to us.

→ I remembered _____.

(2) She was proud that he won first prize.

→ She was proud of _____.

FOCUS 13 동명사와 현재분사

1 밑줄 친 부분이 동명사인지, 현재분사인지 쓰시오.

(1) The <u>driving</u> man in this picture is my uncle.

_____

(2) She is talking to him in the <u>living</u> room.

_____

(3) The baby was <u>crying</u> when she entered the room. _____

(4) This <u>dining</u> room is very cozy. _____

2 우리말과 뜻이 같도록 빈칸에 알맞은 말을 쓰시오.

(1) 우리는 피곤할 때 수면실에서 잘 수 있다.

→ We can sleep in the _____ room when we are tired.

(2) 그가 가장 좋아하는 취미 중 하나는 피자를 만드는 것이다.

→ One of his favorite hobbies is _____ pizza.

1 괄호 안에서 알맞은 것을 고르시오.

(1) I finished (to have / having) a rest in the park.

(2) She hopes (to travel / traveling) in Italy.

(3) He agreed (to play / playing) the game with them.

(4) Would you mind (to wait / waiting) for a minute?

2 빈칸에 들어갈 말을 |보기|에서 골라 알맞은 형태로 쓰시오.

┌─ 보기 ─────────────────────────┐
  play   leave   take   dance
└─────────────────────────────────┘

(1) We decided _____ for Seoul.

(2) Did he keep _____ tennis for an hour?

(3) They enjoyed _____ on the stage.

(4) Tom wants _____ a taxi.

3 우리말과 뜻이 같도록 빈칸에 알맞은 말을 쓰시오.

(1) 그녀는 시험 삼아 소파를 움직이려고 해 보았다.

→ She _____ _____ the sofa.

(2) 그는 너를 그 축제에서 본 것을 기억했다.

→ He _____ _____ you at the festival.

(3) 나는 그 편지를 부칠 것을 잊었다.

→ I _____ _____ _____ the letter.

4 어법상 어색한 부분을 찾아 고쳐 쓰시오.

(1) The boys gave up to play baseball.

_____ → _____

(2) Linda expects studying abroad.

_____ → _____

(3) He agreed not selling his house.

_____ → _____

(4) Why do you avoid to answer my questions?

_____ → _____

1 괄호 안에서 알맞은 것을 고르시오.

(1) It is no use (to cry / crying) over spilt milk.

(2) There is no (avoid / avoiding) a storm.

(3) How about (go / going) out for a walk?

2 빈칸에 들어갈 말을 |보기|에서 골라 알맞은 형태로 쓰시오.

┌─ 보기 ─────────────────────────┐
  join   eat   read
└─────────────────────────────────┘

(1) Do you feel like _____ a movie club?

(2) This novel is worth _____ .

(3) I'm used to _____ spicy food.

3 괄호 안의 말을 바르게 배열하여 문장을 완성하시오.

(1) They _____ for Christmas.
(busy, presents, buying, are)

(2) These worries _____ .
(her, from, kept, sleeping)

(3) I _____ on weekends.
(going, to, am, used, hiking)

4 우리말과 뜻이 같도록 괄호 안의 말을 이용하여 문장을 완성하시오.

(1) 그녀는 너와 사랑에 빠지지 않을 수 없다. (help, fall)

→ _____ in love with you.

(2) 그 파티에 도착하자마자 그는 그녀와 말하기 시작했다.
(on, arrive at)

→ _____ , he began to talk to her.

(3) 나는 너를 곧 방문하기를 고대하고 있다.
(look forward, visit)

→ I'm _____ soon.

» 정답 pp.59~60

16 분사의 역할

- **한정적 용법**: 명사를 꾸며주는 역할을 하며, 분사가 다른 수식어구와 함께 쓰이면 명사의 뒤에서 수식한다.

He has a hidden card. 그는 숨겨진 카드를 갖고 있다.

The girl ¹_____ on a bench is my sister.
벤치에 앉아 있는 그 소녀는 내 여동생이다.

- **서술적 용법**: 문장에서 주격보어 또는 목적격보어 역할을 한다.

You looked excited today. 〈주격보어〉
너는 오늘 흥분되어 보였다.

I saw the moon rising in the sky. 〈목적격보어〉
나는 하늘에서 달이 떠오르고 있는 것을 보았다.

- **감정을 나타내는 분사**: '~한 감정을 느끼게 하는'의 능동 의미일 때는 ²_____, '~한 감정을 느끼는'의 수동 의미일 때는 과거분사를 쓴다.

The game was ³_____. 그 경기는 신이 났다.

I was ⁴_____. 나는 신이 났다.

17 분사구문

- **분사구문 만드는 법**

1. 부사절의 주어가 주절의 주어와 같으면 접속사와 주어를 생략한다.
   As he works at the airport, he can get a free airline ticket.
2. 동사를 「⁵_____ + _____」 형태로 바꾼다.
   Working at the airport, he can get a free airline ticket.
3. 부정은 분사 앞에 not(never)을 쓴다.
   Not working at the airport, he can't get a free airline ticket.
   그는 공항에서 일하지 않기 때문에 무료 비행기 표를 얻을 수 없다.

18 분사구문의 의미 1_시간, 이유

19 분사구문의 의미 2_조건, 양보

- **시간**

While I was walking down the street, I met my homeroom teacher. → Walking down the street, I met my homeroom teacher.
길을 걷는 동안에 나는 내 담임 선생님을 만났다.

- **이유**

Since he didn't feel well, he stayed in bed.

→ ⁶_____ feeling well, he stayed in bed.
그는 몸이 좋지 않으므로 침대에 머물렀다.

- **조건**

If I find Jenny's address, I'll send her an invitation card. → Finding Jenny's address, I'll send her an invitation card. 내가 Jenny의 주소를 찾게 되면 나는 그녀에게 초대장을 보낼 것이다.

- **양보**

Although I live next to his house, I don't know him well. → Living next to his house, I don't know him well. 비록 그의 옆집에 살지만 나는 그를 잘 모른다.

20 분사구문의 의미 3_동시동작, 연속상황

- **동시동작**

As(While) she was looking at me, she stood by the gate. → Looking at me, she stood by the gate.
그녀는 나를 보면서 문 옆에 서 있었다.

- **연속상황**

She studied very hard and passed the exam successfully.

→ She studied very hard, ⁷_____ the exam successfully. 그녀는 매우 열심히 공부했고 성공적으로 시험에 통과했다.

21 완료형 분사구문

22 being, having been의 생략

- **완료형 분사구문**: 부사구의 시제가 주절의 시제보다 앞설 경우 「⁸_____ +과거분사」의 형태로 쓰며, 수동태의 의미인 경우에는 「having ⁹_____ +과거분사」로 쓴다.

Although he had heard the truth about the accident, he still didn't believe it.

→ ¹⁰_____ heard the truth about the accident, he still didn't believe it.
그 사고에 대한 진실을 들었음에도 불구하고 그는 여전히 그것을 믿지 않았다.

- 분사구문의 맨 처음에 나오는 being이나 having been은 생략 가능하다.

(Being) Left alone, she began to listen to music.
그녀는 홀로 남겨졌을 때 음악을 듣기 시작했다.

» 정답 pp.59~60

23 독립분사구문, 비인칭 독립분사구문

- **독립분사구문**: 분사구문의 주어가 주절의 주어와 다를 때 분사구문의 ¹¹_____를 생략하지 않는다.

  As the day was fine, we decided to go swimming.

  → The day being fine, we decided to go swimming.

  날이 좋았으므로 우리는 수영하러 가기로 결정했다.

- **비인칭 독립분사구문**: 주어를 생략하고 관용적으로 쓰는 표현이다.

strictly speaking	엄밀히 말해서	considering	~을 고려하면
generally speaking	일반적으로 말해서	judging from	~로 판단하건대
¹²_____ speaking	솔직히 말해서	speaking of	¹³_____

24 with+명사+분사

- '~인 채로, ~한 상태로'의 의미로, 명사와 분사의 관계가 능동이면 ¹⁴_____, 수동이면 ¹⁵_____를 쓴다.

  Mina came into the room, and everyone stared at her.

  → Mina came into the room with everyone ¹⁶_____ at her.

  미나는 모든 사람들이 주시하는 가운데, 그 방으로 들어왔다.

  He stood there, and his eyes were closed.

  → He stood there with his eyes closed.

  그는 눈을 감은 채 거기에 서 있었다.

FOCUS 16 분사의 역할

1 밑줄 친 부분을 어법상 바르게 고쳐 쓰시오.

(1) Her bag was <u>steal</u>.

→ _____

(2) James is <u>play</u> basketball.

→ _____

(3) I heard my name <u>call</u>.

→ _____

(4) There is a <u>roll</u> ball.

→ _____

2 우리말과 뜻이 같도록 괄호 안의 말을 이용하여 문장을 완성하시오.

(1) 나는 지금 매우 피곤하다. (tire)

→ I am so _____ now.

(2) 분홍색 스웨터를 입은 그 소녀는 내 여동생이다. (wear)

→ The girl _____ a pink sweater is my sister.

(3) 나는 구운 감자를 먹고 싶다. (bake)

→ I'd like to have _____ potatoes.

(4) 잠자는 사자를 깨우지 마라. (sleep)

→ Don't wake up the _____ lion.

3 빈칸에 들어갈 말을 | 보기 |에서 골라 알맞은 형태로 쓰시오.

| 보기 |
| make   paint   break   run |

(1) He is _____ her portrait.

(2) The man _____ in the park is my father.

(3) She found a _____ vase in the room.

(4) I bought a camera _____ in Korea.

4 어법상 어색한 부분을 찾아 고쳐 쓰시오.

(1) Who are those girls wait outside?

_____ → _____

(2) Today was a tired day.

_____ → _____

(3) He always made the students boring.

_____ → _____

(4) The danced woman is my mother.

_____ → _____

FOCUS 17 분사구문

1 괄호 안에서 알맞은 것을 고르시오.

(1) (Entered / Entering) the room, she saw the baby crying.

(2) Not (have / having) money, I can't buy the jacket.

(3) (Walking / To walk) along the beach, we found a strange stone.

2 괄호 안의 말을 빈칸에 알맞은 형태로 쓰시오.

(1) _____ this bus, she will get to the market. (take)

(2) _____ hard, you will lose weight. (swim)

(3) _____ the machine, we can save time. (use)

(4) _____ sick, I couldn't go to the party. (be)

3 어법상 어색한 부분을 찾아 고쳐 쓰시오.

(1) Felt tired, I keep on working.

_____ → _____

(2) Play football, he hurt his leg.

_____ → _____

(3) She does her homework listened to music.

_____ → _____

4 밑줄 친 부분을 분사구문으로 바꿔 쓰시오.

(1) If you leave now, you can get to the train station on time.

→ _____, you can get to the train station on time.

(2) Because Brian didn't know what to do, he asked her for help.

→ _____, Brian asked her for help.

(3) As I saw that building, I was excited.

→ _____, I was excited.

FOCUS 18 분사구문의 의미 1_시간, 이유

1 괄호 안의 말을 바르게 배열하여 문장을 완성하시오.

(1) _____, I could open the door. (forgetting, the, not, password)

(2) _____, we couldn't study any more. (tired, very, being)

(3) _____, she ran away. (the, seeing, dog)

2 밑줄 친 부분을 분사구문으로 바꿔 쓰시오.

(1) Because he spent all of his money, he couldn't buy any food.

→ _____, he couldn't buy any food.

(2) After she watched TV, she cooked dinner.

→ _____, she cooked dinner.

3 밑줄 친 부분을 괄호 안의 접속사를 이용하여 바꿔 쓰시오.

(1) Not knowing the answer, he gave up solving the problem. (since)

→ _____, he gave up solving the problem.

(2) Hearing the news, I jumped with joy. (when)

→ _____, I jumped with joy.

FOCUS 19 분사구문의 의미 2_조건, 양보

1 두 문장의 뜻이 같도록 빈칸에 알맞은 말을 쓰시오.

(1) Taking this subway, you will get to the theater.

→ _____ _____ _____ this subway, you will get to the theater.

(2) Being very sick, he does his homework.

→ _____ _____ _____ very sick, he does his homework.

2 우리말과 뜻이 같도록 빈칸에 알맞은 분사구문을 쓰시오.

(1) 이 상자를 열면, 너는 엄마에게 혼날 것이다.

→ _____, you will be scolded by your mom.

(2) 그녀는 비록 어리지만, 강하고 용감하다.

→ _____, she is strong and brave.

FOCUS 20 분사구문의 의미 3_동시동작, 연속상황

1 우리말과 뜻이 같도록 빈칸에 알맞은 말을 쓰시오.

(1) 천천히 걸으면서, 그녀는 꽃을 꺾었다.

→ _____ slowly, she picked up the flower.

(2) 그는 재킷을 입고 밖으로 나갔다.

→ He put on his jacket, _____ out.

2 어법상 어색한 부분을 찾아 고쳐 쓰시오.

(1) She listened to the radio, driven a car.

_____ → _____

(2) He danced powerfully, to sing loudly.

_____ → _____

(3) Put his hat on, he said, "Good-bye."

_____ → _____

3 두 문장의 뜻이 같도록 빈칸에 알맞은 분사구문을 쓰시오.

(1) As she took a walk, she drank coffee.

→ _____, she drank coffee.

(2) A cloud appeared, and it covered the whole sky.

→ A cloud appeared, _____.

FOCUS 21 완료형 분사구문

1 괄호 안에서 알맞은 것을 고르시오.

(1) (Have found / Having found) the gold, the man went back to his home.

(2) Not (sleeping / having slept) well, he is very tired now.

2 괄호 안의 말을 이용하여 빈칸에 알맞은 말을 쓰시오.

(1) _____ quickly, it has many mistakes. (be, make)

(2) _____ my purse, I have no money. (lose)

(3) _____ my advice, Mark could do the work. (take)

3 우리말과 뜻이 같도록 빈칸에 알맞은 말을 쓰시오.

(1) 그 돈을 써버려서, 나는 그 바지를 살 수 없다.

→ _____ _____ the money, I can't buy the pants.

(2) 파티에 초대받지 못해서 나는 화가 난다.

→ _____ _____ _____ _____ to the party, I'm angry.

FOCUS 22 being, having been의 생략

1 생략할 수 있는 부분을 찾아 밑줄을 그으시오.

(1) Being interested in science, she likes her science class.

(2) Having been made of metal, the table is hard to break.

2 밑줄 친 부분을 분사구문으로 바꿔 쓰시오.

(1) Although the machine was made in a hurry, it works well.

→ _____, the machine works well.

(2) Because she was worried about the test, she couldn't sleep.

→ _____, she couldn't sleep.

3 어법상 어색한 부분을 찾아 고쳐 쓰시오.

(1) Being born in Tokyo, she knows everything about the city.

_____ → _____

(2) Being raised in America, she speaks English fluently.

_____ → _____

1 빈칸에 들어갈 말을 | 보기 |에서 골라 알맞은 형태로 쓰시오.

> 보기
>
> ask   be   set

(1) It _____ fine tomorrow, I'll go to the swimming pool.

(2) The sun having _____, he went home.

(3) I _____ for help, my friend was always there.

2 괄호 안의 말을 바르게 배열하여 문장을 완성하시오.

(1) _____, I had to swim across the river. (being, bridge, no, there)

(2) _____, I could not follow her. (teacher, the, too, speaking, fast)

3 우리말과 뜻이 같도록 빈칸에 알맞은 말을 쓰시오.

(1) 솔직히 말해서, 그 남자는 그렇게 대단한 음악가는 아니다.

→ _____ _____, the man is not such a great musician.

(2) 엄밀히 말해서, 그는 법을 어기고 있다.

→ _____ _____, he is breaking the law.

4 밑줄 친 부분을 분사구문으로 바꿔 쓰시오.

(1) While she was preparing dinner, I cleaned the room.

→ _____, I cleaned the room.

(2) When my friend asked me to join the club, I hesitated.

→ _____, I hesitated.

1 밑줄 친 부분을 바르게 고쳐 쓰시오.

(1) He was watching TV with his wife make dinner. _____

(2) They climbed up the mountain with their hands freeze. _____

2 빈칸에 들어갈 말을 | 보기 |에서 골라 알맞은 형태로 쓰시오.

> 보기
>
> run   cover   fold

(1) He came in with his shoes _____ in mud.

(2) Sally turned around with tears _____ down her cheeks.

(3) He stood there with his arms _____.

3 우리말과 뜻이 같도록 괄호 안의 말을 이용하여 문장을 완성하시오.

(1) 그녀는 눈을 감은 채로 기도를 했다. (close)
→ She prayed _____.

(2) 나는 다리를 꼰 채로 의자에 앉았다. (cross)
→ I sat on the chair _____.

(3) 그는 물이 끓고 있는 상태에서 주방을 떠났다. (boil)
→ He left the kitchen _____.

4 어법상 어색한 부분을 찾아 고쳐 쓰시오.

(1) He sat there with his legs shake.

_____ → _____

(2) I went for a walk with my dog followed me.

_____ → _____

(3) Listen to me carefully with your book closing.

_____ → _____

» 정답 p.60

25 현재완료의 쓰임과 형태

- 현재완료: 「have(has)+¹_____」의 형태로 과거의 어느 시점에서 일어난 동작이나 상태가 현재까지 영향을 미칠 때 쓴다.

부정문	「have(has)+not(never)+과거분사」
의문문	「Have(Has)+주어+과거분사 ~?」

I have ²_____ my purse. 나는 지갑을 잃어버렸다.

cf. 현재완료는 명백한 과거를 나타내는 ~ ago, just now, last ~ 등과 의문사 ³_____과는 같이 쓸 수 없다.

26 현재완료의 의미 1_완료, 결과

- ⁴_____: '막 ~했다'로 해석하며, just, already, yet 등과 함께 쓰인다.

Kevin has ⁵_____ finished his homework.
Kevin은 그의 숙제를 이미 끝냈다.

- 결과: '~했다(그 결과 지금 …하다)'로 해석한다.

cf. have gone to: '~에 가고 그 결과 지금 여기에 없다'(결과)
have been to: '~에 갔다 왔다, ~에 가본 적이 있다'(경험 또는 완료)

He has ⁶_____ to New York.
그는 뉴욕에 갔다. (그 결과 지금 그는 여기 없다.)

He has ⁷_____ to New York. 그는 뉴욕에 가본 적이 있다.

27 현재완료의 의미 2_경험, 계속

- 경험: '⁸_____'로 해석하며 ever, never, before 등과 함께 쓰인다.

Have you ever been to Japan? 너는 일본에 가본 적이 있니?

- 계속: '(계속) ~해왔다'의 의미로, ⁹_____(~ 동안)나 since (~ 이래로)처럼 기간을 나타내는 말과 함께 쓰인다.

She has lived in the house ¹⁰_____ 2008.
그녀는 2008년부터 그 집에 살고 있다.

28 현재완료진행형

- 현재완료진행형: 「have(has) ¹¹_____ +동사원형+-ing」의 형태로 과거의 어느 시점부터 현재까지 진행 중인 동작을 나타내며, '(계속) ~하고 있다, ~하는 중이다'로 해석한다.

It has been ¹²_____ for 2 weeks.
2주 동안 눈이 계속 내리고 있다.

부정문	「have(has) not been+동사원형+-ing」
의문문	「Have(Has)+주어+been+동사원형+-ing ~?」

I have not been using his computer since 5 o'clock.
나는 5시 이후로 그의 컴퓨터를 계속 사용하지 않고 있다.

Have you been using his computer since 5 o'clock?
너는 5시 이후로 그의 컴퓨터를 계속 사용하고 있니?

29 과거완료의 쓰임과 형태

- 과거완료: 「had+과거분사」의 형태로 과거의 어느 시점을 기준으로 그 이전에 일어난 동작이나 상태의 완료, 결과, 경험, 계속을 나타낸다.

When I arrived at the airport, the plane had already left. 〈완료〉 내가 공항에 도착했을 때, 비행기는 이미 떠난 뒤였다.

He had never seen a full moon until he was 10 years old. 〈경험〉 그는 10살이 될 때까지 결코 보름달을 본 적이 없었다.

- 대과거: 과거에 일어난 두 가지 일 중 먼저 일어난 일을 과거완료로 나타낸 것을 말한다.

I lost the letter that he ¹³_____ sent me.
나는 그가 내게 보냈던 편지를 잃어버렸다.

30 과거완료진행형

- 과거완료진행형: 「had been+동사원형+-ing」의 형태로 과거 어느 시점까지 동작이 계속될 때 사용하므로 '(계속) ~하고 있었다, ~하는 중이었다'로 해석한다.

When she entered the room, I ¹⁴_____ _____ _____ the piano for an hour.
그녀가 방에 들어왔을 때, 나는 한 시간 동안 피아노를 치고 있었다.

I hadn't been feeling well for a few days, so I went to see a doctor.
나는 며칠 동안 몸이 계속 좋지 않아서 진찰을 받으러 갔다.

FOCUS 25 현재완료의 쓰임과 형태

1 괄호 안의 말을 이용하여 현재완료 문장을 완성하시오.

(1) He _____ _____ there many times. (be)

(2) She _____ _____ her favorite watch. (lose)

(3) _____ you _____ your homework? (finish)

2 빈칸에 알맞은 말을 | 보기 |에서 골라 알맞은 형태로 쓰시오.

보기		
find	learn	help

(1) Jenny _____ _____ him many times since she met him.

(2) He _____ finally _____ his cap in his room.

(3) She _____ _____ Chinese for 5 years.

3 우리말과 뜻이 같도록 괄호 안의 말을 바르게 배열하시오.

(1) 너는 어떻게 지냈니? (been, have, you, how)

→ _____

(2) 보름달이 방금 언덕 위에 떴다. (the full moon, just, risen, above, has, the hill)

→ _____

4 우리말과 뜻이 같도록 괄호 안의 말을 이용하여 문장을 완성하시오.

(1) 그녀는 유럽에 가본 적이 없다. (be)

→ _____

(2) 그는 3년 동안 여기에 살고 있다. (live)

→ _____

(3) 나는 2000년 이후로 그녀를 알아왔다. (know)

→ _____

FOCUS 26 현재완료의 의미 1_완료, 결과

1 빈칸에 괄호 안의 말을 현재완료 형태로 쓰고, 완료를 나타내면 '완', 결과를 나타내면 '결'이라고 쓰시오.

(1) Jenny _____ just _____ the presentation. (finish) → _____

(2) She _____ _____ to Paris. (go)

→ _____

2 빈칸에 알맞은 말을 | 보기 |에서 골라 알맞은 형태로 쓰시오.

보기		
write	lose	eat

(1) Nick _____ not _____ the letter yet.

(2) John _____ already _____ his sandwich.

(3) I _____ _____ my smartphone and can't find it.

3 괄호 안의 말을 바르게 배열하여 문장을 완성하시오.

(1) Ann _____ without saying good-bye to us. (Canada, has, to, gone)

(2) Linda _____ in the restaurant. (her, has, left, bag)

(3) He _____. (New York, returned, to, has)

4 우리말과 뜻이 같도록 빈칸에 알맞은 말을 쓰시오.

(1) 나는 나의 반지를 찾았다. (그 결과 지금 가지고 있다.)

→ I _____.

(2) 민수는 그의 학교 과제를 막 끝냈다.

→ Minsu _____ his school project.

1 빈칸에 괄호 안의 말을 현재완료 형태로 쓰고, 경험을 나타내면 '경', 계속을 나타내면 '계'라고 쓰시오.

(1) I _____ never _____ such a funny movie before. (see) → _____

(2) How long _____ he _____ in Chicago? (live) → _____

2 괄호 안에서 알맞은 것을 고르시오.

(1) James has ridden a bike (for / since) 3 hours.

(2) She has been ill (for / since) last Saturday.

(3) He has never worked in Ulsan (before / ago).

3 우리말과 뜻이 같도록 괄호 안의 말을 배열하여 문장을 완성하시오.

(1) 그녀는 결코 학교에 가본 적이 없다.
→ She _____ school.
(to, never, has, been)

(2) 나는 그를 전에 만난 적이 있다.
→ I _____ before. (met, him, have)

4 다음 두 문장을 한 문장으로 쓸 때 빈칸에 알맞은 말을 쓰시오.

(1) He started playing the violin in 2011. He still plays the violin.
→ He _____ _____ the violin _____ 2011.

(2) I began to study Japanese 3 months ago. I still study Japanese.
→ I _____ _____ Japanese _____ 3 months.

1 괄호 안의 말을 이용하여 현재완료 진행시제 문장을 완성하시오.

(1) I _____ model cars since last week. (make)

(2) We _____ basketball for 3 hours. (play)

(3) John _____ for 2 hours. (run)

2 우리말과 뜻이 같도록 빈칸에 알맞은 말을 쓰시오.

(1) 너는 그 책을 계속 읽는 중이니?
→ _____ you _____ _____ the book?

(2) 나의 엄마는 오전 내내 쇼핑을 하는 중이다.
→ My mom _____ _____ _____ all the morning.

(3) 그녀는 3시간 동안 케이크를 만드는 중이다.
→ She _____ _____ _____ a cake for 3 hours.

3 밑줄 친 부분을 어법상 바르게 고쳐 쓰시오.

(1) He has been not doing great recently.
→ _____

(2) She has been clean her room for 2 hours.
→ _____

(3) How long have you being jogging?
→ _____

4 두 문장을 한 문장으로 쓸 때 빈칸에 알맞은 말을 쓰시오.

(1) Linda started washing the dishes. She is still washing the dishes now.
→ Linda _____ _____ _____ the dishes.

(2) It started snowing 4 hours ago. It is still snowing now.
→ It _____ _____ _____ for 4 hours.

1 괄호 안에서 알맞은 것을 고르시오.

(1) I didn't know that somebody (had stolen / has been stealing) my book.

(2) We (have cleaned / had cleaned) the house before my mom came home.

(3) When I arrived there, the plane (had taken / had taking) off.

2 빈칸에 알맞은 말을 | 보기 |에서 골라 알맞은 형태로 쓰시오.

| 보기 |
| be   send   leave |

(1) When I met him, he _____ _____ in Seoul for 5 years.

(2) She didn't know that Tom _____ already _____ the house.

(3) She opened the present which he _____ _____.

3 밑줄 친 부분을 어법상 바르게 고쳐 쓰시오.

(1) The conference has already begun when I got there.

→ _____

(2) Brian has injured his leg and couldn't play tennis.

→ _____

4 우리말과 뜻이 같도록 빈칸에 알맞은 말을 쓰시오.

(1) 나는 내 가방을 잃어버린 것을 알았다.

→ I found that I _____ _____ my bag.

(2) 그녀는 여동생이 일어나기 전에 아침을 먹었다.

→ She _____ _____ breakfast before her sister got up.

(3) 그가 모임에 갔을 때 그녀는 이미 집에 가버렸다.

→ When he got to the meeting, she _____ already _____ home.

1 괄호 안의 말을 이용하여 과거완료 진행시제 문장을 완성하시오.

(1) I _____ for 30 minutes before the subway came. (wait)

(2) She _____ him for more than 2 years. (date)

(3) My back hurt because I _____ for a long time. (stand)

2 우리말과 뜻이 같도록 빈칸에 알맞은 말을 쓰시오.

(1) 내가 교실에 들어갔을 때, 그들은 계속 싸우는 중이었다.

→ When I got into the classroom, they _____ _____ _____.

(2) 그녀는 계속 우는 중이었기 때문에 그녀의 눈은 붉었다.

→ Her eyes were red because she _____ _____ _____.

3 괄호 안의 말을 바르게 배열하여 문장을 완성하시오.

(1) _____ for 2 hours when he came? (you, been, had, staying, there)

(2) _____ for a year when we met her. (been, had, traveling, she)

4 어법상 어색한 부분을 찾아 고쳐 쓰시오.

(1) I had been studied hard for 5 hours.

_____ → _____

(2) We had been to play tennis for about an hour when it started to rain.

_____ → _____

(3) She was tired because she has been working hard.

_____ → _____

31 can, could

▪ can

능력 (~할 수 있다)	I can(¹ _____) swim in the sea. 나는 바다에서 수영을 할 수 있다.	
허락, 허가 (~해도 된다)	Can I enter this room now? 제가 지금 이 방에 들어가도 되나요?	
요청 (~해줄래?)	Can you carry the bag for me? 나를 위해 가방을 들어줄 수 있나요?	
가능성 (~일[할] 수 있다)	Anyone can make such a mistake. 누구든 그런 실수를 할 수 있다.	
부정적인 추측 (~일 리가 없다)	He can't(cannot) be an elementary school student. 그가 초등학생일 리가 없다.	

▪ could: can의 과거형 이외에 공손한 요청을 하는 경우에도 쓰인다.

A Could you tell me where the bank is?
은행이 어디 있는지 말씀해 주시겠습니까?

B Sure(Of course). / Sorry, I can't.
물론입니다.   죄송하지만, 할 수 없습니다.

32 may, might

▪ may

허락(= ² _____) (~해도 된다)	You may wear my new coat. 너는 나의 새 코트를 입어도 된다.	
불확실한 추측 (~일지도 모른다)	The gentleman may be the mayor of New York. 그 신사는 뉴욕 시장일지도 모른다.	
기원문 (바라건대 ~하소서)	May the king live long! 바라건대 왕이여 장수하소서!	

▪ might: may의 과거형으로 쓰이거나 may보다 실현 가능성이 희박한, 불확실한 추측을 나타낸다.

His excuse might be true, but I don't believe it.
그의 핑계는 어쩌면 사실일지 모르지만 나는 믿지 않는다.

33 must, have to

▪ must

강한 추측 (~임에 틀림없다)	She has been crying for an hour. She must be very sad. 그녀는 한 시간째 계속 울 고 있다. 그녀는 매우 슬픈 것이 틀림없다.

필요·의무 (~해야 한다)	Students must(³ _____ _____) follow the school rules. 학생들은 교칙을 따 라야만 한다.

▪ must와 have to의 부정형

must not: ⁴ _____ (~해서는 안 된다)	He must not cross the yellow line. 그는 그 노란색 선을 넘어가서는 안 된다.
don't have to: **불필요** (~할 필요가 없다)	You don't have to(don't need to / ⁵ _____ _____) buy a backpack. 너는 배낭을 살 필요가 없다.

34 should, ought to

▪ should, ought to: 의무나 필요와 같은 당연한 행위(~해야 한다)를 나타낸다. 부정형은 「should not / ought not to + ⁶ _____ 」이며 '~해서는 안 된다'라는 의미이다.

We should(⁷ _____ _____) keep our promises.
우리는 우리의 약속을 지켜야 한다.

▪ 제안·주장·요구·명령의 동사(suggest, insist, demand, order 등) 뒤의 that절에서는 대개 should를 생략하고 동사원형만 쓴다.

I suggested that she (should) ⁸ _____ here.
나는 그녀에게 여기 머물러 있으라고 제안했다.

35 had better, would rather

▪ had better: 충고의 의미(~하는 게 낫다, ~하는 게 좋다)로, 부정문은 「had better not + 동사원형」이다.

You had better ⁹ _____ be late.
너는 지각하지 않는 게 좋겠다.

▪ would rather: 선택의 의미(~하는 게 낫다, ~하고 싶다)로, 부정문은 「would rather not + 동사원형」이다.

I ¹⁰ _____ _____ tell him the truth.
나는 그에게 진실을 말하는 게 낫겠다.

▪ 「would rather *A* than *B*」: B 하느니 (차라리) A 하겠다

I would rather watch TV ¹¹ _____ go to a movie.
나는 영화를 보러 가느니 차라리 TV를 보겠다.

» 정답 pp.60~61

36 used to, would

- 「used to+동사원형」: 과거의 ¹² _____ 습관('~하곤 했다, 늘 ~했다')이나 상태('전에는 ~이었다')를 나타낸다.

He used to cook on Sundays. 〈습관〉
그는 일요일마다 요리를 하곤 했다.

They used to live in that house. 〈상태〉
그들은 전에는 저 집에 살았었다.

- 「would+동사원형」: 과거의 ¹³ _____ 습관('~하곤 했다')을 나타내며, 과거의 상태를 나타낼 때는 사용하지 않는다.

In summer we ¹⁴ _____ go to the seaside.
여름에 우리는 바닷가에 가곤 했다.

37 조동사+have+과거분사

¹⁵ _____ +have+과거분사 (~이었음에 틀림없다)	It ¹⁵ _____ have been impossible. 그것은 불가능한 것이었음에 틀림없다.
may(might)+have+과거분사 (어쩌면 ~했을지도 모른다)	She may(might) have been right. 그녀가 어쩌면 옳았을지도 모른다.
¹⁶ _____ +have+과거분사 (~했을 리가 없다)	Jenny ¹⁶ _____ have eaten my chocolate. Jenny가 나의 초콜릿을 먹었을 리가 없다.
should+have+과거분사 (~했어야 했는데 (못했다))	The train should have left at 8 p.m. 그 기차는 오후 8시에 ¹⁷ _____.
should not+have+과거분사 (~하지 말았어야 했는데 (했다))	You should not have seen the scene. 너는 그 장면을 보지 말았어야 했는데.

FOCUS 31 can, could

1 괄호 안에서 알맞은 것을 고르시오.

(1) (Are / Can) you show me the way to the bank?

(2) I (can / could) learn a lot about computers 2 years ago.

(3) She finished the project. She (cannot / must not) be busy now.

2 우리말과 뜻이 같도록 빈칸에 알맞은 말을 쓰시오.

(1) 그녀는 그녀의 드레스를 만들 수 있다.
→ She _____ _____ her dress.

(2) 너무 밝아서 나는 모든 것을 볼 수 있었다.
→ It was so bright that I _____ _____ everything.

(3) 그의 꿈은 실현될 수 있었을까?
→ _____ his dream _____ true?

FOCUS 32 may, might

1 우리말과 뜻이 같도록 빈칸에 알맞은 말을 쓰시오.

(1) 그 소문은 사실일지도 모른다.
→ The rumor _____ _____ true.

(2) 제가 들어가도 됩니까?
→ _____ _____ come in?

(3) 부디 사업에 성공하시기를!
→ _____ _____ _____ in your business!

2 다음 문장을 바르게 해석하시오.

(1) You may not use my computer.
→ _____

(2) He may come to my office.
→ _____

(3) Susan might fail the test.
→ _____

1 우리말과 뜻이 같도록 빈칸에 알맞은 말을 쓰시오.

(1) 그녀는 화장실을 청소해야 한다.
→ She _____ _____ _____ the bathroom.

(2) 너는 그것에 대해 더 이상 걱정할 필요가 없다.
→ You _____ _____ _____ _____ about it any more.

(3) 너는 그를 그 방에 혼자 남겨 두어서는 안 된다.
→ You _____ _____ _____ him alone in the room.

2 다음 문장을 주어진 조건에 맞게 바꿔 쓰시오. (필요한 경우, 단어의 형태를 바꿀 것)

(1) He must do his best in everything. (have to 사용)
→ _____

(2) You must keep the traffic laws. (과거시제로)
→ _____

(3) They must finish their homework. (미래시제로)
→ _____

FOCUS 34 should, ought to

1 다음 괄호 안에서 알맞은 것을 고르시오.

(1) I (should / ought) to help my mother today.

(2) You (ought to not / ought not to) tell what you have in your hand.

(3) He insisted that she (help / helps) them immediately.

2 빈칸에 should, should not 중 내용상 알맞은 말을 골라 쓰시오.

(1) You _____ run in the classroom.

(2) You _____ drink alcohol for your health.

(3) We _____ eat junk food too often.

3 우리말과 뜻이 같도록 괄호 안의 말을 이용하여 문장을 완성하시오.

(1) 우리는 운전할 때 안전벨트를 착용해야 한다. (ought, wear)
→ We _____ while driving.

(2) 내가 이 책을 너에게 돌려줘야 하니? (should, return)
→ _____ to you?

FOCUS 35 had better, would rather

1 괄호 안의 말을 바르게 배열하여 문장을 완성하시오.

(1) You _____ me.
(not, annoy, better, had)

(2) I _____ play games.
(rather, study, would, than)

(3) You _____ because the road is slippery. (down, better, slow, had)

2 어법상 어색한 부분을 찾아 고쳐 쓰시오.

(1) You had not better use his computer.
_____ → _____

(2) I would rather take a walk in the park than going fishing in the lake.
_____ → _____

3 우리말과 뜻이 같도록 빈칸에 알맞은 말을 쓰시오.

(1) 너는 지하철을 타고 학교에 가는 것이 좋겠다.
→ You _____ _____ take the subway to school.

(2) 나는 쇼핑을 가느니 차라리 집에 있겠다.
→ I _____ _____ stay home than go shopping.

(3) 너는 그 옷을 사지 않는 것이 좋겠다.
→ You _____ _____ _____ buy the clothes.

FOCUS 36 used to, would

1 빈칸에 알맞은 말을 | 보기 |에서 골라 used to를 이용하여 쓰시오.

┌─ 보기 ─────────────────────────┐
│   go   be   take   │
└────────────────────────────────┘

(1) I _____ to the river to swim, but I don't swim there now.

(2) I _____ a walk with Nick.

(3) There _____ a fence around the school.

2 어법상 <u>어색한</u> 부분을 찾아 고쳐 쓰시오.

(1) He uses to live in a small town.
_____ → _____

(2) She would to watch TV while she was lying on the sofa.
_____ → _____

(3) He would played basketball in the park.
_____ → _____

3 우리말과 뜻이 같도록 괄호 안의 말을 이용하여 문장을 완성하시오.

(1) 그는 밤새도록 공부를 하곤 했다. (would)
→ He _____ all night.

(2) Brian은 오후에 차를 마시곤 했다. (would)
→ Brian _____ in the afternoon.

(3) 저 건물은 이전에 백화점이었다. (used to)
→ That building _____ a department store.

4 두 문장의 뜻이 같도록 빈칸에 알맞은 말을 쓰시오.

(1) I traveled a lot before, but now I don't.
→ I _____ _____ _____ a lot.

(2) There was a big tree here before, but now it is gone.
→ There _____ _____ _____ a big tree here.

FOCUS 37 조동사+have+과거분사

1 괄호 안에서 알맞은 것을 고르시오.

(1) She (can / must) have done the work by herself.

(2) The guests may have already (arrived / arriving).

2 괄호 안의 말을 바르게 배열하여 문장을 완성하시오.

(1) He _____ today.
(been, have, may, busy)

(2) She _____ breakfast.
(have, cannot, skipped)

(3) The boy _____ his way because he was wandering in the street.
(lost, have, must)

3 우리말과 뜻이 같도록 괄호 안의 말을 이용하여 문장을 완성하시오.

(1) 그가 그 책을 직접 썼을 리가 없다. (write)
→ He _____ _____ _____ the book himself.

(2) 그녀는 그 영화를 보았던 것이 틀림없다. (see)
→ She _____ the movie.

4 빈칸에 알맞은 말을 | 보기 |에서 골라 괄호 안의 단어를 이용하여 과거의 일에 대한 후회를 나타내는 문장을 쓰시오.

┌─ 보기 ─────────────────────────┐
│   go   work   call   │
└────────────────────────────────┘

(1) You _____ too hard last night. (should not)

(2) I _____ _____ _____ you earlier. (should)

(3) They _____ _____ _____ to the forest last summer. (should not)

38 단순 수동태

- 수동태: 「주어+be동사+과거분사+by+목적격(행위자)」의 형태로, 행위자가 일반인이나 분명하지 않을 때 「¹ _____ + _____」은 생략할 수 있다.

Tower Bridge was built in 1894 (by them).
Tower Bridge는 1894년에 (그들에 의해) 지어졌다.

- 부정문은 be동사 뒤에 not을 붙이고, 의문문은 be동사를 문장 맨 앞에 써서 만든다.

The car was not moved by him.
그 자동차는 그에 의해 움직여지지 않았다.

² _____ the chair made by him?
그 의자는 그에 의해 만들어졌니?

39 조동사가 있는 수동태

- 「조동사+be+과거분사」의 형태로 쓴다.

The room must ³ _____ cleaned by you.
그 방은 너에 의해서 청소되어야 한다.

부정문	「조동사+not+be+과거분사」
의문문	「조동사+주어+be+과거분사~?」

This lesson may ⁴ _____ be accepted by him.
이 교훈은 그에 의해서 받아들여지지 않을지도 모른다.

Can the computer be repaired?
그 컴퓨터는 수리될 수 있나요?

40 진행·완료 시제 수동태

- 진행 시제 수동태: 「be동사+being+과거분사」의 형태로 쓴다.

They are making the movie in Hollywood.
그들은 할리우드에서 그 영화를 만들고 있다.

→ The movie is ⁵ _____ _____ (by them) in Hollywood. 그 영화는 할리우드에서 (그들에 의해) 만들어지고 있다.

- 완료 시제 수동태: 「have(has/had) been+과거분사」의 형태이다.

Steven has lost the umbrella. Steven은 그 우산을 잃어버렸다.

→ The umbrella ⁶ _____ _____ _____ by Steven.
그 우산은 Steven에 의해 잃어버려졌다.

41 4형식 문장의 수동태

- 4형식 문장은 간접·직접목적어를 각각 주어로 하는 두 가지 수동태 문장으로 바꿀 수 있는데, 직접목적어가 주어일 때에는 동사에 따라 간접목적어 앞에 전치사 ⁷ _____, _____, _____ 를 쓴다.

She gave Bill a present. 그녀는 Bill에게 선물을 주었다.

→ Bill was given a present by her.
〈간접목적어가 주어〉 Bill은 그녀에 의해 선물을 받았다.

→ A present was given ⁸ _____ Bill by her.
〈직접목적어가 주어〉 선물이 그녀에 의해 Bill에게 주어졌다.

- 동사 buy, make, write, read, sell, get 등은 직접목적어만 주어로 쓴다.

Sam makes me a chair.

→ A chair is made for me by Sam.
의자가 나를 위해 Sam에 의해 만들어졌다.

42 5형식 문장의 수동태

- 5형식 문장의 수동태: 목적어를 수동태의 주어로 하고, 목적격보어는 「be동사+과거분사」 뒤에 그대로 쓴다.

The boys painted the room blue.
그 소년들이 그 방을 파란색으로 칠했다.

→ The room was painted blue by the boys.
그 방은 그 소년들에 의해 파란색으로 칠해졌다.

Andrew asked her to leave. Andrew는 그녀에게 떠나라고 부탁했다.

→ She was asked ⁹ _____ leave by Andrew.
그녀는 Andrew에 의해 떠날 것을 부탁 받았다.

- 지각동사와 사역동사의 수동태: 목적격보어인 원형부정사를 to부정사로 바꾸어 「be동사+과거분사+to부정사」의 형태로 쓴다.

They made him go there. 그들이 그를 거기에 가게 했다.

→ He was made ¹⁰ _____ _____ there by them. 그는 그들에 의해 거기에 가게 되었다.

43 동사구의 수동태

- 「동사+전치사」, 「동사+부사」의 동사구의 문장은 동사구를 하나로 취급하여 만든다.

The boys laughed at her. 그 소년들은 그녀를 비웃었다.

→ She was laughed ¹¹ _____ by the boys.
그녀는 그 소년들에게서 비웃음을 당했다.

» 정답 pp.61~62

44 목적어로 쓰인 that절의 수동태

- 동사 think, say, believe, hope, suppose 등의 목적어로 쓰인 that절은 「It+be동사+과거분사+that ~」의 형태로 수동태를 만든다. 이때 that절의 주어를 수동태의 주어로 하고 that절의 동사를 to부정사로 바꿀 수 있다.

Everyone says that he is a liar.
모든 사람이 그가 거짓말쟁이라고 말한다.

→ It is ¹² _____ that he is a liar. 그는 거짓말쟁이라고 말해진다.
「It(가주어)+be동사+과거분사+that절(진주어)」

→ He is said ¹³ _____ be a liar.
「that절의 주어+be동사+과거분사+to부정사」

45 by 이외의 전치사를 쓰는 수동태

be interested in: ~에 관심이 있다

be caught in: (눈, 비 등을) 만나다

be covered with: ~로 덮여 있다

be worried ¹⁴ _____ : ~에 대해 걱정하다

be made ¹⁵ _____ : ~로 만들어지다 (모양만 바뀜)

be made ¹⁶ _____ : ~로 만들어지다 (성질이 바뀜)

be satisfied with: ~에 만족하다

be surprised ¹⁷ _____ : ~에 놀라다

be disappointed at: ~에 실망하다

be filled ¹⁸ _____ : ~로 가득 차 있다

be known for: ~로 유명하다

be (well) known to: ~에게 (잘) 알려져 있다

be known by: ~에 의해 알려지다

be crowded ¹⁹ _____ : ~로 붐비다

She is interested ²⁰ _____ painting.
그녀는 회화에 관심이 있다.

FOCUS 38 단순 수동태

1 우리말과 뜻이 같도록 괄호 안의 말을 이용하여 문장을 완성하시오.

(1) 교실은 학생들에 의해 매일 청소된다. (clean)
→ The classroom _____ the students every day.

(2) 그는 나에 의해 체포되었다. (arrest)
→ He _____ _____ _____ me.

2 다음 능동태 문장을 수동태 문장으로 바꿀 때 빈칸에 알맞은 말을 쓰시오.

(1) Did you make this doll?
→ Was _____ ?

(2) James didn't break this vase.
→ This vase _____ .

(3) People don't use this road very often.
→ This road _____ .

FOCUS 39 조동사가 있는 수동태

1 빈칸에 알맞은 말을 |보기|에서 골라 괄호 안의 단어를 이용하여 쓰시오.

보기		
fix	give	visit

(1) The palace _____ _____ by a lot of tourists. (will)

(2) A speech _____ _____ in front of the students by him. (may)

(3) The car _____ _____ _____ by the engineer. (can)

2 다음 능동태 문장을 수동태 문장으로 바꿔 쓰시오.

(1) She ought to wash the dishes.
→ _____

(2) We must not waste our time.
→ _____

(3) The man cannot move the heavy box.
→ _____

1 괄호 안에서 알맞은 것을 고르시오.

(1) Cookies are (being / been) baked by my mom.

(2) A car was being (driving / driven) by the man on the highway.

(3) The play isn't (been showing / being shown) by us.

2 우리말과 뜻이 같도록 괄호 안의 말을 이용하여 문장을 완성하시오.

(1) 새 다리가 그들에 의해 건설되고 있는 중이다. (build)

→ A new bridge _____ _____ _____ by them.

(2) 그 집은 지금 수리 중이다. (repair)

→ The house _____ _____ _____ now.

(3) 그녀가 들어갔을 때 방은 청소 중이었니? (clean)

→ _____ the room _____ _____ when she went in?

3 어법상 어색한 부분을 찾아 고쳐 쓰시오.

(1) The radio had being fixed in time by her.

_____ → _____

(2) The gold has been finding by the poor man.

_____ → _____

(3) Has only English be used in the classroom by his students?

_____ → _____

4 다음 능동태 문장을 수동태 문장으로 바꿔 쓰시오.

(1) The girl had already eaten the pie.

→ _____

(2) She has not brought a food basket.

→ _____

(3) Jeff has sent some flowers today.

→ _____

1 괄호 안에서 알맞은 것을 고르시오.

(1) A present was given (to / for) him by Jane.

(2) The tie was bought (to / for) my dad by my sister.

(3) A question was asked (to / of) Sally by the foreigner.

2 우리말과 뜻이 같도록 괄호 안의 말을 이용하여 문장을 완성하시오.

(1) 그 메시지는 나에 의해 그녀에게 보내졌다. (send)

→ The message _____ _____ _____ her by me.

(2) 나는 민수에게서 이 책을 받았다. (give)

→ _____ _____ _____ this book by Minsu.

3 두 문장의 뜻이 같도록 빈칸에 알맞은 말을 쓰시오.

(1) Alice asked me my secret recipe.

→ My secret recipe _____ _____ _____ by Alice.

(2) Cindy gave me a pair of jeans.

→ I _____ _____ a pair of jeans by Cindy.

(3) He bought her a beautiful bracelet.

→ A beautiful bracelet _____ _____ _____ _____ by him.

4 다음을 밑줄 친 부분을 주어로 하는 수동태 문장으로 바꿔 쓰시오.

(1) The woman gave him the car.

→ _____

(2) He made me a muffler.

→ _____

(3) Mary sent him a letter.

→ _____

1 괄호 안에서 알맞은 것을 고르시오.

(1) She was heard (to sing / sung) a song.

(2) The baby (named / was named) Tommy by his parents.

(3) I was made (study / to study) in the library by my teacher.

2 우리말과 뜻이 같도록 괄호 안의 말을 이용하여 문장을 완성하시오.

(1) 그가 창문을 깨뜨리는 것이 우리에게 목격되었다. (see, break)

→ He _____ _____ _____ _____ the window by us.

(2) 그는 친구들에 의해 Jimmy라고 불렸다. (call)

→ He _____ _____ _____ by his friends.

(3) 우리는 그녀에 의해 열심히 일하게 되었다. (make, work)

→ We _____ _____ _____ _____ hard by her.

3 괄호 안의 말을 바르게 배열하여 문장을 완성하시오.

(1) _____ the piano by him.

(was, to, heard, she, play)

(2) _____ by the muddy water.

(shoes, my, were, dirty, made)

(3) _____ by the teacher.

(called, a, he, was, genius)

4 다음 능동태 문장을 목적어를 주어로 하는 수동태 문장으로 바꿔 쓰시오.

(1) We named the dog Mini.

→ _____

(2) Susan advised him to exercise.

→ _____

(3) They made me sign the agreement.

→ _____

1 빈칸에 들어갈 말을 |보기|에서 골라 알맞은 형태로 쓰시오.

> 보기
>
> put off   look for   turn on

(1) The lights on the building were _____ _____ by him.

(2) The festival was _____ _____ by the students.

(3) The luggage was _____ _____ by my brother.

2 우리말과 뜻이 같도록 괄호 안의 말을 이용하여 문장을 완성하시오.

(1) 그 아이는 너에 의해 보살핌을 받았다. (look after)

→ The child _____ _____ _____ by you.

(2) 모든 나무들이 일꾼들에 의해 베어졌다. (cut down)

→ All the trees _____ _____ _____ by the workers.

(3) 그 여자는 그들에게 비웃음을 당했다. (laugh at)

→ The woman _____ _____ _____ by them.

3 어법상 어색한 부분을 찾아 고쳐 쓰시오.

(1) The deer was running over by a car.

_____ → _____

(2) Our teacher has looked up to by us.

_____ → _____

(3) Your son was taken good care by Judy.

_____ → _____

4 다음 능동태 문장을 수동태 문장으로 바꿔 쓰시오.

(1) His teachers spoke well of him.

→ _____

(2) The boss called off the meeting.

→ _____

FOCUS 44　목적어로 쓰인 that절의 수동태

1 우리말과 뜻이 같도록 괄호 안의 말을 이용하여 문장을 완성하시오.

(1) 흡연은 건강에 해롭다고 믿어진다. (believe)

→ It _____ _____ _____ smoking
is unhealthy.

(2) 그는 나에게 친절하다고 생각된다. (think)

→ H e _____ _____ _____ b e
kind to me.

2 어법상 어색한 부분을 찾아 고쳐 쓰시오.

(1) It is expected to being warm tomorrow.

_____ → _____

(2) Cindy is said that be good at dancing.

_____ → _____

(3) It is considering that Hawaii is the best
vacation place.

_____ → _____

3 두 문장의 뜻이 같도록 빈칸에 알맞은 말을 쓰시오.

(1) The woman is said to be a princess.

→ It _____ _____ _____ the woman
is a princess.

(2) It is believed that he is popular among kids.

→ He is _____ _____ _____ popular
among kids.

4 다음을 밑줄 친 부분을 주어로 하는 수동태 문장으로 바꿔
쓰시오.

(1) They think that the man is a millionaire.

→ _____

(2) They expected that the meeting would end
soon.

→ _____

FOCUS 45　by 이외의 전치사를 쓰는 수동태

1 빈칸에 알맞은 말을 | 보기 |에서 골라 쓰시오.

┌─ 보기 ─────────────────────────┐
　　　at　　　　　with　　　　　in
└──────────────────────────────┘

(1) We were caught _____ a shower of rain
on our way home.

(2) Their faces were covered _____ dirt.

(3) The woman was surprised _____ the
news.

2 밑줄 친 부분을 바르게 고쳐 쓰시오.

(1) The mountain is covered <u>by</u> snow.

→ _____

(2) My parents are worried <u>with</u> my grades.

→ _____

(3) These tables are made <u>with</u> wood.

→ _____

3 괄호 안의 말을 바르게 배열하여 문장을 완성하시오.

(1) They _____ all the time.
(satisfied, are, her, food, with)

(2) The garden _____.
(with, was, many, filled, flowers)

(3) He _____ in France.
(a, known, singer, is, popular, as)

4 우리말과 뜻이 같도록 빈칸에 알맞은 말을 쓰시오.

(1) 치즈는 우유로 만들어진다.

→ Cheese _____ _____ _____ milk.

(2) 너는 피아노 연주를 배우는 것에 관심이 있니?

→ _____ you _____ _____ learning
to play the piano?

(3) 그 작은 마을은 일본인들에게 잘 알려져 있다.

→ The small town _____ _____ _____
_____ Japanese.

28　Grammar TAPA

» 정답 p.62

46 원급·비교급·최상급 비교

■ 원급 비교

「as+원급+as」	~만큼 …한
「not as(so)+원급+as」	~만큼 …하지 않은

Sam is as ^{1}_____ as Brian (is).
Sam은 Brian만큼 키가 크다.
Sam is not as(^{2}_____) tall as Brian (is).
Sam은 Brian만큼 키가 크지 않다.

■ 비교급 비교: 「비교급+than」 (~보다 더 …한)
Light is ^{3}_____ than sound (is).
빛은 소리보다 더 빠르다.

■ 최상급 비교: 「the+최상급+of(in) ~」 (~ 중에서 가장 …한)
Jennifer is the prettiest girl ^{4}_____ my class.
Jennifer는 나의 반에서 가장 예쁜 소녀이다.

■ 비교급 강조: much, even, still, far, a lot 등은 비교급 앞에서 비교급을 강조하며, '훨씬'이라는 의미이다.
He looks much younger than his girlfriend.
그는 그의 여자친구보다 훨씬 더 어려 보인다.

47 as+원급+as+주어+can / 배수사를 이용한 비교

■ 「as+원급+as+주어+can」: '가능한 한 ~하게(하도록)'의 의미로, 「as+원급+as ^{5}_____」과 바꿔 쓸 수 있다.
The man tries to explain it as briefly as he can.
→ The man tries to explain it as briefly as possible.
그 남자는 가능한 한 간단하게 그것을 설명하려고 노력한다.

■ 「배수사+as+원급+as」: '~보다 몇 배 더 …한'의 의미로 「배수사+비교급+than」으로 바꿔 쓸 수 있다.
This bag is three times as big as your bag.
→ This bag is three times ^{6}_____ than your bag. 이 가방은 네 가방보다 3배 더 크다.

48 less+원급+than

■ 「less+원급+than」: '~보다 덜 …한', '~보다 …하지 않은'의 의미로 「not as(so)+원급+as」로 바꿔 쓸 수 있다.

The actress is less popular ^{7}_____ the actor.
그 여배우는 그 남자 배우보다 인기가 덜하다.
→ The actress is not as(so) popular as the actor.
그 여배우는 그 남자 배우만큼 인기 있지 않다.

49 비교급+and+비교급 / the+비교급, the+비교급

■ 「비교급+and+비교급」: '점점 더 ~한(하게)'이라는 의미이다.
My English is getting better and better.
나의 영어 실력은 점점 더 좋아지고 있다.

■ 「the+비교급, the+비교급」: '~할수록 더 …한'이라는 의미이다.
^{8}_____ _____ he grows, the weaker he becomes. 그는 나이가 들수록 더 약해진다.

50 one of the+최상급 / 원급과 비교급을 이용한 최상급

■ 「one of the+최상급+복수 명사」: '가장 ~한 것들 중 하나'라는 의미이다.
Betty is one of the most successful ^{9}_____ that I know. Betty는 내가 아는 가장 성공한 사람들 중 한 사람이다.

■ 원급이나 비교급을 이용하여 최상급의 의미를 나타낼 수 있다.
Evan is the strongest boy in the class.
Evan은 반에서 가장 힘이 센 소년이다.
→ Evan is stronger ^{10}_____ any other boy in the class. 〈비교급+than any other+단수 명사〉
Evan은 반에서 다른 어떤 소년보다도 힘이 더 세다.
→ No (other) boy in the class is ^{11}_____ than Evan. 〈No (other) ~ 비교급+than〉
반에서 어떤 소년도 Evan보다 더 힘이 세지 않다.
→ No (other) boy in the class is as strong as Evan.
〈No (other) ~ as+원급+as〉
반에서 (다른) 어떤 소년도 Evan만큼 힘이 세지 않다.

1 괄호 안에서 알맞은 것을 고르시오.

(1) She is as strong (as / than) he.

(2) Chris (not is / is not) as smart as you.

(3) He cooks as (well / better) as his wife.

2 다음 문장을 바르게 해석하시오.

(1) I can't run as fast as you.

　→ _____

(2) Busan is not as large as Seoul.

　→ _____

(3) This sofa is as cheap as that one.

　→ _____

3 우리말과 뜻이 같도록 빈칸에 알맞은 말을 쓰시오.

(1) 민수는 Brian보다 더 어리다.

　→ Minsu is _____ _____ Brian.

(2) 이것이 저것보다 더 작다.

　→ This is _____ _____ that.

(3) 이 도구는 저것보다 더 도움이 된다.

　→ This tool is _____ _____
_____ that one.

4 괄호 안의 말을 이용하여 빈칸에 알맞은 형태를 쓰시오.

(1) The trip was _____ _____ experience ever. (bad)

(2) She is _____ _____ singer in my country. (good)

(3) Jenny is _____ _____ student of the three. (smart)

1 괄호 안에서 알맞은 것을 고르시오.

(1) My room is three (time / times) as big as your room.

(2) Would you come to the school as soon as (can / possible)?

(3) This book is (twice / two) as thick as that book.

2 밑줄 친 부분을 어법상 바르게 고쳐 쓰시오.

(1) Could you read out loud so clearly as you can?

　→ _____

(2) We walked with the kid as slow as possible.

　→ _____

(3) This bridge is four times long as that one.

　→ _____

3 우리말과 뜻이 같도록 괄호 안의 말을 이용하여 문장을 완성하시오.

(1) Sandra는 나보다 무게가 두 배 더 나간다. (much)

　→ Sandra weighs _____ _____
_____ I weigh.

(2) 이 사과는 저것보다 3배 더 크다. (big)

　→ This apple is _____ _____
_____ that one.

(3) 나는 가능한 한 일찍 떠났다. (early)

　→ I left _____ _____ _____
_____.

4 두 문장의 뜻이 같도록 빈칸에 알맞은 말을 쓰시오.

(1) Please come back home as soon as possible.

　→ Please come back home _____
_____ _____ _____.

(2) He studied English as hard as he could.

　→ He studied English _____ _____
_____ _____.

FOCUS 48 less+원급+than

1 다음 빈칸에 알맞은 말을 | 보기 |에서 골라 「less+원급+than」을 이용하여 문장을 완성하시오.

┌─ 보기 ─────────────────────┐
│   new   tasty   cold   │
└──────────────────────────┘

(1) Yesterday was _____ _____ _____ today.

(2) Your cellphone is _____ _____ _____ mine.

(3) This spaghetti is _____ _____ _____ that one.

2 두 문장의 뜻이 같도록 빈칸에 알맞은 말을 쓰시오.

(1) Tim is not as tall as Jeff.
→ Tim is _____ _____ _____ Jeff.

(2) This test is not as easy as you think.
→ This test is _____ _____ _____ you think.

FOCUS 49 비교급+and+비교급 / the+비교급, the+비교급

1 괄호 안에서 알맞은 것을 고르시오.

(1) The better the weather is, the (more happy / happier) I feel.

(2) They felt more and (more / much) tired and went straight to sleep.

(3) (Better and better / More and more) animals are in danger.

2 우리말과 뜻이 같도록 괄호 안의 말을 이용하여 문장을 완성하시오.

(1) 그 대학에 들어가기가 점점 더 어려워지고 있다. (hard)
→ It's becoming _____ _____ to enter the university.

(2) 날씨가 따뜻해질수록 나는 기분이 더 좋아진다. (warm, good)
→ _____ _____ the weather is, _____ _____ I feel.

FOCUS 50 one of the+최상급 / 원급과 비교급을 이용한 최상급

1 어법상 어색한 부분을 찾아 고쳐 쓰시오.

(1) It was one of the bad movies ever made in Korea.
_____ → _____

(2) She is one of the greatest actress in the world.
_____ → _____

2 괄호 안의 말을 바르게 배열하여 문장을 완성하시오.

(1) _____ diamonds.
(no, stone, hard, as, is, other, as)

(2) No boy in his class _____.
(than, more, is, handsome, Evan)

3 우리말과 뜻이 같도록 괄호 안의 말을 이용하여 문장을 완성하시오.

(1) 그 반의 어떤 소녀도 Amy만큼 예쁘지 않다. (pretty)
→ No girl in the class is _____ _____ _____ Amy.

(2) 이것은 세계의 다른 어떤 그림보다 더 크다. (big, painting)
→ This is _____ _____ any other _____ in the world.

4 두 문장의 뜻이 같도록 빈칸에 알맞은 말을 쓰시오.

(1) This is the most difficult problem in the book.
→ No problem in the book is _____ _____ as this.

(2) He is the busiest man in my company.
→ No other man in my company is _____ _____ he.

51 주격 관계대명사_who, which

- 문장에서 주어 역할을 하며, 선행사가 사람일 때는 who, 사물이나 동물일 때는 which를 쓴다.

  I know the girl. + She speaks four languages.

  → I know *the girl* [1]_____ speaks four languages.

  나는 4개 국어를 말하는 그 소녀를 알고 있다.

- who와 which는 that으로 바꿔 쓸 수 있다.

  A lemon is *a fruit* [2]_____ is yellow and sour.

  레몬은 노랗고 신 과일이다.

52 소유격 관계대명사_whose

- 선행사가 사람, 사물 또는 동물이고 관계대명사 뒤에 오는 명사와 소유의 관계일 때 쓴다.

  This is my bike. + Its wheels are red.

  → This is *my bike* [3]_____ wheels are red.

  이것은 바퀴들이 빨간색인 나의 자전거이다.

53 목적격 관계대명사_who(m), which

- 문장에서 목적어 역할을 하며 선행사가 사람일 때는 whom 또는 who를, 사물일 때는 which를 쓴다.

  I like the woman. + Cindy met her yesterday.

  → I like *the woman* [4]_____ Cindy met yesterday.

  나는 Cindy가 어제 만난 그 여자를 좋아한다.

- whom(who)과 which는 that으로 바꿔 쓸 수 있다.

  This is *the house* [5]_____ Jack built.

  이것은 Jack이 지은 집이다.

54 관계대명사 that

- 주격 또는 목적격 관계대명사 who(m), which와 바꿔 쓸 수 있다.

  The waiter [6]_____(that) served us was very rude.

  우리를 시중들었던 종업원은 매우 무례했다.

- 관계대명사 **that**을 쓰는 경우

  선행사가 「사람+동물」, 「사람+사물」일 때 / 선행사에 all, no, any, -thing, 형용사의 최상급, 서수, the only, the same 등이 포함될 때

  This is *the fastest train* [7]_____ I know.

  이것은 내가 알고 있는 가장 빠른 기차이다.

55 관계대명사 what

- '~하는 것(들)'의 의미로 선행사를 포함하며 the thing(s) which (that)로 바꿔 쓸 수 있다.

  What he told me was not true at all.

  → [8]_____ _____ _____ he told me was not true at all. 그가 나한테 말했던 것은 전혀 사실이 아니었다.

56 관계대명사의 계속적 용법

- 관계대명사절이 선행사에 대해 부가적인 설명을 하는 형태로 선행사 앞에 콤마(,)를 쓰며 「접속사+대명사」로 바꿔 쓸 수 있다. 단, 관계대명사 [9]_____과 what은 계속적 용법으로 쓸 수 없다.

  Mr. Kim has *a sister*, who(= [10]_____ _____) is a soccer player. 김 선생님은 여동생이 한 명 있는데, 축구 선수이다.

  cf. 제한적 용법: 관계대명사절이 선행사를 수식하거나 한정할 때 쓴다.

  Mr. Kim has a sister who is a soccer player.

  김 선생님은 축구 선수인 여동생이 있다.

57 전치사+관계대명사

- 관계대명사가 전치사의 목적어인 경우, 관계대명사 앞에 전치사를 쓸 수 있지만, 관계대명사 [11]_____ 앞에는 쓸 수 없다.

  The boy is her brother. + I talked to him.

  → *The boy* to whom I talked is her brother.

  → *The boy* whom(that) I talked to is her brother.

  내가 말을 건 그 남자아이는 그녀의 남동생이다.

» 정답 pp.62~63

58 관계대명사의 생략

■ 제한적 용법의 목적격 관계대명사는 생략할 수 있지만, 앞에 전치사가 있을 경우에는 생략할 수 없다.

The woman (whom[that]) you spoke to is my teacher. 네가 말을 건 그 여자는 나의 선생님이다.

■ 「주격 관계대명사+be동사」도 생략할 수 있다.

The woman (¹²_____ _____) speaking to you is my teacher. 너에게 말을 하고 있는 그 여자는 나의 선생님이다.

59 관계부사 1_when, where
60 관계부사 2_why, how

관계부사	선행사
when	시간(the time, the day, the month 등)
where	장소(the place, the house, the city 등)
¹³_____	이유(the reason)
how	방법(the way) (단, the way와 how는 함께 쓸 수 없음)

61 관계부사와 선행사의 생략

■ 일반적인 선행사가 오는 경우 관계부사 또는 선행사 중 하나를 생략할 수 있지만, 계속적 용법으로 쓰인 경우에는 생략할 수 없다.

Fall is *the time* when students come back to school. 가을은 학생들이 학교로 돌아오는 때이다.

→ Fall is ¹⁴_____ _____ students come back to school. 〈관계부사 생략〉

→ Fall is ¹⁵_____ students come back to school. 〈선행사 생략〉

62 복합관계대명사_whoever, whomever, whichever, whatever

	명사절	양보의 부사절
whoever	anyone who (~하는 누구나)	no matter who (누가 ~할지라도)
whomever	anyone ¹⁶_____ (~하는 누구나)	no matter whom (누구를 ~할지라도)
whichever	anything which (~하는 어느 것이나)	no matter which (어느 것을 ~할지라도)
whatever	anything that (¹⁷_____)	no matter what (무엇을 ~할지라도)

Whoever(= ¹⁸_____ who) arrives first will be the winner. 처음으로 도착하는 누구나 승자가 될 것이다.

Whoever(= ¹⁹_____ _____ who) comes now, I won't open the door. 지금 누가 올지라도, 나는 문을 열지 않겠다.

63 복합관계부사_whenever, wherever, however

복합관계부사	시간·장소의 부사절	양보의 부사절
whenever	at any time when (~할 때는 언제든지)	no matter when (언제 ~해도)
wherever	at any place where (~하는 어디에나)	no matter where (어디에서 ~해도)
however	-	no matter how (아무리 ~해도)

Come and see me whenever(= at ²⁰_____ _____ when) you like. 네가 원할 때는 언제든지 나를 보러 와라.

The baby follows his mom wherever(= at ²¹_____ _____ where) she goes.
그 아기는 그의 엄마가 가는 곳은 어디에나 따라다닌다.

However(= ²²_____ _____ how) hard he exercises, he never loses weight.
아무리 열심히 운동해도 그는 전혀 살이 빠지지 않는다.

FOCUS 51 주격 관계대명사_who, which

1 빈칸에 알맞은 말을 who, which 중 골라 쓰시오.

(1) I bought a bag _____ was made in Korea.

(2) She interviewed the girl _____ won the gold medal.

2 어법상 어색한 부분을 찾아 고쳐 쓰시오.

(1) She didn't get the message who was on the table.

_____ → _____

(2) The woman who wear glasses is my aunt.

_____ → _____

3 두 문장을 관계대명사를 이용하여 한 문장으로 쓰시오.

(1) You have to read the book. The book has 10 chapters.

→ _____

(2) Ms. Brown is a teacher. She is very kind to her students.

→ _____

FOCUS 52 소유격 관계대명사_whose

1 우리말과 뜻이 같도록 빈칸에 알맞은 말을 쓰시오.

(1) Tom은 창문들이 매우 큰 집에서 산다.

→ Tom lives in a house _____ .

(2) 소매가 짧은 셔츠를 보여주시겠어요?

→ Would you show me a shirt _____ ?

(3) 나는 아들이 유명한 배우인 남자를 만났다.

→ I met a man _____ .

2 두 문장을 관계대명사를 이용하여 한 문장으로 쓰시오.

(1) She knew a man. The man's father was a teacher.

→ _____

(2) This is the traditional building. The building's history is very long.

→ _____

FOCUS 53 목적격 관계대명사_who(m), which

1 빈칸에 알맞은 말을 | 보기 |에서 모두 골라 쓰시오.

보기
| which   who   whom   that |

(1) That's the boy _____ I invited to the party.

(2) This is the computer _____ she bought yesterday.

2 우리말과 뜻이 같도록 괄호 안의 말을 이용하여 문장을 완성하시오.

(1) 나는 네가 어제 만났던 그 소녀를 알고 있다. (whom, meet)

→ I know the girl _____ _____ _____ yesterday.

(2) 나는 그가 책상 위에 놓았던 반지를 찾을 수 없다. (that, put)

→ I can't find the ring _____ _____ _____ on the desk.

3 두 문장을 관계대명사를 이용하여 한 문장으로 쓰시오.

(1) This is the book. Lucy lost it yesterday.

→ _____

(2) He is the man. I helped him last night.

→ _____

FOCUS 54 관계대명사 that

1 괄호 안에서 알맞은 것을 모두 고르시오.

(1) This is the girl (who / which / that) you wanted to see.

(2) This is the only woman (what / which / that) I love.

(3) Tell me something (who / whom / that) you know about the test.

2 빈칸에 알맞은 관계대명사를 쓰시오.

(1) He is the first man _____ arrived at the top.

(2) All _____ she wants to do is to go on a picnic.

3 우리말과 뜻이 같도록 that과 괄호 안의 말을 이용하여 문장을 완성하시오.

(1) 나는 길을 걷고 있던 그 여자와 그녀의 개를 보았다. (walk)
→ I saw the woman and her dog _____ _____ _____ on the street.

(2) Petra는 내가 이제껏 본 가장 예쁜 소녀이다. (pretty)
→ Petra is _____ _____ _____ I've ever seen.

(3) 그가 가진 유일한 문제는 충분하지 않은 시간이다. (only)
→ _____ _____ _____ _____ he has is not enough time.

FOCUS *55* 관계대명사 what

1 빈칸에 알맞은 말을 which, what 중 골라 쓰시오.

(1) _____ she made was amazing.

(2) This play shows the things _____ many people already know.

(3) Computer games are _____ he likes most.

2 괄호 안의 말을 바르게 배열하여 문장을 완성하시오.

(1) _____ a baby's smile.
(makes, her, is, what, happy)

(2) This book _____.
(what, he, is, wanted, read, to)

3 우리말과 뜻이 같도록 빈칸에 알맞은 말을 쓰시오.

(1) 나는 네가 말했던 것을 믿지 않는다.
→ I don't believe _____ _____ _____.

(2) 그가 필요한 것은 기회와 돈이다.
→ _____ _____ _____ is a chance and money.

(3) 나는 어젯밤에 발생했던 것에 대해 잊어버렸다.
→ I forgot about _____ _____ last night.

FOCUS *56* 관계대명사의 계속적 용법

1 우리말과 뜻이 같도록 빈칸에 알맞은 말을 쓰시오.

(1) Harry는 두 명의 이모가 있는데, 그들은 가수이다.
→ Harry has two aunts, _____ _____ _____.

(2) 나의 남동생은 카메라가 있는데, 내가 그것을 그의 생일 선물로 그에게 주었다.
→ My brother has a camera, _____ _____ _____ _____ for his birthday present.

2 두 문장을 한 문장으로 쓸 때 빈칸에 알맞은 말을 쓰시오.

(1) You can watch TV. It will help you learn about many countries.
→ You can watch TV, _____ will help you learn about many countries.

(2) Jenny met a man. He told her the truth.
→ Jenny met a man, _____ told her the truth.

3 두 문장의 뜻이 같도록 밑줄 친 부분에 유의하여 빈칸에 알맞은 접속사를 포함하여 쓰시오.

(1) My friend recommended this movie, which is funny.
→ My friend recommended this movie, _____ _____ is funny.

(2) She called Tom, who didn't answer her.
→ She called Tom, _____ _____ didn't answer her.

1 빈칸에 알맞은 말을 |보기|에서 골라 쓰시오.

> 보기
> at　　　on　　　in

(1) Jim is a friend _____ whom I can depend.
(2) Do you know the hotel _____ which she is staying?
(3) This is the house _____ which she was born.

2 우리말과 뜻이 같도록 빈칸에 알맞은 말을 쓰시오.

(1) 우리는 내가 그녀를 만났던 그 모임을 가질 것이다.
　→ We'll have the meeting _____ _____ I met her.
(2) 그는 돌보아야 하는 딸이 있다.
　→ He has a daughter _____ _____ he should take care.

3 어법상 어색한 부분을 찾아 고쳐 쓰시오.

(1) Tommy is the student of that the teacher is proud.
　_____ → _____
(2) The chair with which she is sitting is broken.
　_____ → _____

4 두 문장을 「전치사+관계대명사」 형태의 한 문장으로 쓰시오.

(1) This is the subject. We are interested in it.
　→ _____
(2) Do you like the dog? Luke is playing with it.
　→ _____
(3) She often wears blue jeans. She looks attractive in blue jeans.
　→ _____

1 생략할 수 있는 부분을 찾아 밑줄을 그으시오.

(1) He is not the man whom I want to meet.
(2) What is the movie that she saw last week?
(3) Look at the mountain which is covered with snow.

2 우리말과 뜻이 같도록 밑줄 친 부분을 어법상 바르게 고쳐 쓰시오.

(1) 아름답게 춤추고 있는 소녀들을 보아라.
　→ Look at the girls dance beautifully.
　→ _____
(2) 그 책에 제시된 생각들은 매우 흥미롭다.
　→ The ideas present in the book are very interesting.
　→ _____
(3) 그 집은 초록색으로 칠해진 문이 하나 있다.
　→ The house has a door paint green.
　→ _____

3 다음 문장의 빈칸에 생략된 말을 쓰시오.

(1) This is the bag _____ she likes.
(2) Read many books _____ written in English.
(3) Look at the boy _____ jogging in the morning.

4 두 문장을 관계대명사를 이용하여 한 문장으로 쓰시오. (생략 가능한 부분은 생략할 것)

(1) This is the play. I told you about it.
　→ _____
(2) The bottle is heavy. My sister is holding it.
　→ _____
(3) Look at the baby. The baby is sleeping on the sofa.
　→ _____

FOCUS 59 관계부사 1_when, where

1 괄호 안에서 알맞은 것을 고르시오.

(1) This is the place (which / where) we studied.

(2) Today is the day (which / on which) we will start a new semester.

(3) I remember the date (when / where) we left for our trip to China.

2 어법상 어색한 부분을 찾아 고쳐 쓰시오.

(1) Let's go to the station when the train will start.

_____ → _____

(2) I know the place at where I bought this.

_____ → _____

3 두 문장을 관계부사를 이용하여 한 문장으로 쓰시오.

(1) March is the month. My school starts in March.

→ _____

(2) Cindy went to the shop. She bought her skirt at the shop.

→ _____

FOCUS 60 관계부사 2_why, how

1 빈칸에 알맞은 말을 **how, which, why** 중에서 골라 쓰시오.

(1) I want to know the way in _____ you locked the door.

(2) I have no idea about the reason _____ you left me.

(3) Can you tell me _____ you passed the driving test?

2 우리말과 뜻이 같도록 빈칸에 알맞은 관계부사를 쓰시오.

(1) 그녀가 여기에 왔던 이유는 이상했다.

→ The reason _____ she came here was strange.

(2) 그는 그녀가 어떻게 진실을 알게 되었는지를 몰랐다.

→ He didn't know _____ she found the truth.

3 두 문장의 뜻이 같도록 빈칸에 알맞은 말을 쓰시오.

(1) Do you know why she stopped studying?

→ Do you know the reason _____ _____ she stopped studying?

(2) Ted told me the way he saved money.

→ Ted told me _____ he saved money.

FOCUS 61 관계부사와 선행사의 생략

1 밑줄 친 부분을 생략할 수 있으면 ○, 생략할 수 없으면 ×를 쓰시오.

(1) This is the time, <u>when</u> children can play. (　)

(2) Tell me the reason <u>why</u> you can't join the team. (　)

2 생략할 수 있는 부분을 찾아 쓰시오.

(1) I can remember the day when the Olympics began. _____

(2) I don't know the reason why Kevin left for his hometown. _____

3 생략된 관계부사나 선행사를 넣어 문장을 다시 쓰시오.

(1) Sunday is the day I can play soccer.

→ _____

(2) I know why she ate the food.

→ _____

(3) It is where we can take a walk.

→ _____

1 괄호 안에서 알맞은 것을 고르시오.

(1) (Whatever / Whoever) you eat, I'll have the same thing.

(2) Anyone (who / which) comes will be welcomed.

2 빈칸에 알맞은 말을 | 보기 |에서 골라 쓰시오.

> 보기
> whoever   whichever   whomever

(1) _____ breaks the rules will be punished.

(2) I'll meet _____ you recommend.

(3) Buy me _____ I want to have.

3 두 문장의 뜻이 같도록 빈칸에 알맞은 말을 쓰시오.

(1) Whoever comes first will have this gift.

→ _____ _____ comes first will have this gift.

(2) No matter what she says, I'll agree with her.

→ _____ she says, I'll agree with her.

4 우리말과 뜻이 같도록 빈칸에 알맞은 말을 쓰시오.

(1) 나는 친절한 사람이면 누구나 그 파티에 초대하고 싶다.

→ I want to invite _____ _____ _____ to the party.

(2) 그는 네가 필요한 것은 무엇이든 네게 사줄 것이다.

→ He will buy you _____ _____ _____.

(3) 그녀는 내가 만나고 싶어하는 사람은 누구든지 찾아낼 것이다.

→ She will find _____ _____ _____ to meet.

---

1 빈칸에 알맞은 말을 | 보기 |에서 골라 쓰시오.

> 보기
> whenever   wherever   however

(1) The cat followed her _____ she went.

(2) Please call me _____ you are free.

(3) _____ tired she is, she always smiles.

2 괄호 안의 말을 바르게 배열하여 문장을 완성하시오.

(1) _____, there are crowds of people waiting to see her.
(wherever, goes, she)

(2) _____, I will serve you the best food. (me, you, visit, whenever)

3 두 문장의 뜻이 같도록 복합관계부사를 이용하여 빈칸에 알맞은 말을 쓰시오.

(1) No matter how fast he drives, he is not going to get there in time.

→ _____, he is not going to get there in time.

(2) I will be there for you at any time when you need me.

→ I will be there for you _____.

4 우리말과 뜻이 같도록 빈칸에 알맞은 말을 쓰시오.

(1) 당신이 편하다고 느끼는 곳이면 어디에나 앉으세요.

→ Please sit down _____ _____ _____ comfortable.

(2) 그가 아무리 열심히 노력해도 그녀를 설득하는 것은 불가능하다.

→ _____ _____ _____ _____, it's impossible to persuade her.

» 정답 pp.63~64

64 명사절을 이끄는 접속사_that, whether(if)

- **that**: 문장에서 주어, 목적어, 보어 역할을 하며, 목적어나 보어일 때는 생략할 수 있다.

It is certain that he will come back. 〈가주어와 진주어〉
그가 돌아올 것이 확실하다.

We know (that) he left for America. 〈목적어〉
우리는 그가 미국으로 떠났다는 것을 안다.

- **whether(if)**: '~인지 아닌지'의 의미로 명사절을 이끌며, 뒤에 or not이 오기도 한다.

I don't know whether(if) he will visit us (or not).
나는 그가 우리를 방문할 것인지 아닌지 알지 못한다.

65 시간의 접속사 1_when, while, as

when(~할 때)	시간의 부사절에서는 현재시제로 미래를 표현한다.
while(~하는 동안)	별개의 사건이 동시에 일어날 때 사용한다.
as(~할 때, ~하면서)	관련있는 사건이 동시에 일어날 때 사용한다.

He was talking on the phone ¹_____ I arrived.
그는 내가 도착했을 때 전화 통화를 하고 있었다.

²_____ I was playing the piano, my brother was cooking dinner.
내가 피아노를 연주하는 동안 내 남동생은 저녁을 요리하고 있었다.

Ann ate an apple ³_____ she studied.
Ann은 공부하면서 사과를 먹었다.

66 시간의 접속사 2_before, after, until, since

before/after (~하기 전에 / ~한 후에)	뒤에 동명사나 명사구가 오는 전치사로 쓰이기도 한다.
until(till)(~할 때까지)	-
since(~이후로 (줄곧))	주로 과거시제의 절을 이끌며 현재완료와 쓰인다.

I washed my hands before I had dinner. 〈접속사〉
I washed my hands before having dinner. 〈전치사〉
나는 저녁 식사를 하기 전에 손을 씻었다.

Until(Till) it stops raining, he won't leave.
비가 그칠 때까지 그는 떠나지 않을 것이다.

She has played tennis ⁴_____ she was young.
그녀는 어렸을 때 이후로 (줄곧) 테니스를 치고 있다.

67 조건·이유의 접속사_if, unless / because, as, since

조건	if: (만약) ~라면	조건의 부사절에서는 현재시제로 미래를 표현한다.
	unless: (만약) ~하지 않는다면	if ~ not으로 바꿔 쓸 수 있다.
이유	because: ~이기 때문에	「because of+동명사/명사구」의 형태로 쓴다.
	as, since: ~이므로	이유나 원인을 나타낼 때 쓴다.

Unless you work hard, you won't succeed.
→ ⁵_____ you ⁶_____ work hard, you won't succeed. (만약) 네가 열심히 일하지 않는다면 성공하지 못할 것이다.

We couldn't go to the park ⁷_____ it was raining heavily. 비가 많이 오고 있었기 때문에 우리는 공원에 갈 수 없었다.

As it was cold, I caught a cold.
날씨가 추웠으므로 나는 감기에 걸렸다.

68 양보의 접속사_though, although, even though, even if

- **though(although)**는 '⁸_____'를 의미하고, even though 는 더 강한 양보의 의미를 지닌다.

He went out though(although) it was raining.
비가 오고 있었지만 그는 나갔다.

Even though I knew the truth, I didn't tell him.
나는 사실을 알고 있었음에도 불구하고 그에게 말하지 않았다.

- **even if**: '⁹_____', '비록 ~일지라도', '~에도 불구하고'

Even if I don't agree with him, I respect his opinion.
만약 내가 그의 의견에 동의하지 않을지라도 나는 그의 의견을 존중한다.

- **양보의 전치사 despite / in spite of**: ¹⁰_____

I love her despite her faults.
나는 그녀의 결점에도 불구하고 그녀를 사랑한다.

69 상관접속사 1_both A and B, not only A but also B

- **「both A and B」**: 'A와 B 둘 다'라는 의미로, 주어로 쓰인 경우 동사는 복수형으로 쓴다.

Both Jane and Mary ¹¹_____ at the meeting.
Jane과 Mary 둘 다 회의에 참석했다.

- **「not only A but (also) B」**: 'A뿐만 아니라 B도'라는 의미로 「B as well as A」와 바꿔 쓸 수 있으며, 주어로 쓰인 경우 동사의 수는 ¹²_____에 일치시킨다.

» 정답 pp.63~64

Not only you but (also) he likes soccer.
→ He as well as you ¹³ _____ soccer.
너뿐만 아니라 그도 축구를 좋아한다.

70 상관접속사 2_either A or B, neither A nor B

- 「either A or B」는 'A 또는 B 둘 중 하나', 「neither A nor B」는 'A도 B도 둘 다 아닌'의 의미이다.
He is ¹⁴ _____ a doctor or a lawyer.
그는 의사나 변호사 둘 중 하나이다.
I am ¹⁵ _____ angry nor excited.
나는 화난 것도 신이 난 것도 아니다.
- 주어로 쓰이면 동사는 B의 수에 일치시킨다.
Either she or you ¹⁶ _____ to call him.
그녀 또는 너 둘 중 한 명이 그에게 전화해야 한다.

FOCUS 64 명사절을 이끄는 접속사_that, whether(if)

1 밑줄 친 부분을 생략할 수 있으면 ○, 생략할 수 없으면 ×를 쓰시오.
(1) That he made a mistake is not true. (　)
(2) She thinks that she should help Jack. (　)
(3) I know that she is a famous teacher. (　)

2 괄호 안의 말을 바르게 배열하여 문장을 완성하시오.
(1) I don't know _____.
(will, come, if, she, back, home)
(2) I wonder _____.
(he, will, the, come, whether, to, party)
(3) It is true _____.
(the, her, that, to, belongs, book)

71 접속부사

- 접속부사: 원래 부사(구)이면서 접속사처럼 문장과 문장을 연결하는 말을 접속부사 또는 연결부사라고 한다.

대조	however (그러나), on the other hand (반면에)
결과	therefore (그러므로), as a ¹⁷ _____ (그 결과)
첨가 (게다가)	in addition, besides, moreover
예시 (예를 들면)	for example, for instance

Karen is rich. However, her cousin, Kate, is poor.
Karen은 부자이다. 그러나 그녀의 사촌 Kate는 가난하다.
Nick didn't study. ¹⁸ _____, he failed the test.
Nick은 공부하지 않았다. 그러므로 그는 시험에 떨어졌다.

3 빈칸에 알맞은 말을 that, whether 중 골라 쓰시오.
(1) My wish is _____ my sister gets well.
(2) I wonder _____ he will win the game.
(3) I'm not sure _____ it is gold.

4 우리말과 뜻이 같도록 빈칸에 알맞은 말을 쓰시오.
(1) 문제는 그녀가 그 영화에 관심이 없다는 것이다.
→ _____ _____ _____ _____ she isn't interested in the movie.
(2) 나는 그녀에게 내가 학교에서 인기가 있었는지 없었는지를 물었다.
→ I asked her _____ I was popular in school _____ _____.

1 괄호 안에서 알맞은 것을 고르시오.

(1) (As / While) time goes by, the accident will be forgotten.

(2) (When / While) she was young, she was an actress.

2 우리말과 뜻이 같도록 괄호 안의 말을 이용하여 문장을 완성하시오.

(1) 그녀는 나이가 들면서 자신감을 얻었다. (as, grow)

→ _____ _____ _____ _____, she gained confidence.

(2) 그가 머리를 말리고 있는 동안에 나는 TV를 보았다. (while, dry)

→ I watched TV _____ _____ _____ _____ his hair.

(3) 나는 학교 다닐 때 과학을 좋아했다. (when, in)

→ I liked science _____ _____ _____ _____ school.

3 괄호 안의 말을 바르게 배열하여 문장을 완성하시오.

(1) _____, I drank juice.
(was, as, for, I, waiting, her)

(2) She entered college _____.
(she, only, when, thirteen, was)

4 두 문장을 괄호 안의 접속사를 이용하여 한 문장으로 완성하시오.

(1) Turn off the light. I give the signal. (when)

→ Turn _____.

(2) Someone called you. You were out. (while)

→ Someone _____.

(3) He smiled at me. I looked at him. (as)

→ He _____.

1 괄호 안에서 알맞은 것을 고르시오.

(1) (Before / After) you enter the room, you should take your shoes off.

(2) Let's wait (until / since) the rain stops.

(3) He has thought of her (until / since) he saw her last week.

2 빈칸에 알맞은 말을 | 보기 |에서 골라 쓰시오.

보기			
before	after	until	since

(1) I have eaten well _____ I was young.

(2) _____ you go outside, make sure to put on sunscreen.

(3) We will watch a movie _____ we buy tickets.

(4) You have to do your best _____ you achieve your goal.

3 우리말과 뜻이 같도록 빈칸에 알맞은 말을 쓰시오.

(1) 그녀는 10살 이후로 바이올린 연주를 계속 연습하고 있다.

→ She has practiced playing the violin _____ _____ _____ _____.

(2) 우리는 선생님이 도착하기 전에 교실을 청소해야 했다.

→ We had to clean the classroom _____ _____ _____ _____.

4 두 문장을 괄호 안의 접속사를 이용하여 한 문장으로 완성하시오.

(1) I will be busy. Exams are over. (until)

→ I _____.

(2) I go to bed. I take a shower. (after)

→ I _____.

1 괄호 안에서 알맞은 것을 고르시오.

(1) (If / Unless) you make a noise, you can play here.

(2) If it (will be / is) rainy on Saturday, I'll stay at home.

(3) You will get wet (if / whether) you go out now.

2 괄호 안의 말을 바르게 배열하여 문장을 완성하시오.

(1) _____, people think she is satisfied. (doesn't, she, because, complain)

(2) _____, we should work together to finish it.
(have, as, don't, we, much, time)

(3) Most of the stores are closed _____ _____. (today, a, since, holiday, is)

3 우리말과 뜻이 같도록 괄호 안의 말을 이용하여 문장을 완성하시오.

(1) 그는 정직하기 때문에 나는 그를 믿는다. (as)
→ _____ _____ _____ _____, I trust him.

(2) 너는 내 상황을 알기 때문에 나는 네가 나를 이해할 수 있다고 믿는다. (since)
→ _____ _____ _____ my situation, I believe you can understand me.

4 두 문장을 괄호 안의 접속사를 이용하여 한 문장으로 완성하시오.

(1) We often go to the movies. She lives near me. (since)
→ We _____.

(2) He blinked his eyes. Something went into his eyes. (because)
→ He _____.

1 괄호 안에서 알맞은 것을 고르시오.

(1) (Because / Although) he is a math teacher, he can't solve all the math problems.

(2) (If / Though) she yelled at me, I couldn't hear her.

(3) Jim entered the singing contest (if / even though) he wasn't good at singing.

2 괄호 안의 말을 바르게 배열하여 문장을 완성하시오.

(1) _____, he can do everything by himself. (is, although, Tony, young)

(2) I'll get there _____.
(have to, even, walk, if, I)

3 두 문장을 괄호 안의 접속사를 이용하여 한 문장으로 완성하시오.

(1) She has a lot of money. She is not happy. (although)
→ She _____.

(2) We went on a picnic. We should have gone back to the school. (even though)
→ We _____.

1 괄호 안의 말을 빈칸에 알맞은 형태로 쓰시오.

(1) Not only I but also he _____ wrong. (be)

(2) Wendy as well as you _____ to do the work. (have)

(3) Both James and Jenny _____ interested in music. (be)

2 우리말과 뜻이 같도록 괄호 안의 말을 이용하여 문장을 완성하시오.

(1) 그녀의 아버지와 할아버지 두 분 다 요리사이시다. (both)
→ _____ cooks.

(2) Elly뿐만 아니라 나도 영화 보는 것을 좋아한다. (not only)

→ _____ watching movies.

3 두 문장의 뜻이 같도록 빈칸에 알맞은 말을 쓰시오.

(1) He is learning not only English but also Chinese.

→ He is learning _____.

(2) She enjoys cycling as well as swimming.

→ She enjoys _____.

FOCUS 70 상관접속사 2_either A or B, neither A nor B

1 빈칸에 알맞은 말을 쓰시오.

(1) Either you _____ Jeff has to tell the truth.

(2) You can stay _____ at home or at school.

(3) I went to neither the fast food restaurant _____ the Mexican restaurant.

2 괄호 안의 말을 빈칸에 알맞은 형태로 쓰시오. (현재시제로 쓸 것)

(1) Neither you nor he _____ to go to the hospital. (want)

(2) Either you or your brother _____ to wash the dishes. (have)

(3) Neither my sister nor I _____ fish. (eat)

3 우리말과 뜻이 같도록 빈칸에 알맞은 말을 쓰시오.

(1) 그녀는 지금 화나지도 슬프지도 않다.

→ She is _____ _____ _____ _____ now.

(2) 나는 내일 또는 이번 주말에 소풍을 갈 것이다.

→ I will go on a picnic _____ _____

_____ _____ .

(3) 나의 엄마도 아빠도 일찍 일어나지 않으신다.

→ _____ _____ _____ _____ _____ wakes up early.

FOCUS 71 접속부사

1 괄호 안에서 알맞은 것을 고르시오.

(1) I like playing soccer. (For example / On the other hand), she doesn't like it.

(2) You're just 16 years old. (Therefore / However) you can't vote.

2 빈칸에 알맞은 말을 | 보기 |에서 골라 쓰시오.

| 보기 |
| for example   however   in addition |

(1) She really likes the dog. _____, her mom doesn't allow pets.

(2) The food was delicious. _____, the service was great.

(3) He does many things for his dad. _____, he washes his dad's car and cleans the floor.

3 우리말과 뜻이 같도록 빈칸에 알맞은 말을 쓰시오.

(1) 그는 담배를 끊지 않았다. 그 결과, 그는 건강을 잃었다.

→ He didn't stop smoking. _____

_____ _____, he lost his health.

(2) 내 남동생은 나가서 노는 것을 좋아한다. 반면에 내 여동생은 집에 있는 것을 좋아한다.

→ My brother likes to go out and play.

_____ _____ _____ _____, my sister likes to stay at home.

4 다음 문장을 바르게 해석하시오.

(1) Jenny is smart. Moreover, she is pretty.

→ _____

(2) She didn't like the book. Therefore, she gave it to me.

→ _____

» 정답 p.64

72 가정법 과거

■ 현재의 사실과 반대되거나 불가능한 일을 가정할 때 쓴다. 「If+주어+동사의 과거형 ~, 주어+조동사 과거형+동사원형 …」의 형태로, (만약) ~라면, …일 텐데'라는 의미를 나타낸다. be동사 과거형은 주어의 인칭이나 수에 상관없이 were를 사용한다.

If she [1]_____ rich, she could buy a boat.
만약 그녀가 부자라면, 보트를 살 수 있을 텐데.

→ As she is not rich, she [2]_____ buy a boat.
　　그녀는 부자가 아니라서 보트를 살 수 없다.

73 가정법 과거완료

■ 과거의 사실에 반대되거나 불가능한 일을 가정할 때 쓴다. 「If+주어+had+과거분사 ~, 주어+조동사 과거형+have+과거분사 …」의 형태로, '만약 ~했다면, …했을 텐데'라는 의미를 나타낸다.

If I had left the house on time, I [3]_____ _____ the train. 만약 내가 정각에 집을 떠났다면, 기차를 놓치지 않았을 텐데.

→ As I didn't leave the house on time, I missed the train. 나는 정각에 집을 떠나지 않아서 기차를 놓쳤다.

74 I wish 가정법

■ 「I wish+가정법 과거(주어+동사의 과거형)」: '~라면 좋을 텐데'라는 의미로 현재 사실과 반대되거나 실현 가능성이 희박한 것을 소망할 때 쓴다.

I wish I [4]_____ a big car. 내가 큰 차가 있으면 좋을 텐데.

→ I'm sorry (that) I don't have a big car.
　　나는 큰 차가 없어서 유감이다.

■ 「I wish+가정법 과거완료(주어+had+과거분사)」: '~였다면 좋았을 텐데'라는 의미로, 과거 사실과 반대되거나 실현 가능성이 희박한 것을 소망할 때 쓴다.

I wish he [5]_____ _____ the TV program.
그가 그 TV 프로그램을 보았다면 좋았을 텐데.

→ I'm sorry (that) he didn't see the TV program.
　　그가 그 TV 프로그램을 보지 않아서 유감이다.

75 as if 가정법

■ 「as if+가정법 과거(주어+동사의 과거형) …」: '[6]_____'이라는 의미로 현재 사실과 반대되는 것을 가정하며 주절의 동사와 같은 때를 나타낸다.

She acts as if she [7]_____ a queen.
그녀는 마치 여왕인 것처럼 행동한다.

→ In fact, she is not a queen. 사실, 그녀는 여왕이 아니다.

■ 「as if+가정법 과거완료(주어+had+과거분사) …」: '[8]_____'이라는 의미로 과거 사실과 반대되는 것을 가정하며, 주절의 동사보다 앞선 때를 나타낸다.

He talks as if he had known about the problem.
그는 마치 그 문제점에 대해 알고 있었던 것처럼 말한다.

→ In fact, he didn't know about the problem.
　　〈직설법 전환〉 사실, 그는 그 문제점에 대해 몰랐다.

76 Without(But for) 가정법

■ 「Without(But for) ~, 가정법 과거」: '~가 없다면'이라는 의미로 If it were not for ~로 바꿔 쓸 수 있다.

Without(But for) water, nothing could survive.
물이 없다면 아무것도 생존할 수 없다.

→ If it were not for water, nothing could survive.

■ 「Without(But for) ~, 가정법 과거완료」: '~가 없었다면'의 의미로 If it had not been for ~로 바꿔 쓸 수 있다.

Without(But for) your advice, I would have failed.
네 충고가 없었다면 나는 실패했을 것이다.

→ If it had not [9]_____ for your advice, I would have failed.

77 혼합가정법

■ 혼합가정법: 주로 if절에 가정법 과거완료, 주절에 가정법 과거를 쓴 「If+주어+had+과거분사 ~, 주어+조동사 과거형+동사원형 …」의 형태이다. '만약 ~했다면, …일 텐데'라는 의미로, 과거에 실현되지 못한 일이 현재까지 영향을 미칠 때 쓴다.

If she had left yesterday, she [10]_____ be at home today. 만약 그녀가 어제 떠났다면, 그녀는 오늘 집에 없을 텐데.

→ As she didn't leave yesterday, she [11]_____ at home today. 그녀는 어제 떠나지 않았으므로 오늘 집에 있다.

1　밑줄 친 부분을 어법상 바르게 고쳐 쓰시오.

(1) If I were you, I <u>don't make</u> such a mistake.

　　→ _____

(2) If I <u>live</u> in the country, I would be happier.

　　→ _____

2　괄호 안의 말을 바르게 배열하여 문장을 완성하시오.

(1) If you took a taxi, _____.
　　(take, could, you, the, class)

(2) _____, I would meet the girl.
　　(if, you, were, I)

3　우리말과 뜻이 같도록 빈칸에 알맞은 말을 쓰시오.

(1) 만약 내가 지금 바쁘지 않다면 너와 갈 수 있을 텐데.

　　→ If I _____ _____ b u s y n o w, I
　　_____ _____ with you.

(2) 만약 내가 더 똑똑하다면 퀴즈쇼에 참가할 텐데.

　　→ If _____ _____ smarter, I _____
　　_____ part in the quiz show.

(3) 만약 그녀에게 컴퓨터가 있다면 그 일을 더 빨리 끝낼 수
　　있을 텐데.

　　→ If _____ _____ a computer, she
　　_____ _____ the work faster.

4　두 문장의 뜻이 같도록 빈칸에 알맞은 말을 쓰시오.

(1) As you don't exercise, you aren't in good
　　shape.

　　→ If you _____, you _____ _____
　　in good shape.

(2) If he knew her phone number, he could call
　　her.

　　→ As he _____ _____ her phone
　　number, he _____ _____ her.

1　빈칸에 알맞은 말을 | 보기 |에서 골라 알맞은 형태로 쓰시오.

┌─ 보기 ─────────────────────────────┐
　　　call　　　come　　　be
└────────────────────────────────────┘

(1) If you _____, you could have
　　seen the movie star.

(2) If I _____ him, he wouldn't have
　　been angry.

(3) If he _____ rich, he could have
　　bought the car.

2　밑줄 친 부분을 어법상 바르게 고쳐 쓰시오.

(1) If she <u>has not been</u> sick, she could have
　　attended the meeting.

　　→ _____

(2) If Mary had felt well, she <u>would have go</u> to
　　the party.

　　→ _____

3　우리말과 뜻이 같도록 괄호 안의 말을 이용하여 문장을 완
　　성하시오.

(1) 만약 우리가 더 일찍 떠났다면, 그 버스를 탈 수 있었을
　　텐데. (leave, get)

　　→ If we _____ _____ earlier, we _____
　　_____ _____ on the bus.

(2) 만약 그가 차를 빨리 운전하지 않았다면, 사고가 없었을 텐
　　데. (drive, be)

　　→ If he _____ _____ _____ the car
　　fast, there _____ _____ _____ no
　　accident.

4　두 문장의 뜻이 같도록 빈칸에 알맞은 말을 쓰시오.

(1) As it rained, we couldn't play baseball.

　　→ If _____.

(2) If you had not had good friends, you would
　　not have succeeded.

　　→ As _____.

1 괄호 안에서 알맞은 것을 고르시오.

(1) I wish I (have been / had been) kind to him.

(2) I wish I (can / could) run faster than her.

(3) I wish I (could / were) a brave man.

2 밑줄 친 부분을 어법상 바르게 고치시오.

(1) I wish the man has not been fired yesterday.

→ _____

(2) I wish she had understand my plan then.

→ _____

3 우리말과 뜻이 같도록 빈칸에 알맞은 말을 쓰시오.

(1) Helen이 그 시험을 위해 공부를 더 열심히 했다면 좋았을 텐데.

→ I wish Helen _____ _____ harder for the test.

(2) 그가 진실을 안다면 좋을 텐데.

→ I wish he _____ the truth.

(3) Romeo가 내 파티에 왔다면 좋았을 텐데.

→ I wish Romeo _____ _____ to my party.

4 두 문장의 뜻이 같도록 빈칸에 알맞은 말을 쓰시오.

(1) I wish I had had a lot of friends.

→ I'm sorry that _____.

(2) I'm sorry that I didn't watch the movie.

→ I wish _____.

(3) I wish they listened to my advice.

→ I'm sorry that _____.

(4) I'm sorry I can't get good grades.

→ I wish _____.

---

1 빈칸에 들어갈 말을 | 보기 |에서 골라 알맞은 형태로 쓰시오.

보기		
see	visit	be

(1) You might feel as if you _____ in space.

(2) She looks as if she had _____ a ghost.

(3) He talks as if he _____ _____ France before.

2 괄호 안의 말을 바르게 배열하여 문장을 완성하시오.

(1) The foreigner spoke as if _____. (were, Korean, he)

(2) He acts as if _____. (heard, he, the news, had)

3 우리말과 뜻이 같도록 **as if**를 이용하여 문장을 완성하시오.

(1) 그는 마치 슬픈 것처럼 행동한다.

→ He acts _____.

(2) 그는 마치 Jane을 전에 만난 적이 있었던 것처럼 말했다.

→ He talked _____ before.

4 두 문장의 뜻이 같도록 빈칸에 알맞은 말을 쓰시오.

(1) She talks as if she got an A on the test.

→ In fact, she _____ _____ an A on the test.

(2) In fact, he didn't read the famous novel.

→ He talks as if he _____ _____ the famous novel.

1 두 문장의 뜻이 같도록 빈칸에 알맞은 말을 쓰시오.

(1) If it were not for air, we could not live.
  → _____ air, we could not live.

(2) If it had not been for the accident, he would have arrived earlier.
  → _____ _____ the accident, he would have arrived earlier.

2 괄호 안의 말을 바르게 배열하여 문장을 완성하시오.

(1) Without water, _____.
  (all, would, living things, die)

(2) _____, I could go to the concert. (if, for, were, it, not, my illness)

3 다음 문장을 if를 이용하여 바꿀 때 빈칸에 알맞은 말을 쓰시오.

(1) Without money, you could not buy anything.
  → If _____, you could not buy anything.

(2) Without your help, I couldn't have finished the work.
  → If _____, I couldn't have finished the work.

4 우리말과 뜻이 같도록 빈칸에 알맞은 말을 쓰시오.

(1) 컴퓨터가 없다면, 나는 정보를 얻을 수 없을 것이다.
  → _____ the computer, I _____ _____ information.

(2) 너의 도움이 없었다면, 나는 성공할 수 없었을 것이다.
  → _____ your help, I _____ _____ _____.

1 괄호 안에서 알맞은 것을 고르시오.

(1) If she had not lost her job, she (would take / would have taken) a vacation now.

(2) If you had studied harder, you (might be / might have been) a doctor today.

2 밑줄 친 부분을 어법상 바르게 고쳐 쓰시오.

(1) If you read the letter before, you would understand her now.
  → _____

(2) If it didn't snow yesterday, the road would be better now.
  → _____

(3) If he had worked harder, he would been happier now.
  → _____

3 괄호 안의 말을 바르게 배열하여 문장을 완성하시오.

(1) If she had not lost her smartphone, _____. (use, she, could, it, now)

(2) If he _____, he would not be hungry now. (had, lunch, not, had, early)

4 우리말과 뜻이 같도록 괄호 안의 말을 이용하여 문장을 완성하시오.

(1) 만약 내가 프랑스어를 배우지 않았다면, 그와 지금 말할 수 없을 것이다. (learn, talk)
  → If I _____ _____ _____ French, I _____ _____ with him now.

(2) 만약 지하철이 늦게 도착하지 않았다면, 나는 지금 회의 중일 텐데. (arrive, be)
  → If the subway _____ _____ _____ late, I _____ _____ in the meeting now.

78 수의 일치 1_단수

■ 다음과 같은 경우에는 동사의 수를 단수로 일치시킨다.

every, each, -thing, -one, -body	Every room is clean. 모든 방은 깨끗하다.
시간·거리·금액·무게의 명사 / 학문 이름	Mathematics ¹ _____ my favorite subject. 수학은 내가 가장 좋아하는 과목이다.
「분수, some(most / half / the rest) of the+단수 명사」	Some of the pie ² _____ missing. 그 파이 중 일부가 없다.
「the number of+복수 명사」 (~의 수)	The number of patients increases day by day. 환자들의 수가 나날이 증가한다.

79 수의 일치 2_복수

■ 다음과 같은 경우에는 동사의 수를 복수로 일치시킨다.

「분수, some(most / half / the rest) of the+복수 명사」
Some of the animals are still hungry.
그 동물들 중 일부는 여전히 배가 고프다.

「a number of+복수 명사」 (많은 ~)
A number of cars ³ _____ on the road.
많은 차들이 도로 위에 있다.

「(both) *A* and *B*」 / 항상 짝을 이루는 명사
Are there any socks in the drawer? 서랍 안에 양말이 좀 있니?

80 시제 일치

■ 주절의 동사가 현재시제인 경우 종속절에는 모든 시제를 쓸 수 있다.
He thinks that he is(was / will be) happy.
그는 그가 행복하다고(행복했다고 / 행복할 것이라고) 생각한다.

■ 주절의 동사가 과거시제인 경우 종속절의 시제는 과거나 과거완료가 온다.
He said that he supported the soccer team.
그는 그 축구 팀을 지원한다고 말했다.
He said that he ⁴ _____ supported the soccer team before. 그는 전에 그 축구 팀을 지원했었다고 말했다.

81 시제 일치의 예외

■ 주절의 시제가 과거일지라도 종속절이 불변의 진리, 격언, 현재의 습관, 과학적 사실 등을 나타내면 현재시제를 쓴다.
I learned that light travels faster than sound.
나는 빛이 소리보다 더 빠르게 이동한다는 것을 배웠다.
She said that he ⁵ _____ a walk every morning.
그녀는 그가 매일 아침 산책을 한다고 말했다.

■ 역사적인 사실은 주절의 시제와 상관없이 ⁶ _____ 시제를 쓴다.
He says that Apollo 11 landed on the Moon in 1969.
그는 아폴로 11호가 1969년에 달에 착륙했다고 말한다.

82 평서문의 간접화법

■ 평서문의 간접 화법 전환
1. 전달동사 say는 say (that)로, say to는 ⁷ _____ 로 바꾼다.
2. 쉼표(,)와 인용부호("")를 없앤 후 접속사 that으로 연결한다.
3. that절의 시제는 전달동사의 시제와 일치시키고, 인칭이나 지시대명사와 부사(구)도 알맞게 바꾼다.
cf. 지시대명사와 부사(구)의 전환
this(these) → that(those), here → there, today → that day, tomorrow → ⁸ _____ _____ _____ (the following day), ago → before, now → ⁹ _____, tonight → that night, yesterday → the day before(the previous day)
She said, "I am tired." 그녀는 "나 피곤해."라고 말했다.
→ She said (that) she ¹⁰ _____ tired.
그녀는 피곤하다고 말했다.

83 의문문의 간접화법

■ 의문사가 없는 의문문의 간접화법: 「ask(+목적어)+if(whether)+주어+동사」
He said, "Do you know Mr. Brown?"
그는 "너는 Brown 씨를 아니?"라고 말했다.
→ He asked if(whether) I ¹¹ _____ Mr. Brown.
그는 내가 Brown 씨를 아는지 물었다.

■ 의문사가 있는 의문문의 간접화법: 「ask(+목적어)+의문사+주어+동사」
He said to her, "What are you reading?"
그는 그녀에게 "무엇을 읽고 있니?"라고 말했다.
→ He asked her what she ¹² _____ reading.
그는 그녀가 무엇을 읽고 있는지 물었다.

» 정답 pp.64~65

84 명령문의 간접화법

- **명령문의 간접화법 전환**

  1. 전달동사를 문맥에 맞게 tell, ask, order, advise 등으로 바꾼다.

  2. 인용 부호를 없앤 후, 인용문의 동사를 to부정사로 바꾼다.

  3. 「전달동사+목적어(+not)+to부정사」의 형태로 만든다.

  He said to me, "Do your homework."

  그는 내게 "숙제를 하라."라고 말했다.

  → He told(ordered) me ^{13} _____ _____ my homework. 그는 내게 숙제를 하라고 말(명령)했다.

85 간접화법과 간접의문문

- 간접화법은 다른 사람이 말한 내용을 전달하는 사람의 입장에서 적절히 바꿔서 전달하고, 간접의문문은 직접적인 질문을 공손한 어조로 간접적으로 바꿔서 표현하는 방식이다.

- **간접의문문의 어순**

  1. 의문사가 없는 간접의문문: 「if(whether)+주어+동사」

     Can you tell me? + Is that girl your sister?

     → Can you tell me if(whether) that ^{14} _____ _____ your sister?

     저 소녀가 너의 여동생인지 말해 줄 수 있니?

  2. 의문사가 있는 간접의문문: 「의문사+주어+동사」

     I wonder. + When will you come home?

     → I wonder ^{15} _____ _____ _____ come home. 나는 네가 언제 집에 올 것인지 궁금하다.

FOCUS 78 수의 일치 1_단수

1 괄호 안의 말을 빈칸에 알맞은 형태로 쓰시오. (현재시제로 쓸 것)

   (1) Nobody _____ the truth. (know)

   (2) Every student _____ to be diligent. (have)

   (3) The number of cars in Seoul _____ increasing rapidly. (be)

2 어법상 어색한 부분을 찾아 고쳐 쓰시오.

   (1) Physics are interesting to me.

   _____ → _____

   (2) Some of water are drunk by the dog.

   _____ → _____

   (3) Half of the book were read by the students.

   _____ → _____

FOCUS 79 수의 일치 2_복수

1 괄호 안에서 알맞은 것을 고르시오.

   (1) Most of the Chinese (like / likes) drinking tea.

   (2) The scissors you have (look / looks) dangerous.

   (3) Some of the buildings in this town (is / are) tall.

   (4) His glasses (was / were) broken.

2 괄호 안의 말을 빈칸에 알맞은 형태로 쓰시오. (현재시제로 쓸 것)

   (1) There _____ a number of trees near the lake. (be)

   (2) Three fourths of the students _____ on a field trip. (go)

   (3) Mr. and Ms. Brown _____ in line in front of the theater. (stand)

1 괄호 안에서 알맞은 것을 고르시오.

(1) I thought that it (will / would) rain.

(2) She said that he (has / had) lunch at school.

(3) He thinks that she (is / will be) prettier when she grows up.

2 우리말과 뜻이 같도록 괄호 안의 말을 이용하여 문장을 완성하시오.

(1) 나는 Sam이 피곤하다고 생각했다. (be)

→ I thought Sam _____ tired.

(2) 그녀는 그가 모형 자동차를 만들었다고 생각했다. (make)

→ She thought that he _____ _____ a model car.

(3) 그녀는 Brian이 그 집을 지을 수 있다고 생각했다. (build)

→ She thought that Brian _____ _____ the house.

3 괄호 안의 말을 바르게 배열하여 문장을 완성하시오.

(1) I couldn't believe that _____ for her mom.

(had, the, Linda, done, dishes)

(2) _____ enough to help the old.

(that, he, I, is, think, kind)

4 다음 문장의 시제를 바꿔 쓸 때 빈칸에 알맞은 말을 쓰시오.

(1) We know that something happened.

→ We knew that _____.

(2) She thinks that she did her best to pass the exam.

→ She thought that _____.

(3) Cindy says that she has lived here since 2012.

→ Cindy said that _____.

1 괄호 안의 말을 빈칸에 알맞은 형태로 쓰시오.

(1) He told us that Columbus _____ America in 1492. (discover)

(2) She believed that the early bird _____ the worm. (catch)

(3) Jack said that he _____ a walk every morning. (take)

2 빈칸에 알맞은 말을 |보기|에서 골라 알맞은 형태로 쓰시오.

보기		
take	break	leave

(1) I asked him when the first train _____.

(2) She told me that the Gulf War _____ place in 1991.

(3) She didn't know that the French Revolution _____ out in 1789.

3 어법상 어색한 부분을 찾아 고쳐 쓰시오.

(1) She told me all that glitters was not gold.

_____ → _____

(2) He said the Earth moved around the sun.

_____ → _____

4 우리말과 뜻이 같도록 괄호 안의 말을 이용하여 문장을 완성하시오.

(1) 그는 매일 피아노를 연습한다고 말했다. (say, practice)

→ He _____ that he _____ _____ every day.

(2) 그는 나에게 5 더하기 2는 7이라고 말했다. (tell, make)

→ He _____ me that _____ _____ seven.

1 괄호 안에서 알맞은 것을 고르시오.

(1) He said that he (was / is) free then.

(2) Bill told me that he (does / had done) the work the previous day.

(3) She said that she (had worked / works) very hard the day before.

(4) You said that you (have made / had made) pizza.

2 괄호 안의 말을 바르게 배열하여 문장을 완성하시오.

(1) Steve told them _____.
(was, friend, that, I, his)

(2) He said _____.
(he, a new phone, was going to, that, buy)

(3) Jane told him _____.
(had, his sister, she, the day before, that, met)

3 다음 문장을 간접화법으로 바꿔 쓰시오.

(1) Bill said to his father, "I'm sorry."
→ _____

(2) Jenny said, "I will buy some flowers tomorrow."
→ _____

(3) He said, "I was at home yesterday."
→ _____

4 다음 문장을 직접화법으로 바꿔 쓰시오.

(1) He told me that he couldn't forget me.
→ _____

(2) They said that they had been the best.
→ _____

(3) He said that he had got married three years before.
→ _____

1 괄호 안의 말을 바르게 배열하여 문장을 완성하시오.

(1) I asked her _____ the Internet. (she, use, if, could)

(2) He asked me _____ about the project. (any idea, whether, had, I)

(3) Cindy asked me _____ by him. (had, my house, if, been, built)

2 어법상 어색한 부분을 찾아 고쳐 쓰시오.

(1) He asked to me whether I would wait for him there.
_____ → _____

(2) He asked her that they knew each other.
_____ → _____

(3) She asked me whether did I love her.
_____ → _____

(4) They asked me if I would join them tomorrow.
_____ → _____

3 다음 문장을 간접화법으로 바꿔 쓰시오.

(1) She said to me, "What did you see?"
→ _____

(2) I said to her, "What do you think of me?
→ _____

(3) He said to me, "When will you make dinner?"
→ _____

4 다음 문장을 직접화법으로 바꿔 쓰시오.

(1) She asked me who I was.
→ _____

(2) I asked her when she would finish her work.
→ _____

(3) She asked me what I had in my hand.
→ _____

1 괄호 안의 말을 바르게 배열하여 문장을 완성하시오.

(1) He _____.
(to, me, hard, told, study)

(2) His father _____.
(not, smoke, ordered, to, him)

(3) She _____.
(him, down, asked, sit, to)

(4) Dad _____ in the
morning. (get up, to, advised, early, me)

2 어법상 어색한 부분을 찾아 고쳐 쓰시오.

(1) He told me to not overeat.

_____ → _____

(2) She asked me open the door.

_____ → _____

(3) They ordered me turning off the radio.

_____ → _____

3 다음 문장을 간접화법으로 바꿀 때 빈칸에 알맞은 말을 쓰시오.

(1) Jake said to me, "Work out every day."
→ Jake advised _____.

(2) He said to me, "Don't look at me."
→ He asked _____.

(3) You said to me, "Be careful."
→ You told _____.

4 다음 문장을 전달동사 **say**를 이용하여 직접화법으로 바꿔 쓰시오.

(1) He told me to watch out.

→ _____

(2) I asked them not to make a noise in my class.

→ _____

(3) I ordered Bill not to be late.

→ _____

1 다음 문장을 간접의문문으로 바꿀 때 빈칸에 알맞은 말을 쓰시오.

(1) Did you meet Frank yesterday?
→ I wonder whether _____ _____
_____ yesterday.

(2) Is that boy your brother?
→ Can you tell me _____ _____
_____ _____ your brother?

(3) When will he come?
→ Nobody knows _____ _____
_____ _____.

2 어법상 어색한 부분을 찾아 고쳐 쓰시오.

(1) Do you think what I should do?

_____ → _____

(2) Do you know when is Andy's birthday?

_____ → _____

(3) We want to know when can you start working.

_____ → _____

3 다음 두 문장을 한 문장으로 쓰시오.

(1) Do you think? What did Alex read?
→ _____

(2) Can you tell me? When does he watch TV?
→ _____

(3) I don't understand. Why did Tim cry?
→ _____

4 우리말과 뜻이 같도록 괄호 안의 말을 바르게 배열하시오.

(1) 너는 그녀가 매일 어디에 가는지 알고 있니?
→ _____
(know, goes, do, she, every day, where, you)

(2) 그는 언제 그 사고가 발생했다고 믿고 있니?
→ _____
(believe, when, the accident, he, happened, does)

CHAPTER 12 특수 구문

86 강조 1_동사 강조

■ '정말로', '꼭'의 의미로 일반동사 앞에 do를 이용하여 「do(does/did)+동사원형」의 형태로 써서 동사를 강조한다.

I [1]_____ announce the news every morning.
나는 매일 아침 꼭 소식을 알린다.

87 강조 2_명사, 부정어 강조

■ **명사 강조**: '직접', '바로'의 의미로 명사 뒤나 문장 끝에 재귀대명사를 쓰거나, 명사 앞에 the very를 쓴다.

My sister made this table [2]_____.
내 여동생이 직접 이 탁자를 만들었다.

This is the [3]_____ book that I have lost.
이것은 내가 잃어버린 바로 그 책이다.

■ **부정어(not) 강조**: '전혀', '도무지'의 의미로 문장에 at all, in the least 등을 쓴다.

I was not surprised at all. 나는 전혀 놀라지 않았다.

88 강조 3_It ~ that ... 강조

■ 「It ~ that ...」 **강조 구문**: 동사를 제외한 문장 일부를 강조하며, '...인 것은 바로 ~이다(였다)'라는 의미로 강조 대상에 따라 that 대신 who(m), which, where, when 등을 쓸 수 있다.

Matt had coffee at the cafe yesterday.
Matt은 어제 그 카페에서 커피를 마셨다.

→ It was Matt that(who) had coffee at the cafe yesterday. 〈주어 강조〉

→ It was [4]_____ that(which) Matt had at the cafe yesterday. 〈목적어 강조〉

→ It was at the cafe that([5]_____) Matt had coffee yesterday. 〈장소 강조〉

→ It was [6]_____ that(when) Matt had coffee at the cafe. 〈시간 강조〉

89 도치 1_부사(구)·부정어 도치

■ **부사(구) 도치**: 「부사(구)+동사+주어」의 어순이 된다.

Under the tree [7]_____ sleeping an old man.
나무 밑에서 한 노인이 자고 있었다.

cf. 주어가 대명사인 경우에는 「주어+동사」의 어순을 유지한다.
Here he comes. 여기 그가 온다.

■ **부정어 도치**: 부정어 never, little, hardly, seldom 등이 문장의 맨 앞으로 오면 「부정어+조동사+주어+본동사」의 어순이 된다.

I had never seen so many people in a room.

→ Never [8]_____ I seen so many people in a room. 결코 나는 한 방에 그렇게 많은 사람이 있는 것을 본 적이 없다.

90 도치 2_so / neither+동사+주어

■ 「so+동사+주어」: '~도 또한 그렇다'의 의미로 긍정문 다음에 쓴다.

A He wants to take a rest. 그는 쉬고 싶어 해.
B So [9]_____ she. 그녀도 또한 그래.

■ 「neither+동사+주어」: '~도 또한 아니다'라는 의미로, [10]_____ 다음에 쓴다.

I can't go to New York and neither can she.
나는 뉴욕에 갈 수 없고 그녀 또한 갈 수 없다.

91 부정_부분·전체부정

■ **부분부정**: 「not+every / all / both / always」 등의 형태로 '모두 / 둘 다 / 항상 ~인 것은 아니다'의 의미를 나타낸다.

I do not [11]_____ watch TV.
내가 항상 TV를 보는 것은 아니다.

■ **전체부정**: none, never, neither 등의 부정어를 써서 '아무도 / 결코 / 둘 다 ~하지 않다'의 의미를 나타낸다.

[12]_____ of them are high school students.
그들 중 아무도 고등학생이 아니다.

» 정답 pp.65~66

92 생략 1_공통 부분의 생략

■ 문장에서 공통되는 부분은 다음의 경우 생략할 수 있다.

1. 반복되는 명사(구), 동사(구), 형용사(구)

The moon shines at night and the sun (shines) in the daytime. 달은 밤에 빛나고 태양은 낮에 빛난다.

2. 질문에 대한 응답에서 동사가 반복될 때는 조동사만 쓴다.

A Did you meet John? 너는 John을 만났니?

B Yes, I did (meet John). 그래, 만났어.

3. 비교구문의 than이나 as 뒤의 말이 중복될 때

Jack walks faster than Sam (does). Jack은 Sam보다 더 빠르게 걷는다.

4. to부정사가 반복되면 to만 쓴다.

You may come if you want to (¹³_____). 네가 오고 싶다면 와도 된다.

93 생략 2_「주어+be동사」의 생략

■ 시간·조건·양보 부사절의 주어가 주절의 주어와 같을 때에는 종종 「주어+be동사」를 생략하기도 한다.

Though (she was) poor, she was happy. 비록 그녀는 가난했지만 행복했다.

As (¹⁴_____ was) a boy, he liked playing tennis. 그가 소년이었을 때 그는 테니스 치는 것을 좋아했다.

■ 「if+주어+be동사+necessary(possible / any 등)」구문에서 부사절의 주어가 주절의 주어와 다르더라도 「주어+be동사」를 관용적으로 생략하기도 한다.

Paint all the houses, if (it is) necessary. 필요하다면 그 모든 집을 칠하시오.

FOCUS 86 강조 1_동사 강조

1 괄호 안의 말을 바르게 배열하여 문장을 완성하시오.

(1) _____ the watch.
(her, did, father, she, buy)

(2) _____ although she is not pretty.
(Ann, love, does, he)

(3) _____ he will pass the exam.
(they, believe, that, do)

2 어법상 어색한 부분을 찾아 고쳐 쓰시오.

(1) She does enjoys traveling around the country.

_____ → _____

(2) We did liked to go to the park.

_____ → _____

(3) He did saying good things about her.

_____ → _____

3 우리말과 뜻이 같도록 빈칸에 알맞은 말을 쓰시오.

(1) 그는 정말로 행복해 보인다.

→ He _____ _____ happy.

(2) Sally는 정말로 거기에 갔지만 Tom을 만날 수 없었다.

→ Sally _____ _____ there, but couldn't meet Tom.

(3) 나는 그녀가 시끄러운 음악을 듣는 것이 정말로 걱정된다.

→ I _____ _____ about her listening to loud music.

4 밑줄 친 부분을 강조하는 문장으로 바꿔 쓰시오. (조동사 do를 이용할 것)

(1) I work out in the morning every day.

→ _____

(2) Linda hopes it will clear up tomorrow.

→ _____

(3) He decided to come to the meeting.

→ _____

1 빈칸에 알맞은 말을 | 보기 |에서 골라 쓰시오.

> | 보기 |
> herself   in the least   the very

(1) She wrote the letter to him _____.

(2) This is _____ book I've been looking for.

(3) The machine did not help us do the work _____.

2 어법상 <u>어색한</u> 부분을 찾아 고쳐 쓰시오.

(1) I solved the problem itself.
_____ → _____

(2) This is the much music I wanted to listen to.
_____ → _____

(3) She doesn't like him at least.
_____ → _____

3 우리말과 뜻이 같도록 빈칸에 알맞은 말을 쓰시오.

(1) 그녀는 전혀 피곤하지 않았다.
→ She wasn't tired _____ _____.

(2) Sally가 직접 그 피자를 만들었다.
→ Sally made the pizza _____.

(3) 그는 어제 구매한 바로 그 컴퓨터를 사용하고 있다.
→ He is using _____ _____ computer that he bought yesterday.

4 괄호 안의 말을 이용하여 강조하는 문장이 되도록 빈칸에 알맞은 말을 쓰시오.

(1) She doesn't want to eat spaghetti. (all)
→ She doesn't _____.

(2) This is the place where I was born. (very)
→ This is _____.

(3) I don't like to play soccer. (least)
→ I don't _____.

1 다음 문장에서 강조되고 있는 것이 무엇인지 | 보기 |에서 골라 쓰시오.

> | 보기 |
> 주어   장소   시간

(1) It was Mike that spoke first. → _____

(2) It was yesterday that she met him at the bus stop. → _____

(3) It was on the playground that you lost the necklace. → _____

2 다음 문장에서 강조되고 있는 말을 찾아 밑줄을 그으시오.

(1) It was last weekend when she visited him.

(2) It is the pink skirt that I want to wear.

(3) It was some roses that he sent to me.

3 우리말과 뜻이 같도록 빈칸에 알맞은 말을 쓰시오.

(1) 그가 컴퓨터 게임을 한 것은 바로 어젯밤이었다.
→ It was _____ _____ _____ he played computer games.

(2) 산책을 좋아하는 것은 바로 Sandy이다.
→ It is _____ _____ _____ to take a walk.

(3) Jack이 그때 부러뜨린 것은 바로 그의 안경이었다.
→ It was _____ _____ _____ Jack broke then.

4 밑줄 친 부분을 「It ~ that ...」 구문을 이용하여 강조하는 문장으로 바꿔 쓰시오.

(1) <u>James</u> knows the answer.
→ _____

(2) I was looking for <u>the car key</u>.
→ _____

(3) We went to <u>the beach</u> last month.
→ _____

1 괄호 안의 말을 바르게 배열하여 문장을 완성하시오.

(1) Here _____.
(the, comes, bus)

(2) Down _____.
(a, came, shower)

(3) _____ near my house.
(tree, is, big, a, there)

2 우리말과 뜻이 같도록 괄호 안에서 알맞은 말을 고르시오.

(1) 여기 그가 도착했다.
→ Here (arrived he / he arrived).

(2) 교실에 세 명의 소년들이 있다.
→ (There are three boys / There three boys are) in the classroom.

(3) 나무에 많은 열매들이 있었다.
→ On the tree (many fruits were / were many fruits).

3 우리말과 뜻이 같도록 빈칸에 알맞은 말을 쓰시오.

(1) 나는 그것을 거의 믿을 수 없다.
→ Hardly _____ _____ _____ it.

(2) 그는 춤에 대해서는 거의 모른다.
→ Little _____ _____ _____ about dancing.

(3) 나는 여기에 이사 온 이후로 행복하다고 느껴본 적이 거의 없다.
→ Seldom _____ _____ _____ happy since I moved here.

4 다음 문장을 밑줄 친 단어로 시작하여 다시 쓰시오.

(1) I have never seen such a nice person.
→ _____

(2) My sister seldom met him in the street.
→ _____

1 괄호 안에서 알맞은 것을 고르시오.

(1) Sally passed the exam, and (so / neither) did I.

(2) Brian can't swim, and (so / neither) can Jenny.

(3) I can't believe our team lost the game, and neither (can / does) he.

2 빈칸에 알맞은 말을 so 또는 neither를 이용하여 쓰시오.

(1) **A** I am hungry and tired.
B _____ I.

(2) **A** Tom doesn't like ice cream.
B _____ Jenny.

(3) **A** She saw Mike yesterday.
B _____ we.

3 어법상 어색한 부분을 찾아 고쳐 쓰시오.

(1) I have lost the address, and neither has she.
_____ → _____

(2) Brian isn't good at cooking, and so is Mike.
_____ → _____

(3) Linda would like to travel abroad, and so could I.
_____ → _____

4 밑줄 친 부분을 so 또는 neither를 이용하여 다시 쓰시오.

(1) **A** I'm hungry.
B I'm hungry, too.
→ _____

(2) **A** I must leave now.
B I must leave now, too.
→ _____

(3) **A** I don't like him.
B I don't like him, either.
→ _____

1 우리말과 뜻이 같도록 괄호 안에서 알맞은 것을 고르시오.

(1) 그들 둘 다 한국인인 것은 아니다.

→ Not (both / neither) of them are Korean.

(2) 반짝이는 것이 모두 금은 아니다.

→ (All / Every) that glitters is not gold.

(3) 그들 중 아무도 좋은 고객이 아니다.

→ (No / None) of them are good customers.

2 괄호 안의 말을 바르게 배열하여 문장을 완성하시오.

(1) _____ are like children.

(you, both, not, of)

(2) _____ agree with him.

(do, always, I, not)

(3) You _____.

(none, know, of, them)

3 두 문장의 뜻이 같도록 빈칸에 알맞은 말을 쓰시오.

(1) He doesn't want any of them.

→ He wants _____ of them.

(2) Neither of her parents is alive.

→ _____ of her parents are dead.

4 우리말과 뜻이 같도록 빈칸에 알맞은 말을 쓰시오.

(1) 모든 음식이 맛있어 보이는 것은 아니다.

→ _____ _____ food looks delicious.

(2) 나는 그들 둘 다 좋아하지 않는다.

→ I like _____ _____ _____.

(3) 유명한 그림이 항상 비싸 보이는 것은 아니다.

→ A famous painting does _____

_____ _____ expensive.

1 다음 문장에서 생략할 수 있는 부분을 찾아 밑줄을 그으시오.

(1) They went to the park and they played soccer.

(2) Judy is good at math, but I'm not good at math.

(3) I'll give you a ride if you want me to give you a ride.

2 다음 문장에서 생략된 부분을 넣어 문장을 다시 쓰시오.

(1) My cat is bigger than Mike's.

→ _____

(2) He speaks English well, but I don't.

→ _____

(3) Some boys went to the theater, and others to the lake.

→ _____

1 다음 문장에서 생략할 수 있는 부분을 찾아 밑줄을 그으시오.

(1) Although he is old, he is quite strong.

(2) When he was questioned, he answered quietly.

(3) While I was in Italy, I visited the Colosseum.

2 다음 문장에서 생략된 부분을 넣어 문장을 다시 쓰시오.

(1) If possible, I suggest that you should postpone your departure.

→ _____

(2) Though defeated, he remained a brave man.

→ _____

Answer

요점정리 노트 ··· pp.2~3

1 it   2 what   3 I should   4 in   5 결과   6 …할 수 없
다   7 can't   8 충분히 …하다   9 can   10 for   11 of   12 be
13 have been   14 open   15 bark   16 to   17 사실대로 말하
면   18 to be sure   19 so to speak   20 needless to say

FOCUS 01   p.3

1 (1) To study (2) It (3) to solve   2 (1) to read (2) It, to travel
(3) to win   3 (1) is to be a photographer (2) not to prepare
the party (3) to be friends with you

FOCUS 02   p.4

1 (1) when to leave (2) what to do (3) how to play   2 (1)
when to sleep (2) where to put (3) what to wear   3 (1) who
to invite to dinner (2) where to get off   4 (1) what I should
study (2) how I should apologize to you

FOCUS 03   p.4

1 (1) to visit (2) to do (3) to eat (4) to talk   2 (1) is to go (2)
was not to be (3) is to be   3 (1) no friends to talk to (2)
enough time to do it (3) if we are to get   4 (1) drinking →
drink (2) take care → take care of (3) reading → to read

FOCUS 04   p.5

1 (1) to ask (2) To read (3) to borrow   2 (1) 나는 너를 다시 봐
서 기쁘다. (2) 그는 자라서 영어 선생님이 되었다. (3) Mary는 예술을 공부
하기 위해서 파리로 갔다.   3 (1) He is a thief to steal a ring. (2)
He was sad to hear the bad news.   4 (1) to keep a diary
(2) to lose the game

FOCUS 05   p.5

1 (1) too (2) good enough (3) so   2 (1) too difficult to
understand (2) old enough to get married (3) so small that I
couldn't put   3 (1) too tired (2) enough to be(become) (3)
so dark, couldn't   4 (1) so young that she (2) enough to
buy

FOCUS 06   p.6

1 (1) for (2) of (3) of   2 (1) of → for (2) for → of (3) for → of
3 (1) of you (2) of him (3) for her   4 (1) for him to go (2) for
me to study (3) of you to visit

FOCUS 07   p.6

1 (1) to be (2) seems, you are (3) that he was   2 (1) to be
(2) to have (3) to have been   3 (1) to have had (2) to like

FOCUS 08   pp.6~7

1 (1) play (2) to clean (3) pick   2 (1) know (2) eat (3) swim
3 (1) clean (2) laugh (3) come(coming) (4) sing(singing)

FOCUS 09   p.7

1 (1) wear the cap (2) visit Rome (3) read the book.   2 (1)
make her cry (2) apply for the job (3) help her   3 (1) she
wasn't able to (2) If you want to

FOCUS 10   p.7

1 (1) begin with (2) to say (3) matters worse   2 (1) frank
(honest) with you (2) tell the truth (3) That is to say   3 (1)
확실히 (2) 솔직히 말하면 (3) 말할 것도 없이   4 (1) so to speak (2)
Needless to say

요점정리 노트 ··· p.8

1 To go   2 getting   3 his   4 동명사   5 현재분사   6 reading
7 to   8 watching(to watch)   9 시험 삼아 ~해보다   10 ~하려고 노
력하다   11 ~하게 되어 유감이다   12 ~하자마자   13 help   14 ~하고
싶다   15 worth   16 ~하는 데 익숙하다   17 There   18 ~해도 소용
없다

FOCUS 11   p.9

1 (1) Becoming (2) eating (3) taking (4) winning   2 (1)

reading (2) (To walk)walking (3) (to surf)surfing   3 (1) to wear → wearing (2) Go → Going(To go) (3) Having not → Not having

FOCUS 12   p.9

1 (1) his (2) my (3) Tom, Tom's   2 (1) about her ignoring him (2) of her being late (3) doesn't like his ordering   3 (1) your(you) waving to us (2) his(him) winning first prize

FOCUS 13   p.9

1 (1) 현재분사 (2) 동명사 (3) 현재분사 (4) 동명사   2 (1) sleeping (2) making

FOCUS 14   p.10

1 (1) having (2) to travel (3) to play (4) waiting   2 (1) to leave (2) playing (3) dancing (4) to take   3 (1) tried moving (2) remembered seeing (3) forgot to send   4 (1) to play → playing (2) studying → to study (3) selling → to sell (4) to answer → answering

FOCUS 15   p.10

1 (1) crying (2) avoiding (3) going   2 (1) joining (2) reading (3) eating   3 (1) are busy buying presents (2) kept her from sleeping (3) am used to going hiking   4 (1) She cannot help falling (2) On arriving at the party (3) looking forward to visiting you

CHAPTER 03 분사

요점정리 노트 .... pp.11~12

1 sitting   2 현재분사   3 exciting   4 excited   5 동사원형, -ing
6 Not   7 passing   8 having   9 been   10 Having   11 주어   12 frankly   13 ~에 대해 말하자면   14 현재분사   15 과거분사
16 staring

FOCUS 16   p.12

1 (1) stolen (2) playing (3) called (4) rolling   2 (1) tired (2) wearing (3) baked (4) sleeping   3 (1) painting (2) running

(3) broken (4) made   4 (1) wait → waiting (2) tired → tiring (3) boring → bored (4) danced → dancing

FOCUS 17   p.13

1 (1) Entering (2) having (3) Walking   2 (1) Taking (2) Swimming (3) Using (4) Being   3 (1) Felt → Feeling (2) Play → Playing (3) listened → listening   4 (1) Leaving now (2) Not knowing what to do (3) Seeing that building

FOCUS 18   p.13

1 (1) Not forgetting the password (2) Being very tired (3) Seeing the dog   2 (1) Spending all of his money (2) Watching TV   3 (1) Since he didn't know the answer (2) When I heard the news

FOCUS 19   pp.13~14

1 (1) If you take (2) Though(Although) he is   2 (1) Opening this box (2) Being young

FOCUS 20   p.14

1 (1) Walking (2) going   2 (1) driven → driving (2) to sing → singing (3) Put → Putting   3 (1) Taking a walk (2) covering the whole sky

FOCUS 21   p.14

1 (1) Having found (2) having slept   2 (1) Having been made (2) Having lost (3) Having taken   3 (1) Having spent (2) Not having been invited

FOCUS 22   p.14

1 (1) Being (2) Having been   2 (1) (Having been) Made in a hurry (2) (Being) Worried about the test   3 (1) Being born → (Having been) Born (2) Being raised → (Having been)Raised

FOCUS 23   p.15

1 (1) being (2) set (3) asking   2 (1) There being no bridge (2) The teacher speaking too fast   3 (1) Frankly speaking (2) Strictly speaking   4 (1) She (being) preparing dinner (2) My friend asking me to join the club

FOCUS 24   p.15

1 (1) make → making (2) freeze → frozen   2 (1) covered (2)

running (3) folded **3** (1) with her eyes closed (2) with my legs crossed (3) with the water boiling **4** (1) shake → shaking (2) followed → following (3) closing → closed

CHAPTER **04** 시제

요점정리 노트 ··· p.16

1 과거분사 **2** lost **3** when **4** 완료 **5** already **6** gone **7** been **8** ~한 적이 있다 **9** for **10** since **11** been **12** snowing **13** had **14** had been playing

FOCUS **25** p.17

1 (1) has been (2) has lost (3) Have, finished **2** (1) has helped (2) has, found (3) has learned **3** (1) How have you been? (2) The full moon has just risen above the hill **4** (1) She hasn't(has not / has never) been to Europe. (2) He has lived here for 3(three) years. (3) I have known her since 2000.

FOCUS **26** p.17

1 (1) has, finished, 완 (2) has gone, 결 **2** (1) has, written (2) has, eaten (3) have lost **3** (1) has gone to Canada (2) has left her bag (3) has returned to New York **4** (1) have found my ring (2) has just finished

FOCUS **27** p.18

1 (1) have, seen, 경 (2) has, lived, 계 **2** (1) for (2) since (3) before **3** (1) has never been to (2) have met him **4** (1) has played, since (2) have studied, for

FOCUS **28** p.18

1 (1) have been making (2) have been playing (3) has been running **2** (1) Have, been reading (2) has been shopping (3) has been making **3** (1) has not been doing (2) cleaning (3) been **4** (1) has been washing (2) has been snowing

FOCUS **29** p.19

1 (1) had stolen (2) had cleaned (3) had taken **2** (1) had

been (2) had, left (3) had sent **3** (1) had already begun (2) had injured **4** (1) had lost (2) had had(eaten) (3) had, gone

FOCUS **30** p.19

1 (1) had been waiting (2) had been dating (3) had been standing **2** (1) had been fighting (2) had been crying **3** (1) Had you been staying there (2) She had been traveling **4** (1) studied → studying (2) to play → playing (3) has → had

CHAPTER **05** 조동사

요점정리 노트 ··· pp.20~21

1 am able to **2** can **3** have to **4** 금지 **5** need not **6** 동사원형 **7** ought to **8** stay **9** not **10** would rather **11** than **12** 규칙적인 **13** 불규칙적인 **14** would **15** must **16** cannot **17** 떠났어야 했는데

FOCUS **31** p.21

1 (1) Can (2) could (3) cannot **2** (1) can make (2) could see (3) Could, come

FOCUS **32** p.21

1 (1) may(might) be (2) May(Can) I (3) May you succeed **2** (1) 너는 내 컴퓨터를 사용해서는 안 된다. (2) 그는 내 사무실로 와도 된다. (3) Susan은 시험에서 떨어질지도 모른다.

FOCUS **33** p.22

1 (1) has to clean (2) don't have(need) to worry (3) must not leave **2** (1) He has to do his best in everything. (2) You had to keep the traffic laws. (3) They will have to finish their homework.

FOCUS **34** p.22

1 (1) ought (2) ought not to (3) help **2** (1) should not (2) should not (3) should not **3** (1) ought to wear a seat belt (2) Should I return this book

1 (1) had better not annoy (2) would rather study than (3) had better slow down　2 (1) had not better → had better not (2) going → go　3 (1) had better (2) would rather (3) had better not

1 (1) used to go (2) used to take (3) used to be　2 (1) uses → used (2) to watch → watch (3) played → play　3 (1) would study (2) would drink tea (3) used to be　4 (1) used to travel (2) used to be

1 (1) must (2) arrived　2 (1) may have been busy (2) cannot have skipped (3) must have lost　3 (1) cannot have written (2) must have seen　4 (1) should not have worked (2) should have called (3) should not have gone

CHAPTER 06 수동태

요점정리 노트 ·· pp.24~25

1 by, 목적격　2 Was　3 be　4 not　5 being made　6 has been lost　7 to, for, of　8 to　9 to　10 to go　11 at　12 said　13 to　14 about　15 of　16 from　17 at　18 with　19 with　20 in

1 (1) is cleaned by (2) was arrested by　2 (1) this doll made by you (2) wasn't broken by James (3) isn't used very often (by people)

1 (1) will be visited (2) may be given (3) can be fixed　2 (1) The dishes ought to be washed by her. (2) Our time must not be wasted by us. (3) The heavy box cannot be moved by the man.

1 (1) being (2) driven (3) being shown　2 (1) is being built (2) is being repaired (3) Was, being cleaned　3 (1) being → been (2) finding → found (3) be → been　4 (1) The pie had already been eaten by the girl. (2) A food basket has not (hasn't) been brought by her. (3) Some flowers have been sent by Jeff today.

1 (1) to (2) for (3) of　2 (1) was sent to (2) I was given　3 (1) was asked of me (2) was given (3) was bought for her　4 (1) The car was given to him by the woman. (2) A muffler was made for me by him. (3) A letter was sent to him by Mary.

1 (1) to sing (2) was named (3) to study　2 (1) was seen to break (2) was called Jimmy (3) were made to work　3 (1) She was heard to play (2) My shoes were made dirty (3) He was called a genius　4 (1) The dog was named Mini by us. (2) He was advised to exercise by Susan. (3) I was made to sign the agreement by them.

1 (1) turned on (2) put off (3) looked for　2 (1) was looked after (2) were cut down (3) was laughed at　3 (1) running → run (2) has → is (3) care → care of　4 (1) He was spoken well of by his teachers. (2) The meeting was called off by the boss.

1 (1) is believed that (2) is thought to　2 (1) being → be (2) that → to (3) considering → considered　3 (1) is said that (2) believed to be　4 (1) The man is thought to be a millionaire. (2) The meeting was expected to end soon.

1 (1) in (2) with (3) at　2 (1) with (2) about (3) of　3 (1) are

satisfied with her food (2) was filled with many flowers (3) is known as a popular singer   **4** (1) is made from (2) Are, interested in (3) is well known to

CHAPTER 07 비교 구문

요점정리 노트 ······························ p.29

1 tall   **2** so   **3** faster   **4** in   **5** possible   **6** bigger   **7** than   **8** The older   **9** people   **10** than   **11** stronger

FOCUS **46**   p.30

1 (1) as (2) is not (3) well   **2** (1) 나는 너만큼 빨리 달릴 수 없다. (2) 부산은 서울만큼 크지 않다. (3) 이 소파는 저것만큼 싸다.   **3** (1) younger than (2) smaller than (3) more helpful than   **4** (1) the worst (2) the best (3) the smartest

FOCUS **47**   p.30

1 (1) times (2) possible (3) twice   **2** (1) as clearly as (2) as slowly as (3) as long as   **3** (1) twice as much as (2) three times as big as (3) as early as I could   **4** (1) as soon as you can (2) as hard as possible

FOCUS **48**   p.31

1 (1) less cold than (2) less new than (3) less tasty than   **2** (1) less tall than (2) less easy than

FOCUS **49**   p.31

1 (1) happier (2) more (3) More and more   **2** (1) harder and harder (2) The warmer, the better

FOCUS **50**   p.31

1 (1) bad → worst (2) actress → actresses   **2** (1) No other stone is as hard as (2) is more handsome than Evan   **3** (1) as pretty as (2) bigger than, painting   **4** (1) as difficult (2) busier than

CHAPTER 08 관계사

요점정리 노트 ······························ pp.32~33

1 who   **2** which(that)   **3** whose   **4** whom(who)   **5** which (that)   **6** who   **7** that   **8** The thing which(that)   **9** that   **10** and she   **11** that   **12** who is   **13** why   **14** the time   **15** when   **16** whom   **17** ~하는 무엇이나   **18** Anyone   **19** No matter   **20** any time   **21** any place   **22** No matter

FOCUS **51**   p.34

1 (1) which (2) who   **2** (1) who → which(that) (2) wear → wears   **3** (1) You have to read the book which(that) has 10 chapters. (2) Ms. Brown is a teacher who(that) is very kind to her students.

FOCUS **52**   p.34

1 (1) whose windows are very big (2) whose sleeves are short (3) whose son is a famous actor   **2** (1) She knew a man whose father was a teacher. (2) This is the traditional building whose history is very long.

FOCUS **53**   p.34

1 (1) who, whom, that (2) which, that   **2** (1) whom you met (2) that he put   **3** (1) This is the book which(that) Lucy lost yesterday. (2) He is the man whom(who/that) I helped last night.

FOCUS **54**   pp.34~35

1 (1) who, that (2) that (3) that   **2** (1) that (2) that   **3** (1) that were walking (2) the prettiest girl that (3) The only problem that

FOCUS **55**   p.35

1 (1) What (2) which (3) what   **2** (1) What makes her happy is (2) is what he wanted to read   **3** (1) what you said (2) What he needs (3) what happened

FOCUS **56**   p.35

1 (1) who are singers (2) which I gave him   **2** (1) which (2)

who 3 (1) and it (2) but he

FOCUS 57　　p.36

1 (1) on (2) at (3) in　2 (1) at which (2) of whom　3 (1) that → whom (2) with → on　4 (1) This is the subject in which we are interested. (2) Do you like the dog with which Luke is playing? (3) She often wears blue jeans in which she looks attractive.

FOCUS 58　　p.36

1 (1) whom (2) that (3) which is　2 (1) dancing (2) presented (3) painted　3 (1) which(that) (2) which(that) are (3) who(that) is　4 (1) This is the play I told you about. (2) The bottle my sister is holding is heavy. (3) Look at the baby sleeping on the sofa.

FOCUS 59　　p.37

1 (1) where (2) on which (3) when　2 (1) when → where (2) where → which　3 (1) March is the month when my school starts. (2) Cindy went to the shop where she bought her skirt.

FOCUS 60　　p.37

1 (1) which (2) why (3) how　2 (1) why (2) how　3 (1) for which (2) how

FOCUS 61　　p.37

1 (1) (x) (2) (o)　2 (1) the day 또는 when (2) the reason 또는 Why　3 (1) Sunday is the day when I can play soccer. (2) I know the reason why she ate the food. (3) It is the place where we can take a walk.

FOCUS 62　　p.38

1 (1) Whatever (2) who　2 (1) Whoever (2) whomever (3) whichever　3 (1) Anyone who (2) Whatever　4 (1) whoever is kind (2) whatever you need (3) whomever (whoever) I want

FOCUS 63　　p.38

1 (1) wherever (2) whenever (3) However　2 (1) Wherever she goes (2) Whenever you visit me　3 (1) However fast he drives (2) whenever you need me　4 (1) wherever you feel (2) However hard he tries

CHAPTER 09 접속사

요점정리 노트 ·························· pp.39~40

1 when　2 While　3 as　4 since　5 If　6 don't　7 because 8 비록 ~일지라도　9 (만약) ~할지라도　10 ~에도 불구하고　11 were 12 B　13 likes　14 either　15 neither　16 have　17 result 18 Therefore

FOCUS 64　　p.40

1 (1) (x) (2) (o) (3) (o)　2 (1) if she will come back home (2) whether he will come to the party (3) that the book belongs to her　3 (1) that (2) whether (3) whether　4 (1) The problem is that (2) whether(if), or not

FOCUS 65　　p.41

1 (1) As (2) When　2 (1) As she grew older (2) while he was drying (3) when I was in　3 (1) As I was waiting for her (2) when she was only thirteen　4 (1) off the light when I give the signal (2) called you while you were out (3) smiled at me as I looked at him

FOCUS 66　　p.41

1 (1) Before (2) until (3) since　2 (1) since (2) Before (3) after (4) until　3 (1) since she was 10(ten) (2) before the teacher arrived　4 (1) will be busy until exams are over (2) go to bed after I take a shower

FOCUS 67　　p.42

1 (1) Unless (2) is (3) if　2 (1) Because she doesn't complain (2) As we don't have much time (3) since today is a holiday　3 (1) As he is honest (2) Since you know 4 (1) often go to the movies since she lives near me (2) blinked his eyes because something went into his eyes

1 (1) Although (2) Though (3) even though　**2** (1) Although Tony is young (2) even if I have to walk　**3** (1) is not happy, although she has a lot of money (2) went on a picnic, even though we should have gone back to the school

1 (1) is (2) has (3) are　**2** (1) Both her father and grandfather are (2) Not only Elly but (also) I like　**3** (1) Chinese as well as English (2) not only swimming but (also) cycling

1 (1) or (2) either (3) nor　**2** (1) wants (2) has (3) eat　**3** (1) neither angry nor sad (2) either tomorrow or this weekend (3) Neither my mom(mother) nor dad(father)

1 (1) On the other hand (2) Therefore　**2** (1) However (2) In addition (3) For example　**3** (1) As a result (2) On the other hand　**4** (1) Jenny는 똑똑하다. 게다가, 그녀는 예쁘다. (2) 그녀는 그 책을 좋아하지 않았다. 그러므로 그녀는 그것을 나에게 주었다.

CHAPTER **10** 가정법

요점정리 노트 ·· p.44

1 were　2 can't　3 wouldn't have missed　4 had　5 had seen　6 마치 …인 것처럼　7 were　8 마치 …였던 것처럼　9 been　10 wouldn't　11 is

1 (1) wouldn't make (2) lived　**2** (1) you could take the class (2) If I were you　**3** (1) were not, could go (2) I were, would take (3) she had, could finish　**4** (1) exercised, would be (2) doesn't know, can't call

1 (1) had come (2) had called (3) had been　**2** (1) has not been → had not been (2) would have go → would have gone　**3** (1) had left, could have gotten (2) had not driven, would have been　**4** (1) it hadn't(had not) rained, we could have played baseball (2) you had good friends, you succeeded

1 (1) had been (2) could (3) were　**2** (1) had not been (2) understood　**3** (1) had studied (2) knew (3) had come　**4** (1) I didn't have a lot of friends (2) I had watched the movie (3) they don't listen to my advice (4) I could get good grades

1 (1) were (2) seen (3) had visited　**2** (1) he were Korean (2) he had heard the news　**3** (1) as if he were sad (2) as if he had met Jane　**4** (1) doesn't get (2) had read

1 (1) Without (2) But for　**2** (1) all living things would die (2) If it were not for my illness　**3** (1) it were not for money (2) it had not been for your help　**4** (1) Without, couldn't get (2) Without, couldn't have succeeded

1 (1) would take (2) might be　**2** (1) had read (2) had not snowed (3) would be　**3** (1) she could use it now (2) had not had lunch early　**4** (1) had not learned, couldn't talk (2) had not arrived, would be

CHAPTER **11** 일치와 화법

요점정리 노트 ·· pp.48~49

1 is　2 is　3 are　4 had　5 takes　6 과거　7 tell　8 the

next day 9 then 10 was 11 knew 12 was 13 to do
14 girl is 15 when you will

FOCUS 78 p.49

1 (1) knows (2) has (3) is 2 (1) are → is (2) are → is (3) were
→ was

FOCUS 79 p.49

1 (1) like (2) look (3) are (4) were 2 (1) are (2) go (3) stand

FOCUS 80 p.50

1 (1) would (2) had (3) will be 2 (1) was (2) had made (3)
could build 3 (1) Linda had done the dishes (2) I think
that he is kind 4 (1) something had happened (2) she
had done her best to pass the exam (3) she had lived here
since 2012

FOCUS 81 p.50

1 (1) discovered (2) catches (3) takes 2 (1) leaves (2) took
(3) broke 3 (1) was → is (2) moved → moves 4 (1) said,
practices the piano (2) told, five and two makes

FOCUS 82 p.51

1 (1) was (2) had done (3) had worked (4) had made 2 (1)
that I was his friend (2) that he was going to buy a new
phone (3) that she had met his sister the day before 3 (1)
Bill told his father that he was sorry. (2) Jenny said that
she would buy some flowers the next(following) day. (3) He
said that he had been at home the day before(the previous
day). 4 (1) He said to me, "I can't forget you." (2) They
said, "We were the best." (3) He said, "I got married three
years ago."

FOCUS 83 p.51

1 (1) if she could use (2) whether I had any idea (3) if my
house had been built 2 (1) asked to → asked (2) that →
if(whether) (3) did I love → I loved (4) tomorrow → the next
(following) day 3 (1) She asked me what I had seen. (2) I
asked her what she thought of me. (3) He asked me when
I would make dinner. 4 (1) She said to me, "Who are

you?" (2) I said to her, "When will you finish your work?" (3)
She said to me, "What do you have in your hand?"

FOCUS 84 p.52

1 (1) told me to study hard (2) ordered him not to smoke
(3) asked him to sit down (3) advised me to get up early
2 (1) to not → not to (2) open → to open (3) turning → to
turn 3 (1) me to work out every day (2) me not to look
at him (3) me to be careful 4 (1) He said to me, "Watch
out!" (2) I said to them, "Don't make a noise in my class."
(3) I said to Bill, "Don't be late."

FOCUS 85 p.52

1 (1) you met Frank (2) if(whether) that boy is (3) when he
will come 2 (1) Do you think what → What do you think
(2) is Andy's birthday → Andy's birthday is (3) can you →
you can 3 (1) What do you think Alex read? (2) Can you
tell me when he watches TV? (3) I don't understand why
Time cried. 4 (1) Do you know where she goes every
day? (2) When does he believe the accident happened?

CHAPTER 12 특수 구문

요점정리 노트 ·· pp.53~54

1 do 2 herself 3 very 4 coffee 5 where 6 yesterday
7 was 8 had 9 does 10 부정문 11 always 12 None
13 come 14 he

FOCUS 86 p.54

1 (1) She did buy her father (2) He does love Ann (3) They
do believe that 2 (1) enjoys → enjoy (2) liked → like (3)
saying → say 3 (1) does look (2) did go (3) do worry
4 (1) I do work out in the morning every day. (2) Linda
does hope it will clear up tomorrow. (3) He did decide to
come to the meeting.

FOCUS **87** p.55

1 (1) herself (2) the very (3) in the least   **2** (1) itself → myself (2) much → very (3) at least → at all(in the least)   **3** (1) at all (2) herself (3) the very   **4** (1) want to eat spaghetti at all (2) the very place where I was born (3) like to play soccer in the least

FOCUS **88** p.55

1 (1) 주어 (2) 시간 (3) 장소   **2** (1) last weekend (2) the pink skirt (3) some roses   **3** (1) last night that(when) (2) Sandy that(who) likes (3) his glasses that(which)   **4** (1) It is James that(who) knows the answer. (2) It was the car key that (which) I was looking for. (3) It was the beach that(where) we went to last month.

FOCUS **89** p.56

1 (1) comes the bus (2) came a shower (3) There is a big tree   **2** (1) he arrived (2) There are three boys (3) were many fruits   **3** (1) can I believe (2) does he know (3) have I felt   **4** (1) Never have I seen such a nice person. (2) Seldom did my sister meet him in the street.

FOCUS **90** p.56

1 (1) so (2) neither (3) can   **2** (1) So am (2) Neither does (3) So did   **3** (1) neither → so (2) so → neither (3) could → would   **4** (1) So am I. (2) So must I. (3) Neither do I.

FOCUS **91** p.57

1 (1) both (2) All (3) None   **2** (1) Not both of you (2) I do not always (3) know none of them   **3** (1) none (2) Both   **4** (1) Not all (2) neither of them (3) not always look

FOCUS **92** p.57

1 (1) they (2) good at math (3) give you a ride   **2** (1) My cat is bigger than Mike's cat. (2) He speaks English well, but I don't speak English well. (3) Some boys went to the theater, and others went to the lake.

FOCUS **93** p.57

1 (1) he is (2) he was (3) I was   **2** (1) If it is possible, I suggest that you should postpone your departure. (2) Though he was defeated, he remained a brave man.

Memo

New
Reading
Master

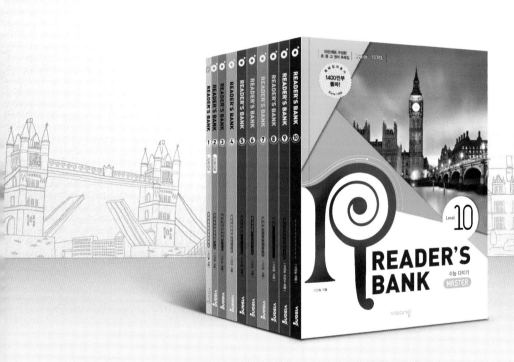

10단계 맞춤 영어 독해서의 표준! **리더스뱅크**

영문 독해에 평생을 바친 이장돌 선생님의 역작

1,400만 권 돌파

- 초등부터 고등까지 탄탄하게 잇는 **10단계 맞춤형 독해 시스템**
- 학생들의 관심사를 고려한 **흥미로운 지문**과 내신·수능 대비 최적화 문제 수록
- 모든 지문에 중등 교과과정 **필수 문법 항목 적용**
- 학습 효과를 더욱 높여주는 **지문 QR코드, 단어장, 워크북** 제공

T·A·P·A 영역별 집중 학습으로 영어 고민을 한 방에 타파 합니다.

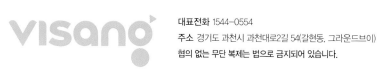

LEVEL 3

핵심문법으로 격파하는

GRAMMAR
TAPA
정답과 해설

GRAMMAR
TAPA
정답과 해설

LEVEL 3

CHAPTER 01 to부정사

FOCUS 01   p.11

A 1 To stop   2 to return   3 to go   4 not to give up
B 1 It, to improve   2 It, to paint   3 It, to get along
C 1 to finish   2 to sell shoes   3 To play soccer
4 not(never) to lend

교과서 문장 응용하기   1 Alison wants to go to L.A.   2 It is not easy to read this book.

FOCUS 02   p.12

A 1 how to speak   2 who to invite   3 where I should get off   4 when I should go   **B** 1 what I should bring to your house   2 when they should finish their homework   **C** 1 what to read   2 how to open   3 who(m) to lend

교과서 문장 응용하기   1 Tell me where to send the flowers.   2 Do you know how you should solve the problem?

FOCUS 03   p.13

A 1 something to tell   2 chair to sit on   3 no children to take care of   **B** 1 aren't to smoke   2 is to speak   3 was to be   4 are to see   5 are to pass the test

교과서 문장 응용하기   1 Amy needed a spoon to eat with. 2 We are to meet him at 3(three) in the afternoon.

FOCUS 04   p.14

A 1 to help   2 to have   3 to send   4 to see   5 to fail
B 1 to do   2 grew up to be   3 difficult to learn
4 disappointed to hear   5 to ask you   6 sad to miss

교과서 문장 응용하기   1 She sat down to read a book.
2 I am happy to meet you again.

FOCUS 05   p.15

A 1 enough to carry   2 too tired to work   3 too big to put   4 enough to travel   **B** 1 too late   2 warm enough   **C** 1 too expensive to buy   2 foolish enough to trust   3 sweet enough to eat

교과서 문장 응용하기   1 This coffee is too hot to drink. 2 My little sister isn't old enough to go to school.

FOCUS 06   p.16

A 1 Brandon to go   2 of her to spend   3 us to provide   4 for him to find   **B** 1 him to speak
2 her(Grace) to be   3 of you to say   **C** 1 me to bring   2 for you to laugh   3 for us to swim

교과서 문장 응용하기   1 The book is necessary for you to understand the history.   2 It is honest of her to tell us the truth(tell the truth to us).

FOCUS 07   p.17

A 1 to have been   2 to be   3 to have been
B 1 to have worked   2 to have been   3 to have passed   4 to have happened   **C** 1 to be   2 to read   3 to have lost

교과서 문장 응용하기   1 He seems to like dogs.   2 They seem to have lived here before.

FOCUS 08   p.18

A 1 follow   2 call   3 touch   4 cross   5 stealing
6 play   **B** 1 made him go   2 helped her mother wash   3 heard him knock on the window   4 smell the pie burning   **C** 1 somebody(someone) call
2 saw my sister go out   3 repair the fence

교과서 문장 응용하기   1 I watched him play the drums.
2 Dad made me clean the living room.

FOCUS 09   p.19

A 1 have dinner   2 go climbing   3 go abroad this

summer **4** move into the new house **5** come home
B **1** need to **2** wasn't able to **3** would like to
4 have to **5** told us not to

교과서 문장 응용하기 **1** You don't have to talk about it if you don't want to. **2** I want to go there, but I won't be able to.

FOCUS 10   p.20

A **1** To tell **2** To make **3** to mention **4** to say
B **1** Needless to say **2** so to speak **3** To be honest with you **4** To begin with **5** To be sure   **C** **1** That is to say **2** To tell the truth **3** To be frank(honest) with you

교과서 문장 응용하기 **1** Needless to say, he is not(isn't) a doctor. **2** To be sure, the movie is interesting.

내신적중 실전문제   pp.21~24

01 ④   **02** how to use   **03** ④   **04** ②   **05** for, of
06 ②   **07** ①   **08** ④   **09** ②   **10** ⑤   **11** ⑤   **12** ④
13 ④   **14** is to start   **15** ④   **16** ②   **17** ④   **18** ⓐ
too ⓑ enough   **19** ④   **20** ⑤

서술형 평가

01 (1) to do (2) to arrive (3) (in order/so as) to meet   **02** (1) important for children to eat (2) careless of him to wear   **03** (1) so small that we can travel (2) small enough to travel   **04** (1) how to swim (2) how I should swim   **05** (1) ⓓ (2) ⓑ, ⓒ (3) ⓐ   **06** That is to saying → That is to say

01 첫 번째 문장에는 '가난한 사람들을 돕는 것'이라는 의미로 주어 역할을 하는 명사적 용법의 to부정사 형태나 동명사 형태가, 두 번째 문장에는 '돌봐 줄'이라는 의미로 명사 dogs를 수식하는 형용사적 용법의 to부정사 형태가 알맞다.

02 '어떻게 사용해야 하는지를'의 의미로 동사 teach의 목적어 역할을 하는 「의문사+to부정사」가 알맞다.

03 |보기|와 ④는 감정의 원인의 의미를 나타내는 to부정사의 부사적 용법이다. ①, ⑤는 형용사적 용법 ②, ③은 명사적 용법이다.

04 목적격보어로 원형부정사가 쓰였는데, ② tell은 목적격보어로 to부정사를 취하므로 알맞지 않다.

05 to부정사의 의미상 주어는 일반적으로 「for+목적격」의 형태로 쓰고 사람의 성질이나 성격을 나타내는 형용사가 있으면 「of+목적격」의 형태로 쓴다.

06 원래 문장인 I'd like to improve it.에서 앞 문장의 반복되는 부분인 improve it을 생략하고 대부정사 to만 쓸 수 있다.

07 '영어는 말할 것도 없이'의 의미가 가장 자연스러우므로 빈칸에는 ①이 알맞다.

08 주어진 문장은 '모든 학생은 기말시험을 봐야 한다.'라는 의미로 be to 용법의 의무를 나타내므로 '~해야 한다'의 의미인 조동사 should나 must를 쓴 문장으로 바꿔 쓸 수 있다.

09 나머지는 to부정사의 의미상 주어로 「for + 목적격」을 쓰므로 for가, ②는 사람의 성질·성격을 나타내는 형용사 cruel이 있으므로 of가 알맞다.

10 ⑤ needless to say는 '말할 필요도 없이'라는 뜻이다.

11 나머지는 앞의 명사를 수식하는 to부정사의 형용사적 용법이고, ⑤는 '~해서 …하다'라는 결과의 의미를 나타내는 to부정사의 부사적 용법이다.

12 ④ 지각동사 saw는 목적격보어로 원형부정사나 현재분사가 오는데, 여기서는 cross와 병렬구조를 이루어야 하므로 enter를 써야 한다.

13 「so+형용사+that+주어+can't」는 '너무 ~해서 …할 수 없다'는 의미로 「too+형용사+to부정사」로 바꿔 쓸 수 있다. 여기서는 주절과 that절의 주어가 일치하지 않으므로 의미상 주어 「for+목적격」을 to부정사 앞에 써야 한다.

14 '~할 예정이다'라는 의미는 be to 용법으로 나타낸다.

15 ④ when he was young은 과거를 뜻하므로 to부정사의 시제가 주절의 시제보다 앞서기 때문에 to be는 완료부정사인 to have been으로 써야 한다.

16 ② '나에게 쓸 펜을 빌려 줄 수 있니?'라는 뜻으로 to write는 to부정사의 형용사적 용법으로, 명사 a pen이 전치사의 목적어로 쓰였으므로 to write with로 써야 한다.

17 ⓐ, ⓑ는 주어, 보어로 쓰인 to부정사의 명사적 용법이며, ⓒ, ⓓ는 결과, 근거의 의미를 나타내는 부사적 용법이다. ⓔ는 '~하려고 하다'는 뜻으로 의지를 나타내는 be to용법으로 형

용사적 용법이다.

18 ⓐ '너무 ~해서 …할 수 없다'의 의미가 되어야 하므로 「too+형용사+to부정사」를 쓴다. ⓑ '~할 만큼 충분히 …하다'의 의미가 되어야 하므로 「형용사+enough+to부정사」를 쓴다.

19 ④ to부정사의 부정은 to 앞에 부정어를 써야 하므로 not to fall이 되어야 한다.

20 ⑤ 「so+형용사+that+주어+can」은 '너무 ~해서 …할 수 있다'의 의미로 「형용사+enough+to부정사」와 바꿔 쓸 수 있다.

서술형 평가

01 문장의 의미를 파악하여 알맞은 동사를 to부정사로 나타낸다. (1) 숙제를 할(형용사적 용법) (2) 도착할 예정인(형용사적 용법) (3) 만나기 위해 (목적의 부사적 용법)

02 (1) 「It ~ for+목적격(의미상 주어)+to부정사」 (2) 형용사가 사람의 성격을 나타내므로 「It ~ of+목적격+to부정사」로 쓴다.

03 '~할 정도로 충분히 …하다'의 의미는 「so+형용사(부사)+that+주어+can」이나 「형용사+enough+to부정사」로 쓴다.

04 '~하는 방법'이라는 의미로 목적어 역할을 하는 「how+to부정사」와 「how+주어+should+동사원형」으로 쓸 수 있다.

[05~06]

> 우리의 오늘날 생활 방식은 매우 분주하다. 다시 말하면, 우리는 한정된 시간 안에 끼워 맞춰야 하는 가족, 학교, 스포츠, 여가, 사회적 약속이 있다. 우리는 일상생활의 요구에 대처하기 위해 건강해야 한다. 건강한 생활 방식을 갖기 위해 우리는 다음과 같이 해야 할 필요가 있다.
> • 대부분 건강에 좋은 다양한 음식을 먹는다.
> • 규칙적인 운동을 한다.
> • 충분한 수면을 취하기 위해 일찍 잔다.
> 다른 것들보다 한 가지에 더 중점을 두기보다는, 이러한 생활의 여러 면에서 균형을 맞추는 것이 중요하다.

05 (1)은 to부정사의 명사적 용법(ⓓ), (2)는 to부정사의 부사적 용법(ⓑ, ⓒ), (3)은 to부정사의 형용사적 용법(ⓐ)이다.

06 '말하자면, 즉'의 뜻으로 that is to say로 써야 한다.

CHAPTER 02 동명사

FOCUS 11   p.27

A 1 is listening to jazz **2** quit eating junk food **3** the advantages of living **4** Cycling on mountains is **5** Not following his advice was   **B 1** finished writing **2** developing **3** going back **4** Making plans **5** Drinking

교과서 문장 응용하기 1 Singing is one of his hobbies. **2** She is good at playing basketball.

FOCUS 12   p.28

A 1 her talking loudly **2** his(him) welcoming us **3** a dragonfly('s) flying **4** the driver('s) driving   **B 1** your(you) coming **2** her smiling **3** my brother('s) passing **4** Her cleaning **5** his(him) carrying

교과서 문장 응용하기 1 She is proud of my(me) winning the gold medal. **2** Luke admitted the students(') ignoring the rule.

FOCUS 13   p.29

A 1 ⓐ 동명사 ⓑ 현재분사 **2** ⓐ 동명사 ⓑ 현재분사 **B 1** 규칙적으로 운동하는 것은 정말 좋은 습관이다. **2** 아침에 자전거를 타는 것은 너의 기분을 상쾌하게 한다. **3** 나의 할머니는 지팡이를 가지고 산책하러 가셨다.   **C 1** twinkling eyes **2** boiling water **3** Reading history books

교과서 문장 응용하기 1 Her hobby is taking photos of flowers. **2** Owen is writing an essay now.

FOCUS 14   p.30

A 1 to rain, raining **2** drinking **3** to work, working **4** taking **5** to pass **6** to go **7** to become   **B 1** to drink, singing **2** to wash, bringing **3** to submit, going

교과서 문장 응용하기 **1** Luna always avoids cleaning her room. **2** I remember living with my grandmother.

FOCUS 15 p.31

A **1** denying **2** watching **3** drawing **4** preparing
B **1** having trouble finding **2** busy talking(calling)
3 look forward to working **C** **1** visiting, 우리는 다음 주에 Brown 씨를 방문하고 싶다. **2** hearing, 그 캠핑 프로그램에 대해 듣자마자, 나는 참여하고 싶었다.

교과서 문장 응용하기 **1** I feel like sleeping on the bed now. **2** She cannot help crying during the movie.

내신적중 실전문제 pp.32~36

01 ④ 02 ② 03 ② 04 ① 05 ⑤ 06 ⓐ to bring, ⓑ bringing 07 ⑤ 08 ③ 09 ⑤ 10 ⑤ to meet → meeting 11 ② inviting → to invite 12 ④ 13 ③ 14 ③ 15 ① 16 ④ 17 ⓐ lending, ⓑ lending 18 ② 19 ⑤ 20 ③ 21 ②, ③ 22 ① 23 ① 24 ⑤ 25 ⓐ, ⓓ / ⓑ, ⓒ, ⓔ

서술형 평가

01 are used to handling 02 Sally's taking care of her little sister 03 (1) 쿠폰을 가지고 갔던 것을 기억한다 (2) 쿠폰을 가지고 갈 것을 기억한다 04 (1) Jean에게 이야기하는 것을 멈추었다 (2) Jean에게 이야기하기 위해 멈추었다 05 (1) Walking(To walk) (2) to walk (3) walking (4) walking(to walk) (5) walking 06 On(Upon) getting up 07 ⓐ studying(to study) ⓑ to insert

---

01 '마음을 여는 것'이라는 의미로 주어 역할을 하는 동명사가 알맞다.

02 '패션 모델이 되는 것'이라는 의미로 보어 역할을 하는 동명사가 알맞다.

03 동사 enjoy는 목적어로 동명사를 취한다.

04 전치사 다음에 동사가 올 경우에는 동명사 형태로 쓰며, 동명사의 부정은 동명사 앞에 not을 쓴다.

05 빈칸에는 동명사와 to부정사를 모두 목적어로 취하는 동사가

알맞다. ⑤는 동명사만을 목적어로 취하므로 알맞지 않다.

06 ⓐ 「remember + to부정사」: (앞으로) ~할 것을 기억하다 ⓑ 「remember + 동명사」: (과거에) ~했던 것을 기억하다

07 | 보기 |와 ⑤는 문장에서 보어의 역할을 하는 동명사이다. ①, ②, ④는 목적어, ③은 주어 역할을 한다.

08 첫 번째 문장은 '~하곤 했다'의 뜻이 되어야 하므로 「used to + 동사원형」이, 두 번째 문장은 '~하는 데 익숙하다'의 뜻이 되어야 하므로 「be used to -ing」가 알맞다.

09 동명사의 관용 표현인 feel like -ing는 '~하고 싶다'는 의미이며, look forward to -ing는 '~하기를 기대하다'의 의미이다. 따라서 첫 번째 빈칸에는 taking이 두 번째 빈칸에는 to joining이 알맞다.

10 ⑤ avoid는 동명사를 목적어로 취하는 동사이므로 meeting으로 써야 한다.

11 ② 다음 주에 초대할 것을 기억한다는 의미여야 하므로 remember 다음에 to부정사를 써야 한다.

12 동명사의 부정은 동명사 앞에 부정어 not을 쓴다.

13 imagine은 동명사를 목적어로 취하며, 주절의 주어와 동명사의 주어가 다르므로 의미상 주어 he의 소유격 his를 동명사 앞에 쓴다.

14 ⓑ 전치사의 목적어로 동사가 올 때는 동명사 형태로 쓴다. ⓓ 여기서 stop은 '~하는 것을 멈추다'의 의미로 동명사가 목적어로 온다. ⓔ 「spend + 시간(돈) + -ing」의 형태여야 한다.

15 목적어가 동명사인 것으로 보아 to부정사를 목적어로 취하는 ① want는 알맞지 않다.

16 동명사의 의미상 주어가 문장의 주어와 다르므로 의미상 주어를 소유격(my)으로 써야 한다.

17 ⓐ 전치사의 목적어는 동명사 형태여야 한다. ⓑ 내용상 '빌려주었던 일'을 '잊어버렸었다'는 말이 되어야 하므로 과거의 뜻을 나타내는 「forget + 동명사」가 알맞다.

18 나머지는 동명사이고, ②는 현재분사이다.

19 ⑤ promise는 to부정사만을 목적어로 취할 수 있다.

20 '~하는 데 어려움을 겪다'는 의미는 have trouble -ing로 나타낸다.

21 ① 부정어 not은 동명사 앞에 쓴다.(going not → not going) ④ 문맥상 '~하려고 노력하다'는 의미가 되어야 하므로 동명사가 아니라 to부정사를 써야 한다.(explaining → to explain) ⑤ 동명사의 의미상 주어이므로 소유격을 써야 한다.(he → his)

22 동사 deny는 목적어로 동명사를 취하며, 동명사의 의미상 주어는 소유격으로 쓴다.

23 주어진 문장은 '화성에서 사는 것은 불가능하다.'라는 의미로 '~라는 것은 불가능하다'라는 There is no -ing의 표현으로 바꿔 쓸 수 있다.

24 ⑤ 문맥상 '휴식을 취하기 위해서'라는 목적의 의미를 나타내야 하므로 to부정사로 고쳐야 한다. (→ to take)

25 ⓐ, ⓓ는 현재분사, ⓑ, ⓒ, ⓔ는 동명사로 쓰였다.

서술형 평가

01 '~하는 데 익숙하다'는 의미는 be used to -ing로 나타낸다.

02 it은 'Sally takes care of her little sister'를 가리키며, about 다음에 동사가 올 때는 동명사의 형태이다. 문장의 주어와 의미상 주어가 일치하지 않으므로 소유격으로 의미상 주어를 쓴다.

03 (1) remember + 동명사: ~했던 것을 기억하다
(2) remember + to부정사: ~할 것을 기억하다

04 (1) stop + 동명사: ~하는 것을 멈추다
(2) stop + to 부정사: ~하기 위해 멈추다

05 (1), (4) 동사가 주어나 보어로 올 때는 동명사나 to부정사로 쓴다. (2) want는 목적어로 to부정사를 취한다. (3) enjoy는 목적어로 동명사를 취한다. (5) feel like -ing는 '~하고 싶다'는 의미이다.

[06~07]

> 미소는 아침에 일어나자마자, 교실로 들어갔다. 교실은 그녀의 침실 바로 옆에 있었다. 인공지능 로봇 선생님이 켜져 있는 상태에서 그녀를 기다리고 있었다. 선생님은 토요일과 일요일을 제외하고는 매일 같은 시각에 켜져 있다. 스크린이 환해졌고 선생님이 말을 했다. "복제에 관한 공부를 시작해 봅시다. 어제 과제물을 적당한 구멍에 넣는 것을 잊지 마세요." 미소는 숙제를 넣었다. 인공지능 로봇 선생님은 스크린에서 반짝거리고 있었다.

06 '~하자마자'는 on(upon) -ing로 나타낸다.

07 ⓐ begin은 목적어로 동명사와 to부정사를 모두 취할 수 있다.
ⓑ '~하는 것을 잊지 마라'는 의미여야 하므로 forget 다음에 to부정사를 써야 한다.

CHAPTER 03 분사

FOCUS 16　　　　p.39

A 1 delighted **2** interesting **3** bored **4** wearing **5** Frozen **6** going **7** stolen　**B 1** the room cleaned **2** The frightened child **3** the boy running **4** his friends dancing **5** the girl reading

교과서 문장 응용하기　1 The movie was disappointing. **2** I found a broken computer.

FOCUS 17　　　　p.40

A 1 Opening **2** Being **3** Entering **4** Not being
B 1 Taking **2** Leaving **3** Waiting
C 1 Washing(Doing) **2** Turning **3** Not hearing

교과서 문장 응용하기　1 Being alone, he listens to music. **2** Taking this train, you will get there.

FOCUS 18　　　　p.41

A 1 Playing **2** Traveling **3** Not having **4** Smiling
B 1 Opening the drawer **2** Taking off his shirt **3** Having no time **4** Being late for school
C 1 Crossing **2** Walking **3** Living

교과서 문장 응용하기　1 Finishing our homework, we went swimming. **2** Being a child, he couldn't drive.

FOCUS 19　　　　p.42

A 1 Meeting Brian **2** Working hard **3** Being honest **4** Not studying harder **5** Being free in the afternoon
B 1 Missing **2** Being **3** Losing **4** Eating **5** Not having

교과서 문장 응용하기　1 Walking along this street, you will find the park. **2** Being rich, she is not happy.

FOCUS 20　　　　p.43

A 1 As(While) we were walking **2** and went out

3 and left for Rome 4 As(While) he was saying
5 and drove to the airport **B** 1 finishing 2 going
3 Smiling 4 Listening

교과서 문장 응용하기 1 The man ate(had) a sandwich, reading a magazine. / Reading a magazine, the man ate(had) a sandwich. 2 I arrived at the train station, taking a taxi.

FOCUS 21 p.44

A 1 Having watched the movie 2 Having been told the rumor 3 Not having read the book before
B 1 Having been taught 2 Having finished 3 Having passed 4 Having lived **C** 1 Having worked
2 Having been decorated 3 Not having met

교과서 문장 응용하기 1 Having arrived at the station, Tyler entered the building. 2 Having been written in Chinese, the book looked difficult.

FOCUS 22 p.45

A 1 Being seen, Seen 2 Having been written, Written **B** 1 Shocked 2 Broken 3 Surrounded
4 Born **C** 1 Alarmed 2 Delighted 3 Given
4 Taken

교과서 문장 응용하기 1 (Being) Tired from working, my father (being) took a rest. 2 (Having been) Repaired by Luke, the machine works well.

FOCUS 23 p.46

A 1 My father cooking 2 The sun having risen
3 Their homework (being) done **B** 1 It being
2 Judging from 3 Considering 4 Strictly speaking
5 Generally speaking

교과서 문장 응용하기 1 The painting (being) completed, she felt satisfied. 2 Speaking of sports, I like baseball best.

FOCUS 24 p.47

A 1 shining 2 crossed 3 with tears flowing

4 with the door locked 5 with the phone ringing
B 1 painted 2 pointing 3 closed 4 folded
5 broken

교과서 문장 응용하기 1 Emma studied with TV turned on.
2 He was running with his dog following.

내신적중 실전문제 1회 pp.48~50

01 ② 02 ③ 03 ② 04 ③ 05 ② 06 ③ 07 ①
08 surprised, surprising 09 ② 10 ⑤ switching
→ switched 11 ① made → making 12 ③ 13
③ 14 ④ 15 ② 16 ① 17 ⑤ 18 ⓐ Dinner
being ⓑ Having visited 19 ③ 20 ⑤

01 '깜박이는'이라는 능동의 의미가 되어야 하므로 현재분사 형태가 알맞다.

02 '튀겨진'이라는 수동의 의미가 되어야 하므로 과거분사 형태가 알맞다.

03 '바쁘지 않았기 때문에'의 이유의 의미를 나타내는 분사구문 부정으로 부정어 not은 분사 앞에 쓴다.

04 '나는 노래를 부르면서, 목욕을 하고 있었다.'는 의미인 동시동작을 나타내는 분사구문으로 「동사원형＋-ing」 형태인 ③이 알맞다.

05 분사구문으로 부사절에서 접속사와 주어를 생략하고 동사는 「동사원형＋-ing」 형태가 되어야 한다. 따라서 첫 번째 빈칸에는 의미상 While the girl walked slowly, ~이므로 Walking이, 두 번째 빈칸에는 Because he was shocked by the news, ~이므로 Being shocked가 알맞은데, 여기서 Being은 생략할 수 있으므로 shocked가 알맞다.

06 첫 번째 빈칸에는 「with+명사+분사」의 형태로 명사와 분사의 관계가 능동이므로 현재분사인 running이, 두 번째 빈칸에는 As there was nothing to do ~의 분사구문으로 주절과 분사구문의 주어가 일치하지 않으므로 주어 There를 맨 앞에 쓴 There being이 알맞다.

07 문맥상 '매우 배가 고팠기 때문에'라는 이유를 나타내는 분사구문으로 접속사 since, as, because 등을 이용해서 부사절로 바꾼 ①이 알맞다.

08 감정을 나타내는 동사 surprise는 사람의 감정을 나타낼 때는 과거분사로, 사물을 수식할 때는 현재분사로 쓴다.

09 '개들끼리 남겨졌을 때'라는 뜻의 수동태 분사구문이 알맞으며, Being left의 Being은 생략할 수 있다.

10 ⑤ 「with + 명사 + 분사」의 형태에서 명사와 분사의 관계가 수동이므로 과거분사로 써야 한다.

11 ① 문맥상 '거리에서 소음을 내는 사람들'이라는 능동의 의미가 되어야 하므로 현재분사 making으로 써야 한다.

12 ③은 '일어나면서'라는 의미의 동시동작을 나타내는 분사구문이다.

13 ③ considering은 '~을 고려하면'이라는 의미를 나타낸다.

14 ① 화가에 의해 '그려진'의 수동 의미로 과거분사를 써야 한다. ② 분사구문의 부정은 not을 분사 앞에 쓴다. ③ 「with + 명사 + 분사」에서 명사와 분사가 수동 관계이므로 과거분사를 써야 한다. ⑤ '전에 파리에 살았던 것'이 주절의 시제보다 먼저 일어난 행위이므로 완료형 분사구문으로 써야 한다.

15 ② 문맥상 '떨어지는 빗소리'가 되어야 자연스러우므로 fallen은 능동을 나타내는 falling으로 고쳐야 알맞다.

16 ① '일요일이라서 대부분의 가게가 문을 닫았다.'라는 의미로 분사구문의 주어가 주절의 주어와 일치하지 않으므로 분사구문의 주어를 써야 한다. (Being Sunday → It being Sunday)

17 독립분사구문의 부정이 알맞다. '돌아오지 않은 것'은 그녀이므로 분사구문의 주어(she)를 맨 앞에 쓰고, 부정어 not을 분사 앞에 쓴다.

18 ⓐ는 주절의 주어와 분사구문의 주어가 같지 않으므로 주어를 생략할 수 없다. ⓑ는 부사절의 시제가 주절보다 앞서므로 완료형 분사구문인 「having + 과거분사」 형태가 알맞다.

19 ⓐ, ⓒ는 양보의 의미를, ⓑ는 시간을, ⓓ는 이유를 나타내는 분사구문이다.

20 ⑤ 부사절의 시제가 주절보다 앞선 완료형 분사구문이므로 After I had finished가 되어야 한다.

내신적중 실전문제 2회 pp.51~54

01 ② **02** ④ **03** ⑤ **04** ① **05** ② **06** ③ **07** ②, ③ **08** ① **09** ② **10** ② **11** Not knowing **12** ⑤ **13** ⓒ Been → It being **14** ② **15** ⑤ **16** ⑤ **17** ③ **18** ⓐ sailing ⓑ called **19** ⓐ Cleaning ⓑ Located **20** ②

서술형 평가

01 (1) boring, bored (2) moving, moved **02** (1) 돈이 충분하지 않았지만 (2) 돈이 충분하지 않았기 때문에 **03** (1) As(Because/Since) she was born (2) Having been born (3) Born **04** (1) Reading the book, I'll be very moved. (2) Hearing a big sound, she went upstairs. (3) Wearing his duck-down parka, he was very cold. **05** Being embarrassed **06** (1) To see → Seeing (2) confusing → confused

01 '끓고 있는 주전자'라는 능동의 의미의 현재분사로 명사 kettle 앞에서 수식하는 형태가 알맞다.

02 '부서진 창문'이라는 수동의 의미의 과거분사로 명사 window를 수식하는 형태가 알맞다.

03 목적격보어인 me가 '~한 감정을 느끼는 것'이므로 빈칸에는 과거분사가 알맞다.

04 '난 시골에 살기 때문에'라는 의미의 이유를 나타내는 문장이어야 하므로 As I live 또는 분사구문 형태인 Living이 되어야 한다.

05 '~하면'이라는 의미의 조건의 분사구문이 알맞다. if절을 쓰려면 「if + 주어 + 현재동사」의 조건부사절이 되어야 한다.

06 As the kitten was cute, Sora wanted ~.에서 주절의 주어와 부사절의 주어가 다르므로, 분사 앞에 주어를 쓴 분사구문을 만든다.

07 수동형의 분사구문 Being frightened ~에서 Being은 생략할 수 있다.

08 '내려다 보았을 때'라는 의미가 자연스러우므로 「접속사+주어+동사」의 역할을 하는 분사구문 형태가 되어야 한다. (→ Looking)

09 ② '눈을 감은 채'라는 의미인 「with+명사+분사」 형태로 명사와 분사가 수동의 관계이므로 과거분사 closed가 되어야 한다.

10 |보기|와 ②는 '비록 ~이지만'이라는 양보의 의미를 나타낸다. ① 이유 ③ 시간 ④ 조건 ⑤ 동시동작

11 이유를 나타내는 분사구문의 부정이 알맞으므로 「동사원형 + -ing」 형태인 knowing 앞에 부정어 not을 쓴다.

12 '솔직히 말하면'의 의미는 Frankly speaking으로 쓴다.

13 ⓒ 주절의 주어와 부사절의 주어가 다르므로 분사구문으로

바꿀 때 날씨를 나타내는 비인칭주어 It을 생략할 수 없다.

14 ⓐ는 '잃어버린'이라는 수동의 의미로 과거분사가, ⓑ는 '싸우고 있는'이라는 능동의 의미로 현재분사가, ⓒ는 '서 있는 것'이라는 능동의 의미로 현재분사가 알맞다.

15 ⑤ '흥미진진한'이라는 뜻으로 감정을 느끼게 만드는 능동의 의미가 알맞으므로 현재분사로 써야 한다. (→ exciting)

16 ① 동시동작을 나타내는 분사구문이 알맞으므로 Hoped는 Hoping이 되어야 한다. ② 수동태 분사구문에서 Being이 생략된 wounded로 시작해야 한다. ③ ~에 대해 말하자면'은 speaking of로 나타낸다. ④ '반창고가 붙은 채로'는 「with + 명사 + 분사」 형태로 명사와 분사가 수동의 관계이므로 bandaging은 bandaged가 되어야 한다.

17 ⓑ '도난당한'이라는 수동의 의미로 명사를 수식해야 하므로 stealing은 과거분사 stolen이 되어야 한다. ⓔ 수동태 분사구문을 이용하여 (Being) Taken으로 시작하는 것이 알맞다.

18 ⓐ '인도로 항해하는'이라는 능동의 의미는 현재분사로, ⓑ '불리는'이라는 수동의 의미는 과거분사로 쓴다.

19 ⓐ '방을 청소할 때(when she cleaned ~)'라는 시간의 의미를 나타내는 분사 구문으로 「동사원형 + -ing」형태가 알맞다. ⓑ Being located ~ 에서 being이 생략된 분사구문으로 과거분사 형태가 알맞다.

20 ② Being shocked로 Being은 생략할 수 있으므로 Shocked로 써야 한다.

서술형 평가

01 감정을 나타내는 동사가 사람이 느끼는 감정을 나타낼 때는 과거분사로, 감정을 느끼게 만드는 사물의 상태를 나타낼 때는 현재분사로 쓴다.

02 뒤 문장과의 맥락을 파악하여 밑줄 친 부분의 의미를 찾는다. ⑴은 양보를 나타내는 분사구문이고, ⑵는 이유를 나타내는 분사구문이다.

03 이유를 나타내는 부사절과 분사구문을 쓰는 것이 알맞다. 태어난 것이 유명한 영화배우들을 아는 것보다 한 시제 앞선 일이므로 완료분사구문으로 나타내며, Having been은 생략할 수 있다.

04 ⑴ 조건, ⑵ 때, ⑶ 양보의 의미를 나타내는 분사구문 문장이 되어야 하므로 동사는 「동사원형 + -ing」의 형태로 쓴다.

[05~06]

> 잘못된 언어 소통은 문화와 언어의 차이 때문에 발생

할 수 있다. 당신은 얼굴 표정 또한 다른 문화권에서 잘못 전달될 수 있다는 것을 아는가? 예를 들어, 많은 문화권에서 미소는 행복함이나 즐거움을 나타낸다. 그러나, 몇몇 아시아 국가의 사람들은 당황스러울 때, 미소 짓거나 웃는다. 이것을 본다면, 서양 사람들은 혼동이 되어 그 아시아 사람이 즐거워서 웃고 있다고 생각할 수 있다.

05 부사절의 주어가 주절의 주어와 일치하므로 접속사와 부사절의 주어를 생략하고 동사는 「동사원형 + -ing」 형태로 쓴다.

06 ⑴ '이것을 본다면'이라는 조건을 의미하는 분사구문 문장이어야 한다. ⑵ confuse는 사람이 느끼는 감정을 나타내야 하므로 과거분사 형태여야 한다.

CHAPTER 04 시제

FOCUS 25   p.57

A 1 has gone **2** have written **3** have known
B 1 has bought **2** has broken   **C 1** didn't go
2 has not eaten(had) **3** Have, heard

교과서 문장 응용하기 **1** I have bought a smartphone.
2 She has lived in Busan.

FOCUS 26   p.58

A 1 has gone **2** have, watched **3** has, finished
4 has, had   **B 1** has lost **2** has left **3** have,
arrived **4** has, sent   **C 1** have lost **2** have not
visited **3** Has, taken

교과서 문장 응용하기 **1** Gabriel has gone to London.
2 She has just arrived at the airport.

FOCUS 27   p.59

A 1 has been **2** Have, met **3** has, tasted **4** has taught **B 1** Have, worn **2** have ridden **3** has swum **4** has, changed **5** have, seen **C 1** have not seen **2** has been **3** has snowed

교과서 문장 응용하기 **1** Daniel has read the book three times. **2** They have lived in the dormitory since July.

FOCUS 28　　　　　p.60

A 1 has been raining **2** have been studying **3** have, been working **4** have, been learning **5** Has, been playing **B 1** has been eating **2** has, been exercising **3** Has, been cleaning **4** has been talking **5** has been saving **C 1** Has she been sleeping **2** have been planning **3** have been looking

교과서 문장 응용하기 **1** I have been talking on the phone for an hour. **2** They have not been building the library since June.

FOCUS 29　　　　　p.61

A 1 had lived **2** had taken **3** had, been **4** had left **B 1** had lent **2** had fallen **3** had gone **4** had been **C 1** had not seen **2** had bought **3** had given **4** had, disappeared

교과서 문장 응용하기 **1** I read the report (that(which)) she had written. **2** When he returned, Carol had washed the car. / Carol had washed the car when he returned.

FOCUS 30　　　　　p.62

A 1 had been surfing **2** had been overeating **3** had been living **B 1** had been looking **2** had been working **3** had not been watching **4** Had Jim been praying **C 1** had been waiting **2** had been standing **3** had been singing **4** had, been learning

교과서 문장 응용하기 **1** Somebody(Someone) had been smoking before I came. **2** They said(that) they had been fishing for an hour.

● ● ● ●
내신적중 실전문제　　　　　pp.63~66

01 ⑤　**02** ⑤　**03** has　**04** ④　**05** ②　**06** ④　**07** ⑤　**08** has been taking care of　**09** ③　**10** ③　**11** for, since　**12** ②　**13** ⑤　**14** have been cleaning　**15** ③　**16** ②　**17** ④　**18** ①　**19** ⓐ have learned, ⓑ have been lying, ⓒ had left　**20** ②, ⑤

서술형 평가
01 (1) has acted　(2) had acted　**02** (1) has gone to Russia　(2) has taught(has been teaching) math for 5 years　**03** (1) Pedro had seen a hippo in the picture book　(2) My club members had been discussing the project　**04** She has been taking swimming lessons for two years.　**05** ⓐ was → has been　ⓑ has been appointed → was appointed　**06** how human had walked on the moon

---

01 2시간 동안 기다리는 동작이 계속되고 있다는 것이 자연스러우므로 현재완료진행형이 알맞다.

02 '발견한 것'보다 '영어책을 집에 두고 온 것'이 먼저 일어난 일이므로 과거완료가 알맞다.

03 첫 번째 문장은 '현재까지 비가 내리고 있다'는 의미여야 하므로 현재완료진행형(have been + 동사원형 + -ing)이 알맞다. 두 번째 문장은 '이미 책을 샀다'는 의미로 완료를 나타내는 현재완료(have + 과거분사)가 알맞다.

04 '세수를 할 수 없었던 것'보다 '팔이 부러진 것'이 먼저 일어난 일이므로 과거완료가 알맞다.

05 '지금까지 본'이라는 의미는 과거부터 현재에 이르기까지의 경험을 나타내므로 현재완료가 알맞다.

06 어제 차가 고장이 났고 그 이전에는 계속해서 잘 달렸으므로 과거 이전의 일을 나타내는 과거완료진행형이 알맞다.

07 첫 번째 빈칸에는 과거를 나타내는 부사구 last night으로 보아 과거시제가, 두 번째 빈칸에는 '10시 이후로 지금까지 컴퓨터 게임을 하고 있다'는 뜻이어야 하므로 현재완료진행형(「have been + 동사원형 + -ing」)이 알맞다.

08 지금까지 3일 동안 계속 돌보고 있으므로 현재완료진행형인 「have been + 동사원형 + -ing」로 써야 한다.

09 ③ 그를 발견한 것보다 그를 찾고 있었던 것이 먼저이며, 두 번째 문장은 문맥상 '계속해서 찾고 있는 중이었다'가 되어야 자연스럽다. 따라서 ③은 「had been + 동사원형 + -ing」의 과거완료진행형으로 써야 한다.(→ looking)

10 '엄마가 전화를 한 것'은 과거로, '숙제를 이미 끝낸 것'은 그 이전의 일이므로 과거완료로 쓴다.

11 현재완료의 계속 용법으로 for는 '~동안'으로 기간을, since는 '~ 이후로 (지금까지)'로 어떤 기간의 시작점을 나타낸다.

12 '프랑스에 가서 지금 여기에 없다'라는 의미이므로 결과를 나타내는 현재완료로 쓴다.

13 |보기|와 ⑤는 경험, ①②는 계속, ③ 결과, ④ 완료의 의미를 나타낸다.

14 2시간 전에 시작한 청소를 지금도 하고 있는 중이므로 현재완료진행형으로 쓴다.

15 ③ '뉴욕에 한 번 가본 적이 있다'라는 의미가 되려면 has gone to가 아닌 has been to가 알맞다.

16 ①③④는 현재완료이고, ⑤는 현재완료진행형이므로 have가, ②는 말하기 전에 이미 의자를 망가뜨렸다는 뜻이 되어야 하므로 과거완료 「had + 과거분사」의 had가 알맞다.

17 ④ 눈이 온 것이 버스가 도착하지 않은 것보다 먼저 일어난 일이므로 과거완료 시제가 되어야 한다.(→ had snowed)

18 ⓐⓒ는 현재완료의 계속을, ⓑ는 완료를, ⓓ는 경험을 나타낸다.

19 ⓐ는 '작년부터 계속 배웠다'는 뜻이어야 하므로 계속 용법의 현재완료가, ⓑ는 1시간 동안 계속 진행 중인 일을 나타내므로 현재완료진행형이, ⓒ는 '누군가가 두고 간 것'이 핸드백을 찾은 것보다 먼저 일어난 일이므로 과거완료가 알맞다.

20 ① yesterday는 명백한 과거를 나타내는 부사이므로 현재완료가 아닌 과거시제로 표현해야 한다. (→ bought) ③ 휴가 중이라 가고 없다는 뜻이므로 been to는 gone to가 되어야 한다. ④ 고친 것이 다시 망가진 것보다 먼저 일어난 일이므로 has는 had가 되어야 한다.

서술형 평가

01 (1) '작년 이후로'라는 의미이므로 현재완료로 쓴다. (2) 과거 이전에 시작한 일이 과거의 어느 시점까지 영향을 미치므로 과거완료로 쓴다.

02 (1) Sally는 러시아에 가서 지금 여기 없으므로 결과를 의미하는 현재완료로 쓴다. (2) 김 선생님은 5년 전에 수학을 가르치기 시작해서 지금도 여전히 가르치고 있으므로 계속을 의

미하는 현재완료나 현재완료진행형으로 쓴다.

03 (1) 과거에 시작한 일이 과거 어느 시점까지 영향을 미치면 과거완료로, (2) 그 동작이 계속되고 있었다면 과거완료진행형으로 쓴다.

04 질문의 시제에 맞도록 현재완료진행형으로 대답하며, 일정한 기간을 말할 때는 그 앞에 전치사 for를 쓴다.

[05~06]

> Green 여사는 20년 동안 대도시에서 과학 선생님이었다. 지난주에 그녀는 외딴 마을로 발령을 받았다. 그녀는 수업 첫날, 현대 과학과 그것이 인류의 발전에 얼마나 도움을 주고 있는가에 관한 이야기를 했다. 그녀는 우주선에 대해서 이야기했고 인간이 어떻게 달 위를 걸었는가에 관한 이야기도 했다. 강의를 끝냈을 때, 그녀는 학생들에게 질문이 있는지를 물었다. "선생님,"하고 한 학생이 물었다. "우리 마을을 통과하는 버스 노선이 언제 생길지 말씀해 주시겠습니까?"

05 ⓐ 20년이라는 기간 동안 선생님이었다는 '계속'을 나타내므로 현재완료로 써야 한다. ⓑ 과거를 나타내는 부사구(Last week)는 현재완료와 함께 쓸 수 없으므로 과거 시제를 써야 한다.

06 이야기를 한 것보다(She told about ~) 달 위를 걸은 것이 먼저 일어난 일이므로 동사는 과거완료 형태가 알맞으며 「의문사(how) + 주어(human) + 동사(had walked) + 부사구(on the moon)」의 순서대로 쓴다.

CHAPTER **05** 조동사

FOCUS 31 p.69

A 1 borrow 2 can't 3 Could you 4 couldn't
B 1 can walk 2 Can you carry 3 will be able to play 4 can't be a liar   **C** 1 can solve 2 Could(Can) you tell me 3 will be able to speak

교과서 문장 응용하기 1 Can(Could) you answer the question? 2 You can't(cannot) be bored.

A 1 may go **2** may have **3** May I have   **B 1** may not smoke **2** May(Can) I see **3** might study **C 1** 그녀는 그녀의 친구의 목소리를 알아들을지도 모른다. **2** 바라건대 신께서 너를 도우시기를! **3** 너는 도서관에서 크게 말해서는 안 된다.

교과서 문장 응용하기   1 May(Can) I sit(have a seat) here? **2** It may(might) rain this afternoon.

A 1 had to **2** have to **3** must **4** must not **B 1** has to wear **2** must not use **3** had to take(catch) **4** doesn't have to wait **5** must be

교과서 문장 응용하기   1 You must be afraid of ghosts. **2** You must not go out at night.

A 1 should **2** ought not to **3** should not **4** attend **5** ought not   **B 1** should(ought to) follow **2** should(ought to) call **3** should(ought to) spend **4** should(ought to) drink   **C 1** should take **2** ought not to tell **3** should visit

교과서 문장 응용하기   1 He should(ought to) quit smoking. **2** You should not(ought not to) touch the artworks in gallery.

A 1 would **2** would rather **3** better not **4** go **5** better   **B 1** had better wear **2** would rather not swim **3** had better not say **4** would rather study   **C 1** would rather read **2** had better run **3** had better not leave

교과서 문장 응용하기   1 Mike had better be(keep) quiet for a while. **2** I would rather live in a crowded city.

A 1 visit **2** used **3** used to **4** used to   **B 1** used to watch **2** used to have **3** used to go **4** used to collect   **C 1** used to have **2** would wait **3** used to teach

교과서 문장 응용하기   1 That room used to be a kitchen. **2** I would(used to) work on weekends.

A 1 may have won **2** might have arrived **3** must have done **4** cannot have forgotten **5** should have decided   **B 1** must have lost **2** may(might) have lost **3** cannot have repaired(fixed) **4** should not have gone **5** must have bought

교과서 문장 응용하기   1 I must have broken the window. **2** Joshua should not have slept last night.

내신적중 실전문제   pp.76~80

01 ② **02** ⑤ **03** may(May) **04** used to **05** ②
06 ③ **07** ③ **08** ④ **09** ④ **10** ① playing → play
11 ④ **12** ② **13** ② **14** ⑤ **15** ④ **16** ③ **17** ④
18 ③ **19** ① **20** ⑤ **21** ① **22** ③ lives → live
23 ② **24** ⑤ **25** ④ **26** ③

서술형 평가

01 (1) had to (2) used to (3) might   **02** ⓐ 떠나도 된다, 허락 ⓑ 올지도 모른다, 추측 ⓒ 제가 사용해도 될까요?, 요청   **03** (1) Kate has to use a coupon by tomorrow. (2) Students must(should) not leave bicycles here.   **04** (1) can't have gone (2) might have studied (3) should have called   **05** They don't have to leave their homes   **06** ⓐ can ⓑ can ⓒ can't ⓓ can

01 문맥상 '자신을 자랑스러워함에 틀림없다'가 자연스러우므로 강한 추측을 나타내는 must가 알맞다.

02 '가게에서 쿠키를 사느니 차라리 스스로 쿠키를 굽겠다'는 의미가 자연스러우므로 선택을 나타내는 「would rather A than B」가 알맞다.

03 첫 번째 문장에는 허락, 두 번째 문장에는 추측, 세 번째 문

장에는 기원을 나타내는 may가 알맞다.

04 첫 번째 문장에는 과거의 규칙적인 습관을, 두 번째 문장에는 과거의 상태를 나타내는 used to가 일맞다.

05 '~일 리가 없다'라는 부정적 추측은 cannot으로 쓴다.

06 '~하지 않는 게 좋겠다'라는 충고의 의미는 「had better not + 동사원형」으로 쓴다.

07 '어딘가에 귀걸이를 떨어뜨렸을지도 모른다'는 과거의 불확실한 추측의 의미이므로 「may(might) have + 과거분사」로 쓴다.

08 'James는 (과거에) 여행 가이드였지만, 지금은 더 이상 아니다.'라는 의미로 과거의 상태는 「used to+동사원형」으로 쓴다.

09 '~했어야 했는데(못했다)'라는 의미의 과거 사실에 대한 유감은 「should have + 과거분사」로 나타낸다.

10 ① 과거의 규칙적인 습관을 나타내는 used to 다음에는 동사원형을 쓴다.

11 문장을 완성하면 I would rather sleep than eat breakfast.이다. 「would rather A than B」는 'B하느니 차라리 A하겠다'라는 뜻이다.

12 첫 번째 빈칸에는 '우산을 가져가야 한다'의 뜻으로 '~해야 한다'는 의무를 나타내는 should가, 두 번째 빈칸에는 정중한 요청을 나타내는 could가 알맞다.

13 첫 번째 빈칸에는 '알러지가 있으니 땅콩 파이를 먹었을 리가 없다'의 의미가 되도록, 「cannot have + 과거분사」를, 두 번째 빈칸에는 '졸려보이는 게 일 때문에 피곤했음에 틀림없다'의 의미가 되도록 「must have + 과거분사」를 쓴다.

14 |보기|와 ⑤는 과거의 불규칙적인 습관을 나타낸다. ①, ③은 추측의 의미를 나타내고, ②는 주절과의 시제 일치를 위한 will의 과거형이다. ④는 정중한 요청의 의미이다.

15 첫 번째 빈칸에는 과거의 일에 대한 가능성을 나타내는 could가, 두 번째 빈칸에는 접속사 but으로 보아 can't가 알맞다.

16 첫 번째 빈칸에는 '물지도 모른다'는 추측의 의미인 may가, 두 번째 빈칸에는 '만지면 안 된다'는 금지의 의미인 ought not to가 알맞다.

17 ④ had better의 부정형은 had better not이다.

18 '~해야 한다'라는 의미로 must와 have to를 모두 쓸 수 있지만, 시제가 과거일 때에는 have to의 과거형 had to를 쓴다.

19 ① must가 '~임에 틀림 없다'의 뜻일 때는 have to로 바꿔 쓸 수 없다.

20 나머지는 '~해야 한다'의 의미이고, ⑤는 '~임에 틀림 없다'의 의미이다.

21 '그녀는 아팠음에 틀림없다'는 의미로 과거에 대한 강한 추측을 말하고 있으므로 「must have + 과거분사」가 알맞다.

22 ③ 「would rather A than B」 구문에서 A와 B는 같은 형태여야 하므로 live가 알맞다.

23 ② '날씨가 지금 흐리니 오후에 비가 올지도 모른다.'는 추측의 의미를 나타내야 하므로 may로 써야 한다.

24 ⓐ 과거에 했어야 하는 행동에 대한 후회를 나타내므로 「should have + 과거분사」를 쓴다. ⓑ than 뒤에 비교 대상이 있으므로 「would rather A than B」를 쓰는 것이 알맞다.

25 ⓐ '~할 수 있을 것이다'라는 의미는 will be able to로 쓴다. ⓓ ought to의 부정형은 ought not to이다.

26 ③ 'Alex가 30분 일찍 오지 않아서 유감이다.'라는 의미는 '~했어야 했는데 하지 못했다'는 과거의 일에 대한 후회를 나타내는 「should have+과거분사」로 써야 한다. 「should not have+과거분사」는 '~하지 말아야 했는데 (했다)'의 의미이다.

서술형 평가

01 (1) '~해야 했다'는 had to(have to의 과거형)로, (2) 과거의 상태는 used to로, (3) '~일지도 모른다(추측)'는 might로 쓴다.

02 may는 ⓐ 허락 ⓑ 추측 ⓒ 요청의 뜻을 나타낸다.

03 (1) '~해야 한다'는 의미는 has to로 쓴다. 여기서는 to가 있으므로 must나 should는 쓸 수 없다. (2) '~해서는 안 된다(금지)'의 의미는 must not이나 should not으로 쓴다.

04 과거 사실에 대한 추측은 「조동사 + have+과거분사」로 쓴다. (1) ~이었을 리가 없다: can't have + 과거분사 (2) ~이었을지도 모른다: might have + 과거분사 (3) ~했어야 했다: should have + 과거분사

[05~06]

인터넷 쇼핑, 즉 온라인 쇼핑은 점점 더 인기 있어지고 있다. 점점 더 많은 사람들이 물건을 사기 위해 인터넷을 이용하고 있다. 사람들은 왜 쇼핑하기 위해 인터넷을 이용할까? 어떤 사람들은 그것이 더 편리하다고 말한다. 그들은 물건을 주문하기 위해 집을 나갈 필요가 없고, 밤낮 상관없이 언제든 원하는 것을 쇼핑할 수 있다. 다른 사람들은 집 근처의 상점에서 찾을 수 없는 상품들을 찾을 수 있다고 말한다. 그리고 또 다른 사람들은 인터넷에서 더 좋은 가격의 물건들을 찾을 수 있다고 말한다.

05 '집을 떠날 필요가 없다'는 의미여야 하므로 must not이 아니라 don't have to로 써야 한다.

06 ⓐ 쇼핑할 수 '있다' ⓑ 찾을 수 '있다' ⓓ 찾을 수 '있다'는 가능을 나타내므로 can이 알맞다. ⓒ 찾을 수 '없다'는 의미여야 하므로 can't가 알맞다.

CHAPTER 06 수동태

FOCUS 38   p.83

A 1 was bitten 2 was 3 opened 4 is not spoken B 1 is played 2 was destroyed 3 was not broken by C 1 The key was found by my sister. 2 The bug was not(wasn't) caught by the old man. 3 Is the play seen by her?

교과서 문장 응용하기 1 The table was bought by the woman yesterday. 2 Were the cups broken by you?

FOCUS 39   p.84

A 1 ought to be washed 2 might be played by 3 could not be understood 4 Waste should be recycled B 1 may be invited 2 Will, be replaced 3 must(should) be obeyed by C 1 Our environment must be protected by us. 2 The blue ribbon may not be bought by Emily. 3 The new English teacher will be loved by everyone. 4 A new restaurant is going to be opened by Mr. Jones next week.

교과서 문장 응용하기 1 Children can be taught by the teacher. 2 This car will not be stolen.

FOCUS 40   p.85

A 1 A cup of water is being drunk by Charlie.

2 Was the desk being painted by you? 3 My bike has been found by me in the park. 4 Blue shoes had been worn by him before he bought the new ones. B 1 is being built 2 were being caught 3 have not been washed 4 had been cleaned

교과서 문장 응용하기 1 The man was being chased by the police officer. 2 Her songs have been recorded by him for 2(two) months.

FOCUS 41   p.86

A 1 was sent 2 is given 3 be made B 1 was sent to 2 were bought for 3 will be given to C 1 Science is taught to us by Mrs. Brown. 2 I was told surprising news by him. 3 Some questions were asked of the students by Michael. 4 A cup of coffee will be made for you by Victoria.

교과서 문장 응용하기 1 He was asked a question by a guest. 2 The postcard was written to me by Leo.

FOCUS 42   p.87

A 1 to walk 2 to turn on 3 made to sign B 1 Lucy was elected the vice president by the members. 2 Kate was heard to shout at a man by us. 3 She was made to run faster for a good time by him. 4 He was advised to exercise regularly by them. C 1 was asked to go 2 was made happy 3 was made to water

교과서 문장 응용하기 1 The door was left open. 2 Violet was seen to enter the room.

FOCUS 43   p.88

A 1 are taken care of by all parents 2 will be set up by the company 3 was picked up by her on her way to the office B 1 is looked up to 2 was handed in 3 will be carried out C 1 The birds were looked after by my brother. 2 I was spoken to by a stranger on the street. 3 The broken chairs were taken away last night (by someone).

교과서 문장 응용하기 **1** The meeting was put off by her. **2** The man is looked down on by everyone(everybody).

FOCUS 44 p.89

A **1** Their marriage is said to be in trouble. **2** He is hoped to win the gold medal. **3** She is thought to be the right person for the job. **B** **1** It is said that **2** was found to be **3** It was thought that **C** **1** It was believed that he would come back soon., He was believed to come back soon. **2** It is thought that turtles live longer than monkeys., Turtles are thought to live longer than monkeys.

교과서 문장 응용하기 **1** It is believed that they are very kind. **2** The children are expected to pass the exam(test).

FOCUS 45 p.90

A **1** with **2** at **3** from **4** to **B** **1** is interested in **2** is made of **3** are satisfied with **4** is known for **C** **1** was crowded with **2** is covered with **3** is worried about

교과서 문장 응용하기 **1** The ship was caught in a storm. **2** Paper is made from wood.

내신적중 실전문제 pp.91~94

01 ⑤ **02** ④ **03** in **04** ② **05** ② **06** ⑤ **07** ⑤ **08** ① been → being **09** ③ to buy → to be bought **10** ④ **11** to, of **12** ②, ④ **13** ③ **14** being taken **15** ④ **16** has not been caught by **17** ③ **18** ③ **19** ⑤ **20** ②

서술형 평가

01 was written by Hemingway **02** have been painted by his wife **03** (1) was given a piece of advice (2) was given to Jessica **04** (1) was heard to come up the stairs (2) was made to keep a diary in English **05** (1) are being sold (2) was being repaired **06** (1) They said that the dog's constant barking was always disturbing their peace. (2) The dog's constant barking was said to be always disturbing their peace. **07** is being taken care of

01 '스페인어가 말해진다'라는 의미여야 하므로 현재시제의 수동태로 쓴다.

02 '행해져야 한다'는 수동의 의미여야 하며, 조동사가 있는 문장의 수동태는 「조동사 + be + 과거분사」로 쓴다.

03 • be interested in: ~에 관심이 있다
• be caught in: (눈, 비 등을) 만나다

04 '비웃다'는 뜻의 동사구 laugh at은 한 단어로 취급하여 수동태로 쓴다.

05 직접목적어가 주어로 쓰인 동사 buy의 수동태 문장은 간접목적어 앞에 전치사 for를 쓴다.

06 지각동사와 사역동사의 수동태는 목적격보어인 원형부정사를 to부정사로 써야 한다.

07 ⑤ 5형식 문장의 수동태는 목적어 him을 주어로, 목적격보어는 동사 뒤에 그대로 써야 한다.(make → to make)

08 ① 진행 시제의 수동태는 「be동사 + being + 과거분사」로 쓴다.

09 ③ '시계가 구입될 필요가 있다'라는 말이 되어야 하므로 to부정사를 수동태로 써야 한다.

10 '올해에 두 번째로 뽑혔다'라는 경험의 완료 시제 수동태여야 하므로 「has been + 과거분사」의 형태가 알맞다.

11 4형식 문장을 수동태로 바꿀 때 동사에 따라 간접목적어 앞에 전치사를 써야 하는데, give는 to가, ask는 of가 알맞다.

12 동사 think의 목적어로 쓰인 that절을 「It + be동사 + 과거분사 + that ~」의 형태나 「that절 주어 + be동사 + 과거분사 + to부정사 ~」의 형태의 수동태로 만든다.

13 조동사가 있는 수동태는 「조동사 + be + 과거분사」로 쓴다.

14 수동태의 진행시제는 「be동사 + being + 과거분사」로 쓰는데, 여기서는 의문문이므로 be동사가 문장의 맨 앞에 있다.

15 ④ '전세계 어린이들에게 알려져 있다'는 의미이므로 be

known to를 써야 한다.

16 완료시제 수동태의 부정문은 「has not been + 과거분사 + by」로 쓴다.

17 ③ 수동태 It is believed that ~의 능동태는 현재시제 is와 시제가 일치하도록 People believe that ~이 되어야 한다.

18 ③ 동사구가 쓰인 수동태 문장으로 '태워주다'는 동사구는 pick up으로 한 단어로 취급하여 써야 한다.(picked → picked up)

19 ⑤ 행위자가 특정한 사람이므로 생략할 수 없다.

20 ⓑ 현재완료 수동태의 의문문은 Has가 문장 맨 앞에 와야 한다.(Did → Has) ⓔ 조동사가 있는 문장의 수동태는 「조동사 + be + 과거분사」의 형태여야 한다.(dry → dried)

서술형 평가

01 사물이 주어인 수동태 문장은 「be동사 + 과거분사」로 쓴다.

02 주어가 they인 문장의 현재완료 수동태는 「have + been + 과거분사」로 쓴다.

03 4형식 문장으로 간접목적어와 직접목적어를 주어로 하는 두 개의 수동태가 가능하며, 직접목적어가 주어이고, 동사가 give인 수동태의 경우 간접목적어 앞에 전치사 to를 써야 한다.

04 지각동사와 사역동사의 수동태는 「be동사 + 지각동사(사역동사)의 과거분사+to+동사원형」으로 쓴다.

05 진행시제 수동태는 「be동사 + being + 과거분사」로 쓴다. (1) 현재진행 수동태 (2) 과거진행 수동태

[06~07]

> Pear Tree Street의 400번지에 사는 어떤 가족이 소유한 짖어대는 개 한 마리는 이웃들 사이에서 골칫거리의 원인이었다. 일요일 오후, 옆집 사는 가족에 의해 불만 사항이 경찰서에 접수되었다. 그들은 그 개가 계속 짖어대서 그들의 평화가 늘 방해 받고 있다고 말했다. 그들은 그들이 그 소리를 참을 수 없으며 그 개를 주인에게서 데려가기를 원한다고 진술했다. 결국, 그 개는 일시적으로 시립 동물 보호소에서 보호되고 있다.

06 ⑴ that절이 목적어인 문장의 능동태는 they say that ~으로 나타내며, be동사가 was이므로 said를 쓴다. ⑵ 종속절의 주어가 주절의 주어로 오고 시제가 일치하면 that절의 동사는 「to+동사원형」이 된다.

07 '개가 보호되고 있다'는 동사구가 쓰인 현재진행형 수동태이므로 is being taken care of의 순서가 되어야 한다.

CHAPTER 07 비교 구문

FOCUS 46   p.97

A 1 yours **2** as **3** faster **4** highest **5** most familiar **6** a lot   **B 1** as(so) polite as **2** more difficult than **3** much better than **4** the most useful of **5** as early as

교과서 문장 응용하기 1 He is not as(so) healthy as Susan. **2** I am a lot more optimistic than my friends.

FOCUS 47   p.98

A 1 possible **2** they could **3** twice as tall as   **B 1** twice as heavy as **2** four times as old as **3** as fast as she could **4** as slowly as possible **C 1** two times harder than **2** as often as I could **3** five times as tall as

교과서 문장 응용하기 1 He jumped as high as possible(he could). **2** This desk is twice as big as mine.

FOCUS 48   p.99

A 1 less brave than **2** less fast than **3** less tired than **4** less interested, than **5** less excited, than **B 1** less comfortable than **2** less clever than **3** less exciting than **4** not as(so) adventurous as

교과서 문장 응용하기 1 My hometown is less famous than London. **2** He is not as(so) polite as his friend.

FOCUS 49   p.100

A 1 sooner **2** smarter, smarter **3** busier, busier **4** higher **5** less, less   **B 1** darker **2** the happier **3** more **4** the more **5** better and better   **C 1** The longer, the angrier **2** more and more popular **3** the easier

교과서 문장 응용하기 1 The world is getting smaller and smaller. **2** The older we grow, the wiser we get(become).

A 1 one of the most famous **2** the cleanest, cleaner than any other, No, cleaner than, No, as clean as   **B 1** higher than, higher than any other, the highest of **2** more(as) famous than(as), more famous than any other

교과서 문장 응용하기 1 The shirt is one of the most colorful shirts in this shop. **2** Sam is smarter than any other student in my class.

내신적중 실전문제
pp.102~106

01 ① **02** ④ **03** she can **04** The more, the **05** ④ **06** ① **07** ③ **08** ① **09** ⑤ **10** ② **11** ④, ⑤ **12** ④ **13** ⓐ, ⓒ, ⓓ **14** ② **15** less, than **16** three times as, as **17** ① **18** ① **19** ④ **20** ④ **21** ③, ④ **22** ⑤ **23** ⑤ **24** ⓐ tall as ⓑ faster than ⓒ the largest **25** ② **26** ②

서술형 평가

01 (1) as fast as possible (2) as fast as you can
02 (1) is less nutritious than (2) isn't as(so) nutritious as **03** (1) more popular (2) most popular (3) as popular **04** (1) No (other) country in the world is as(so) small as the Vatican City. (2) No (other) country in the world is smaller than the Vatican City. (3) The Vatican City is smaller than any other country in the world. **05** one of the most famous American poets **06** ⓐ the more often she wanted to be alone ⓑ she ran upstairs to hide as fast as she could ⓒ Dickinson was becoming worse and worse

01 '~만큼 …하지 않은'이라는 의미의 원급 비교는 「not as(so) + 원급 + as」의 형태로 쓴다.

02 방문했던 곳 중 '가장 오래된' 성이라는 의미여야 하므로 「the + 최상급」의 형태로 쓴다.

03 '가능한 한 ~하게'라는 의미인 「as + 원급 + as possible」은 「as + 원급 + as + 주어 + can」으로 바꿔 쓸 수 있다.

04 '만약 네가 더 많이 연습한다면, 너는 더 빨리 무대에 설 수 있다.'라는 뜻은 '더 많이 연습할수록, 더 빨리 무대에 설 수 있다'는 의미인 「the + 비교급, the + 비교급」을 이용한 표현으로 바꿔 쓸 수 있다.

05 ⓐ '가장 …한'의 의미는 「the + 최상급」의 형태로 쓴다. ⓑ 두 개의 사람이나 사물을 비교하는 '~보다 더 …한'의 의미는 「비교급 + than」의 형태로 쓴다

06 ⓐ 「less + 원급 + than」: ~보다 덜 …한 ⓑ 「배수사(twice) + as + 원급 + as」: ~보다 두 배 더 …한

07 나머지는 'Ethan은 세상에서 (그 누구보다도) 가장 운이 좋다.'라는 의미인데, ③은 'Ethan은 세상에서 다른 사람들만큼 운이 좋다.'는 의미이다.

08 비교급을 강조하고 있으므로 원급을 강조하는 부사 very와는 바꿔 쓸 수 없다.

09 ⑤ 뒤에 than으로 보아 비교급 형태가 되어야 한다. (→ safer)

10 「as + 원급 + as」의 형태여야 하므로 빈칸에는 비교급인 worse 또는 better는 알맞지 않다.

11 「A + 비교급 + than B」 = 「B + less + 원급 + than A」 = 「B + not as(so) + 원급 + as A」

12 '~할수록 …하다'는 의미는 「the + 비교급, the + 비교급」의 형태로 쓴다.

13 ⓑ는 '타이타닉은 다른 영화만큼 좋지 않다.'는, ⓔ는 '타이타닉은 모든 다른 영화보다 덜 좋다.'는 뜻이다. 나머지는 '타이타닉이 영화 중에서 가장 좋다.'는 뜻이다.

14 '가장 ~한 것 중 하나'라는 뜻은 「one of the + 최상급 + 복수 명사」로 쓰므로 배열하면 one of the largest islands가 된다.

15 검은 우산이 흰색 우산보다 비싸지 않으므로 「less + 원급 + than」의 형태로 쓴다.

16 Aron이 Jack보다 만화책을 3배 더 많이 가지고 있으므로 「배수사(three times) + as + 원급 + as」의 형태로 쓴다.

17 ① 「be(get / become) + 비교급 + and + 비교급」: 점점 더 ~ 해지다

18 비교급 강조 부사(even)는 비교급 앞에 오며, '~보다 덜 …한'은 「less + 원급 + than」의 형태로 쓴다.

19 ④ 「비교급 + and + 비교급」 구문에서 비교급이 「more + 원급」의 형태인 경우에는 「more and more + 원급」으로 쓴다. (→ more)

20 Package D가 제일 무거우므로 'Package D는 다른 소포들만큼 무겁지 않다.'는 ④는 알맞지 않다.

21 '가능한 ~하게[하도록]'의 의미는 「as + 원급 + as possible」 또는 「as + 원급 + as + 주어 + can[could]」의 형태로 쓴다.

22 ⑤는 「one of the + 최상급 + 복수 명사」이므로 invention은 복수인 inventions가 되어야 한다.

23 ⑤ 'A가 다른 ~보다 더 …한'이라는 최상의 의미는 「A + 비교급+than any other + 단수 명사」로 나타내므로 magazines는 magazine이 되어야 한다.

24 ⓐ '~만큼 …지 않다'라는 원급 비교는 「not as[so] + 원급 + as」로, ⓑ '~보다 더 …한'의 의미는 「비교급 + than」으로, ⓒ '가장 ~한'의 의미는 「the + 최상급」의 형태로 쓴다.

25 ⓑ '세 배'는 three times로 써야 한다. ⓓ '점점 더 ~해지다'는 「get + 비교급 + and + 비교급」의 형태로 warm and warm은 warmer and warmer가 되어야 한다. ⓕ 「one of the + 최상급 + 복수 명사」의 형태로 driest는 the driest가 되어야 한다.

26 ② 첫 번째 문장은 카나리아보다 독수리의 색채가 덜 화려하다는 의미이므로 두 번째 문장의 isn't는 is가 되어야 한다.

서술형 평가

01 '가능한 한 ~하게[하도록]'라는 의미는 「as + 원급 + as possible」이나 「as + 원급 + as + 주어 + can」의 형태로 쓴다.

02 '~보다 덜 …한, ~만큼 …하지 않은'이라는 의미는 「less + 원급 + than」이나 「not as[so] + 원급 + as」의 형태로 쓴다.

03 ⑴ 인터넷 서핑이 운동하기보다 인기가 있으므로 비교급 비교가 알맞다. ⑵ 영화 감상이 가장 인기가 있으므로 최상급이 알맞다. ⑶ 독서와 음악 감상의 인기가 같으므로 원급 비교가 알맞다.

04 「the + 최상급」 = 「부정 주어 + as[so] + 원급 + as」 = 「부정 주어 + 비교급 + than」 = 「비교급 + than any other + 단수 명사」

[05~06]

> Emily Dickinson은 미국의 가장 유명한 시인 중 한 명이었다. 그녀는 나이가 들면 들수록 더욱 더 자주 혼자 있고 싶어 했다. 누군가 집에 오면 그녀는 가능한 빨리 이층으로 가서 숨었다. 그녀의 인생의 마지막 16년 동안, 그녀는 집을 떠나지 않았다. 커튼이 항상 가리워져 있었다. 그녀는 흰색 옷만 입었다. 어느 날, Dickinson은 점점 더 아팠지만, 그녀는 의사를 방으로 들어오지 못하게 했다. 그는 현관에서만 그녀를 볼 수 있었다.

05 「one of the 최상급 + 복수 명사」: 가장 ~한 것 중 하나

06 ⓐ 「the + 비교급, the + 비교급」: ~할수록 더 …한 ⓑ 과

거 시제이므로 can 대신 could를 써야 한다. ⓒ 「비교급 + and + 비교급」: 점점 더 ~한[하게]

CHAPTER 08 관계사

FOCUS 51   p.109

A 1 which 2 which 3 that 4 that 5 who
B 1 who(that) admires 2 which(that) was written 3 who(that) is wearing   **C** 1 I know Adam who(that) lives in the Netherlands. 2 Look at the house which(that) has just one small window. 3 The cafe which(that) sells the best milkshake in town is not open.

교과서 문장 응용하기 1 Sally is a girl who plays soccer well. / Sally is a girl who is good at soccer.
2 A monkey is an animal that lives in trees.

FOCUS 52   p.110

A 1 whose 2 whose 3 whose 4 whose 5 whose
B 1 whose course 2 whose cover 3 whose hobby   **C** 1 James knows a girl whose father is a TV producer. 2 Look at the flower whose color is bright orange. 3 The boy whose bike was broken yesterday is over there. 4 This is the picture whose price is really high.

교과서 문장 응용하기 1 This is the girl whose mother is from Canada. 2 He has a bag whose price is 20(twenty) dollars.

FOCUS 53   p.111

A 1 that 2 which 3 whom 4 which 5 which
B 1 whom(who/that) I told 2 which(that) Olivia recommended 3 which(that) she composed
C 1 The pizza which(that) Grace made was delicious. 2 The boy whom(who/that) my sister

dated is very handsome. **3** Is the movie which(that) you are watching scary?

 **1** Did you find the key which(that) you lost? **2** The woman whom(who/that) I met was a famous singer.

FOCUS 54   p.112

A 1 who, that **2** that **3** that **4** that   **B 1** that I put **2** that attended **3** boy that I know **C 1** That's the same wallet that I have lost. **2** Peter is the first boy that Julie loved in life. **3** Did you see the man and his dog that I am looking for?

 **1** Daniel is the only person that she likes. **2** You may take any book that you want.

FOCUS 55   p.113

A 1 what **2** What **3** what **4** which   **B 1** What **2** what **3** which(that)   **C 1** What, The thing which(that) **2** what, the thing which(that) **3** what, the thing which(that)

 **1** What she said made me happy. **2** I didn't listen to what he advised me to do.

FOCUS 56   p.114

A 1 which **2** whose **3** whom **4** who **5** which **B 1** for(as / because) he **2** but I **3** and it **C 1** who explained **2** which was **3** who asked

 **1** Sarah is my classmate, whom(who) I don't like. **2** I have a friend, who lives in London.

FOCUS 57   p.115

A 1 to which **2** for whom **3** to which **4** whom **B 1** to which **2** in which **3** with whom **C 1** These are her cats for which she was looking. **2** Do you know the man to whom Spencer is speaking? **3** The man should follow the directions for which she asked. **4** Victoria with whom he fell in love left him.

 **1** The sofa on which you are sitting looks comfortable. **2** I know the girl with whom Jessica played.

FOCUS 58   p.116

A 1 ○ **2** × **3** ○ **4** ×   **B 1** he can **2** I wanted **3** he stayed   **C 1** The peaches (which(that)) I bought yesterday are delicious. **2** The lady (whom(who/that)) Joe married is a science teacher. **3** The ice hockey match (which(that)) Sean played in was exciting. **4** It is a very old statue (which(that) was) made of bronze.

 **1** She is the woman (whom(who/that)) I met last year. **2** My uncle (whom(who/that)) I live with is very kind. / My uncle with whom I live is very kind.

FOCUS 59   p.117

A 1 where **2** when **3** in which   **B 1** day on which **2** library where **3** time when   **C 1** She didn't forget the day when her son went to school. **2** This is the place where the accident happened. **3** Do you know the time when the soccer game will start?

 **1** This is the office where(at which) my mother works. **2** Winter is the season when(in which) mountains are covered with snow.

FOCUS 60   p.118

A 1 how **2** why **3** in which **4** the way **5** why **B 1** how **2** the way **3** the reason why   **C 1** There were some reasons why I missed the train. **2** I know how Emily operated the machine. **3** The horror movie was the reason why Dylan couldn't sleep.

 **1** That's the reason why he crossed the road. **2** He wondered how she learned to play the guitar.

A 1 The day 2 why 3 where 4 How 5 when
B 1 why he went 2 the day she saw 3 how he makes **C** 1 Could you tell me the time when the train will leave? 2 He wondered the reason why she didn't invite him. 3 I look forward to the day when our school festival begins.

교과서 문장 응용하기 1 That's why she got angry at me.
2 This is where I lost my bracelet.

A 1 Whatever 2 whomever 3 whichever
4 Whoever **B** 1 Whatever 2 No matter who
3 whomever **C** 1 whatever 2 anyone who
3 No matter whom

교과서 문장 응용하기 1 Whoever comes here will be my friend. 2 Whatever other people think, do your best.

A 1 However 2 Wherever 3 whenever 4 when
B 1 whenever 2 Whenever 3 However 4 Wherever
C 1 However 2 Whenever I read 3 wherever she goes 4 No matter how

교과서 문장 응용하기 1 I'll follow you wherever you go. / Wherever you go, I'll follow you. 2 I get sick whenever I eat ice cream. / Wherever I eat ice cream, I get sick.

내신적중 실전문제　　pp.122~126

01 ⑤ 02 ① 03 what 04 Whoever 05 ④ 06 ③ 07 ② 08 ⑤ 09 which was 10 ⑤ 11 ③
12 ⑤ 13 ④ 14 What(what) 15 ① 16 but he
17 ③ 18 ③ 19 ②, ④ 20 ③ 21 ② 22 ⑤ 23 ③ 24 ②, ⑤ 25 ②

서술형 평가

01 (1) which(that) were sent (2) sent 02 (1) 내가 원하는 것은, 주어 (2) 내가 읽기를 원했던 것, 보어 03 (1) in which you grow plants (2) (which(that)) you grow plants in (3) where you grow plants 04 (1) the shop where (2) the season when (3) the reason why 05 ⓐ and they are called ⓑ which
06 ⓒ Whoever(Anyone who) ⓓ Whoever(Anyone who)

01 빈칸 앞의 선행사와 빈칸 뒤의 명사가 소유 관계이므로 소유격 관계대명사 whose가 알맞다.

02 선행사가 사물이고 계속적 용법이므로 관계대명사 which가 알맞다.

03 빈칸에는 '~한 것'을 의미하는 선행사를 포함하는 관계대명사 what이 알맞다.

04 빈칸에는 '~하는 누구나'를 의미하는 복합관계대명사 whoever가 알맞다.

05 ④ forget의 주어가 my father이므로 forgets가 되어야 한다.

06 the same이 선행사를 수식하고 있으므로 관계대명사 that으로 연결한다.

07 선행사가 시간을 나타내므로 관계부사 when을 이용하여 연결한다.

08 ⑤ '네가 원하는 것은 어느 것이든'의 의미이므로 복합관계대명사 whichever가 되어야 한다.

09 「주격 관계대명사+be동사」는 생략할 수 있다.

10 첫 번째 빈칸에는 선행사가 사람이고 빈칸 이하가 주어 역할을 하므로 관계대명사 who 또는 that이 알맞다. 두 번째 빈칸에는 선행사가 사물이고 빈칸 이하가 목적어 역할을 하므로 관계대명사 which 또는 that이 알맞다.

11 첫 번째 빈칸에는 선행사가 이유를 나타내므로 관계부사 why가 알맞다. 두 번째 빈칸에는 생략된 선행사가 방법을 나타내므로 관계부사 how가 알맞다.

12 선행사를 포함하며 명사절을 이끄는 복합관계대명사 whoever를 사용하여 whoever made this cake를 주어로 쓴다.

13 ④ 전치사 뒤에는 that을 쓸 수 없다.

14 '~하는 것'의 뜻으로 선행사를 포함하여 명사절을 이끌면서 주어, 보어, 목적어 역할을 하는 관계대명사 what이 알맞다.

15 ① 주격 관계대명사 which는 that으로 바꿔 쓸 수 있다. ② 선행사가 -thing인 경우에는 that만 쓴다. ③ whose는 다른 것으로 바꿔 쓸 수 없다. ④ 「전치사＋관계대명사」가 연달아 올 경우에는 that을 쓸 수 없으므로 which만 가능하다. ⑤ 계속적 용법에는 that을 쓸 수 없다.

16 관계대명사의 계속적 용법은 「접속사＋대명사」로 바꿔 쓸 수 있다. 문맥상 접속사 but이, 대명사는 her teacher이자 Mr. Kim을 가리키는 he가 알맞다.

17 ③ 관계부사 how는 선행사인 the way와 함께 쓰지 않는다. (→ the way 또는 how)

18 문맥상 '네가 가는 어디에나'의 의미여야 하므로 복합관계부사 wherever가 자연스럽다.

19 '무슨 일이 일어나든지'라는 의미는 선행사를 포함한 복합관계대명사 whatever로 나타내며, 양보의 의미이므로 no matter what으로도 바꿔 쓸 수 있다.

20 나머지는 선행사를 수식하는 관계대명사로, ③은 명사절을 이끄는 접속사로 쓰였다.

21 ② 단독으로 쓰인 주격 관계대명사는 생략할 수 없다.

22 ⑤ '그가 아무리 나이가 들었다 해도'라는 양보의 의미여야 하므로 복합관계부사 however로 고쳐야 한다.

23 ⓐ 선행사 the girl 뒤에 주격 관계대명사 who를 쓰거나 「주격 관계대명사＋be동사」를 생략하여 is를 삭제해야 한다. ⓑ 관계대명사 that은 계속적 용법으로 쓸 수 없다. ⓓ 선행사 the way와 관계부사 how는 함께 쓸 수 없다.

24 선행사가 장소를 나타내므로 관계부사 where로 연결한다. 관계부사는 「전치사＋관계대명사」로 바꿔 쓸 수 있으며, 이때 that은 쓸 수 없다.

25 ⓐ 관계대명사의 계속적 용법이므로 whom은 주격 관계대명사 who가 되어야 한다. ⓒ 선행사가 「사람＋동물」이므로 관계대명사 who는 that이 되어야 한다. ⓓ 「주격 관계대명사＋be동사」인 which was가 생략된 문장으로, '지어진'이라는 수동의 의미이므로 building은 built가 되어야 한다.

서술형 평가

01 선행사가 사물이므로 (1) 주격 관계대명사 which 또는 that으로 연결하거나 (2) 「주격 관계대명사＋be동사」를 생략하고 쓸 수 있다.

02 관계대명사 what은 선행사를 포함하면서 명사절을 이끌어 문장에서 주어, 보어, 목적어 역할을 하며, '~(하는)것'이라는 뜻을 나타낸다.

03 관계대명사가 전치사의 목적어인 경우 「전치사＋관계대명사」로 쓰며, 이때는 that을 쓸 수 없고 관계부사로 바꿔 쓸 수 있다. 전치사를 문장의 끝에 쓸 때는 생략 가능하다.

04 「선행사＋관계부사」를 이용한다. (1) '샌들을 산 가게', (2) '많은 사람들이 소풍을 가는 계절', (3) '남극이 북극보다 추운 이유'라는 의미가 자연스럽다.

[05~06]

> 인간의 뇌는 두 부분으로 나뉘는데, 그것은 우뇌와 좌뇌라고 불린다. 좀 더 논리적인 좌뇌는 언어를 통제한다. 좌뇌는 사물의 이름을 정하고 그것들을 분류한다. 철자나 문법적인 규칙을 기억하는 사람은 누구나 이 부분을 사용한다. 오른쪽 뇌는 좀 더 창조적이다. 시각, 청각, 후각, 촉각, 그리고 미각으로부터 정보를 얻는다. 그림을 그리거나 음악을 듣는 사람은 누구나 이 부분을 사용한다.

05 ⓐ 관계대명사의 계속적 용법은 「접속사＋대명사」로 바꿔 쓸 수 있다. 의미상 접속사는 and가, 주어는 two sides이므로 대명사 they가 알맞다. ⓑ 선행사가 사물이므로 which로 바꿔 쓸 수 있다.

06 둘 다 '~하는 사람은 누구나'의 의미여야 하므로 Anyone who 또는 Whoever가 되어야 한다.

CHAPTER 09 접속사

FOCUS 64   p.129

A 1 주어 **2** 주어 **3** 목적어 **4** 보어   **B 1** That Mr. Johnson will not return **2** that you had a traffic accident **3** I wonder if Noah **4** whether she will quit the job **5** It is important that   **C 1** that, enough time **2** that, will be hard **3** Whether he will agree **4** whether(if), attend the meeting

교과서 문장 응용하기 **1** Jeff doesn't know (that) she is sick. **2** Emily doesn't know whether(if) I am a teacher (or not).

FOCUS 65 p.130

A 1 seem very happy when you help other people **2** made some cookies while I was taking care of my sister **3** came up to me as he was singing **4** watched the movie while Violet was taking a test **5** got a lot of experience as time passed **6** will tell her the truth when she comes here tomorrow **B 1** As you are chewing **2** when you have free time **3** While she was listening to

교과서 문장 응용하기 **1** When she was younger, she enjoyed surfing. / She enjoyed surfing when she was younger. **2** As time goes by, I love you more. / I love you more as time goes by.

FOCUS 66 p.131

A 1 until this bakery opens **2** after we graduate **3** since he moved to his hometown **B 1** stayed outside until the guests arrived **2** haven't seen him since he went to the USA **3** packed their luggage before they left for Thailand **C 1** Until(Till) he spoke **2** since she got married **3** After, ended

교과서 문장 응용하기 **1** Come back before he comes. **2** I will read the book until(till) Ben arrives home.

FOCUS 67 p.132

A 1 as **2** unless **3** if **4** since **5** Because **B 1** unless, is fine **2** if, use **3** Since Monday is **4** because he was standing **5** As they knew

교과서 문장 응용하기 **1** Unless you attend the party, I will not(won't) go. / I will not(won't) go unless you attend the party. **2** Since he arrived, she left early. / She left early since he arrived.

FOCUS 68 p.133

A 1 Although **2** even if **3** though **4** Even though **B 1** went out without a coat though it was very cold **2** will be played even if it rains **3** won't give up even though he failed **4** has to do her homework although she doesn't like doing it **C 1** though she is only four **2** Even if you don't like **3** Although, is younger than

교과서 문장 응용하기 **1** Although Tim is poor, he is honest. / Tim is honest although he is poor. **2** Even if she is hungry, she won't have(eat) dinner. / She won't have(eat) dinner even if she is hungry.

FOCUS 69 p.134

A 1 both, and **2** not only, but also **3** as well as **4** but also, is **B 1** but also attractive **2** both, and math **3** Both, I **4** but, mine **C 1** Both Jack and Petra **2** not only, but **3** as well as

교과서 문장 응용하기 **1** I will meet both Brian and his wife. **2** She is studying not only English but (also) science. / She is studying science as well as English.

FOCUS 70 p.135

A 1 or **2** neither **3** nor **B 1** neither, nor **2** Either, or **3** Neither, nor **C 1** neither hot nor **2** either a bus or **3** Either, or Tom

교과서 문장 응용하기 **1** She eats(has) either bread or salad. **2** They went neither camping nor fishing.

FOCUS 71 p.136

A 1 However **2** Therefore **3** In addition **4** As a result **5** For instance **B 1** Moreover **2** However **3** Therefore **4** For example **C 1** Besides (Moreover / In addition) **2** Therefore **3** On the other hand

교과서 문장 응용하기 **1** It rained heavily. As a result, the tennis match(game) was cancelled. **2** She is very popular. On the other hand, she is not kind.

내신적중 실전문제

pp.137~140

01 ② 02 ⑤ 03 as 04 if 05 ④ 06 ⑤ 07 ④, ⑤ 08 ④ 09 ⑤ 10 before, after 11 because (since / as), Therefore 12 ④ 13 ①, ④ 14 ③ 15 ③ 16 Unless 17 ① 18 ①, ③ 19 ① 20 ④

서술형 평가

01 (1) before I go to bed (2) since I came to this city (3) because(since / as) I didn't have breakfast (4) until I got up 02 (1) Unless you read these articles (2) If you don't read these articles 03 (1) that there are many bad people in the world (2) if(whether) they smell good 04 (1) Both Jessy and her parents have (2) Not only Jessy but also her parents have (3) Her parents as well as Jessy have 05 ⓐ Though(Although) ⓑ because(as / since) ⓒ When(As) ⓓ after 06 I didn't know that in Kuwait, people serve coffee at the end of a visit.

01 첫 번째 빈칸에는 '비록 ~하지만'의 의미인 양보의 접속사 though가, 두 번째 빈칸에는 명사절을 이끌며 '~인지 아닌지'라는 의미인 접속사 whether가 알맞다.

02 첫 번째 빈칸에는 '~할 때까지'라는 시간의 의미를 나타내는 접속사 until이, 두 번째 빈칸에는 앞 문장에 대한 이유를 나타내는 접속사 because가 알맞다.

03 첫 번째 빈칸에는 '~하면서'라는 시간의 의미를 나타내는 접속사 as가, 두 번째 빈칸에는 '~ 때문에'라는 이유의 의미를 나타내는 접속사 as가 알맞다.

04 첫 번째 빈칸에는 '만약 ~라면'이라는 조건의 의미의 접속사 if가, 두 번째 빈칸에는 '~인지를'이라는 의미로 동사 know의 목적어 역할을 하는 접속사 if가 알맞다.

05 '~하는 동안'의 의미는 시간의 접속사 while로 쓴다.

06 '~하지 않으면'이라는 부정의 조건은 접속사 unless로 쓴다.

07 'A뿐만 아니라 B도'의 의미는 「not only A but also B」와 「B as well as A」로 쓴다.

08 ④ 한국어를 못 했었지만 지금은 잘한다는 내용이므로 대조를 나타내는 접속부사 however나 on the other hand를 써야 한다.

09 ⑤ 두 번째 문장은 문맥상 '그녀가 가지 않으면 그도 가지 않을 것이다.'라는 의미가 되어야 하므로 ⑤는 '(만약) ~하지 않는다면'의 의미인 접속사 unless를 써야 한다.

10 첫 번째 빈칸에는 '~하기 전에'라는 의미의 접속사 before가, 두 번째 빈칸에는 '~ 후에'라는 의미의 접속사 after가 알맞다.

11 첫 번째 빈칸에는 빈칸의 뒤가 이유를 나타내므로 because (as / since)가, 두 번째 빈칸에는 빈칸 뒤의 문장이 결과를 나타내므로 접속부사 therefore가 알맞다.

12 시간을 나타내는 부사절에서는 현재시제가 미래시제 대신 쓰인다.

13 |보기|와 ①, ④는 '~인지 아닌지'의 의미인 명사절을 이끄는 접속사이다. ②, ③은 '(만약) ~라면'의 의미의 조건의 접속사이다. ⑤ even if와 함께 쓰여 '만약 ~할지라도'라는 의미를 나타낸다.

14 빈칸에는 앞 문장의 결과를 나타내는 접속부사 as a result를 이용하여 '걸어서 출근해야만 한다'는 내용이 이어지는 것이 자연스럽다.

15 Harry와 Jack 둘 다 좋아하지 않으므로 「neither A nor B」로 나타낸다.

16 「If ~ not」은 '(만약) ~하지 않는다면'이라는 의미로 접속사 unless와 바꿔 쓸 수 있다.

17 '비록 화가 났지만'이라는 양보의 의미를 나타내야 하므로 in spite of로 쓸 수 있다.

18 ① 「both A and B」가 주어로 쓰일 경우 동사는 복수형으로 쓴다. (is → are) ③ 「either A or B」가 주어로 쓰일 경우 동사는 B의 수에 일치킨다. (have → has)

19 첫 번째 빈칸에는 since(~이므로), 두 번째 빈칸에는 when(~할 때), 세 번째 빈칸에는 that(~라는 것을), 네 번째 빈칸에는 though(비록 ~일지라도)가 알맞다.

20 ⓐ, ⓓ, ⓔ는 '~ 이므로'라는 의미인 이유의 접속사이고, ⓑ, ⓒ의 since는 '~ 이후로'의 의미인 시간의 접속사이다.

서술형 평가

01 (1) 일기를 쓰는 것은 잠자리에 들기 '전(before)'이다. (2) 도시에 온 '이후로'라는 의미여야 하므로 since가 알맞다. (3) 배가 고픈 것은 '아침을 먹지 않았기 때문(because(since/as))'이다. (4) '내가 일어날 때까지' 계속 울었다는 의미여야 하므로 until이 알맞다.

02 '~하지 않으면'이라는 부정의 조건은 접속사 unless나 if ~ not으로 나타내며, 조건의 부사절에서는 현재시제가 미래시

제를 대신한다.

03 (1) 접속사 that을 넣어 진주어 역할을 하는 명사절을 연결한다.
　　(2) '~인지 아닌지'의 의미로 목적어 역할을 하면서 명사절을 이끄는 접속사 if(whether)를 쓴다.

04 'Jessy와 부모님 모두 스쿠버 다이빙을 해본 적이 있다.'는 의미로, 주어로 쓰인 경우 「both A and B」는 동사를 복수 취급하고, 「not only A but also B」와 「B as well as A」에서 동사는 모두 B의 수에 일치시킨다.

[05~06]

> 　　내 이름은 Arpi이다. 나는 미국인이지만, 이란에서 자랐다. 지금은 미국에 산다. 어느 날 나는 쿠웨이트에서 온 두 명의 자매를 만났는데 그들의 가족은 미국인이었다. 나는 그들의 친구가 되고 싶어서 그들을 우리 집으로 초대했다. 그들이 도착했을 때, 우리는 아주 다정하게 이야기하기 시작했다. 나는 즉시 그들에게 과자와 과일을 가져다 주었다. 그런 다음 커피를 주었다. 갑자기 그들은 당황해 보였다. 그들은 도착한 20분 쯤 후에, 인사를 하고는 가버렸다. 나는 쿠웨이트에서는 사람들이 방문 끝부분에 커피를 제공한다는 것을 몰랐다.

05 ⓐ 양보, ⓑ 이유, ⓒ '~할 때(시간)', ⓓ '~ 후에(시간)'의 의미를 나타내는 접속사가 알맞다.

06 동사 know의 목적어 역할을 하는 접속사 that으로 문장을 연결한다.

CHAPTER 10 가정법

FOCUS 72　　　　　p.143

A 1 had　2 could　3 failed　4 were　　**B** 1 tried, might succeed　2 were not, would go　3 doesn't have, can't(cannot) learn　　**C** 1 If, were, would build　2 were, could meet　3 If, had, could take

교과서 문장 응용하기　1 If she were not sick, I would invite her to the party.　2 If he met her again, he would be happier.

FOCUS 73　　　　　p.144

A 1 didn't take, regretted　2 lost his money, walked　3 hadn't been, have invited　　**B** 1 would have gone　2 had not(hadn't) trained　3 could have sent　　**C** 1 had not encouraged, could not have finished　2 hadn't known, wouldn't have bought　3 had not been, would have gone

교과서 문장 응용하기　1 If I had seen Evan, I would have returned his smartphone.　2 If she had done (her) homework, the teacher would not have punished her.

FOCUS 74　　　　　p.145

A 1 don't own　2 didn't know　3 had studied　4 had　　**B** 1 were　2 had brought　3 met　　**C** 1 could talk　2 had had　3 hadn't spent

교과서 문장 응용하기　1 I wish I could speak Italian.　2 I wish he hadn't(had not) bought the car.

FOCUS 75　　　　　p.146

A 1 were　2 had visited　3 ate cucumbers　　**B** 1 he had watched the movie　2 she were a police officer　　**C** 1 were German　2 as if she were rich

교과서 문장 응용하기　1 Patrick acts as if he were a teacher.　2 She acts as if she had been an architect.

FOCUS 76　　　　　p.147

A 1 Without　2 But for　　**B** 1 If, had not been for　2 If, were not for, might not overcome　　**C** 1 would have lost　2 couldn't buy　3 couldn't have stopped(quit)

교과서 문장 응용하기　1 Without your help, I couldn't do my homework.　2 But for the firefighter, they would have died.

FOCUS 77　　　　　p.148

A 1 had rained　2 would not be　3 had taken, could

understand **4** had taken, would be   **B 1** had left
2 had majored, would be **3** had eaten(had) **4** would
not feel

교과서 문장 응용하기 1 If I had studied hard last night,
I would get a good mark today. **2** If he hadn't(had
not) broken his arm last month, he could play
basketball now.

・・・・・ 내신적중 실전문제   pp.149~152

01 ② **02** ⑤ **03** ② **04** But for(Without) **05** ④
06 ② **07** ④ **08** ⑤ is → were **09** ① learned →
had learned **10** ⑤ **11** ③ **12** ⑤ **13** ⑤ **14** ④
15 ⑤ **16** ③ **17** ② **18** wouldn't buy **19** ④
20 ②

서술형 평가

01 ⑴ If there were a time machine, could go
⑵ As there isn't a time machine, can't go
02 ⑴ didn't eat → hadn't eaten ⑵ wouldn't get
→ wouldn't have gotten   **03** ⑴ Without ⑵ If it
were not for ⑶ Were it not for   **04** ⑴ didn't
have an allergy, could eat ⑵ had had my
shopping list, wouldn't have forgotten to buy
05 ⓐ If she went to Lake House ⓑ she might
get to spend time in real space capsule
06 (that) she can't go to the both places

01 주절이 「주어 + 조동사의 과거형 + 동사원형」 형태로 쓰였으므
로, if절은 가정법 과거인 「주어 + 동사의 과거형」으로 쓴다.

02 과거 사실과 반대되는 내용을 가정하며 '마치 ~였던 것처럼'
이라는 의미는 「as if + 가정법 과거완료」로 쓴다.

03 현재 사실과 반대되는 소망을 나타내야 하므로 I wish 뒤에
는 가정법 과거 형태인 「주어 + 동사의 과거형」이 알맞다.

04 문맥상 '~가 없(었)다면'의 의미인 But for(Without)가 알맞다.

05 주어진 문장이 과거 사실에 대한 유감을 나타내는 가정법 과
거완료이므로, 직설법 문장의 명사절은 과거시제로 쓰며, 긍
정의 내용은 부정으로 바꾼다.

06 '어제 ~하지 않았다면, 지금 …하지 않을 것이다.'라는 의미이

므로 혼합가정법을 써서 주절은 가정법 과거로 표현한다.

07 '만약 ~했다면 …했을 텐데'의 의미이므로 가정법 과거완료
형태인 「If + 주어 + had + 과거분사 ~, 주어+조동사의 과거
형 + have + 과거분사 …」를 쓴다.

08 '마치 노인인 것처럼 행동한다'라는 의미여야 하므로 「as if +
가정법 과거」로 써야 한다.

09 ① '만약 ~했다면, …일 텐데'라는 의미여야 하므로 「가정법
과거완료 + 가정법 과거」의 혼합가정법으로 써야 한다.

10 「as if + 가정법 과거(주어 + 동사의 과거형)」는 현재 사실과 반대
되는 것을 가정하는 '마치 ~인 것처럼'의 의미이다. 따라서 빈칸
에는 현재의 사실인 ⑤ '그녀는 나의 엄마가 아니다'가 알맞다.

11 현재 사실에 반대되는 것을 소망하고 있으므로 「I wish + 가
정법 과거(주어 + 동사의 과거형)」가 알맞다.

12 첫 번째는 would have eaten으로 보아 가정법 과거완료의
문장이며, 두 번째는 혼합가정법 문장으로 if절에 가정법 과
거완료가 온다.

13 현재 있는 것을 없다고 가정할 때는 가정법 과거 앞에
Without(But for / If it were not for ~ / Were it not for ~)
를 쓴다. ⑤는 과거에 있었던 것을 없다고 가정하고 있다.

14 주어진 문장의 시제는 과거이므로 과거 사실을 반대로 표현
하는 가정법 과거완료인 「if + 주어 + had + 과거분사 ~, 주
어 + 조동사의 과거형 + have + 과거분사」가 알맞다.

15 ⑤ 현재 사실과 반대되는 내용을 가정하며 '마치 ~인 것처럼'
이라는 의미여야 하므로 as if 뒤에는 가정법 과거가 알맞다.
(is → were)

16 ③ last night으로 보아 과거 사실에 대한 소망을 나타내는
가정법 과거완료이므로 hadn't eaten으로 고쳐야 된다.

17 ⓐ if절의 then으로 보아 가정법 과거완료이므로 asked는
had asked가 되어야 한다. ⓔ '~이 없다면'이라는 뜻은 If it
were not for ~로 쓴다.

18 현재 이룰 수 없는 일은 가정법 과거로 쓰며, 주절은 「주어 +
조동사의 과거형 + 동사원형 ~」의 형태이다.

19 ⓒ as if 가정법 과거완료 문장이 되어야 하므로 haven't는
hadn't로 고쳐야 한다. ⓓ 혼합가정법이 되어야 하므로 주절
이 「조동사의 과거형 + 동사원형」이 되도록 could have been
은 could be로 고쳐야 한다.

20 ② 「as if + 가정법 과거」의 긍정은 직설법에서 부정이 된다.
(is → isn't)

01 현재 사실에 대한 가정은 가정법 과거로 나타내며, 직설법의 시제는 현재로 쓴다. 가정법의 긍정은 직설법에서 부정으로 바뀐다.

02 B의 마지막 말은 내용상 과거의 사실과 반대되는 가정을 나타내므로 가정법 과거완료인 「If+주어+had+과거분사 ~, 주어+조동사의 과거형+have+과거분사 ~.」 형태가 알맞다.

03 '~이 없다면'이라는 가정법 과거문장 But for는 Without / If it were not for ~ / Were it not for ~로 바꿔 쓸 수 있다.

04 ⑴ 현재 사실에 대한 가정은 가정법 과거로, ⑵ 과거 사실에 대한 가정은 가정법 과거완료로 쓴다.

[05~06]

> Molly는 걱정스럽다. 그녀의 가장 친한 친구인 Sally가 Lake House에서 1주일을 보내자고 그녀를 초대했다. 하지만 그것은 Space Camp와 같은 주이다. Molly는 언젠가 우주 비행사가 되는 것을 꿈꿔왔다. 만약 Molly가 Lake House에 간다면, 그녀는 수영을 하고 야외에서 잠을 잘 수 있을 것이다. 반대로 Space Camp에 간다면 진짜 우주선에서 시간을 보내게 될 것이다. 두 여행 모두 재미있을 것이다. Molly가 양쪽 모두를 갈 수 있으면 좋으련만. 그녀는 어떻게 해야 할까?

05 둘 다 가정법 과거 문장이므로 ⓐ의 if절에는 동사의 과거형이 ⓑ의 주절에는 「조동사의 과거형+동사원형」이 쓰여야 한다.

06 가정법 과거이므로 직설법의 시제는 현재로, 가정법의 긍정은 부정으로 바꿔 쓴다.

CHAPTER 11 일치와 화법

FOCUS 78   p.155

A 1 is 2 was 3 is 4 has   B 1 is 2 wears 3 is 4 is 5 is 6 feels   C 1 Everyone(Everybody) is 2 Some of, was 3 The number, is increasing

교과서 문장 응용하기   1 Each student has to submit a history report.   2 Most of the lecture was very difficult.

FOCUS 79   p.156

A 1 are 2 are 3 are 4 are 5 are 6 are
B 1 was → were 2 is → are 3 visits → visit 4 is → are 5 is → are   C 1 Both, and, like 2 Some of, were made

교과서 문장 응용하기   1 A number of buildings were destroyed.   2 There were many people in the museum.

FOCUS 80   p.157

A 1 would 2 said 3 can 4 had made 5 had been 6 will complete   B 1 ○ 2 ○ 3 × → was 4 × → had been 5 ○   C 1 the price was 2 would give 3 had visited 4 had broken

교과서 문장 응용하기   1 He says (that) he can finish his homework.   2 He thought that she had admired him.

FOCUS 81   p.158

A 1 makes 2 is 3 was 4 invented 5 gets
B 1 The teacher said that World War II ended in 1945.   2 Lisa told me that practice makes perfect.   3 The scientists said that the Earth is getting warmer.   4 My father said that Madrid is the capital of Spain.   C 1 moves 2 boils 3 is

교과서 문장 응용하기   1 She told me that the Earth is round.   2 I learned that Edison invented the light bulb.

FOCUS 82   p.159

A 1 told, he was 2 told, had been inspired 3 said, didn't, that 4 said, would not go, the next day
B 1 I want to visit my friends this weekend.   2 We have lived here for a long time.   3 I will finish this report tonight.

교과서 문장 응용하기   1 Rose told him (that) she was busy then.   2 Noah said (that) he had been sick the day before(the previous day).

FOCUS 83 — p.160

A 1 if(whether) she liked   2 if(whether) I could, the next(following) day   3 had moved   4 who had given him that   5 if(whether) I was free that night(evening)
B 1 asked, who(m) I was   2 asked, would do that day   3 if(whether) he could speak

교과서 문장 응용하기 1 She asked me if(whether) I liked butterflies.   2 I asked her what she had done two days before.

FOCUS 84 — p.161

A 1 ordered, to try   2 told, to help   3 asked, to lend her   4 advised, not to skip   5 told, not to use
B 1 Walk your dog.   2 Don't be too noisy in the museum.   3 Drink enough water.   4 Join the baseball team.

교과서 문장 응용하기 1 She ordered him not to run.   2 I asked her to take me to the party.

FOCUS 85 — p.162

A 1 the boy is   2 Why do you think   3 he went
B 1 if(whether) he can play   2 why you were   3 Who, will be   **C** 1 Do you know who wrote this poem?   2 Nobody knows when the accident happened.   3 Where do you suppose she comes from?

교과서 문장 응용하기 1 Do you know what she wanted?   2 Who do you think will win the game?

내신적중 실전문제 — pp.163~166

01 ③   02 ②   03 if(whether)   04 ④   05 ③   06 ④   07 ④   08 ②   09 ④ my → his   10 ④ flew → had flown   11 ⓐ is ⓑ keep ⓒ was   12 ⑤   13 ⑤   14 ⑤   15 ②   16 ⑤   17 ⑤   18 ②   19 ③   20 ④

서술형 평가

01 (1) Some of the pumpkin pies are missing.
(2) Both Bill and Sora want to ride a camel around the desert.   02 (1) had escaped   (2) was invented   03 (1) if(whether) Ted eats   (2) what Sally is doing   04 Ann asked Peter what the librarian had said to him.   05 (1) if(whether) she was reading the detective novel then   (2) (that) it was very exciting / (that) she was reading it(the book)   06 ⓐ has ⓑ weighs   07 How much do you think the same woman weighs on the Moon?

01 주어는 each로 단수이며 yesterday로 보아 시제가 과거이므로 be동사는 was가 알맞다.

02 주어가 시간으로 문맥상 하나의 단위를 나타내면 단수로 취급한다.

03 첫 번째는 의문사 없는 의문문의 간접화법 문장이며, 두 번째는 동사 tell의 목적어 역할을 하는 간접의문문이므로 if절은 「if(whether)+주어+동사」의 어순으로 쓴다.

04 의문사가 있는 간접의문문의 어순은 「의문사+주어+동사」이며, 시제는 주절의 시제와 일치시킨다.

05 주절의 동사가 said로 과거형이므로 미래형인 ③은 올 수 없다. ⑤는 규칙적인 습관을 나타내므로 현재시제를 쓴다.

06 명령문의 간접화법은 전달동사는 tell로 바꾸고, 피전달문은 to부정사를 이용한다. 부정문인 경우 「not+to부정사」의 형태로 쓴다.

07 의문사가 없는 간접화법으로 asked는 said to로, 인용 부호를 쓰고, 과거진행형은 현재진행형으로, 주어 I는 you로 바꾼다.

08 ② a number of는 '많은 ~'이라는 의미로 뒤에 복수 명사가 와야 한다. (→ students)

09 ④ 직접화법의 my는 Richard를 가리키므로 his가 되어야 한다.

10 ④ 직접화법에서의 과거는 전달동사가 과거인 경우 간접화법에서 과거완료가 되어야 한다.

11 「부분(some/most) / 분수+of the+명사」에서는 of 다음의 명사가 주어의 수를 결정한다. ⓐ 단수(our body), ⓑ 복수(my friends), ⓒ 단수(time)이다.

12 상관접속사 「both *A* and *B*」가 주어일 때는 복수 취급하여 복수 동사를 쓴다.

13 문맥상 의사가 '규칙적으로 운동하시오.'라고 말한 것이 자연스럽다. 명령문을 간접화법으로 바꿀 때는 to부정사를 이용한다.

14 ⑤ 주절의 동사가 생각이나 추측을 나타내는 guess이므로 의문사가 문장의 맨 앞으로 오고 간접의문문의 어순은 「의문사 + 주어 + 동사」가 되어야 한다. (→ How do you guess she can get first prize?)

15 ② 「the number of + 복수 명사」는 '~의 수'의 의미로 단수 취급한다. (→ has)

16 ⑤ 역사적 사실은 항상 과거형으로 쓴다. (had discovered → discovered)

17 ① 직접화법 피전달문의 주어는 she가 아닌 I이다. ② 부사구 the next day는 tomorrow가 되어야 한다. ③ 「not + to부정사」는 부정명령문인 Don't ~. 의 형태로 바꾼다. ④ 주절과 피전달문의 시제가 과거이므로 Did는 현재형 Do로 써야 한다.

18 간접의문문에서 의문사가 앞에 온 것을 보아 빈칸에는 think, imagine, suppose, guess 등 추측이나 생각을 나타내는 동사가 알맞다.

19 ⓐ 길이의 단위는 단수 취급한다. (are → is) ⓔ 격언이나 속담은 항상 현재시제로 나타낸다. (tasted → tastes)

20 ④ 부정명령문의 간접화법은 「전달동사 + 목적어 + not + to부정사」로 쓴다. (sing → not to sing)

서술형 평가

01 (1) some of는 다음에 오는 명사에 동사를 일치시키므로 pies 뒤에는 복수 동사가 온다. (2) 「Both *A* and *B*」는 동사를 복수로 쓴다.

02 주절의 동사가 현재에서 과거로 바뀌면 (1) 종속절의 과거는 과거완료가 되고, (2) 역사적인 사실은 시제가 변하지 않고 그대로 과거가 된다.

03 (1) 동사 wonder의 목적어 역할을 하면서 의문사가 없으므로 「if(whether) + 주어 + 동사」의 순서이다. (2) 동사 know의 목적어 역할을 하면서 의문사가 있으므로 「의문사 + 주어 + 동사」의 순서이다.

04 전달문에 의문사가 있는 경우 「의문사 + 주어 + 동사」의 순서로 쓰며, 전달동사가 과거일 때 과거시제는 과거완료가 된다.

05 전달문에 의문사가 없는 의문문의 간접화법은 「if

[whether] + 주어 + 동사」의 순서로 쓰며, 전달동사가 과거일 때, 현재진행형은 과거진행형, 부사 now는 then으로 바뀐다. (2) 평서문의 간접화법은 that으로 연결하거나 생략하며, 현재시제는 과거시제가 된다.

[06~07]

> 달이 지구의 1/6의 중력을 가지고 있다는 것을 알고 있는가? 모든 것이 달에서는 6배가 덜 나간다. 어떤 여자가 지구에서는 120파운드다. 같은 여성이 달에서는 얼마의 무게가 나갈 거라고 생각하는가? 맞다. 그녀는 달에서 20파운드가 될 것이다. 그녀는 지구에서 보다 달에서 더 높이 뛰어 오를 수 있다. 흰긴수염고래는 150톤이다. 만약 흰긴수염고래가 달에 갈 수 있다면 25톤이 될 것이다.

06 ⓐ 달의 중력이 지구의 1/6이라는 것은 과학적 사실이므로 항상 현재형으로 써야 한다. ⓑ 주어가 everything일 때는 단수 취급한다.

07 동사가 think인 경우의 간접의문문에서 의문사는 문장 앞으로 와야 한다.

CHAPTER **12** 특수 구문

FOCUS **86**　　　　p.169

A 1 does like **2** do believe **3** did wait **4** did train **5** did become　**B 1** did sell **2** Do be **3** did warn **4** does read **5** does take care of **6** did take

교과서 문장 응용하기 1 He does study music in Boston. **2** I did give her your letter and present(gift). / I did give your letter and present(gift) to her.

FOCUS **87**　　　　p.170

A 1 myself **2** in the least **3** at all **4** himself **5** the very　**B 1** herself **2** at all **3** the very **4** themselves **5** in the least　**C 1** at all **2** himself **3** the very house

교과서 문장 응용하기 1 This is the very book she is looking for. **2** I'm not interested in movies at all.

A 1 It was she that(who) met the popular actor at the airport. 2 It was the money that(which) Noah returned last night. 3 It was last week that(when) they started a dancing class. 4 It is a true story that(which) this movie is based on.   B 1 It, his smartphone that(which) 2 It, Mike that(who(m)) 3 It, yesterday that(when) 4 It, at(in) the restaurant that(where) 5 It, Helen that(who) picked up

교과서 문장 응용하기   1 It is Finn that(who) knows her well. 2 It was this jacket that(which) she bought yesterday.

A 1 begins the meeting 2 are two bats 3 does she make 4 did I dream   B 1 are some apples 2 rushed the girl 3 have I seen 4 did we meet

교과서 문장 응용하기   1 On the plate is the cheese cake. 2 Little did she understand him.

A 1 So did 2 Neither will 3 So has 4 Neither does   B 1 neither can 2 so am   C 1 So can Leo 2 Neither do I 3 Neither would I 4 so did his 5 neither did Hannah

교과서 문장 응용하기   1 Fiona likes Brandon and so do we. 2 He couldn't believe her and neither could I.

A 1 never 2 Neither 3 all   B 1 None 2 Not both 3 Not everyone(everybody) 4 not always 5 Neither of the stories

교과서 문장 응용하기   1 She doesn't always have(eat) dinner at the same time. 2 Neither of his parents is alive.

A 1 can't swim well 2 can run 3 Adam's hair 4 to go to concerts   B 1 She met her friends and ordered some food. 2 Ivy does the dishes more often than Isaac. 3 This is the most beautiful and expensive hotel in China.   C 1 Susan's 2 want to 3 I couldn't

교과서 문장 응용하기   1 His book and Eva's (book) are on the desk. 2 Her dress is simpler than Sophia's (dress is).

A 1 she was 2 I was 3 it is 4 he was 5 it is   B 1 As she was a young artist, she was not famous. 2 When you are in danger, you should call me. 3 If it is necessary, you can use a dictionary. 4 Though he is in Paris, he has not visited the Louvre Museum.   C 1 if possible 2 when swimming 3 Though(Although) lazy

교과서 문장 응용하기   1 While (she was) listening to music, she drew a picture. 2 Call me tonight, if (it is) necessary.

내신적중 실전문제   pp.177~180

01 ② 02 ② 03 can 04 ⑤ 05 ④ 06 ⑤ 07 ②
08 did 09 ③ got → get 10 ② 11 ④ 12 ③
13 ④ 14 ② 15 ③ 16 ⑤ 17 so is Jenny 18
③ 19 ⓑ, ⓓ 20 ④

서술형 평가

01 On a hill in front of the hotel stood a great castle. 02 (1) Some people went to the park on foot and others went to the park by bus.
(2) Always stay with your parents when you are camping in the woods. 03 (1) Not all (2) Not every 04 Neither can I. 05 (1) It was Sally that(who) met the prince at the party last night.
(2) Sally did meet the prince at the party last night. (3) It was the prince that(who(m)) Sally met at the party last night. (4) It was at the party

that(where) Sally met the prince last night. (5) It was last night that(when) Sally met the prince at the party.　06 ⓐ Jack himself is determined to jog today, as he does every day. ⓑ he now does feel better than he did in years ⓒ It is in the rain that Jack begins jogging.　07 (4행) never he wants → never does he want

01 문맥상 '정말 가기를 원한다'라는 뜻이 되어야 한다. 동사를 강조할 때는 「do(does, did)+동사원형」으로 나타내며, 주어가 3인칭 단수 현재형이므로 ②가 알맞다.

02 빈칸에 들어갈 말인 to come with you에서 to 뒤의 중복되는 부분은 생략할 수 있다.

03 '~도 또한 아니다'라고 응답하려면 「neither+동사+주어」의 어순으로 쓰며, A의 말에 쓰인 조동사 can을 이용한다.

04 접속사로 연결된 절에서 앞 문장의 동사가 뒤 문장에서 반복될 때에는 조동사만 쓰고 나머지는 생략할 수 있다.

05 부정어가 문장의 맨 앞에 있고 동사가 일반동사이므로 「조동사 do+주어+동사원형」의 형태로 쓴다.

06 첫 번째 빈칸에는 「It ~ that ..」 강조 구문이므로 it, 두 번째 빈칸에는 「Here+대명사 주어+동사」의 형태이므로 대명사 she가 알맞다.

07 ② 동사는 「It ~ that ...」 강조구문으로 강조할 수 없다.

08 • '~ 또한 그렇다'의 의미는 「so+동사+주어」의 어순으로 쓰며, 동사는 앞 문장의 동사의 종류, 시제와 일치시킨다.
• 접속사로 연결된 문장에서 앞 문장의 어구가 반복되면 조동사만 남기고 생략할 수 있다.

09 ③ 동사를 강조하는 did 다음에 나오는 동사는 동사원형으로 써야 한다.

10 ② none of us는 '우리 중에 아무도 ~하지 않다'는 뜻으로 전체부정을 나타낸다.

11 부정어를 강조해서 문장 앞에 쓰게 되면 「부정어+조동사+주어+본동사」의 어순이 되며, 의미상 현재완료 시제가 알맞다.

12 ③은 '외국 손님들 중 오지 않은 사람이 없다'는 의미로 전체부정을 나타낸다.

13 ⓒ 시간의 부사절 뒤의 「주어+be동사」는 부사절의 주어와 주절의 주어가 같을 때만 생략 가능하다. 주절의 주어는 the bell이고 부사절의 주어는 I이므로 생략할 수 없다.

14 ② 첫 번째 문장은 '모두가 그 소식을 알지는 못했다.'는 부분

부정의 의미이고, 두 번째 문장은 '모두들 그 소식을 모르고 있었다.'는 전체부정의 의미이다.

15 ③ do one's homework는 '숙제하다'의 의미로 do는 일반동사로 쓰였다.

16 |보기|와 나머지는 모두 「It ~ that ...」 강조 구문에 쓰인 it이고, ⑤는 진주어인 that 절을 대신하여 쓰인 가주어이다.

17 '~도 또한 그렇다'라는 의미로 「so+동사+주어」의 형태로 쓴다.

18 ③ 부사로 쓰인 here가 문장 앞에 쓰이면 「Here+동사+주어」의 순서로 쓴다. (→ Here are two apples and three oranges.)

19 ⓑ 양보 부사절의 주어가 주절의 주어와 같을 때 「주어+be동사」는 생략할 수 있다. ⓓ 비교 구문에서 than 뒤의 말이 중복되면 생략할 수 있다.

20 ④ 부사구가 도치되면 「조동사+주어+동사」의 어순이다. (→ Only after lunch can you play baseball.)

01 부사구의 도치는 「부사구+동사+주어」의 순서로 쓴다.

02 (1) 반복되는 어구가 생략되었다. (2) 시간의 부사절의 주어가 주절의 주어와 같으므로 「주어+be 동사」가 생략되었다.

03 네 사람 모두 찬성한 것은 아니라는 의미여야 하므로, 부분부정으로 나타낸다. (1) 동사가 복수형(are)이므로 not all이 알맞다. (2) 단수 동사 is가 있으므로 not every가 알맞다.

04 '~도 또한 아니다'의 의미는 「neither+조동사+주어(부정문)」으로 쓴다.

05 (1), (3), (4), (5)는 주어, 목적어, 장소, 시간을 강조하는 「It ~ that ...」 강조 구문을, (2)는 조동사 do를 이용한 「do+동사원형」의 과거시제를 써서 강조한다.

[06~07]

> 나쁜 날씨에도 불구하고, Jack은 다른 날과 마찬가지로 오늘도 조깅을 하기로 결심한다. 그는 두 달 전에 그의 운동 프로그램을 시작했는데, 전혀 방해받고 싶지 않다. Jack은 살을 뺐을 뿐 아니라 수년 동안의 그보다 지금 좋아진 것을 느낀다. 그래서 우스워 보일지 모르겠지만, 빗속에서 조깅을 시작한다.

06 ⓐ 명사를 강조하므로 명사 뒤에 재귀대명사를 쓴다. ⓑ 현재형 동사를 강조하므로 「does+동사원형」의 형태로 쓴다. ⓒ 부사구를 강조하므로 「It ~ that...」 강조 구문으로 쓴다.

07 부정어인 never가 앞으로 오면 「부정어+조동사+주어」의 순서로 쓴다.

Memo